STALIN'S SINGING SPY

STALIN'S SINGING SPY

The Life and Exile
of Nadezhda Plevitskaya

PAMELA A. JORDAN

ROWMAN & LITTLEFIELD
Lanham • Boulder • New York • London

Published by Rowman & Littlefield
A wholly owned subsidiary of The Rowman & Littlefield Publishing Group, Inc.
4501 Forbes Boulevard, Suite 200, Lanham, Maryland 20706
www.rowman.com

Unit A, Whitacre Mews, 26-34 Stannary Street, London SE11 4AB,
United Kingdom

British Library Cataloguing in Publication Information Available

Library of Congress Cataloging-in-Publication Data
Names: Jordan, Pamela A., 1965–
Title: Stalin's singing spy : the life and exile of Nadezhda Plevitskaya / Pamela A.
  Jordan.
Description: Lanham : Rowman & Littlefield, 2016. | Includes bibliographical
  references and index.
Identifiers: LCCN 2015031863 | ISBN 9781442247734 (cloth : alkaline paper) |
  ISBN 9781442247741 (electronic)
Subjects: LCSH: Plevitskaia, Nadezhda Vasil'evna, 1884–1940. | Plevitskaia,
  Nadezhda Vasil'evna, 1884–1940—Trials, litigation, etc. | Women spies—
  Soviet Union—Biography. | Spies—Soviet Union—Biography. | Miller,
  Evgeniĭ Karlovich, 1867–1939—Kidnapping, 1937. | Trials (Kidnapping)—
  France—Paris—History—20th century. | Women singers—Russia—
  Biography. | Soviet Union—History—1917–1936—Biography. | Russia—
  History—Nicholas II, 1894–1917—Biography.
Classification: LCC DK268.P55 J67 2016 | DDC 327.12470092—dc23
  LC record available at http://lccn.loc.gov/2015031863

Printed in the United States of America

CONTENTS

ACKNOWLEDGMENTS

I could not have completed my book without the helpful and generous assistance of several institutions and individuals. First of all, I would like to thank the President's SSHRC Committee of the University of Saskatchewan for awarding me a grant in support of my archival research, and the Text and Academic Authors Association for awarding me an Academic Publications Grant. At the Bakhmeteff Archive of Russian & East European Culture, Rare Book & Manuscript Library, Columbia University, Tanya Chebotarev kindly answered my many document-related queries in person and over e-mail. Protodeacon Vladimir Tsurikov, dean of Holy Trinity Seminary in Jordanville, New York, did the same. Nicolas Buat, archivist at Archives de la préfecture de police, Paris, tracked down the musty files of the Kutepov and Miller kidnapping cases for me. I thank the Davis Center for Russian and Eurasian Studies at Harvard University for providing me with access to Harvard University's libraries as one of its center associates. Hugh K. Truslow, librarian for the Davis Center's collection, helped me locate Soviet-era periodicals.

Russian organizations assisted me as well. At the State Archives of the Kursk Region in Russia, the staff fulfilled my photo request in record time, and at the Kursk public library, the librarians photocopied materials for me after closing. Down the street from the archives and the library, at the Trinity Convent, where Plevitskaya had once studied to be a nun, Sister Iustina welcomed me into her office and tried her best to locate information about the singer's time there. When I visited the N. V. Plevitskaya Museum in nearby Vinnikovo, its director, Irina Solodova, accompanied me on a tour of its exhibits, patiently answered my questions, and offered me materials that gave me a clearer understanding of Plevitskaya's early years.

As any researcher knows, presenting your work to your peers can be a daunting experience. Fortunately, my peers were merciful and fair. Two research groups in particular served as collegial spaces where I could present my research on Plevitskaya and receive encouragement and thoughtful advice: the Department of History's Research Workshop at the Faculty Club, University of Saskatchewan, and the Davis Center's Gender, Socialism and Postsocialism Working Group. Edythe C. Haber, Rochelle G. Ruthchild, Valerie Sperling, and Nikolay Valkov—scholars who have participated in the Davis Center's Gender, Socialism and Postsocialism Working Group—made a special effort to help advance my Plevitskaya research and encourage my progress. I would also like to give a nod to the students in my Female Spies in the Modern Age seminar at the University of Saskatchewan; they kept me on my toes.

I am grateful for the support of many other knowledgeable people who have been most generous with their time, whether in person, over the phone or e-mail, or all three. In terms of the many individuals whom I contacted for assistance on this project, I first want to thank the relatives of my research subjects, who were giving of their time. During my visit to Moscow in 2012, Irina Raksha graciously shared her family memories about Plevitskaya. She showed me mementos, including sheet music of Plevitskaya's songs and the singer's gramophone recordings, and provided me with digitized copies of family photos. In addition, Irina helped arrange for my driver during my visit to Kursk and Vinnikovo. Mary-Kay Wilmers, a relative of Max Eitingon and the Eitingon family biographer, answered a specific query I had about his whereabouts in 1938. Alexander S. Franckel and Philip L. Franckel, Esq.—the son and grandson of Isidore Franckel, one of Plevitskaya's criminal defense attorneys—shared valuable information with me about their relative.

Many experts responded to my queries with enthusiasm. From the initial stage of my project, Gennady Barabtarlo offered me his advice, particularly on interpreting sources about the Miller kidnapping, and he forwarded me additional information that helped me better flesh out the story. John Puckett, a fellow researcher on Soviet espionage, shared with me his opinions about Plevitskaya, Skoblin, and the Miller kidnapping. In addition, John put me in touch with Lazar Fleishman, who helped me better assess the "Bolshevik" nature of the Amtorg. Julie Fedor, Mark Kramer, and Nikita Petrov gave me further insight into the FSB archives. Jean-Marc Berlière, Jacqueline Hodgson, and Francois Le Goarant helped me navigate the labyrinth of French archives and better understand the French legal system. In response to my e-mail message, Laurence Tauzin quickly obtained a photocopy of Plevitskaya's prison file, housed in the state archive in Rennes, and mailed it to me. Vladimir Alexandrov kindly answered my query about the Russian entertainment world in the late tsarist era, and Robert Shenk provided me with fascinating detail about the U.S. Navy's assistance to White Army soldiers and their families during their evacuation from Crimea in 1920. Richard Robbins confirmed that Plevitskaya had performed at the celebration of the tricentennial anniversary of the founding of the Romanov dynasty. Paul Robinson's comments gave me a more nuanced perspective on the lives of specific White Army veterans in exile.

I am especially indebted to Susan McEachern, my superb editor at Rowman & Littlefield Publishers, and her thoughtful assistant, Audra Figgins, for greatly improving the quality of my manuscript and for making the editing process more enjoyable. Many thanks as well to acquisitions editor Carolyn Broadwell-Tkach, for believing in me, and to Janice Braunstein, Matt Evans, and Jacqline Barnes, for their creativity and their meticulous attention to detail. I would also like to thank the two anonymous evaluators of my manuscript, who offered me constructive criticism.

I am very grateful to my friends who are language specialists. Lubov Yakovleva helped me decipher Plevitskaya's handwriting in select passages of her prison diary and the handwriting of White Army colonel Georgy Poliansky in a letter he wrote in 1939. Ludmilla Voitkovska and Sofia Vorontsova helped me translate a passage from a French-language transcript of Plevitskaya's trial, and Charles Savoie helped me read a French official's notes scrawled at the bottom of a letter about Plevitskaya's death.

To my friends and family who are not specialists on topics related to this project, yet still endured my incessant talk about Plevitskaya and offered their moral support, I owe you a special debt of gratitude. You know who you are.

I would like to extend my deepest thanks and love to my mom, Karen Wyles Feighan, who always champions my work, and to my husband, John McCannon, who encouraged me to stay the course whenever I wanted to quit and provided invaluable advice and editing support on my manuscript. Our first meeting—on February 28, 1992, in a small flat on Bakhrushin Street in Moscow—is still my dearest memory of my time in Russia. I dedicate this book to our daughter Miranda, who probably knows more about Russian history than most other American kids do.

Finally, it is important for readers to understand that none of the people or organizations that I acknowledge as having assisted me along the way is responsible for the views expressed or any of the errors made in this book.

ABBREVIATIONS

AFSR   Armed Forces of Southern Russia, 1919–1920
AN   National Archives, Paris
APP   Paris Police Archives
BA   Bakhmeteff Archive of Russian & East European Culture,
            Rare Book & Manuscript Library, Columbia University
Cheka   Extraordinary Commission for Combating Revolution and
            Sabotage, 1918–1922
Comintern   Communist International, 1919–1943
FSB   Federal Security Service of the Russian Federation, 1995–
GPU   State Political Department, 1922–1923
GRU   Military Intelligence Agency, 1918– (officially named GRU
            in 1942)
HIA   Hoover Institution Archives, Stanford University
HTOS   Holy Trinity Orthodox Seminary, Jordanville, New York
INO   Foreign Department of the Soviet secret services, 1920–1941
KGB   Committee for State Security, 1954–1991
NKVD   People's Commissariat for Internal Affairs, 1934–1945
NTSNP   National Labor Union of the New Generation, 1930s (later
            renamed NSNP)
OGPU   United State Political Department, 1923–1934
ROVS   Russian General Military Union, 1924–
TREST   The OGPU's deception operation against White Guardists,
            1921–1927

INTRODUCTION

"I am an orphan. I have no witnesses." These were among the last words spoken by Nadezhda Vasilievna Plevitskaya, once one of Russia's most popular folk singers, at her criminal trial in Paris in 1938. At the time, Plevitskaya was indeed orphaned, not to mention stateless and nearly friendless. To her horror, her former admirers had become her principal attackers. As during the Dreyfus affair forty years before, the entire European public, both on the left and the right, followed Plevitskaya's trial eagerly. One German embassy official in Paris described it as "so gripping that it can be ranked among the great political show trials and is probably destined for movies, the stage, or novels."[1] With the gathering of World War II's storm clouds to occupy everyone's attention, why had Plevitskaya, so suddenly estranged from her close-knit expatriate community, become the subject of such widespread interest?

The year before her trial, in 1937, the Paris police had arrested the singer as an accomplice in the kidnapping of a White Russian general, Evgeny Miller. Miller headed the Russian General Military Union (ROVS), the leading anti-Soviet military organization among Russian political exiles. Within hours of learning about Miller's disappearance, Russian émigrés and Paris investigators suspected that Stalin's secret police, the People's Commissariat for Internal Affairs (NKVD), had planned and executed his kidnapping. Due to a note that Miller had left in his office on the morning of his disappearance, the police also began to suspect that Nikolai Skoblin—a former White Army general and Plevitskaya's husband—had infiltrated ROVS on behalf of the Soviets and had taken part in Miller's abduction. To twist the plot even further, Skoblin vanished for good, hours after Miller did.

1

After Skoblin disappeared, Plevitskaya was left as the lone suspect. While in custody, she swore to investigators that she had not been involved in the kidnapping. She claimed to have been oblivious to her husband's business affairs. Given what they knew of the nature and extent of Soviet intelligence activities in Europe, French officials found her story unconvincing. To bolster their own interests, French authorities, the press, and fellow émigrés portrayed "La Plevitzkaïa" as a Soviet Mata Hari—as a Red seductress who masterminded Miller's kidnapping and used her feminine wiles to pressure her younger husband into becoming a Soviet agent.

This book maintains that the popular image of Plevitskaya as a femme fatale, while unsurprising, is overdrawn. Even so, if Plevitskaya's detractors overstepped the bounds of accuracy, this does not mean she was innocent. Recently available evidence makes it clear that she knew of, and was complicit in, several aspects of Skoblin's espionage activities.

In contrast to her later years, Plevitskaya's early life reads like a fairy tale. Over a half century before her Paris trial, she was born in an isolated Russian village. Due to her strong drive for personal fulfillment and artistic expression, she challenged the dead-end cycle of illiteracy, drudgery, and poverty that trapped many peasant girls in tsarist Russia. Her initial ambition was to become the best singer in her village. By the time she was thirty, she was striving to join the ranks of Russia's most famous singers. Her career goals were more than fully realized: by 1910, she was celebrated nationwide and had become one of Tsar Nicholas II's favorite singers. It was the tsar himself who coined her most famous sobriquet—the "Kursk Nightingale."

Plevitskaya transcended the restrictions of gender that Russian peasant culture imposed on her and became a top-paid performer who understood her audience and made astute business decisions. But her stage persona as a peasant was not altogether an act. It reflected her own self-identity as the daughter of hardworking peasants, even as her new life as a popular entertainer distanced her from her rural roots. Historian Hubertus F. Jahn describes Plevitskaya as "the superstar among the singers of popular songs" and credits her as "instrumental in displacing the gypsy craze with patriotic and sentimental songs of village life in the prewar years."[2] Decades before the mass media revolution of the late twentieth century, her famous brand triggered a "'Plevitskomania' all over the country and among all social strata."[3] Plevitskaya always declared that she was foremost an artist who sang for all people, regardless of their ideological leanings or socioeconomic background. Plausibly or not, she claimed throughout her career to be fundamentally apolitical.

Plevitskaya's privileged life changed drastically when, along with Skoblin and thousands of other anti-Bolshevik Whites, she fled from Russia as Red victory in Russia's civil war cemented Lenin and his Bolshevik regime in power. After living briefly in Turkey and Bulgaria, she and Skoblin settled in France in 1924. The couple spent much of their time in Paris, which hosted the largest and most diverse Russian émigré population in Europe.

Plevitskaya became a cherished symbol of the anti-Soviet White movement in exile. In 1924, émigré artist Filipp Maliavin painted her dressed in an elaborate costume of a Boyar noblewoman from Kursk, and the painting was unveiled at an exhibit in Paris later that year. She sought adulation and financial backing from her fellow émigrés and had no desire to assimilate into French society. Like many of her compatriots, Plevitskaya experienced homesickness and hoped to return to Russia someday. She coped poorly with her marginalized existence, especially as her health deteriorated and her music, whose appeal rested on a steadily fading nostalgia, failed to attract wider audiences. When asked about her life abroad, she insisted that she was living in exile. She refused to speak of herself as an émigré, because the latter term implied permanent residence abroad.

Plevitskaya noted in her memoirs, "In life, I knew two joys: the joy of artistic glory and the joy of the soul, achieved through suffering."[4] She compared the first joy to being inebriated. The second joy, Plevitskaya explained, made her feel lighter, calmer, and happier: "The first joy passes, while the soulful one brings joy till the end of your days." But by the late 1920s, she had tired of exile, and no ambition was more important to her than returning home, at whatever cost. Skoblin, disillusioned with his military superiors and the White cause, felt the same way.

The price of homecoming for Plevitskaya and Skoblin was to serve Stalin's regime, and the official history of Soviet intelligence has acknowledged that they were recruited as agents in 1930.[5] The Skoblins were far from the only Russian émigrés to be recruited by Soviet intelligence. Dozens were, and the majority of these agents have yet to be identified. NKVD chief Nikolai Yezhov once boasted that "no matter how many foreign intelligence officers were purged, the NKVD could always find agents among the White Russians."[6]

In fulfilling their tasks for Soviet intelligence, Skoblin and Plevitskaya did not need to invent alternative selves. They simply remained in place, deceiving those around them. The use of couples was standard practice in intelligence agencies, both in the USSR and elsewhere. In their archive-based book on Soviet espionage in the West, Christopher Andrew and Vasili Mitrokhin, a KGB officer who defected to Britain, name over two dozen couples who served Soviet intelligence agencies between the 1920s and 1970s, including Ethel and Julius Rosenberg.[7] (Andrew and Mitrokhin mention Skoblin, but not Plevitskaya.) Soviet intelligence officials made use of couples because of the widespread assumption that they shared information and interests, trusted each other, and already functioned as a team. They also provided each other with cover for clandestine activities. Husbands were typically given more critical tasks than their wives, who tended to play supporting roles. This was the case for the Skoblins as well as the Rosenbergs.

Gender-based prejudices abound in the world of espionage, whatever the national context, although women's roles in this line of work have evolved in response to cultural, social, political, and technological changes. During the Soviet era, female recruits tended to face more scrutiny, if only because many Soviet intelligence officials stereotyped women as the weaker sex. A manual of the Soviet secret services instructed intelligence officials to "exercise farsightedness in the selection of women spies and avoid recruitment of females 'who might prove to be the wrong types because mentally and physically they cannot withstand the difficult situations likely to confront them.'"[8] Soviet intelligence officials preferred to use women as lower-level agents rather than as spy handlers or senior officers, although there were noteworthy exceptions, including Elizabeth Bentley, who ran two Soviet spy networks on the East Coast of the United States between 1939 and 1944, and Ruth Werner, who was a courier for the Soviets' key atomic spy, Klaus Fuchs, during the 1940s.

Skoblin's and Plevitskaya's clandestine work appeared to be divided along gender lines, as Skoblin carried the weightier assignments. However, their careers and skill sets, which themselves were shaped by gender stereotypes, also determined their usefulness to Soviet intelligence. Skoblin, a former White Russian general, worked for an anti-Soviet, male-dominated Russian émigré military organization. Plevitskaya—deemed the "mother-commander" of Skoblin's regiment in exile—was a popular entertainer whose peasant songs soothed large audiences of Russian émigrés who missed their homeland. Each persona was potentially useful to the couple's Soviet handlers.

Stalin's Singing Spy is the first biography of this fascinating antiheroine written for a Western audience. Plevitskaya's story is a gripping narrative that has been the subject of literary fiction (Vladimir Nabokov's "The Assistant Producer") and film (Éric Rohmer's *Triple Agent*). Plevitskaya built her successful performing career in the late tsarist era on her peasant roots, but was then nearly destroyed by one of the greatest dramas of the twentieth century, Russia's revolution and civil war. Her years in exile shed light on how Russians and other immigrant groups struggled to maintain their national identity in Europe during an interwar era of political and economic upheaval. Moreover, her and Skoblin's activities as spies usefully illustrate how Soviet foreign intelligence operated and what factors motivated certain émigrés to change sides and serve its deadly cause.

Works published about Plevitskaya and Skoblin before the early 1990s tend to depict their lives with limited accuracy. For one thing, any author before then had little to no access to Soviet secret police files. Moreover, many of those writing about the couple were biased or self-serving in their assessments. This was especially the case with former Soviet spies or Russian émigrés, most of whom turned against Plevitskaya after she was arrested.[9] Yet several of the books published about Plevitskaya during the 1990s, when NKVD files about the Skoblins and Miller briefly opened, have also proved disappointing.[10] Reading more like spy novels, these weave excerpts from the archives and other sources into their narratives without providing references and often romanticize their subjects.

In contrast, I aim to provide a more nuanced interpretation of Plevitskaya's life, analyzing primary and secondary sources in Russian, French, and English. I have researched key secondary sources and émigré memoirs, and I have conducted research in the main repositories of White Russian émigré papers in the United States and France. I have examined Plevitskaya's prison file from France, and I have visited the museum dedicated to her life in her birthplace of Vinnikovo, Russia.

The first photo I ever saw of Plevitskaya appears on the cover of a standard reference work, *A Biographical Dictionary of the Soviet Union 1917–1988*. She is wearing a Russian folk costume with an elaborate headdress and is glancing off to her right, her left hand resting coquettishly on her cheek. I found the dictionary's entry about the singer herself, particularly its last sentence, compelling: "The true story of her extraordinary life has never been fully established."[11]

In accepting the challenge of reconstructing Plevitskaya's life, I have sifted through thousands of documents and newspaper articles. Readers will see that parts of her story are harder to elucidate than others, and that no honest researcher can claim to provide the last word on every question pertaining to her complex and eventful life. I have gone a long way in shedding useful light on major issues. But where points of uncertainty arise, I make the reader aware of them—offering what I believe to be the most plausible explanations and outcomes, based on my extensive research.

1

DEZHKA'S JOURNEY

During her criminal trial, Plevitskaya portrayed herself as a barely literate woman whose childhood in a Russian village formed her character and outlook. She told the presiding judge, "Oh, it's very difficult for me, dear sir, to remember now what was said about this affair, for how can I, a peasant woman, understand those educated people?"[1] Her contemporaries knew her rags-to-riches story, in which a peasant-ingénue became a singing sensation. But few witnesses at her trial believed that she was still the innocent peasant girl she once had been.

What was Plevitskaya's childhood like, and how did it shape the woman she became? Place plays an important role in this story. Plevitskaya was born and raised in southwestern Russia's Kursk province, a farming region best known as the site of the pivotal 1943 tank battle that bears its name. For centuries, Russians have viewed the rural, black-earth regions of European Russia, including Kursk, as cradles of national identity.

Kursk is also known for its strong folk music traditions. Plevitskaya described her childhood, and especially her passion for folk music, in her first volume of memoirs, entitled *Dezhkin karagod*.[2] It is this text on which scholars must rely almost solely for direct information about Plevitskaya's early years, and the memories and impressions recounted throughout this and the next chapter are drawn from it and the singer's second volume of memoirs. The word "Dezhkin" is an adjectival form of Nadezhda's childhood nickname, Dezhka, and *karagod* is a form of singing and ring dancing popular in the Kursk region, typically performed by young women. Singing in a karagod offered many girls their first experience of ecstasy, a spiritual communing with nature, friends, and relatives. As Plevitskaya mused, "How can one not be transported by the joyful surges of songs? Rushing, flying around the circle, a multicolored and exultant vortex. I am carried from karagod to karagod." Plevitskaya was attracted to movement, whether through song and dance or through her travels, which took her far beyond Kursk. In her memoirs, she frequently referred to the movement of birds and their melodic voices. She fancied herself a bird, with the freedom to fly and make music.

From her childhood onward, Plevitskaya had an irrepressible drive for personal fulfillment and expression, and she hated conforming to others'— particularly her family's—expectations of her. But beyond her strong will and talent, her success was also shaped by her relatives, as well as by artists, managers, and political and business elites. Cultural influences also played their part, as Plevitskaya came to inhabit the dynamic entertainment world of prerevolutionary Russia.

Plevitskaya was raised in a village called Vinnikovo, just over twenty miles northeast of Kursk, the province's capital city. Vinnikovo's few hundred residents were the descendants of state peasants, who, during the era of serfdom, were not the property of large private landowners. Instead, they had cultivated small plots of government-owned land that were passed down within one's family from generation to generation.[3] They took pride in their heritage as stewards of the land. Their songs bore the marks of old regional influences, including the dominance of Muscovite-era nobles, or boyars, and the distinct form of urban culture that arose around Kursk in the seventeenth century.

According to records in Vinnikovo's Trinity Church and also in a village museum dedicated to her life, Plevitskaya was born in September 1879, likely on September 17 or 18.[4] Interestingly, Plevitskaya herself, reportedly due to some early career advice about the need to appear younger, often cited 1886 as her birth year. Whatever her real age, she wrote of Vinnikovo with great longing during her exile in France, and it is the memory space most vividly recalled in her memoirs. Plevitskaya was the youngest of twelve children in the Vinnikov family, whose name derived from that of their village. Seven of her siblings died in childhood, which was not unusual at the time, given the poor state of health care.

Plevitskaya's surviving siblings included a brother named Nikolai and three sisters: Anastasia (Nastenka), Dunya, and Maria (Masha), who was closest in age to her. The family patriarch, Vasily, nicknamed Vasya, served as a rifleman in the Nikolaev Division of the Russian Imperial Army for eighteen years. (Plevitskaya's middle name, or patronymic, was Vasilievna.) One day Vasya was injured in a gunpowder accident, severely impairing his eyesight. He was discharged from the military and returned to farming. Back in Vinnikovo, he was affectionately called "the Soldier."[5] Vasya often

Nadezhda Plevitskaya's sister
Masha, with her mother Akulina
and Masha's two children, circa
1912. Courtesy of Irina Raksha

Nadezhda Plevitskaya, left, with her
three sisters, circa 1912. Courtesy
of Irina Raksha

regaled Plevitskaya, who worshipped him, with tales of his military exploits. It is likely no coincidence that four of her five romantic partnerships would be with military men.

Plevitskaya inherited her musical talent from her mother, the strong-willed, judgmental, and charitable Akulina Frolovna. Like many other Russian peasants, Akulina had little formal schooling and remained illiterate. According to Russian law during this period, women had few legal rights and could not be granted land. They were not masters of their own fates. The Russian feminine ideal, until the turn of the century at least, was selflessness and self-sacrifice.[6] But female peasants were important to households: they clothed their families, labored in the fields, and organized the home. By the late nineteenth century, female peasants of all ages began to supplement their families' incomes by selling homemade goods such as gloves, socks, or baskets, and even working in the mines. Akulina's life revolved around her family and the farm, with Russian Orthodox Church holidays and the pleasure of fishing in a nearby lake to break up her routine. Plevitskaya affectionately recalled that her mother was "self-sacrificing, and offered her children food first."

Akulina was the most influential person in Plevitskaya's youth and early adulthood. Mother and daughter shared a strong bond, and Akulina doted on her youngest child. Plevitskaya sought her approval even at the height of her fame. However, their relationship was at times strained, especially as Plevitskaya began desiring more independence. Akulina's attitudes reflected the Russian feminine ideal prevalent in her own childhood, while Plevitskaya's mirrored those of the fin de siècle, when women were granted greater license to express their own individuality.[7] Their strong personalities clashed whenever the stubborn and impulsive girl tried to challenge Akulina's plans for her. Plevitskaya came to blame her mother for everything bad that befell her. In turn, Akulina would accuse her of being cunning and evil.

The Vinnikovs's house, located only steps away from Trinity Church, was a typical peasant hut, with a thatched roof and wooden floor. Its main room had a large stove, a customary "red corner" shelf on which the family icon stood, a wooden table and chairs, and benches and shelves. A portrait of Tsar Alexander III and his family hung on the wall. According to Plevitskaya's memoirs, her family was not destitute. Like most other peasant households, the Vinnikovs survived on food derived from their livestock and land, which amounted to seven *desyatinas*, or about nineteen acres. When times were bountiful, Plevitskaya later recalled, her family enjoyed a variety of vegetables, fruits, and nuts, as well as fresh meats such as goose, ham, and corned beef. "A family of seven is not a lot," she noted, "but my parents were strong managers and with a good harvest, we had enough to survive on."

Plevitskaya assisted her mother with housework and fishing, while her father and siblings worked in the fields. Goose herding, which she abhorred, was her main outdoor responsibility from around the age of six. Akulina would remind her that a "hardworking girl is a treasure in the home." In late Imperial Russia, to become desirable as a potential farm wife, a girl needed to show that she was a stout laborer.[8] As she grew older, Plevitskaya supplemented the family income by selling cabbage and meat *pirozhki*, or pastries, at the nearby train station, not an unusual way for peasant girls and women to earn extra cash. She also made money for her family doing piecemeal jobs around the village. From an early age, Plevitskaya was being groomed to become a treasure in the home someday, although she increasingly found this role less attractive.

Plevitskaya grew up listening to and singing a variety of folk songs that were the most widely sung in Russia's heartland. Between 1860 and 1917, Russia experienced a sweeping folk music revival, and, as an adult, Plevitskaya became one of its principal beneficiaries.[9] Characteristic songs concerned soldiering, weddings, holidays, and the annual cycle of peasant and village life, including the bittersweet experiences of women and girls. Female performers dressed in traditional folk costumes. These included a long-sleeved dress called a *rubakha*, which was sufficient for unmarried girls and women, and a bright, often floral-patterned scarf. A married singer typically wore a *sarafan*, a kind of jumper, over her rubakha, as well as a head covering. Fancier headgear included a crown-shaped headdress or *kokoshnik*. During her performances as an adult singer, Plevitskaya usually wore parts of these folk costumes. She sometimes dressed as a peasant fresh from the fields. At other times, she dressed in elaborate costumes made of brightly colored fabrics and accented with pearls.

Plevitskaya first performed on Vinnikovo's streets, and she learned to sing in a stylized way by imitating her mother's voice and that of an in-law she admired named Tatiana. Tatiana, an orphan, had provided for herself by performing in taverns.[10] In her memoirs, Plevitskaya described the first time her singing was rewarded. She was nine years old, seated outside with her sisters and Tatiana, whom she aimed to impress. While she sang, a carriage approached containing a baron and his wife. They waved their handkerchiefs and then threw a paper bag down to her containing cakes and candies.

Plevitskaya also detailed Tatiana's wedding to one of her cousins, a man named Afoniak. Plevitskaya remembered that Tatiana "sang songs, but did not yell, as girls in the countryside usually yelled songs. Her voice was like pure silver." The guests, including her father and mother, sang popular wedding songs at the reception. According to Plevitskaya,

> Everyone knew that Akulina Frolovna was a great singer and player. I saw how my mother's light eyes were burning, how hard it was for her to keep from leaping up . . . but members of the wedding party were not supposed to dance: they had to remain seated at the table of honor. I fell in love with my mother—she was so alive. She tied a scarf on her head, a strand of her hair peeked out from under it . . . everything was breaking loose. . . . No one has a better mother.

Four decades apart in age, mother and daughter were inseparable, and Akulina was in many ways Plevitskaya's role model in singing as in life. However, whereas Akulina's spirit was circumscribed by her role as a village wife, Plevitskaya wanted to live a free life—breaking loose and singing wherever and however she wished.

The origins of Plevitskaya's singing career stemmed as much from her experiences in the village church as from events like the ones described

Trinity Church, Vinnikovo. Courtesy of Pamela A. Jordan

above. Like her mother and the majority of peasants at the time, Plevitskaya embraced Russian Orthodoxy and its rituals as beacons of daily life. Trinity Church featured (and still does) simple white plastered walls, hung with icons, as well as an icon screen, or iconostasis, located, as in all Russian Orthodox churches, on the center wall of the sanctuary. Believers not just from Vinnikovo, but from surrounding villages too, worshipped at the church, which was known for incorporating inspirational liturgical music into its masses.[11]

Plevitskaya noted that in church her mother "stood like a candle before God, and had no other thoughts but about God." In villages across Russia, women like Akulina were often the standard-bearers of rural Christianity. In contrast to her pious mother, Plevitskaya often struggled to focus on God while in church, and instead looked around curiously at the other parishioners, silently critiquing their outfits. Yet she learned some of her first songs there, surrounded by her loved ones and the priests she trusted and turned to for spiritual guidance. A well-liked village teacher, Vasily Gavrilovich, directed the choir—but to Plevitskaya's frustration, only boys were allowed to sing in it, a restriction that fueled her determination.

In May 1889, when Plevitskaya was nine years old, she and her mother traveled around the countryside and visited the city of Kursk. They began by walking nearly ten miles to a monastery called Korennaia Pustin to mark Pentecost. During Plevitskaya's childhood, the monastery housed a famous icon that drew many pilgrims, and she and her mother likely worshipped in its presence. Plevitskaya and her mother traveled next to Kursk. On warm evenings, in Vinnikovo, at sunset on her front porch, the young girl could hear the faraway ringing of the bells hanging in Kursk's baroque cathedral. Now she could enjoy in person the hustle and bustle of the capital city. She could admire the fancy dresses and peek into clothing stores and cafés. She and Akulina entered the city's cathedral and observed a service. As recounted in her memoirs, with her mother kneeling beside her, Plevitskaya prayed silently that she would never have to marry.

Plevitskaya and Akulina stayed overnight at nearby Trinity Convent, which is located near the edge of the hilltop on which central Kursk stands and affords pleasant views of the steppe. Mother and daughter attended a service in the convent church, and Plevitskaya was moved by the music performed by the female choir. At last, a sacred place where she could sing! She now set her sights on becoming a nun.

First, however, she planned to attend Vinnikovo's village school, which Akulina, who wanted her at home doing chores, opposed. After all, why would Dezhka need schooling when none of her older siblings could read fluently or sign their names? At this time, the majority of Russian peasant girls did not attend school. Like Akulina, most parents still believed that their daughters' main duty was to work hard. However, Plevitskaya was fortunate to have been born at a time when the Russian government, starting with Tsar Alexander II's 1864 reform program for the newly freed peasants, began expanding basic education for peasants in a drive to modernize Russia economically. More peasant parents wanted their children attending school, especially as better-paying jobs in the cities, which demanded more skills, became available. Children were eligible to attend school once they reached the age of eight, although many were forced to drop out due to family circumstances.

Nothing would deter Plevitskaya from attending school. She got her way partly because of a fight she had with her mother, who struck a blow to her head and felt guilty about it later. To compensate for hitting her, Akulina offered to buy new shoes and clothes for Dezhka and to send her to school. Plevitskaya recalled, "This was the first time mother got so angry with me, but also the first time I was so happy: Glory to God, I will go to school."

Knowing that the school was operated by the local Orthodox parish might also have made Akulina more amenable to letting her daughter attend it. The school was housed in a small wooden structure next to the church. Its entire curriculum lasted three years, the standard length of schooling for peasants at the time. Plevitskaya attended for only two and a half years, from the time she was nine until almost twelve years old. This was the only formal education she would have. Plevitskaya later reminisced how nervous she was on her first day of school, but she derived confidence by wearing her finest clothes and a fancy hair ribbon, a gift from a friend. Plevitskaya admired her teacher, Vasily Gavrilovich. It was unusual for her to have a male teacher, as over half the teachers in rural schools were women. In rural schools, students typically learned only the rudiments of reading and writing.[12] Unlike most schools in the area, Vasily also taught his students the fundamentals of singing.

Plevitskaya's education proved valuable in more ways than one, but she continued to maintain her childhood superstitions; a belief in pagan magic was widespread in peasant communities and meshed syncretically with rural Christianity. Her strong imagination played a role as well. She felt traumatized by the death of a classmate and dear friend, Misha Kozyrka, who was buried alive in grain. A woman in the village claimed to have seen a demon at the moment Misha was killed. Plevitskaya believed her and was afraid to leave her house. She remained superstitious and impulsive throughout her life and assigned deep symbolic meaning to her dreams.

Sadly, her stable family life ended abruptly when Vasya died. The exact year is not noted in Plevitskaya's memoirs, but it may have been 1893, when she was thirteen years old. The death of her father marked her first bout of genuine grief. Vasya had left Vinnikovo for three days to visit a mill and returned feeling ill and feverish. He struggled to breathe and died shortly afterward. Plevitskaya described how her father's death aged her and added a new layer of pensive moroseness to her personality.

As a widow, Akulina now bore full responsibility for farm operations and her family's welfare. For her youngest daughter, she wanted an early marriage to a neighbor boy named Yakushka. Plevitskaya, though, showed no interest in the match, and Akulina eventually stopped pestering her about him. Not only was Plevitskaya not attracted to the boy, but she knew that, once married, she would be expected to live with and act as a servant to her in-laws.[13]

Within a year of her father's death, Plevitskaya begged her mother to take her to the Kursk convent. This time Akulina relented. "And I remember her words," Plevitskaya wrote: "'It's clear that God directed Dezhka on the path of righteousness and truth.'" During the late 1800s, when the Russian government began to pursue economic modernization, a growing number of peasants, especially young men, left for the cities to find work.[14] At the same time, many peasants looked down on cities as places of decadence and temptation. Peasant girls in particular, if they left for the city, badly compromised their chances of marrying well back in their hometowns.[15] Akulina may have felt less worried about her youngest daughter's living in a convent in Kursk because she would be insulated from the city's dark side.

When Plevitskaya entered the convent, it was run by Mother Superior Miletina and Mother Konkordia, who had served there forty years and twenty years respectively. They informed Dezhka that all but the oldest nuns performed labor. If they did not receive funds from home, younger women had to work for their room and board. Plevitskaya's time at the convent began without incident. She would need to live there three years, first as a postulant, then as a novice, before taking the veil. She had to pay 300 rubles for tuition, a significant sum for a peasant family. Instead of giving the sisters money, which Plevitskaya's mother could not afford to do, she paid them in kind with geese, a pig, and wheat from the family farm. Plevitskaya herself sold icons and other religious items at a bazaar as a part of her regular duties. Much of her life centered on the convent's church. She conformed to the daily liturgical routine without objection, waking up at 6:00 a.m. and attending prayers in the church. By the time she turned sixteen, she was dressing in black and singing in the choir, the activity she had most looked forward to upon first visiting the convent.

Despite her many hopes and her promising start, Plevitskaya left the convent at age sixteen, after only two years of training. Realizing that not all the nuns were happy or truly righteous and kind, she had gradually become disillusioned. She later described the example of Polia, a lay sister who had been at the convent for six years. Not only did Plevitskaya observe how miserable, exploited, and unfulfilled Polia was, but she also identified with Polia's feeling of entrapment. She herself felt the pull of what lay beyond the convent's walls. The young Dezhka came to believe that the devil could lurk anywhere, inside a convent or outside it. In this sense, the convent was no better a place to pursue her life's purpose than the bazaar or a restaurant, or anywhere else she might take up commerce—or follow her dream of performing publicly. Abandoning her childhood intention to become a nun, Plevitskaya now faced, for the first time, the challenge of how to provide for herself.

After leaving the convent, most likely in 1897, Plevitskaya stayed for a few days with her sister Dunya, who worked in a factory in Kursk. It was around Easter, and a popular circus, operated by the Zaikin Theater Company, came to town for the holiday. Dunya agreed to take her little sister to one of their shows. This was the first time Plevitskaya had ever seen a professional performance. She and her sister bought tickets and sat on the bleachers. Plevitskaya long remembered the clowns, the acrobats, the trained animals, and the tightrope walkers. Her eye alit on a female acrobat around her age, dressed in red, and it occurred to her that, with some training, she could tumble just as well. A grand choir, wearing the costumes of old boyar nobility, sang and danced. Another female performer cantered about on horseback. Observing how much pleasure the audience took from the spectacle, she elected on the spot to join the circus and work as an acrobat. She gleefully spoke of this decision to Dunya, who dismissed her sister's talk as nonsense. Undeterred, Dezhka sought Mr. Zaikin out the very next day.

Approaching the manager, she was very nervous, but she had no need to worry. Zaikin accepted her immediately: "He didn't even ask about my relatives, or anything about my background." He introduced her to his daughter, Lelia, the girl in the red dress. It was his wife who had ridden the horse. Plevitskaya noticed that Madame Zaikina did not look as pretty as she had the day before, and realized from this how much cosmetics could change a person's appearance under stage lights. Lelia took her to her family's apartment, which looked exactly like the sort of place where

The Zaikin Theater Company, Kursk, circa 1897. Dezhka Vinnikova (Plevitskaya) stands in the middle, wearing a boyar noblewoman's costume, with a dark kokoshnik on her head. Courtesy of the Museum of N. V. Plevitskaya, Vinnikovo

she had imagined artists would live. Lelia invited the peasant girl to stay in her room. That first night at the Zaikins, Dezhka began to feel guilty about leaving the convent and worried about her mother's reaction.

The next day, Plevitskaya set out to participate as a full-fledged member of the Zaikin Theater Company. In the morning, she appeared for a group photo, standing in the center of the group and wearing a boyar costume. Then she began training on a tightrope, which she enjoyed. It is perhaps no surprise that Plevitskaya would be attracted to tightrope walking—an activity associated in the popular imagination with defying gravity and taking risks, habits that naturally came to Plevitskaya, both as a child and a woman.[16] During her brief flirtation with tightrope walking, she experienced her first vision of herself on stage as something to behold. But after that first day as a circus performer, she began to notice dark forces at play behind the scenes and started having second thoughts. In one noteworthy episode, a clown approached her, smelling of alcohol. He scared her with his curious talk, "unbecoming of a married man," and she ran from him into Lelia's room.

Her family worried about her too. Discovering that Dezhka had vanished, Dunya first rushed to the convent, only to learn that her headstrong little sister had left. Then she alerted Akulina, who was mortified. How could a child of hers embrace the sinful life of the circus? She raced to Kursk to find her daughter. There she encountered the drunken clown, who at least had the decency to disclose her daughter's whereabouts. Akulina reproached Zaikin for not seeking her permission before hiring Dezhka. At first, Plevitskaya refused to quit. But hours later, she relented, after Akulina promised that she would not be forced to return to the convent. "Mama, calm down, I did not abandon God. God is strong in my heart," the girl reassured her.

Akulina literally dragged her from the big top. "I took refuge in a corner at my sister's place and cried from shame," Plevitskaya wrote. Her mother tried to soothe her: "We'll live in the country until July, and then Aunt Aksiniya will go to Kiev on a religious pilgrimage. I'll send you with her. You'll visit grottos and, at the same time, your sister Nastenka. She's already been in Kiev for three months." Rather than focusing on the pilgrimage, Plevitskaya immediately began to plot her next move: finding another circus to join.

Before Plevitskaya left for Kiev, Akulina secured a few months' work for her in Kursk as a maid to the daughter of a wealthy merchant named Nikolai Gladkov. "The house was rich, important, and I soon grew used to it," Plevitskaya recalled. Although she considered Mr. Gladkov "annoying," Mrs. Gladkov was kind to her. "Only the older daughter, Manya, who was lame, behaved haughtily and in a chilly manner," Plevitskaya wrote. Here she observed how the upper class lived, and she came to feel dissatisfied with her lowly status. Although social mobility was extremely limited in Imperial Russia, she was not deterred by this fact.

Sometime over the summer, Plevitskaya fell ill with a sore throat, and her mother nursed her back to health. She never worked at Gladkov's house again. By this point, her sister Nastenka was in Kiev, married to a soldier, and all her other siblings had left the family farm as well. Plevitskaya stayed with her mother a while longer before leaving for Kiev. She noticed that her Vinnikovo friends "had already married, conducted themselves as adults, and went to the karagods as older people." Akulina wanted to set her up with a nice young man named Sergei, but Plevitskaya again refused. Now was the time for her to move on.

Recalling her first train ride, which took her to Kiev and away from her mother's watchful eyes, Plevitskaya remembered how the train set off: "Mother began crying. I tried to be cheerful, but not for long. We passed familiar houses, the green dome of the bell tower came into view over the tall poplars. A golden cross flashed. We passed the brooks in the pasture and departed from my village into the radiant distance." Vinnikovo would never again be her permanent residence.

Plevitskaya and her Aunt Aksiniya arrived at the train station in Kiev. Aksiniya showed her around town, window-shopping for clothes and worshipping at St. Sophia's Cathedral. She saw her sister Nastenka and her niece Niusia. After two weeks, her aunt left, and she stayed on with Nastenka. Her sister's landlord had a niece named Nadya who was Plevitskaya's age, and the two became friends.[17] Nadya invited her to a show given by a professional choir in a park called Arkadia. Students and artists were in the audience. Plevitskaya felt self-conscious about being the only one there wearing a peasant scarf while others wore urbane-looking hats. A military band played, and a half circle of women sang a light march. After the performance, the girls approached the group's manager about auditioning, and he said that they could sing in the choir if they wished.

The following day they met the choir director, Alexandra Lipkina. Plevitskaya recalled her as "a tall woman with a proud bearing, smoothly combed hair, without any makeup. I liked her very much." Plevitskaya and Nadya made a positive first impression on her, and she told them to come the next day to receive an advance, to have their voices evaluated, and to order the black-and-white dresses they would wear as their costumes. Lipkina, a music teacher and folk singer in her own right, crucially influenced Plevitskaya's musical career path. The two girls were excited about their new opportunity but decided not to tell their relatives for fear of reprisal. They also did not inform their director that they had not received permission from their families to join the group.

The next day, Plevitskaya had her first rehearsal. Alexandra's husband, Lev Lipkin, played the piano, and the first song was a march. Lev suggested that Dezhka sing the contralto part. This was the first time her voice was judged by a professional to be in the lower range, although for the balance of her career, she was more often described as a mezzo-soprano than a contralto. The Lipkina Choir, forty members strong, performed a wide repertoire of songs, including classical opera pieces. Plevitskaya quickly determined that singing in a choir would be better than performing in a circus, and she enjoyed earning a salary, however modest. Plus, Lipkina's folk singing inspired her, and she imitated her style. Despite a lack of formal voice training and an inability to read music, Plevitskaya soon impressed crowds with her expressive voice. Lipkina began to assign her solos, and she worked diligently to improve her technique and performance style.

Soon Plevitskaya learned that the choir would be touring southern Russia, stopping in Kursk. She fretted about how to keep her family from noticing her presence. "I know that I behaved cruelly toward my relatives, not writing them," she reminisced. "In my soul I suffered, but I was afraid to write, for fear that they'd go searching for me." Her family considered any form of stage life sinful—at least at this point, before she had become one of Russia's highest-paid singers and one of the tsar's favorite performers.

Once in Kursk, Plevitskaya stayed with the choir at the Evropeiskaya Hotel, which her sister Dunya had denounced as indecent. When she strolled around Kursk, she disguised herself. Her pretense, though, did not fool Dunya, who spotted her on the street and urged her to return home. Plevitskaya tried to resist but ended up at Dunya's apartment before escaping back to the hotel. Dunya later tracked her down at the hotel and pointed out their mother, who was weeping on the street. Feeling a sense of defeat, Plevitskaya escorted Akulina to Alexandra's room. Unexpectedly, Akulina saw a burning icon lamp and noticed Alexandra's mother playing affectionately with her granddaughter. Akulina was positively impressed by the choir director's religiosity and dedication to family togetherness.

Alexandra told Akulina that her daughter was talented. "We're drilling her, and she will be a good artist," Alexandra reassured her.

Akulina asserted that it was a "very big sin to be an actor. . . . And you, Dezhka, what do you say: is it possible not to live and make your soul miserable?" Plevitskaya insisted that she wanted to remain in the hotel with the choir.

"If only your father were still alive," Akulina sighed. Then she sat quietly for a few minutes, pondering the situation. Finally she said, "Well, Alexandra Vladimirovna, you take her, and beat her if she doesn't listen. As God is my witness, I give you Dezhka." She wept and blessed Dezhka before the icon. Akulina was comforted by at least knowing what had become of her daughter. Akulina and Dunya accompanied Plevitskaya to the train station, where the choir was leaving for the next stop on their concert tour, the city of Tsaritsyn.

In Tsaritsyn, Plevitskaya saw Alexandra perform for an audience for the first time and admired her rendition of folk songs. The young woman imagined herself one day performing solos on stage. Alexandra's singing also reminded her of her own mother's singing. In some respects, Alexandra had become Plevitskaya's surrogate mother.

Plevitskaya worried about maintaining a moral code while staying in hotels and traveling with the choir. Half of its members seemed hardworking and humble, and Plevitskaya sought to emulate them. Otherwise, she feared, singing in lowlife taverns might lead to a life of debauchery. She remembered her mother's warnings to stay on the right side of God. "My mother's simple instruction became for me a staff that I strongly leaned on," Plevitskaya wrote. Plevitskaya also took strength from her dedication to performing folk songs: "A Russian folk song does not know slavery," she wrote, as it comes from the hearts of ordinary people, rather than from the brains of trained musicians.

Then, a series of unforeseen circumstances transformed Plevitskaya's life. A year or so after the concert tour of southern Russia, Alexandra mysteriously disappeared. Plevitskaya speculated in her memoirs that her mentor had been hauled away—possibly kidnapped—by a Persian man who then sailed on to the Azerbaijani city of Baku. Alexandra's husband was distraught and tried to commit suicide. He lacked the strength to lead the choir, and it broke up. Around this time, a Polish ballet troupe, the Shtein Company, arrived in Kiev to perform in the Château des Fleurs Theater. The balletmeister, named Vankovsky, invited all former Lipkina members, including Plevitskaya, to join the troupe. Shtein featured dancers from the Warsaw State Theater, including one Edmund Miacheslavovich Plevitsky, whom she soon befriended.

Within a year of joining Shtein, Plevitskaya was dancing in addition to singing. Plevitsky gave her pointers, and she came to admire his intelligence, stately mannerisms, and humility. She now kept in better touch with her mother, feeling less shame because she was establishing herself as a performer and working with respectable artists. In other words, she saw herself as standing on more equal ground with Akulina. In one letter, she begged her mother for her blessing to marry Plevitsky, describing him as like a baron in his comportment. According to Plevitskaya's memoirs, Akulina approved of the couple's marriage and grew to love Edmund as a son. The two married in 1902. From this point forward, Dezhka Vinnikova would be known as Nadezhda Plevitskaya.

The Plevitskys were forced to look for new work when Shtein went bankrupt after a concert tour of Ukrainian cities that took in less revenue than predicted. Fortunately, in 1903, before they became destitute, they managed to secure positions with the Minkevich Choir, named after its director, a former opera singer. Minkevich mentored Plevitskaya, encouraging her to focus exclusively on the Russian folk genre. He hired Plevitsky as the group's choreographer. The pair performed with Minkevich for five years, until 1908.

Nadezhda Plevitskaya with her first husband, Edmund Plevitsky, circa 1905. Courtesy of Irina Raksha

Touring with the Minkevich group, Plevitskaya visited St. Petersburg, the empire's grand metropolis, for the first time. Here, she sang in café *chantants*, where members of the growing middle class gathered. These small stages offered various artists—singers, choirs, dancers, acrobats, comedians, and even trained animals—a chance to perform.[18] She also soloed in a Petersburg restaurant called the Krestov Garden. In her free time, Plevitskaya attended other groups' concerts and theatrical performances. "Theater was my form of relaxation and my school," she noted. She visited the opera and ballet for enjoyment and to learn, and she wondered why only classical pieces, and not folk songs, were performed in large halls.

In an account published thirty years after Plevitskaya's death, an émigré named G. Breitman wrote an article about his early acquaintance with her.[19] A young newspaper publisher in Kiev at the time, Breitman met Nadezhda Vinnikova shortly after her arrival in the city, when she was living with a friend—likely Nadya—near its famous Golden Gates. Then, possibly in the summer of 1908, he was sitting in a Kiev nightclub when two performers in Polish costumes appeared on stage dancing the mazurka. The girl looked familiar, and the pair turned out to be the Plevitskys. Next

Breitman watched as Plevitskaya sang a solo. She was a real singer, he noticed, original, fresh, self-taught. Afterward, he met her and Plevitsky. Breitman also described how Plevitskaya had sometimes performed in the private rooms of certain nightclubs. This sort of performance carried more than a whiff of sexual allure. Such establishments attracted shady characters, and the women who sang in them were often desperate for money.

Plevitskaya, Breitman reminisced, impressed the nightclub's owners and clientele because of her ability to perform what some might have called "boorish songs." One night she appeared alone on stage at the nightclub, and the audience was ecstatic. "I can't say that I played an important role in her career development, but I did play a part," Breitman continued. In his Kiev paper, he depicted Plevitskaya as a talented interpreter of folk songs. More importantly, he persuaded her not to settle for a career of nightclub singing, but to pursue instead a serious career, possibly in the popular variety show format, which the Russians called *estrada*. Breitman claimed that she and Plevitsky accepted his advice. "Within two years," Breitman wrote, "she became a well-known singer. . . . Knowing that I was always proud of her success . . . who could have guessed how she'd finish her life!"

Plevitskaya gained a national reputation as a popular singer during the so-called Silver Age, a cultural era lasting from approximately 1890 to 1920 and marking Russia's transition to artistic modernism. Key figures of the Silver Age included poets Alexander Blok, Anna Akhmatova, and Boris Pasternak; the writer Maxim Gorky; the ballerina Anna Pavlova; the impresario Sergei Diaghilev, of Ballets Russes fame; and those who designed or composed for Diaghilev, such as Léon Bakst and Igor Stravinsky. Plevitskaya was fortunate that, along with this cultural revival, the leisure industry flourished and new recording technology emerged. According to scholar Louise McReynolds, "leisure broadened the category of 'arts' to include the growing number of public spaces that had become commercialized, such as nightclubs, racetracks, and tourist hotels."[20]

Estrada variety shows originated in Moscow and St. Petersburg in the nineteenth century and usually took place during the summer. Choirs and soloists performed a diverse assortment of songs, from popular urban tunes to folk and gypsy numbers, and were joined by virtuoso musicians on the balalaika and other folk instruments. The estrada's format was new: for the first time, it featured songs performed as "individual numbers," with no shared narrative.[21] By the early twentieth century, the folk music revival that began in the mid-1800s had become big business, boosted by the estrada's popularity. In Russia in 1907, there were around fifty variety shows; by 1912, their number had almost doubled.

Estrada art represented the most elementary aesthetic pursuit—easily accessible, popular singing, featuring sentimental prose that manipulated listeners' emotions. Singers like Plevitskaya were not expected to have received any formal musical training, which was one reason she could use this style to gain fame.[22] The estrada, which in Russian also means "stage," was an important part of a new commercial synergy that linked together gramophone recordings, mass audiences, films, and popular entertainment magazines and newspapers. Initially, it acted as a democratizing force, as middle-class and even lower-class Russians could afford to buy tickets. But as the industry grew more profitable, ticket prices increased and performances became less accessible to lower-class fans. Either way, the estrada's stars profited greatly. "They enjoyed wide recognition in the most diverse ranks of Russian society, competing with writers, artists, and painters," Soviet musicologist I. V. Nestev notes, and "their influence on the musical daily life of the masses was enormous."[23]

The variety show featured a significant number of female singers. They came to personify the new modern urban woman, who was more publicly engaged, more independent, and sexually freer.[24] Two singers in particular paved the way for Plevitskaya's rise to stardom and shared similar career paths: Varya Panina (1872–1911) and Anastasia Vialtseva (1871–1913). There is no surviving evidence that Plevitskaya knew either of these women, although they may have crossed paths when she was performing in St. Petersburg. Panina, affectionately proclaimed "Queen of the Romance," gained fame as a gypsy singer, at a time when Russian audiences were passionate about the exotic allure of that style. She first performed in Moscow's top restaurants and then became an estrada star. She died in 1911 at age thirty-nine, as Plevitskaya's fame was growing.

Anastasia Vialtseva, who lived and performed in St. Petersburg, was a famous actor, businesswoman, and singer of gypsy romances. Her listeners expected an escape from their daily routine, and she delivered. In addition to her performing career, Vialtseva operated her own restaurant and the Monte Carlo Casino, which was rumored to have housed an upscale brothel servicing the capital's elite men. She was admired for her talent but viewed as scandalous and decadent. Like Panina, Vialtseva died fairly young, at age forty-two, in 1913.

Mirroring Panina and Vialtseva, Plevitskaya used a wide range of emotions in performing her repertoire. However, in contrast to them, she cultivated a more wholesome and less glamorous stage presence. Plevitskaya typically appealed to audiences' sense of national identity, particularly to their sentimentalized views of Russian peasant life. She comforted her

Nadezhda Plevitskaya, posing in an early publicity shot, wearing a boyar noblewoman's costume, circa 1907. Courtesy of Irina Raksha

urban listeners, reassuring them that they still shared common values with each other and their countryside kin, even as modernity and decadence threatened to fracture the Russian social order. According to Laura Olson, "musical producers not only sought to engender 'Russian character' through their performances, but aimed to define and evoke 'authenticity' through their manipulation of potent symbols of untouched folk nature."[25] Plevitskaya became expert at portraying folk simplicity. She even seems to have convinced herself of her genuineness—although this, of course, remains unknowable.

Plevitskaya, then, was a key beneficiary of the Silver Age's new spirit. By 1908, she had been performing for several years in ensembles and nightclubs. She increasingly wanted to have her own billing, but felt guilty about abandoning her husband and the other Minkevich performers for a solo career. "For a while, I had been invited to Moscow to [perform in a restaurant called] Yar," she later recalled. "But I didn't want to leave the troupe."

Yar was a prestigious restaurant in northwest Moscow that had opened in the early 1800s. In its luxurious setting, Russia's rich and powerful flocked in the evenings to be seen and entertained. The lure of opulence and the thought of her own solo billing were too great for Plevitskaya to reject. Whether or not Breitman's advice played any part in her decision, she, with her husband's support, sought the advantages of relocating to Moscow. Her invitation came courtesy of an ambitious businessman named Aleksei Sudakov, who had managed Yar since 1896.[26] Like Plevitskaya, Sudakov came from peasant stock and had climbed the career ladder through a combination of effort, talent, and luck. He expected his performers to work as hard as he did.

Sudakov wanted his female performers to look attractive, but not to dress too sexily. He was concerned that Yar maintain its reputation for decency, as its rich male clients frequently brought their wives. At his first meeting with Plevitskaya, Sudakov reportedly asked her whether she performed in an outfit with a revealing décolletage, and she was taken aback by his directness. Nevertheless, she signed a contract to perform for him regularly, beginning in the winter of 1909. She deemed her first show at Yar a success, and her subsequent concerts there cemented her image as a premier interpreter of Russian folk songs. "Muscovites fell in love with me, and I with them," she wistfully recalled in her memoirs.

In 1908, Plevitskaya made the first recording on disk of a popular folk song, "The Happy-Go-Lucky Merchant" (*Ukhar-kupets*), in the Moscow studio of the Pathé record company, and it was one of her first recordings.[27] Based on lyrics by Russian poet Ivan Nikitin (1824–1861), the version Plevitskaya recorded was arranged by Yakov Prigozhi, a pianist at Yar. The song is about a rakish and wealthy young merchant who, passing through a village, rapes a beautiful young woman during a night of debauchery and against her mother's protests; the merchant gives her silver and gold before departing, but she is left without her "maidenly conscience." Vsevolod Meyerhold, one of modern Russia's most acclaimed theater directors, wrote that Plevitskaya's stirring rendition of this song influenced audiences no less than stage dramas.[28] She was already establishing herself as a gifted storyteller.

Within months of signing on at Yar, and at approximately the age of thirty, Plevitskaya had her biggest break yet. In the fall of 1909, in the famed market town of Nizhnyi Novgorod, she attracted the attention she needed to vault to a position of national prominence. In a word, she was "discovered." That September, Nizhnyi Novgorod, which lies 250 miles to the east of Moscow, held its annual trade fair, which had been celebrated far and wide for years in the Russian folk calendar. As part of the festivities, the Naumov Restaurant hired her to perform nightly as the fair ran its course. Each evening, she was the final act; little did she imagine the triumph that would result. Each night, "it was usually loud in the hall," Plevitskaya recalled, "but when they hung a sign on the curtain with my name on it, the audience fell silent." During one of the Naumov concerts, a wealthy old merchant named Nikolai Bugrov found himself reduced to tears by Plevitskaya's rendition of "Quietly the Small Horse Drags Herself Along" (*Tikho tashchitsia loshadka*). Tears streaming, Bugrov tried to hide his face due to pride.

Another of her admirers that night—and a far more important one— was opera tenor Leonid Sobinov, also performing in Nizhnyi Novgorod. Sobinov had earned his fame as an opera singer at Moscow's Bolshoi Theater and later performed in famous opera houses in Europe, including Milan's La Scala. After her performance, Sobinov introduced himself to her backstage. Bursting with admiration, he told her, "Only talent can compel such a crowd to fall silent. You've got that talent."

Sobinov invited Plevitskaya to sing with him at a charity concert in the Grand Fair Theater later in the week. They were joined by another famous opera singer, Renée Radina-Figner. Plevitskaya could not believe that she was singing with stars such as these. She felt nervous as she entered the stage, but after one song she felt united with the audience. Sobinov was immensely pleased with her performance. The next day a newspaper reviewer noted how this virtual unknown was singing with noteworthy artists. Plevitskaya was grateful to Sobinov for offering her this immense ar- tistic leg up. "Thanks to Sobinov," she wrote, "I grew strong wings." Like Breitman, Sobinov took credit for persuading her to perform in variety shows.[29] Once he returned to Moscow from Nizhnyi Novgorod, Sobinov told musicians and theater literati about her talent and invited her to his home to sing for them. Within weeks, Plevitskaya had signed numerous lu- crative contracts for concerts at large halls across Russia. To commemorate the good fortune that had come to her in Nizhnyi Novgorod, she made a point of returning there every fall to perform at the fair.

In the meantime, in late September and early October of 1909, after her concerts in Nizhnyi Novgorod had concluded, Plevitskaya performed in the Summer Theater in Yalta, a popular resort on the Black Sea. By now, she was overflowing with hope and felt a sense of boundless possibil- ity. In Yalta, everyone was anticipating the arrival of the tsar and his family, who vacationed at Livadia Palace. Plevitskaya felt emotional when thinking of Nicholas II, for whom she would sing only six months later.

The thought of Nicholas II evoked Plevitskaya's childhood memories of the photo of his father, Alexander III, which had hung on the wall of her peasant hut in Vinnikovo. She imagined her father kneeling before the portrait, with the rest of her family beside him, praying for the royal family's safekeeping. The socioeconomic gulf between the two families, along with Alexander III's right-wing despotism, had been irrelevant to the Vinnikovs, who had essentially been patriotic but apolitical.

Now, as an adult, Plevitskaya was mixing with Russia's elite, including members of the nobility who were charmed by her seeming Russian authenticity and her lack of airs. Looking back on her time in Yalta, Plevitskaya recalled, "My heart was young and winged then. It seemed to tear itself loose from my chest and fly off into the sunny expanse."

2

YEARS OF FAME AND FORTUNE

Plevitskaya's performances in Yalta in September 1909 were well received by audiences and marked the first of many concert tours. In her memoirs, she recalled feeling eager to build on her success. Back in Moscow, she broke her contract with Yar Restaurant, bitterly angering her patron there, the manager Sudakov. In a rage, Sudakov sent Plevitskaya's wardrobe across town to the Bouffe Theater, where she would be performing under the direction of Alexander Blumenthal-Tamarin. Before long, though, Sudakov and Plevitskaya repaired their relations. Sending for her in a sleigh that whisked her to his restaurant, Sudakov treated her to drinks while musicians performed gypsy music in the background. Once he cooled down, Sudakov, a pragmatic businessman, understood that Plevitskaya needed to move on. She would be singing in the Grand Hall of the Moscow Conservatory—Moscow's premier concert hall—and ticket sales were brisk, so he did not try to convince her to return to Yar to perform on his small stage.[1] He and she parted company as friends.

At this time, Plevitskaya secured Vladimir D. Reznikov as her first impresario. The two met during one of her Yalta performances, where he immediately discerned her star potential.[2] Widely considered one of Russia's foremost talent agents, Reznikov laid the groundwork for Plevitskaya's financially successful career. Within months of signing on with him, Plevitskaya became one of Russia's top-paid performers. She would eventually record at least sixty songs on many of the top national and international record labels at the time—including Amour Gramophone, Beka-Grand-Plastinka, His Master's Voice, Lirophone, Pathé, and Zonophone (Gramophone)—and further widen her popular appeal. By 1915, nearly twenty million records were being produced a year in Russia, and many of them featured Plevitskaya's voice.[3] Due to her popularity and Reznikov's help, she earned between 50,000 to 60,000 rubles a year, which was then a princely sum.[4] "I was not greedy for money," Plevitskaya asserted. "Only success truly gladdened me."

Plevitskaya's fan base spanned all social classes, and her songs touched a chord in the national self-consciousness at a time when the folk music revival was at its height. Audiences felt she interpreted folk songs authentically and symbolized the eternal soul of the Russian people; her heartland origins served to strengthen this impression. Her admirers found her entire persona captivating. On stage, she wore glistening folk costumes, incorporated choreography, particularly delicate hand gestures, and used a broad range of emotions and her expressive brown eyes to connect with her audiences.[5] Alexandre Benois, one of the most prominent painters to design sets for the Ballets Russes in Paris, described Plevitskaya as a performer who "enchanted everybody, from the monarch to his least distinguished subject, by her typical Russian beauty and the vividness of her talent."[6] Pioneering film director Sergei Eisenstein later said that her singing helped shape his entire aesthetic.[7] Today's audiences would likely find her style too folksy and sentimental, but her strong popular appeal caused her to be widely emulated, with numerous would-be imitators trying to cash in on her fame.

Not all perceptions were so glowing. Some of Plevitskaya's contemporaries criticized her music as pseudo-artistic and lowbrow. Humorists parodied her. Her detractors found her voice unexceptional, even screechy. Music critics reviewed her concerts less frequently than journalists and literary figures, who were more attracted to her performance style, appearance, and interpretation of songs than the quality of her voice or its range, which was undeniably limited.

Success transformed the singer's private life and her worldview. The former peasant from Vinnikovo could now afford luxury apartments in Moscow and St. Petersburg. She hired several servants, including a Chinese butler and a personal assistant named Masha, whom Plevitskaya called her "devoted companion." Upon learning that two other servants, a maid and a nurse, had stolen valuables from her, she philosophized that "truth and beauty are found only up above, where the clear stars twinkle—and not below, where we are." As a result, "my relations with people changed so much."

As his wife's schedule grew busier and her social circle expanded, Edmund Plevitsky came to play an increasingly minor role in her life. They apparently remained childless; other than an unsubstantiated family rumor, there is no evidence that Plevitskaya ever gave birth.[8] The singer would have had access to contraceptives, given that she was living in Russia's largest cities and could afford them, and she could also have had abortions, which were illegal at the time but available to women of financial means.[9] Nor do her memoirs contain any expression of an interest in becoming a mother, although her childlessness may have had more to do with her demanding career and fragile health than with a conscious effort not to conceive. There is evidence that Plevitskaya, despite standing five feet, six inches tall and possessing a strong build, may have suffered from chronic nephritis, a form of kidney disease that can be mitigated now, but was highly debilitating in the early 1900s.[10] Plevitskaya frequently wrote about her anxieties and the exhaustion she suffered as a result of her long concert tours. While the career stress exacted a toll on her health, "the love of the crowd," in her opinion, made any price worth paying. As it happened, "the crowd" now included her country's monarch.

On the morning of March 27, 1910, the servant girl Masha opened the front door to Plevitskaya's apartment and was shocked to find Moscow's governor, General Vladimir Dzhunkovsky, standing there. He had arrived with an announcement from the commander of his Excellency's Regiment, General Vladimir Komarov, that she had been invited to sing for Tsar

Nadezhda Plevitskaya, wearing the Order of St. Anna that Tsar Nicholas II had awarded her, circa 1914. Courtesy of Irina Raksha

Nicholas II in honor of a regimental holiday the next day in Tsarskoe Selo, the famed palace suburb outside St. Petersburg. Plevitskaya was thrilled, but also placed in a bind: her debut performance in the Grand Hall of the Moscow Conservatory was scheduled for the very same evening. Of course, the orders of the "Little Father," as Russia's peasants customarily thought of the tsar, could not be disobeyed, and Plevitskaya unhesitatingly assured General Dzhunkovsky that she and Reznikov would change the conservatory concert date to accommodate the tsar's wishes. As commanded, Plevitskaya performed the next evening for Tsar Nicholas II in the Alexander Palace, the royal family's main residence. It is at this concert that Nicholas is said to have dubbed Plevitskaya the "Kursk Nightingale." In his diary entry of March 28, 1910, he wrote,

> After supper with the Composite Regiment, we all listened to Plevitskaya's singing. She sang Russian songs that I enjoyed. During the intermission, Leonardi's Romanians played, but the singer was a much greater success.[11]

Not surprisingly, Plevitskaya devoted more space to the event in her own memoirs. Upon reaching Tsarskoe Selo, she was first taken to the home of Vladimir Dediulin, the palace commandant. There she was given a room in which to prepare. At 10:00 p.m., an officer came to fetch her by royal carriage. At the entrance to the palace, Commander Komarov presented her with a floral bouquet. She requested a cup of coffee and a shot of cognac to calm her nerves, but these were unavailable. Instead her handlers gave her twenty tablets of valerian, a mild sedative, but even this failed to help.

When the time came to perform, servants opened the door to a drawing room where the tsar was seated beside several distinguished guests. Plevitskaya noticed that "only a table decorated with pale pink tulips separated me from the tsar." She looked directly into Nicholas's face and "met the calm light of his radiant eyes." He seemed surprised that she was so nervous. At that moment, "something miraculous happened. My fear passed, and I suddenly calmed down."

"By outward appearance," Plevitskaya observed, "the tsar was not majestic, and the generals seated nearby seemed more imposing." Still, Nicholas's bright eyes and humble demeanor struck her as befitting a tsar. She sang more than she had expected to. The tsar listened attentively and asked her, through Komarov, whether she was tiring. She said that she was too happy to feel tired. She worried about the lyrics to some of the songs she sang, which were written for peasants and other commoners, not for royal ears. "I was presented a list of songs, and I sang them from the soul," she remembered. "I even sang a revolutionary song about an unlucky fellow who was sent to Siberia because of unpaid debts, but no one took any notice of it." This was wholly in keeping with her self-professed lack of political awareness. (In a telling example from her memoirs, Plevitskaya confessed not knowing what the Cadet Party—from the initials "C" and "D," for "Constitutional Democrat"—was, thinking that the name referred literally to officers in training.)

As the tsar sat listening to her, Plevitskaya noticed a wistful light in his eyes. "I sang out of a sense of joy, joking in my songs, and the tsar laughed," she later wrote. "He understood the joke as simple, peasant-like, and plain." During the intermission, Komarov asked her to open the second half of her performance with a song in the tsar's honor. When her concert resumed, she stood by the piano:

> We will sing a toast, glorious soldiers,
> Thus sang in olden times our forefathers, with goblet in hand,
> Hurrah, hurrah, we soldiers strike up a song,
> Long live our Russian falcon, His Majesty.

Her hands shaking, she then carried a golden goblet to the tsar, and he rose. She continued:

> Little red sun, our radiant Tsar, we ask you to drink,
> Thus in olden time sang our forefathers, goblet in hand!
> Hurrah, hurrah, we soldiers strike up a song,
> Long live our Russian falcon, His Majesty!

Nicholas then drank the contents of the goblet and bowed to her. He said a hearty "hurrah," and tears filled his eyes. Before he left, he took her hand and said, "Thank you, Nadezhda Vasilievna. I have listened to you with great pleasure. They told me that you have never taken voice lessons before. You should remain as you are. I have heard well-trained nightingales many times, but they sang only for the ear. You sing for the heart."

Placing his hand on his own heart, he expressed his hope that this would not be the last time he would hear her sing. Choked with emotion, she could only answer, "I am happy, Your Majesty. I am happy." At this point, Nicholas walked out, surrounded by his entourage.

Plevitskaya's sentimental narrative suggests that she felt a strong spiritual connection to Russia's last tsar. What Nicholas's diary entry and the singer's narrative do not reveal is how the concert may have benefited them personally. The event offered Plevitskaya a unique opportunity to promote her career and afforded her an entrée into high society. In return, the tsar, as well as members of the nobility and top military officers, may have shown an interest in Plevitskaya not just because of Nicholas's well-documented admiration for the Old Russian folk style, but also because openly displaying that interest offered them a way to show the wider public their purported "democratic" artistic interests.[12]

Nicholas, who ascended to the throne in 1894 and was formally crowned tsar in 1896, had an abiding interest in art, music, and ballet. Plevitskaya put it simply: "His Majesty loved everything Russian."[13] On the other hand, Nicholas was an authoritarian ruler with weak political skills, ill equipped to lead Russia at a time when it needed to modernize economically and politically. He reluctantly agreed to share his power with the Duma, a legislative body formed out of desperation after the 1905 Revolution, when his subjects across the empire demanded economic and political freedoms. Meanwhile, radical left-wing parties, including the Bolsheviks, were agitating for his overthrow. Nicholas may have felt that after 1905 he needed to show that he still commanded the loyalty of the peasants, who comprised the vast majority of his empire's population. Plevitskaya may have appeared to him as a convenient stand-in for her class when he awarded her with the distinction of "people's singer," granted to only a handful of performers.

In her memoirs, Plevitskaya conveyed how lucky she felt to have gone from such humble beginnings to being one of the tsar's honored singers. She sang for Nicholas and his family several more times, including another performance at the Alexander Palace the following March, which Nicholas noted in his diary. Thanks to these growing ties with the royal family, her health was looked after by the tsar's own physician, Dr. Nikolai Simanovsky.[14] Her most treasured royal gift was a diamond brooch in the shape of the two-headed Russian imperial eagle. Perhaps inevitably, rumors emerged that Nicholas had taken Plevitskaya as a mistress. This was not impossible, as he is known to have had an affair with the ballerina Mathilde Kschessinska. Still, that was in his youth, before his marriage, and in the absence of any concrete or circumstantial evidence, it seems doubtful that Nicholas and Plevitskaya were ever lovers.

On March 29, the evening after her first concert for the tsar, Plevitskaya performed in the Grand Hall of the Moscow Conservatory. The conservatory had been founded in 1866 as a premier music school, and its distinguished roster of faculty members included Pyotr Tchaikovsky and

Alexander Scriabin. The Grand Hall, built in 1901, was its main concert venue, where classical music was performed but folk music rarely heard. Plevitskaya was the first folk artist to sing in this prestigious venue, and she performed there on at least one more occasion. Excitement about her March 2010 concert ran so high that a number of fans bought expensive overflow tickets for seats in the foyer after tickets for seats inside the hall had sold out.[15] The audience gave her a standing ovation. As she exited the building and walked toward her chauffeured car, dozens of well-wishers, including music students, were waiting to greet her. Plevitskaya noted in her memoirs how overwhelmed with attention she felt.

That same night she boarded a train to St. Petersburg for more concerts. Her compartment was filled with flowers from her admirers. Masha gave her some warm milk to soothe her. Plevitskaya could not sleep: "In my head, bells were ringing and my heart was expanding from the grateful love I felt for all people, all the world. Unexpectedly and undeservedly—I myself don't know for what—people loved my simple artistry, my peasant songs."

In the capital, Plevitskaya's next major concert took place in Tenishevsky Hall, which glistened with the shine of the diamond tiaras and the sheen of furs worn by well-heeled audience members. Prince Yuri Trubetskoi, who commanded the tsar's bodyguard, helped arrange the concert and encouraged other aristocrats to patronize it. Plevitskaya was now socializing with St. Petersburg's elite at soirées and other high-society gatherings. She sang at St. Petersburg's most distinguished venues, including the Mariinsky Theater and the Hermitage Theater. She could afford to stay in the magnificent—and expensive—European Hotel, as clear a sign as any that she was well on her way to becoming one of Russia's most celebrated performers.

Now established as a popular folk singer and estrada star, Plevitskaya gave light opera a try on the advice of some of her friends. In June 1910, in the Hermitage Theater, which adjoined the Winter Palace, she debuted as an operatic performer in a musical adaptation of Aristophanes's play *Lysistrata*. Immediately after each performance, she changed idioms and sang Russian folk songs in a variety show hosted by the same theater. Right away, she noticed how much more fulsome the applause was that she received after these folk performances than after the operas. If she had any doubt about her proper métier, it was now gone: the operetta would bring her neither glory nor satisfaction, and her fleeting dream about a career as an opera diva faded.[16] From that time forward, she focused her efforts on her solo career.

By this juncture, Plevitskaya's repertoire combined three song genres: the urban popular song, the folk song, and the military-patriotic song. She owed her initial fame largely to her renditions of urban popular songs, which featured themes about daily life. Based often on nineteenth-century poetry, these songs were arranged by estrada composers; perhaps the example best known to Western audiences is "Kalinka," composed in 1860 by Ivan Larionov. A noteworthy theater critic, A. R. Kugel, felt that such numbers appealed to lower middle-class tastes, and Plevitskaya's detractors sometimes accused her of crass materialism and pandering when she performed these urban tunes.[17] Reasoning along the same lines, Moscow music critic Yuri D. Engel panned a Plevitskaya concert as sentimental schlock, appetizing to the masses but lacking in musical skill.[18] If Plevitskaya's interpretations of these trendy urban tunes were indeed of dubious artistic value, this did not stop gramophone industry executives from recording them—they originally preferred these numbers to her Kursk peasant songs, which they assumed would be less profitable.[19]

Plevitskaya's second genre was the folk song. Initially, she avoided performing these, because she feared, as had the gramophone executives she worked with, that the urban public would reject them. However, she gradually introduced folk songs, many from Kursk, into her repertoire, and by 1914 they formed the largest part of it. She recorded lyrics from her youth and checked her memory of them with her former Vinnikovo neighbors. The words to one darkly humorous folk song, "Powder and Paint" (Belilitsy, rumianitsy vy moi), were conveyed by an older woman resident of Vinnikovo and later reinterpreted by Plevitskaya.[20] The lyrics, which illustrate the prevalence of domestic violence in peasant society, tell the story of a wife who flirted with another man in public and fears that her husband will whip her if he finds out.[21] Plevitskaya's most famous recording of this song, made in 1926 in New York City, was arranged by Sergei Rachmaninoff, who also accompanied her on piano. Included here is the chorus:

> Quickly, quickly, from my cheeks the powder off!
> And remove the rosy paint without delay!
> That my face be white and not betray the tale,
> For I hear my jealous husband stepping near.
> Lo, he brings, he brings a costly gift to me.
> What, a gift? A precious woven whip of silk![22]

Some of the folk songs Plevitskaya interpreted were based on the texts of old epic poems, called *byliny*, about Slavic knights-errant. Other folk numbers introduced urban audiences to lyrical themes about daily life in

Sheet music for "Quietly the Small Horse Drags Herself Along," which Nadezhda Plevitskaya often performed, 1911. Courtesy of Pamela A. Jordan

the provinces, providing details about weddings and major holidays. But they sometimes told of the hardships of life in Russia, depicting unhappy convicts stuck in exile, the misfortunes of factory workers, and the death and burial of poor peasants.[23] These songs resonated widely. For example, a Russian film actress named Sofia Goslavskaya recalled that in her youth, Plevitskaya had been her favorite concert singer. Of her songs, Goslavskaya noted that "she communicated the tragedy of them in such a way as to shake your soul, and we, the audience, were ready to listen to her endlessly."[24] Similarly, the best-selling author Alexander Kuprin, who saw Plevitskaya perform in 1913 in Yessentuki, near the base of the Caucasus Mountains, found that her singing—whether humorous or sorrowful—reflected Russian village life.[25]

Plevitskaya declared that one of her goals was to heighten public awareness of peasant songs, and to this end she recorded almost twenty songs from the Kursk region.[26] In 1910, when she learned that some ethnographers had been criticizing her efforts, she defended herself. In a newspaper interview, she said how sickened she was by these scholars' accusations of inauthenticity. Turning the tables, she lambasted them for only spending brief periods in the countryside, whereas she herself had grown up in a village. What could be more genuine? she asked. More-over, she knew the scholarly provenance as well: "Believe me, I studied all the articles—Filipov, Rimsky-Korsakov, Melgunov, and Ilinsky—and took everything possible from them. But no one would listen to me if I sang everything from [these older collections]."[27] Firing off a second salvo, Mitrofan Piatnitsky, director of the Piatnitsky Russian Folk Chorus, took Plevitskaya to task in an open letter for not performing even more archaic folk songs—ones that she had not grown up with or ever studied, but which ethnographers had researched.[28] Such interchanges show the constant friction between Plevitskaya and academic experts over the true meaning of "folk" and her deep-seated resentment of critics who belittled her for her lack of musicological training, when, to her mind, they were pretentious pedants who understood nothing of the environment in which she had been born and bred.

Given her lack of training in music theory, several composers—in-cluding the folk musician Stepan Skitalets, a friend of the writer Maxim Gorky—arranged new renditions of folk songs from the Kursk region for her, and these became publicly available in sheet music form.[29] Composer Ilya Sats was inspired by her songs after hearing her perform. Sats dreamed of creating a Theater of Folk Art and Performance where multinational ethnographic concerts would be staged. With this goal in mind, he formed a group of artists and music patrons called Music of the People, which Plevitskaya gladly joined.[30]

Plevitskaya began performing military and patriotic songs in 1910, on the initiative of General Pavel Plehve, who at the time was the commander of forces in the Moscow district. She sang for Plehve and his men at the theater in Moscow's Hermitage Garden on July 19. One author wrote in the journal *Russkii invalid* that soldiers in many regiments sang Plevitskaya's songs and that she was very much in the hearts of the troops.[31] As discussed below, this would particularly be the case during World War I.

Typically, Plevitskaya's sole form of accompaniment was a piano, and she was fortunate to have accomplished musicians by her side. Often these pianists shared in the glory of estrada singers like Plevitskaya and served as their trainers. For several years, Plevitskaya's most loyal accompanist was Alexander M. Zarema, who composed the popular folk song "Moscow Fire" (about the burning of the city during Napoléon's invasion).[32] While on a concert tour of Siberia, she ended up nursing Zarema back to health when rheumatoid arthritis laid him low. Another of her accompanists, V. Ia. Krushinin, later became a prominent Soviet-era songwriter.

Louise McReynolds argues that Plevitskaya only became a star after "she took the nationalist turn and specialized in stylized renditions of folk songs."[33] However, she was already a household name before 1914, when she was singing more urban and military-patriotic songs and making a number of recordings. It seems more precise to say that her popular appeal increased due to her adoption of a more gendered stage presence, that of a romanticized female peasant with natural, homegrown talent. McReynolds explains that Plevitskaya's costumes often resembled those worn in the pre-imperial era by women belonging to the noble boyar class, and that this look promoted "nostalgia for Russian exceptionalism, a heady theme especially during the First World War."[34] Indeed, Plevitskaya shaped herself into a unifying symbol of Russian identity, and her entire persona, not just her repertoire, helped to create a sense of Russian exceptionalism. In 1914, when she decided to devote more concert time to performing the folk songs she had sung in her childhood, she began appearing on stage in a peasant dress from the Kursk region.[35]

Given what many of her contemporaries said about her, the latter image rang more true. It appears that her average fans viewed her more as a common peasant woman whom they could relate to and sympathize with.

Nadezhda Plevitskaya, posing in peasant dress from the Kursk region, circa 1912. Courtesy of the State Archive of the Kursk Oblast

Whatever the case, the critic Kugel observed at the time that Plevitskaya's songs "strengthened national consciousness a thousand times more than many other voices put together."[36] He praised her "wonderful Russian nostrils," an attribute he associated with many great Russian singers, including the renowned bass virtuoso, Feodor Chaliapin.[37] To Nestev, the Soviet musicologist, the deeper reason for Plevitskaya's popularity, and that of many other estrada singers, was the "earthy and clearly nationalistic cast of the 'maliavinskaia baba,' the simple peasant in country dress with a smiling face with high cheekbones, personifying for many listeners Russia's awakening grassroots strengths, to which the future belonged."[38] In addition to her physical bearing, audiences appreciated Plevitskaya's adherence to the rules of dramatic expressive speech, a method that enhanced her storytelling abilities while she sang.[39]

Plevitskaya consciously portrayed herself as a singer of the people and for the people. While she enjoyed socializing with members of Russia's aristocracy and often acted deferentially toward them, she did not always agree with the advice they gave her about managing her image. In one revealing and humorous anecdote, she recounted how her high-placed friends unsuccessfully tried to mold her to their expectations:

> One time, at an evening at [Senator] Polovtsev's, in the presence of the Grand Duke and Duchess, I did not hold myself back and danced gypsy songs, which I love very much. A few days later, at an evening at the Grand Duchess Maria Pavlovna's house, Prince Trubetskoi, leaving the palace at the end of the concert, took me by the hand, as he would a young child, led me to his wife, Maria Alexandrovna, and said: "Mary, I'm going now and leave her to your care. Keep an eye on her, so she doesn't take any more foolish actions." A foolish action, in his opinion, was my gypsy dancing. He suggested that a "people's singer" should not dress in gypsy costumes.

Despite the occasional disagreements over style that she had with her sometimes uptight and prejudiced patrons, the apolitical Plevitskaya felt that she had no enemies during the prerevolutionary years. She apparently had affection for anyone who showed an interest in her music, regardless of his or her political leanings. Her mentality, however, came with a price. Her ties to Nicholas II and his courtiers may have enhanced her reputation in general, but they discredited her in the eyes of certain members of the intelligentsia. Many among this well-educated and cultured class denounced the monarchy as antiquated, anti-Semitic, and dictatorial—and an increasingly sizable proportion of them longed for a new government altogether.[40]

Disapproval came in the form of anonymous letters from a surprising number of people who did not like her performing for the tsar. One letter begged her not to go to Tsarskoe Selo for a concert, warning of a possible attempt on her life. She handed the letter to the commander of her escort. That night, after the concert, she thought she saw two people following her back to her hotel, but Prince Trubetskoi assured her that they were only officers dispatched to guard her.

One rumor had it that she belonged to a royalist, anti-Semitic right-wing organization called the Union of the Russian People. But while she may have befriended the group's leaders, how strong her ideological affiliation was for it remains unclear. On the other end of the political spectrum—and showing how indiscriminately she defined her circle of acquaintances—she befriended the landowner Mikhail Stakhovich, a writer and liberal Duma deputy. Stakhovich gave her books by Tolstoy to read, and she especially liked *Anna Karenina* and *War and Peace*.

Plevitskaya particularly appreciated the attention she received from noteworthy Russian artists, theater directors, and performers. Many of these figures welcomed her into their circles and mentored her. The famed

Nadezhda Plevitskaya, circa 1912. Courtesy of Irina Raksha

theater director Konstantin Stanislavsky, for example, offered Plevitskaya advice about the practicalities of performance and promoted her career. She once appeared at a star-studded concert that Stanislavsky hosted at the renowned Moscow Art Theater (MKhAT). Founded in 1898 by Stanislavsky and Vladimir Nemirovich-Danchenko, MKhAT produced plays by Anton Chekhov and Maxim Gorky, earning international renown for its innovative, top-notch dramatic offerings. The night Stanislavsky brought Plevitskaya to MKhAT, a galaxy worth of Russia's artistic luminaries were gathered to hear her sing. As she repeatedly said of herself, Plevitskaya felt that her singing was more understandable to artists than to trained singers, who she thought focused more on voice quality than on the interpretation of lyrics before a live audience. Stanislavsky, whose theatrical writings gave rise to "method acting," passed on to Plevitskaya a useful stage technique she turned to many times in the future: when she was not feeling up to singing but had to perform, she should look directly at someone whose face she liked and sing only to him or her.

The poet and musician Sergei Mamontov, son of the railroad tycoon and celebrated patron Savva Mamontov—who launched some of Silver Age Russia's brightest artistic careers from the "colony" he founded on his Abramtsevo estate outside Moscow—took an interest in Plevitskaya as well. In his 1910 memoirs, the younger Mamontov wrote that, despite her lack of training and refined musical taste, Plevitskaya had "a divine spark in her" and could win over the most sophisticated audiences. She "soulfully experiences everything she sings about and transmits it sincerely and strongly," he continued, "a gift lacked by many who finish the music conservatory with gold medals. When she sings, Plevitskaya's typical Russian face becomes inspired, she breathes with inspiration and is charmingly pretty." Mamontov observed further that, when Plevitskaya stopped singing, her face grew more humble and average looking.[41] He introduced her to Chaliapin, who had been discovered by the elder Mamontov.

The first time Chaliapin invited Plevitskaya to his apartment, he taught her how to sing one of his favorite folk songs. She remembered his telling her, "God help you, my dear Nadiusha. Sing your own songs that you brought from the land. I have no such songs, for I am an inhabitant of a *sloboda* [an urban industrial area], not the countryside." In 1913, Plevitskaya and Chaliapin performed at a concert in the Mariinsky Theater in St. Petersburg, attended by the royal family, in honor of the twenty-fifth anniversary of the founding of Vasily Andreev's Great Russian Orchestra. Ilya Shneider, a journalist who wrote for theater journals and one of

Plevitskaya's later impresarios, wrote that she was at one point even more popular than the great Chaliapin.[42]

While she did not begrudge herself the fruits of her fame, such as valuable properties and jewelry, Plevitskaya was not selfish. She performed in charity concerts, as famous performers of her generation were expected to do. In the Kursk area, her concerts raised funds for war veterans and the victims of a fire in Vinnikovo.[43] She paid for the education of her nieces and nephews and for a family wedding in Vinnikovo. She also had a home built for her brother Nikolai, gave village children gifts, and donated a bell for the church belfry.

In 1911 Plevitskaya signed a contract with Reznikov for forty concerts, beginning in mid-September. They would take her across Russia, including to Kursk. Newspapers chronicled her success and the enthusiasm of the audiences who packed her shows. In 1911, to honor her visit there, a candy company in Crimea created a new confection called the "Plevitskaya."[44] While performing in Kursk, she took advantage of the opportunity to visit Vinnikovo for the first time in several years. Her oldest sister Dunya was engaged to a man whom she had been unable to marry for some time because of her poverty. Plevitskaya paid for the dowry and wedding and attended the ceremony. She spent time as well with her mother, her brother Nikolai, and his wife Parasha. At the wedding dinner, Akulina toasted Dunya and Nadezhda and sang to the bride and groom. Nadezhda noticed how her mother "looked younger when she was singing," despite being over eighty years old. During her free time between concerts in Kursk, Plevitskaya visited the sisters at Trinity Convent.

Plevitskaya performed at a large concert hall in Kursk called the Velikolepnyi, or "Magnificent." As usual, she was nervous before the concert, but even more so because this would be the first time Akulina would see her perform on stage. "I will sing to her today, to her alone," Plevitskaya resolved. Akulina and other relatives sat in the second row. Plevitskaya nodded to them, and the audience clapped louder because they knew that her relatives were present. The Kursk governor and other officials approached her mother during the intermission to congratulate her on her daughter's success. Her mother felt uncomfortable with all the attention.

The journalist Shneider wrote in his memoirs about a subsequent concert in Kursk that Akulina attended. He observed that, although the crowd enthusiastically applauded her daughter's singing after every number, Akulina, wearing a traditional black peasant dress, sat rigidly and held her hands together tightly. But when Plevitskaya finished and took her final bow,

Nadezhda Plevitskaya, center, with two of her sisters, in front of her dacha, Vinnikovo, circa 1911. Courtesy of Irina Raksha

Akulina stood up and bowed deeply, saying, "Thank you, daughter," in a soft but distinct voice, and she quietly lowered herself back into her chair.[45]

Plevitskaya now used Vinnikovo to give herself a respite from city life and her exhausting tour schedule. In 1911, she bought her own plot of land on the west side of the village, near a picturesque ravine, and commissioned a renowned Moscow engineer, Vasily Kardo-Sysoev, to build a house. The land included part of the Moroskin forest, where she had played in childhood. She herself planted trees lining the driveway to her house. The sprawling house was smartly designed. It possessed the homey qualities of a cottage and the splendor of a wealthy dacha, complete with a terrace overlooking Plevitskaya's favorite countryside. In the only surviving photograph of the house under construction, Plevitskaya is shown playing croquet in the front yard with two of her sisters. The trees are mere saplings. Once her house was built, she spent portions of each summer there, visiting with family and friends and entertaining guests, such as the poet Nikolai Kliuev. She also rehearsed her new repertoire there with Zarema and other musicians.[46]

Before traveling to Vinnikovo in 1911, Plevitskaya returned to Moscow from her forty-stop concert tour drained of energy. As soon as she settled into her apartment, her phone began to ring, as people knew she was back in town and had various favors to ask. On top of this, she still had concerts to perform in Moscow and as far away as the Caucasus before she could relax in Vinnikovo. At one concert in Moscow, the audience numbered in the tens of thousands. Its huge size made her even more fearful of crowds, especially because she was swarmed by her fans and had to be rushed to her car. "I love the crowd, but only when I'm standing on stage," she joked.

In the summertime, Plevitskaya visited Vinnikovo whenever she had a break between concerts. She attended services at the village church, whose belfry now boasted the new bell she had donated. Taking a special interest in the upbringing of her young nieces and nephews, who adored her, she helped run the parish school. Edmund joined her in Vinnikovo, and the couple welcomed various friends into their home. During one visit, she learned that the father of one of her close in-laws, a woman named Nastya, had died. His death and Nastya's grief touched Plevitskaya, who resolved that "when my old age approaches, I will spend the last years of it here," in Vinnikovo.

This sad news also made her reflect on her mother's mortality. Akulina lived in Plevitskaya's house year round, and it was equipped with everything she needed. She liked her daughter's new home and was proud of her accomplishments. But Akulina felt uncomfortable around wealth and warned her daughter that "a person's soul grows stiff from being rich." Despite being in her eighties and contending with her own health problems, she continued to help the poor and infirm. By this point, her and Dezhka's past conflicts had lost their importance, and mother and daughter felt at peace in each other's company. Plevitskaya reassured herself that, at eighty-three years old, Akulina had more vitality than she herself did.

In fact, in the spring of 1912, Akulina stayed with Plevitskaya in her Moscow apartment for two days and attended one of her concerts at the Grand Hall of the Moscow Conservatory. Afterward, Plevitskaya asked Akulina about her impressions and received something of a lecture. "Well, what can I say, daughter?" she replied. "You were marked by God, and talent was sent to you. You sing such songs that would not be a sin to sing in church, my tears are overflowing. Yes, as a mother, I will not begin to praise you. . . . Many already praise you, as I saw this very night." It seems from Akulina's remarks that she was pleased her daughter was using a God-given gift, but out of fear of spoiling her, she remained reluctant to grant her unqualified approbation. Once the concert was over, Akulina, who missed Vinnikovo, quickly grew bored with Moscow and returned home with relief.

The year 1912 also marked the end of Plevitskaya's marriage to Edmund Plevitsky. In her memoirs, she does not detail exactly how their marriage fell apart, but one can read between the lines. By this point in their marriage, Edmund appeared to be dependent on Plevitskaya financially, and she seemed to treat him like a child rather than her spouse. In February 1912, she went with Edmund to the French Riviera, on the advice of her doctors, who had urged her to convalesce there after her latest bout of exhaustion. In the seaside resort of Beaulieu-sur-Mer, Plevitskaya relaxed on the balcony of her hotel while cooks fixed her salads. By March she had recovered and, before returning to Russia, decided to visit Monte Carlo. She criticized the famous casino there as an "insane asylum," recalling the obsession with which the gamblers crouched behind tables, scribbled numbers, and calculated their winnings and losses. During a game of roulette, which she was dominating, she suspected that the other gamblers were wondering how "such a scatter-brained person could get a hold of sables and jewels." Back in Beaulieu, she felt depressed by the rain and the sight of a destitute, forgotten old man—perhaps a former performer—who sang "O Solo, Mio" on the street under her balcony. She tossed some of her winnings down to him. "Plevitsky laughed at my tears," she recalled, "and, calming me, said that everyone is occupied with his own affairs."

"A singer sings, you cry, the English drink their coffee, and I am busy resolving whether or not you'll set me free today in Monte Carlo," he continued. "I dreamed about the number 22, and I definitely must play it." Plevitskaya let him go back to Monte Carlo to realize his dream, and in an hour, Plevitsky returned. "The dream turned out to be prophetic," she wrote. "He lost all his money. As they say, he was completely routed. I did not let him recoup his money." Symbolically, this point marked the end of their marriage, although not the end of their close relations.

According to family rumor, the marriage dissolved because Edmund was gay, although there is no evidence to support this claim.[47] Divorces in Russia at this time were hard to obtain due to restrictions in the civil code and the strong influence of the Russian Orthodox Church on conjugal life. However, if the Plevitskys in fact did not have sexual relations, then Plevitskaya could have used "sexual incapacity" as grounds for a divorce.[48] Whatever the case, Plevitsky eventually remarried and lived with his new wife in Poland after the Bolshevik Revolution, so if he was gay, he kept that secret largely to himself. Nadezhda and Edmund's divorce was relatively amicable, and they managed to remain friends for the rest of her life. Mindful of the importance of name recognition to her career, she chose to keep her married name rather than revert to her birth name. Akulina loved Plevitsky and was distressed when the couple divorced. Reportedly, Plevitsky's parents and sister lived with Akulina at Plevitskaya's house in Vinnikovo at least until the beginning of World War I. His parents were later buried in the cemetery there.[49]

Another possible reason for their divorce in 1912—perhaps the most likely one—is that Plevitskaya met her next love. One Sunday evening that spring, Plevitskaya performed at the invitation of the Grand Duchess Olga Alexandrovna, Nicholas II's sister, in her two-hundred-room palace in St. Petersburg. The grand duchess introduced her to two of the tsar's children, the Grand Duchesses Olga Nikolaevna and Anastasia Nikolaevna, in addition to several other guests. One of these was a young army officer named Vladimir Antonovich Shangin, a cousin to Olga Alexandrovna. A graduate of the Academy of the General Staff, Shangin had volunteered to serve in the Russo-Japanese War (1904–1905) and earned the prestigious St. George's Cross. Plevitskaya and Shangin were immediately attracted to each other and struck up a conversation. On the second day of their acquaintance, and certainly before the finalization of Plevitskaya's divorce, she and Shangin decided they loved each other.[50] They seem not to have become engaged until 1914. Some sources claim that they married, but in her memoirs, Plevitskaya described Shangin only as her fiancé.

With her romantic life so much in flux, Plevitskaya continued to perform, including for the royal family in the spring of 1912, at Yalta's Livadia Palace. Here, she planned to sing a number of old folk songs, but fretted that Tsar Nicholas II and Tsarina Alexandra would dislike them. Once the royal couple arrived at 10:00 p.m., the tsar's brother, Grand Duke Mikhail, led Plevitskaya to her seat; then the tsar approached her, squeezed her hand, and asked whether she was nervous. "Yes," she said. He told her not to worry, that the thick rug would help with acoustics in the room. Plevitskaya felt relieved when Prince Trubetskoi asked her whether she wanted some coffee. This, to those cued to the subtleties of royal behavior, indicated that the tsar was enjoying her performance. During the intermission, Alexandra told her that she liked the sad songs best. Plevitskaya apologized to Nicholas for the plainness of her songs that evening, but he reassured her that they were not musically deficient, as they were "our own."

Plevitskaya's memoirs suggest that, still, even years after becoming famous, she felt a sense of childlike awe about her celebrity when she sang for the crème de la crème of Russian society. Once in St. Petersburg

Nadezhda Plevitskaya, circa 1914. Courtesy of Irina Raksha

before a 1912 concert, she arrived at the hall and saw a group of beggars waiting to hand her petitions, pleading for financial assistance and other favors. After collecting some of their pleas, she entered the hall and saw, in stark contrast, the glittering surfaces of privileged society—the luster of the crystal chandeliers; the attractive, well-dressed crowd taking their seats in anticipation of hearing her; the tsar's occupied box. Here, she injected into her reminiscences a rare reference to the revolutionary changes that lay ahead. On stage that night, "I felt tipsy from the songs and the applause, and I could hardly have thought then that an awful phantom stood behind our backs; a wild threat was approaching that would bend our backs and burn our eyes with tears, as with a fire."

Through the end of 1912 into the first half of 1914, Plevitskaya remained blissfully ignorant of the events unfolding throughout Europe that would lead to total war. Her career continued in a blur of concerts, and her romance with Shangin shaped her private hours. She was one of a handful of "people's singers," a group that included her mentor Sobinov—with whom she performed at a concert in Yaroslavl in May 1913 marking the three-hundredth anniversary of the founding of the Romanov dynasty.

In June 1914, the singer was on holiday with Shangin in Switzerland, relaxing along the shores of Lake Neuchâtel in the western part of the country. During this Swiss idyll, on the morning of June 29, the young army officer read a newspaper article to Plevitskaya about the previous day's assassination of Archduke Franz Ferdinand, the heir apparent to the Austro-Hungarian throne, in Sarajevo, the capital of Austria-Hungary's recently annexed territory of Bosnia and Herzegovina. Understanding full well the wider diplomatic ramifications of this latest Balkan crisis, Shangin knew that he would be immediately called to duty.

"Gather up your things," he said stoically. "Tomorrow we must return to Russia."

"I didn't understand anything about politics and was surprised," Plevitskaya remembered. "Why did my affairs have to do with the murder of a foreign duke somewhere in Serbia? [*sic*: Serbia was independent at the time, and Sarajevo did not belong to it.] I didn't know that great grief was drawing nearer to us. Here it had burst out, and the earth shuddered and blood began to flow."

World War I would bring no glory to Russia's soldiers or civilians. On the war's eastern fronts, Russian units fought a formidable coalition of German, Austrian, and Turkish foes. The Russian army suffered from a constant lack of munitions, weapons, and basic supplies—and, as time went on, from poor morale and incompetent officers. By the end of Russia's tragic war experience, in March 1918, 1.7 million soldiers had been killed, and civilian deaths have never been satisfactorily calculated.[51]

Vladimir Shangin was one of approximately 1.5 million Russians who were immediately mobilized for war. He served as a lieutenant of His Majesty's Cuirassier Regiment in the Seventy-Third Infantry Division, under the command of Lieutenant General Georgy (Yuri) Levitsky. His division fought in Eastern Prussia as a part of Russia's First Army, which was under the less than inspired command of General Paul von Rennenkampf. Plevitskaya followed behind him near the front lines from the fall of 1914 to January 1915 while volunteering, like many other women, as a nurse in field hospitals. Proud to join her compatriots in contributing to the war effort, she wondered in exultation, "Who wouldn't love Mother Russia?" For months, she shed her "silk clothing and costumes" in favor of the "gray cotton dress and white scarf" of the Red Cross nurse.

Early in the war, Shangin and Plevitskaya were based in Kovno (present-day Kaunas, in Lithuania). She joined the Nikolaev Nurses' Association and worked twelve-hour shifts in an eight-bed ward for severely wounded soldiers. The best evidence indicates that she left this front for

Nadezhda Plevitskaya, dressed in her nurse's uniform, 1914. Courtesy of the Museum of N. V. Plevitskaya, Vinnikovo

good in late January 1915. (At her 1938 trial in Paris, a rumor surfaced that, in the summer of 1915, she had somehow manipulated the commandant of the Kovno fortress, General Vladimir Grigoriev, into betraying Russian forces to the Germans.[52] General Grigoriev was later court-martialed and executed. However, there is no evidence to support this long-after-the-fact allegation, and Plevitskaya testified at her trial that she never even knew Grigoriev.)

Plevitskaya wove her memories of World War I into a literary narrative in which the songs she performed inside field hospitals offered soldiers an emotional balm, while the men outside were shattered by enemy fire. Although she felt that she lacked the strength a nurse ought to have, she compensated for it with kindness and gifts. "I knew each of them and grew so accustomed to them," she wrote, "that, whenever someone was discharged, I missed him."

She gave special attention to men who were badly injured and unlikely to survive. In one instance, in the fall of 1914, she helped a disabled soldier who wanted to celebrate his patron saint's day. She brought back some communion bread from a nearby church, bought some wine and fruit, and managed to hold a saint's day celebration on the ward. She regaled the soldiers, most of whom had been raised in villages similar to her own, with folk songs. They asked her how she knew their songs. "Are you from the countryside too?" they would inquire, not knowing Plevitskaya's true identity. They sometimes proposed to her. One time, another nurse asked her to sing for a badly injured soldier whose pain was not fully deadened by morphine. Plevitskaya serenaded him softly until he fell asleep.

She also sang concerts elsewhere in the hospitals and in army installations. "Sometimes my songs were demanded, like medicine," she recalled. What Plevitskaya described was not an exaggeration. Journalists reported how soldiers in hospitals listened in rapture to recordings of military marches, folk choirs, and songs like Plevitskaya's.[53]

During the war, Plevitskaya's military-patriotic repertoire offered people solace not only in field hospitals, but in soldiers' and officers' quarters along the eastern front, on board naval vessels, and in homes across Russia.[54] When she was not serving as a field nurse, her impresario, Ilya Shneider, arranged for her to perform for Russian army units near the front.[55] But she performed for civilian audiences as well. In 1915, at a benefit concert in Kislovodsk, a city in the Northern Caucasus, she sang "O, Rus!," a song about village children fighting for their motherland, which was personified as a peasant woman. As Hubertus F. Jahn argues in *Patriotic Culture in Russia during World War I*, Plevitskaya, by emphasizing such themes as heroism and death, "regularly moved her audiences to tears and perfectly reflected the general ambivalence toward the war in 1915. Her songs reflected a mood of retreat into the shell of a secure communal identity and at the same time a hesitant hope for victory. By expressing what many people were longing for or afraid of, she conquered the hearts of mass audiences."[56]

Between September 1914 and January 1915, Plevitskaya followed Shangin's regiment along the front by automobile. She described the horror of battle and its effects on young Russian recruits. The field hospital where she was posted stood just over a mile from the staff headquarters and near the town of Verzhbolovo (Virbalis in Lithuanian), on southwest Lithuania's border with East Prussia. One night, as Verzhbolovo burned, she and the other medical staff waited for incoming wounded. "The wounded were brought in at 2:00 a.m.," Plevitskaya recalled. "A medical orderly passed around a large kettle with boiling water, and to whomever could drink it, I gave cognac, occasional shots of which I nabbed from the doctor. Although I felt some shame at this, I thought that a glass of cognac was necessary for a person who had just been injured by military fire—in shock and bloodied."

But hospital personnel had to keep moving along with the regiment, and soon Plevitskaya found herself driving to another field hospital, closer to the front. She experienced firsthand what it meant to be near enemy lines. Fortunately, another unit came to their aid. Later that night she helped prepare surgeries by cutting gauze. She slept soundly after surviving her first day this close to the front. That night, although she did not know until months later (when she read his diary), Shangin came into the camp and looked in on her as she lay dozing on a bundle of straw surrounded by strangers.

For a few weeks before January 1915, Shangin's regiment was not engaged in battle. He and Plevitskaya were posted near the East Prussian town of Gumbinnen, the site of one of Russia's few early military victories, in August 1914. Being of Orthodox faith, the Russians were celebrating Christmas, which fell two weeks later than among non-Orthodox Christians. Plevitskaya listened as the officers argued around a table one night about who had proved brave and who had not. She was pleased to hear that they described Shangin as having shown particular courage in battle.

A few days later, Plevitskaya pushed on with the regiment to Trakehnen in East Prussia. She was accompanied by the administrative head of the Nikolaev nurses, Grand Duchess Vasilchikova, who gave her a scarf and headdress. As they were leaving Trakehnen, the Grand Duchess's car, with Plevitskaya on board, encountered enemy fire. "It never occurred to the Germans," Plevitskaya later joked, "that a Grand Duchess in the last month of her pregnancy and a folk singer were in that car. If it had, they would not have wasted their shells."

Indeed, at this moment, the German command was putting into motion a plan to penetrate deep into Russian lines. Fighting quickly intensified, and Shangin's regiment was forced to retreat from East Prussia. The Russian army suffered nearly two hundred thousand casualties during these operations, and Shangin was one of them. He died on January 28, 1915. It would take a number of days for Plevitskaya to learn of her fiancé's passing.

In the meantime, Plevitskaya, who later claimed to have had premonitions of Shangin's death, was thrown by the retreat into a riot of confusion and uncertainty. Her superior, General Nikolai Epanchin, ordered the nurses to a regimental hospital closer to Russia's border. During this transfer, an orderly named Yakov accompanied her eastward on an open sleigh. Surrounded by Russian army transports, singing to pass the time on the road, Plevitskaya and Yakov approached a shabby and gloomy house. As they were passing by it, Plevitskaya felt a sudden stab of unexplained dread. Heart racing, she wondered why this place unnerved her so much.

Then, only two miles short of their destination, a snowstorm hit. Despite the heavy weather, an enemy plane, "like a winged demon," flew low overhead, dropping its bombs in the vicinity.[57] German forces were overtaking the Russians, cutting off their transports and taking prisoners. Yakov whipped the fatigued horse into action and tried to avoid the mass panic.

> Racing at a full gallop, the artillery transports pushed us into a snowdrift. The divisional doctor and I found ourselves sprawled in the snow, covered by our overturned sleigh, and we would have spent a long time there had Yakov not freed us. The senior doctor, wiping off the snow from his sheepskin coat, softly upbraided Yakov for not giving way to the artillery units. The doctor, with shaking hands, tried to light a cigarette, and my heart was beating so quickly that I complained of a heart attack.

The group continued its nighttime flight. The snowstorm had blanketed the dark hills. Plevitskaya's heart continued to pound.

> I closed my eyes and imagined the dying white face of my beloved. "Where is he?" I wondered. I had last seen him with the division's general staff, but the staff had long ago flown past us. [A few days later], in a small town, I tracked down the staff general at the division headquarters. There, I learned of my misfortune. The most terrible thing conceivable had happened: an iron curtain fell and the light was extinguished from my eyes. Saving others, my fiancé had been killed—right by the same house I had been unable to pass in the night without severe anguish.

Sometime later, Plevitskaya traveled by train through the same area. According to her memoirs, her journey brought her to the mound of earth where a white wooden cross marked Shangin's grave. Stopping for a last farewell, she "bowed before the mound and before the man who was buried alone in the foreign soil." "Now," she lamented, "the cross is probably not there anymore and the wind has swept the mound away." Even if some of this story's details have been embellished for the sake of drama, Plevitskaya's grief was no less genuine for that.

Shortly after Shangin's death, Plevitskaya returned to St. Petersburg, or Petrograd as it had been renamed to avoid sounding too German. She stayed at the home of Shangin's mother, Elena Shangina, and devoted her time to grieving his death and that of a nephew of hers, her brother Nicholas's firstborn son, also killed in action. When Plevitskaya felt ready to perform again, in March 1915, she chose to sing at a charity concert in the Mikhailovsky Theater. The purpose of the concert, which was sponsored by the tsar's eldest daughter, the Grand Duchess Olga, was to raise money for the families of Russian soldiers killed in the war. Elena Shangina attended the event to lend her support. Before going on stage, Plevitskaya confessed to Shangina that she did not think she could sing because she still felt too distraught. Once on stage, she leaned against the piano to steady herself. "There was deathly silence in the hall," she recalled, "and I could not sing. Suddenly, in the semidarkness, and with a flash from the passionate eyes of [my accompanist] Logranzh, I remembered the lyrics to a song that had been written for today's concert." She sang its first stanza:

> Amidst the faraway fields in a foreign country,
> On cold and frozen land,
> The Russian war wounded languished,
> In the joyless gloom of the approaching dawn.[58]

Unable to sing any further, she spoke the remaining lyrics. When she finished, the audience did not know whether to clap or remain silent, given the solemnity of the occasion. Then, after a pause, they erupted in applause. Plevitskaya was handed a collection bucket and solicited donations from the crowd. "How great it is to realize that there are moments when people think alike and are equally good," she exulted.

While Plevitskaya recovered in 1915 from the deaths of her fiancé and nephew, she was also compelled to help her mother, whose health was failing. She and other family members gathered in Vinnikovo to celebrate the Easter holidays—the most important in the Russian Orthodox calendar— with Akulina. At first, Plevitskaya felt buoyed up to find that her mother appeared younger than her eighty-six years, with few gray hairs and strong teeth. Plevitskaya's sister Dunya was in Vinnikovo, cooking for the holiday, and she brought along her son. Soon Plevitskaya's brother Nikolai arrived, still grieving the loss of his son in the war.

This early optimism faded. Akulina told her daughter that she felt she was going to die soon. Her eyesight was failing, and she cried often. Plevitskaya worried about the day when she would no longer hear her mother's voice or see her eyes. They wept together. For the past two decades, since Vasya's death, Akulina had been preparing for her own demise. She had already planned her funeral, right down to the lilacs she wanted placed on her grave.

Plevitskaya returned to Vinnikovo that summer to join her mother. One day, probably in late June or early July, Akulina felt ill and complained of severe headaches. Her family called in a priest, Father Nikolai. The family kneeled around Akulina's bed, and she lay peacefully as the priest performed the rite of holy unction, in which a sick person asks for God's forgiveness and mercy. But she did not die that day, and so Plevitskaya thought she would have time to perform in Kislovodsk, in the Caucasus, before returning to Vinnikovo.

On July 5, in Kislovodsk, Plevitskaya visited a friend's dacha. The afternoon was spent in relaxing conversation, and she returned to her hotel that night feeling refreshed. Unfortunately, there a telegram awaited her with the sorrowful news that her mother had died earlier that day. "I was orphaned," she exclaimed. "How empty the world had become. There was no one. I was alone in the world. Who could take my mother's place? There's no purer or truer love than that of a mother. Her love never lied and never changed." Plevitskaya's doctors urged her not to travel to the funeral, a journey of some eight hundred miles, because of her own frail health. At first, she agreed. But it did not take long for her to reconsider. She had to be present when her mother—her greatest teacher and influence in her life—was laid to rest, her own health be damned. Edmund Plevitsky and Dunya had been with Akulina when she died. Dunya told her sister that, at first, when Plevitskaya had telegrammed that she could not attend the funeral, their mother's dead visage had been devoid of expression. But as soon as Plevitskaya cabled to say she was coming after all, Akulina's face seemed to be smiling. Edmund corroborated this bizarre account, which, whether or not it was true, brought his ex-wife comfort.

Plevitskaya arrived in Vinnikovo in time to attend her mother's funeral. The church bell rang solemnly, as the pallbearers carried her lilac-covered coffin to the cemetery. Once the priest completed the burial ceremony, Plevitskaya, along with the male members of the family, threw a handful of soil into the grave. Nikolai reacted angrily, saying that it was inappropriate for a woman to do so. Plevitskaya pled ignorance of this prohibition, but apologized for her mother's sake. In her memoirs, Plevitskaya recounted a dream she had shortly after the funeral:

> I was standing in the belfry of our church and the plowed field and open meadows were visible in the distance. And suddenly I saw flying in confusion, a white dove, racing a school of black birds. The dove rushed

about, and the black birds overtook it. I yelled in anguish, "They'll harm the poor dove." The dove fell into the talons of a black bird and hung breathlessly. Then I saw my mother, coming from the side of the cemetery. Seeing her, I yelled to someone below that mother should not try to meet me, that it was difficult for her to climb the stairs, that I'd come to her myself. I ran down from the belfry. Usually the stairs were unsteady, but now they were carpeted. I ran down and mother embraced me. She held a white wing in her hand, gave it to me, and said, "Here you are, Dezhka, a dove's wing, which the crows tore off." Mother's voice was sorrowful and tender. I took the wing from her hand and woke up. At that time, I could only guess what the dream meant, and only now, it seems, I understand. . . . Now when I'm writing these words, a bird is singing under my window in a thick mulberry tree; it's bursting with song. Is it delivering a greeting from my own land? Did it visit the Moroskin forest? Did the little bird sing at the lilac bush by my mother's grave? Thank you, dear songstress. I send you a song. You have swift wings. Wherever you wish to go, you fly there. I have only one wing, one injured wing.

During the summers of 1915 and 1916, Plevitskaya found a new outlet for her sorrow: she acted in two films, *The Power of the Land* and *The Cry of Life*. They were produced by Russian filmmaker Vladimir R. Gardin on Plevitskaya's Vinnikovo property. Gardin had begun his career as a stage actor and director in provincial theaters. As his reputation grew, he came to work in Moscow and St. Petersburg theaters and then broke into Russia's film industry. He produced early film versions of Tolstoy's works, including *Anna Karenina* (1914), *The Kreutzer Sonata* (1914), and *War and Peace* (1915). After the Bolshevik Revolution, he continued to make films and was later awarded the distinction of People's Artist of the Soviet Union.

Gardin, the other actors, and the crew stayed at Plevitskaya's dacha during the filming. In his memoirs, Gardin noted that her appearance in the films caused a sensation across Russia, indicating that she still had star power in 1915 and 1916.[59] Plevitskaya's agent, probably Ilya Shneider, brought Gardin a six-page contract to sign, which stipulated a 15,000-ruble honorarium. Gardin quickly learned that Plevitskaya was not particularly interested in the cinema as an artistic endeavor and instead looked forward every day to finishing the shoots and performing her music in the evenings. "Besides her voice," wrote Gardin, "she possesses a broad emotional range. We heard her. There was not one empty phrase; the entire song was permeated with feeling." Gardin observed that she filled the room where she was performing with sound and emotional force, enough to reach the back of a large concert hall—the kind of venue she was now more accustomed to performing in. "Plevitskaya worked with amusing enthusiasm," he wrote. "She was completely disinterested in the film script, and she could act in any scene without having any connection to what preceded it. However, we encouraged her enthusiasm, insofar as it was necessary to shoot her at the same time for two separate pictures . . . and curiously one of them was about an estrada singer who was a born actress." In one scene, Plevitskaya's character poisoned herself to death in her bedroom. She executed this scene by climbing down from an armchair and falling to the floor in dramatic fashion.

While Plevitskaya was filming in Vinnikovo and performing in concerts, Russia's war effort continued to falter. As the Germans advanced farther eastward, Russia's First Army retreated from East Prussia to Poland, and then to present-day Ukraine and Belarus. In September 1915, Tsar Nicholas II took direct command of the Russian army, forcing his uncle, Grand Duke Nikolai Nikolaevich, to step down. With her husband at the front, Tsarina Alexandra remained in Petrograd helping to run the government. She relied heavily for advice on the infamous Grigory Rasputin, a Siberian mystic healer who had cultivated a faddish appeal among the St. Petersburg elite before the war. The royal couple had come to trust Rasputin with the health of their only son and heir, Alexei, who suffered the crippling effects of the blood disease hemophilia. As the months passed, more Russians, including those who held positions of power, grew to resent Rasputin's ever-expanding influence over public life. Meanwhile, many average Russians, frustrated by severe food shortages and discouraged by repeated military setbacks, were becoming disillusioned with the tsar's government. Alexandra, because of her German descent, was widely—if unfairly—suspected of spying for the enemy. In December 1916, Rasputin was murdered by aristocrats in Petrograd. As the new year approached, the tsar's days in power were numbered.

There is no evidence suggesting that Plevitskaya was anything but loyal to the monarch. In her memoirs, she wrote about her disappointment in losing the diamond brooch he had given her. It had been in a suitcase left behind when she fled from the Germans in 1915. Distancing herself from politics, she continued to perform in concerts and gave occasional press interviews. In one interview, she discussed how other female singers were trying to imitate her. She advised them that they did not "need to be anyone's slave. After all, a song is a person's soul. . . . People pour out their grief in a song, the song unfolds, tears flow, and . . . the soul becomes lighter."[60] Such words reveal the unhealed rawness of her emotions. However, she did not share her opinions about Russia's political future, nor could she have been expected to predict the drastic changes that lay ahead.

3

REVOLUTION AND WAR

In 1917, while Plevitskaya performed for soldiers, Russia experienced two revolutions. The first, which occurred in late February (early March under the West's Gregorian calendar), was spontaneous. In the midst of food shortages and news of food rationing, Petrograd workers began to protest on the streets, calling for bread and peace. Over the next three days, demonstrations expanded to other cities in the Russian Empire. Factories closed, and daily routine collapsed. Tsar Nicholas II ordered the police and military to quell the unrest. However, many soldiers disobeyed his orders, and some prevented him from returning to Petrograd. On March 2 (March 15) the Duma called for his abdication. He agreed to step down, marking the end of Russia's three-hundred-year-old Romanov dynasty.

After the February Revolution, a Provisional Government was formed, but it lacked legitimacy in the eyes of many Russians. In the meantime, leftist parties, such as the Bolsheviks and Mensheviks (both communist in orientation) and the non-Marxist Socialist Revolutionaries, created councils called "soviets" across the Russian Empire. They advocated for even more radical change, including pulling Russia out of the war, transferring gentry-owned land to the peasants, instituting worker control of factories, and eclipsing the power of the Provisional Government. Over the summer of 1917, workers on the left protested with greater militancy, while, from the right, General Lavr Kornilov staged a failed coup against the Provisional Government. Catastrophic defeats at Germany's hands caused mass desertions and fatally depressed the public mood.

Consequently, a second, more famous revolution occurred that autumn. This was planned by members of the Bolshevik Party, including Vladimir Lenin, its leader. On the night of October 24–25 (November 6–7), Bolshevik forces seized control of the Winter Palace—formerly the tsar's residence in Petrograd, but now the headquarters of the Provisional Government—and arrested key government officials. In Moscow and other cities, including Kursk, the Bolsheviks organized successful uprisings. Elections for a national Constituent Assembly were held in November, but when the Bolsheviks did not win a plurality of the vote, they dissolved it. The new Bolshevik government pulled Russia out of World War I in March 1918 with the signing of the Brest-Litovsk Treaty.

Soon a massive civil war erupted between the Reds—the Bolsheviks and their supporters—and the Whites: a jumble of disparate groups that included conservative monarchists, liberals, and members of left-wing parties opposed to Bolshevik rule. In a sprawling conflict that lasted from the spring of 1918 until the early 1920s—although the war is conventionally considered to have ended in early 1921—an estimated eight to ten million people died as a result of combat, disease, and widespread famine. Fighting took place countrywide, but this chapter will focus on southern Russia and the Ukraine, where Plevitskaya lived at the time. This was also an area that witnessed some of the civil war's deadliest combat.

Did Plevitskaya, once so fond of the tsar, come to sympathize with the Bolsheviks? It seems that she did not, at least initially. During Russia's years of revolution and civil strife, she never publicly commented about politics, except when she reportedly expressed her opposition to the tsar's abdication.[1] In a newspaper interview shortly after the Bolshevik Revolution, she said nothing negative about the deposed monarch.[2] Nor did she protest or join a political party. During the Provisional Government's tenure during the first half of 1917, Plevitskaya performed in benefit concerts in Moscow for Russian soldiers. Once the civil war began, she sang for both Red and White audiences, a choice that left her vulnerable to condemnation from both ends of the political spectrum. The events that unfolded between 1919 and 1920—and the decisions she made then—overturned Plevitskaya's life and forced her into exile, along with hundreds of thousands of other Russians.

During the late summer and fall of 1917, Plevitskaya based herself in the Kursk area, traveling occasionally to Crimea for concerts. A Kursk newspaper announced that she was performing in the city on August 11, 1917, and she was in Vinnikovo on the day of the Bolshevik Revolution.[3] At this watershed moment for the country, a major development in her own life occurred. On November 8, in Vinnikovo's Trinity Church, Plevitskaya married a twenty-five-year-old lieutenant in the Imperial Army named Yuri Levitsky. This was the son of Lieutenant General Levitsky, Shangin's former commander. On the marriage registry, Plevitskaya gave her age as thirty-seven and made note of her divorce. Levitsky recorded the event as his first marriage.[4]

Although the circumstances under which Plevitskaya and Levitsky met remain obscure, two accounts describe their early married life. The first is by her concert manager Ilya Shneider, who wrote about his first encounter with Levitsky in the fall of 1917. One day, Plevitskaya called Shneider about arranging some concerts in Yalta and elsewhere in Crimea. When Shneider arrived in Crimea, he was surprised to see Plevitskaya with "an ungainly, tall, red-haired officer. She understood my startled look and quietly said to me, 'I myself don't know why. It's hard for me to be alone.'"[5] The other account is by one of Plevitskaya's friends, Evdokiya Evdokimova. Evdokimova dropped by Plevitskaya's apartment in Kursk one day that fall and met Levitsky, whom she described as "a tall, interesting young man."[6]

After her concerts in Yalta in the fall of 1917, Plevitskaya planned to visit the Dulber Palace, located nearby on the southern coast of Crimea. Dulber was the estate of Grand Duke Pyotr Nikolaevich Romanov, first cousin once removed to Tsar Nicholas II. Apparently Levitsky was unable to come, and she urged Shneider to join her.[7]

"Why?" he asked.

"You'll see something interesting."

"And what exactly?"

"After all, you're now so committed to the ballet. Would you like to see the evil fairy Karbos from *Sleeping Beauty*?"

"Has she come to Russia?"

"Yes, a long time ago already. They call her the evil genius of Russia. . . . She's the Dowager Empress Maria Feodorovna."

Shneider refused Plevitskaya's invitation, although he thought it would have been interesting to meet the mother of the deposed tsar. The dowager empress was visiting Dulber with her daughter Olga Alexandrovna, Nicholas II's sister and a friend to Plevitskaya before the war. Olga was glad to see the singer and kissed and hugged her. They took tea in a room where, according to Shneider, Maria Feodorovna sat imperiously, as if on a throne. Unlike her son and his family, the dowager empress and the other royals with her were not killed by the Bolsheviks. They were rescued by the British in 1919 and never returned to Russia.

In December 1917, in preparation for civil war, Generals Mikhail Alexeev and Lavr Kornilov formed the Volunteer Army to fight the Reds in southern Russia. In 1919, this body combined forces with the Don

Army, and the new organization was named the Armed Forces of Southern Russia (AFSR). In total, six major White armies—which all scattered across the now defunct Russian Empire—aimed to defeat the Bolsheviks. Their officers valued the chivalric ideal of honor and were willing to shed blood to defend it.[8] But the White armies had many weaknesses. They lacked a unitary structure, making it impossible to plan and implement joint strategies. They also lacked the Reds' manpower. In October 1919, the AFSR fielded 100,000 troops, compared to 150,000 for the Red Army.[9] Although the Whites had some support from Allied forces, this aid could not compensate for the Reds' numerical advantage. Worse still, White officers, despite their advantages in technical and tactical training, tended to be politically naive.

During the civil war, White officers often viewed their struggle solely in military terms and failed to formulate political and economic strategies for winning over local populations and consolidating their power. Another White weakness involved the significant political and generational divisions within the movement's officer ranks. Most officers—fearing modernity—supported right-wing authoritarianism and a restored monarchy, but a sizable minority were republicans and even favored a democratic system. Senior officers tended to operate in more disciplined ways, while younger firebrands tended to act more impulsively.[10] As the civil war continued, increased dissention and insubordination undermined the command structure, and such splits led to low morale among the rank and file.[11]

In contrast to the Whites, the Bolsheviks were more unified in their political and economic objectives, and the Red Army was more cohesive and less corrupt. The Reds enjoyed many strategic advantages, including control over railroad lines, communication links, and industrial and agricultural areas in central Russia. Both sides terrorized their military foes and carried out pogroms against Jews, although the Reds used terror more effectively, with the assistance of their new secret police, the Cheka, to eliminate opposition and impose discipline. Perhaps most crucially, the Reds earned more popular support than the Whites did. Marxist ideology appealed to broad segments of the population, especially youth, ethnic minorities, and the lower classes. Moreover, the Bolsheviks often rewarded their supporters with powerful positions. For example, Plevitskaya's mentor, Leonid Sobinov, chose to cooperate with the Bolsheviks and was handsomely compensated with the directorship of Moscow's Bolshoi Theater.

During the civil war, every individual faced an existential crisis, and many—out of fear, desperation, or opportunism—let baser instincts gain the upper hand. Former AFSR commander Anton Denikin recalled, "Not only did the experience [of civil war] cripple the body. It deformed the soul as well."[12] Most Russians tried to remain politically neutral. Some stood by passively as control over their towns changed hands several times before the war finally ended, while others changed sides less for ideological reasons than out of a need for survival. Others fought one side or the other to maintain their community's ideals. Many peasants in the Kursk region and in other rural areas, exhausted by the war and enraged at the grain confiscations inflicted on them by both sides, joined independent "green" rebellions to defend their traditional way of life. Ukrainian nationalists fought both Whites and Reds in their failed struggle for independence.

Where did Plevitskaya fit into this complex web? Was she, in fact, as apolitical as she claimed, or did she harbor sympathies for the Bolsheviks and even serve as an informant, as some argue? Unfortunately, for the civil war years, there is little reliable information on Plevitskaya's political allegiances, her exact movements, or the people with whom she fraternized. Clues to her whereabouts and motives can only be gleaned from newspaper articles and the personal recollections—not all of them completely trustworthy—of a dozen or so of her contemporaries. Plevitskaya seems to have calculated that her best chance for survival was to earn income by performing for both Red and White Army audiences. Her other chief priority was to remain close to Vinnikovo, to Levitsky (at least at first), and to her relatives. Along the way, she was forced to make choices that, to an unsympathetic or uncomprehending observer, might seem to signal a concrete commitment to one side or the other. As with countless other Russians during this painful, tumultuous time, the reality behind Plevitskaya's actions was far more complicated.

During the civil war, Plevitskaya, like so many Russians, lived in places that experienced multiple changes of government. The Kursk region, her home base, passed back and forth between Red and White hands until the Reds' final victory there in November 1919, and German occupiers remained in the vicinity until the end of 1918. The Ukrainian port of Odessa, where Plevitskaya also spent much time in 1918 and 1919, was controlled by the Bolsheviks from the second half of 1917 to December 1918. Then, for several months in early 1919, it was occupied by a coalition of anti-Bolshevik groups, including Volunteer Army units, Ukrainian nationalists, and—as part of the Allies' pro-White intervention—French, Greek, and Serbian troops. The Reds threatened Odessa once more in the spring of 1919, and thousands evacuated in late March and early April when Allied interventionists pulled out for good. At that point, the Bolsheviks retook Odessa, forcing White Army personnel and their families to flee.

Plevitskaya, however, continued to move freely between there and Kursk, over six hundred miles away.

Why, then, could Plevitskaya—a tsarist-era singer and the wife of a White officer—travel without hindrance over such great distances through Red-dominated war zones? As it happens, Levitsky switched sides sometime in 1918 and commanded a Red Army unit, possibly for over a year. Levitsky's motivation for switching sides is unknown, but he may have been captured by the Reds and given the stark choice to cooperate or die. (During her 1938 trial, Plevitskaya testified that her husband had been pressed into service as a rank-and-file soldier in the Red Army for only two weeks, but this was less than honest.[13]) Levitsky's defection explains Plevitskaya's back-and-forth shuttling between Kursk and Odessa. It also explains why she performed with some regularity for Red Army soldiers in 1918 and 1919. Did it also, as her detractors claim, cause her to become a Bolshevik collaborator, or even a spy?

In the spring and summer of 1918, Bolshevik-controlled newspapers reported on performances by Plevitskaya for Red Army units in Kursk and Odessa.[14] She also sang for wounded Red Army soldiers at hospitals in Kursk.[15] Plevitskaya was seen in the Kursk region in September 1918, at which point the Germans occupied half the area, including the city of Belgorod, while the Bolsheviks occupied the other half. Plevitskaya reportedly arrived in the German-occupied zone after entering from the Bolshevik side. She appealed to a local boss to provide her with the documents needed to travel to southern Russia, somewhere near the Caucasus, to be closer to the Volunteer Army. While her documents were prepared, she stayed in a Belgorod hotel for a few days and performed in the city. When she left, she did not travel to the Caucasus, but to Odessa instead. Allegedly, the Belgorod boss, whose name is lost to history, met her there for some unknown reason.[16]

It is impossible to trace all of Plevitskaya's movements between the fall of 1918 and the fall of 1920, but she clearly moved with a great deal of freedom through Bolshevik-controlled territory. Was this simply because of her husband's new allegiance to the Reds? Or because she herself was sought by them as an entertainer? Or was she up to something more nefarious, especially in Odessa? Certainly she mingled with high-ranking Reds there. In 1918 or 1919, for instance, she joined the Moscow artist Igor Nezhnyi, the singer Isabelle Kremer, and several other actors and singers in a command performance for Red Army officers.[17] Similarly, a writer named P. Trubnikov claimed that he often saw Plevitskaya at this time in an Odessa club that "swarmed with Bolshevik sympathizers."[18]

Plevitskaya's Odessa visits appear even more controversial when we factor in additional accounts claiming that she had close relations with two Bolshevik officials (possibly Cheka operatives) and may even have worked in Cheka prisons. As part of Lenin's call to unleash a nationwide "Red Terror" against the revolution's enemies, the Odessa branch of the Cheka regularly tortured and executed White prisoners.[19] During the Red occupation of Odessa in 1918 and 1919, two Bolshevik commissars, a Captain Dombrovsky and a Cheka official named Shulga, ruled through mass terror.

Two reports about Plevitskaya's supposed activities in Odessa come from Russians who testified against her in 1937–1938 during the investigation of General Miller's kidnapping. The first, a woman identified as Nurse G., claimed to have been in Odessa in 1919 at the same time as Plevitskaya, when the city was in Bolshevik hands. In Bolshevik circles, she said, Plevitskaya was considered "one of their own."[20] Captain A. Baranov, a White counterintelligence officer for the Volunteer Army, said much the same in the other report. One of his Odessa informants—possibly Nurse G.—told him that Plevitskaya was "with the Reds" and friendly with Dombrovsky and Shulga, who were "up to their elbows in blood."[21]

Two other accounts were even more sordid. Journalist Alexander Miakin had no doubt that Plevitskaya was a Bolshevik agent during the civil war.[22] He lived in Odessa in April 1919, when the Reds seized control, and in his unpublished memoirs, he recalled Plevitskaya's appearance there with Levitsky. According to Miakin, the Chekists Shulga and Dombrovsky often socialized with a circle that included Plevitskaya, Levitsky, and another singer, Tamara Gruzinskaya. Allegedly, Shulga made advances on Plevitskaya, and Dombrovsky on Gruzinskaya. One night, Miakin attended Gruzinskaya's birthday party with another journalist, Konstantin Shumlevich, and an assistant of Levitsky's, a Lieutenant Kallinikov. When the two arrived at the banquet hall, two Red Army guards asked to see their documents. Plevitskaya and Gruzinskaya were the only women there. Plevitskaya sat next to Shulga, and Levitsky sat some distance from her. Plevitskaya and Gruzinskaya ignored Miakin. A month later, in May 1919, Miakin and Kallinikov received job offers in Tiflis, and they needed Shulga to authorize their transfer. They asked Plevitskaya to intercede on their behalf, but she demurred. When they met with Shulga, he denied their request and, oddly, denied even knowing Plevitskaya.

The fourth and final source about Plevitskaya's acquaintance with the Odessa Chekists is a journalist named Lev M. Kamyshnikov, who later emigrated to the United States. In his memoirs, Kamyshnikov, who was in Odessa at the time, claimed that Dombrovsky scheduled entertainments that featured Plevitskaya. He included titillating detail about how Shulga made sexual advances toward her: "Drunk from wine and love, the sailor Shulga, with loving eyes, glanced at his female friend. A violent disturbance took place after the concert. . . . Cheka officials whipped out their guns. Shulga took Plevitskaya by the hand and led her from the hall. Soon after this event [around January 1919], Denikin's forces seized Odessa. Dombrovsky fled. Shulga took the last train out of Odessa with his friend Dezhka."[23]

When questioned at her trial about her acquaintance with Dombrovsky and Shulga, Plevitskaya insisted that she had met them only once and that her main concern was protecting her own safety and that of Levitsky and his family:

> In Odessa my father-in-law, Lieutenant General Levitsky, his brother, and his aunt were with me. When the French suddenly evacuated Odessa [in March 1919], we were desperate. We lived in hotel rooms. When the Bolsheviks arrived, they surrounded the hotel and, twenty-four minutes later, threw us out on the pavement. The artists Roshina-Inearova and Tamara Gruzinskaya were with me. When they expelled us, we went searching for refuge, to the commandant's office. Dombrovsky was the commandant, and his assistant was Shulga. They assigned us an apartment. This is all of my acquaintance with these men. Of course, in order to save my father-in-law and husband, I tried to have good relations with them. But I had no other dealings with them.[24]

In addition to the controversy over her ties to Dombrovsky and Shulga, Plevitskaya came under suspicion of something far worse: actively serving as a Cheka jailer. Many years later, in 1937 or 1938 in Paris, a Russian émigré woman whose last name was Kharitonova testified that Plevitskaya had helped operate a Bolshevik prison for White captives in Kursk.[25] Kharitonova was in the city during the revolution, and her husband was imprisoned by the Cheka. When Kharitonova vainly petitioned for his release, she confronted a woman who, she later insisted, resembled Nadezhda Plevitskaya. Kharitonova offered to this woman some jewelry in exchange for her husband's release, but the bribe was rejected. Kharitonova's Paris statement additionally noted that another émigré woman, surnamed Soren, had also claimed to have encountered Plevitskaya in a Cheka-run prison.[26] Nothing besides these two unsubstantiated accusations supports the rather fanciful notion of Plevitskaya's working as a Cheka jail matron.

Far-fetched or plausible, the above allegations all imply that Plevitskaya not only socialized with Chekists but may have been one herself. Are they sufficient proof? Thousands of Russians became Cheka informants during the civil war period, so why not Plevitskaya, whose husband commanded a Red Army unit? Chekists boasted that 25 percent of city dwellers during the civil war were informants, and they certainly recruited spies from diverse socioeconomic backgrounds.[27] Plevitskaya, moving in and out of White circles regularly, would have proved quite useful to the Cheka, even as a messenger.

The charge most easily dispensed with is that of having worked in a Cheka prison. Some women were known to have done so, among them the example of Vera Grevenivkova (or Grebennikova), also known as Dora. Dora, described as the daughter of a colonel, was said to have been romantically tied to a Chekist and reputedly killed almost seven hundred prisoners while serving for two months with the Odessa Cheka.[28] But the story of Dora is thought by many to be apocryphal. And why a wealthy, high-profile performer like Plevitskaya would agree to serve as a Cheka jailer, whether in Odessa or in Kursk, is difficult to explain and even harder to substantiate. Indeed, it seems quite possible that Kharitonova, lodging her accusation against Plevitskaya years after the fact, either conflated the sensational tale of Dora with her memory of the singer, or used it as the inspiration for a deliberate calumny.

As for associating with Bolshevik officials or even cooperating with them more actively, Plevitskaya may well have done either or both. Still, it is important to bear in mind the extent of rumormongering and after-the-fact "remembering" that surrounds cases like Plevitskaya's. During the World War I era, the Mata Hari scandal made nothing easier to believe than the notion that female spies lurked around every corner.[29] Tales of femme fatale seductresses proliferated throughout World War I Europe, and the "Dora" story shows how widely the idea of Red temptresses circulated during the Russian Civil War. It must be remembered that, during the war itself, few if any would have dreamed of placing Plevitskaya in such a category. Most of the rumors about her proliferated only after her arrest in 1937. This does not rule out the possibility that such rumors were true, or at least partly so.

However, the Cheka did not keep archival records of their informants and jailers, and no Soviet intelligence official later admitted that Plevitskaya played these roles. It is therefore impossible to prove that she was an agent during these early years. It seems best to suppose that if she had dealings with the Reds during the civil war, it was not as a spy, but as someone who skillfully used her social capital and access to powerful men on both sides to survive and to protect her husband and father-in-law. But Plevitskaya did not expend social capital solely on herself and her relatives. In one instance, she saved the lives of a handful of Volunteer Army soldiers in 1918, when she was in Red-controlled territory in southern Russia, by intervening on their behalf with Bolshevik officials there. When Plevitskaya was under investigation for her role in General Miller's kidnapping, she claimed that she had saved these men. Among them were two brothers of Colonel Sergei Matsylev, who verified the story, despite serving as a witness for the prosecution during her 1938 trial.[30]

Accounts about Plevitskaya's time in Odessa indicate that she was there at least through the spring of 1919. The next mystery is what happened to her that summer, when she and Levitsky were spotted in the Kursk province. Why would they have returned there, other than to stay in her home in Vinnikovo? Levitsky's Red Army unit was reportedly stationed in the area in August and September 1919. The recollections of Prince Alexander Ratiev, who served in a Red Army artillery battery under a commander named Suvorov, shed light on Plevitskaya's and Levitsky's activities during this time. According to Ratiev, Suvorov "was often in the company of Levitsky, who was then a military instructor, and his then mistress, the well-known singer Nadezhda Vasilievna Plevitskaya. . . . One morning Levitsky chose to go on a reconnaissance mission. He took with him Nadezhda Plevitskaya, from whom he was inseparable. Neither of them ever returned."[31]

They never returned because the Whites apparently captured them near Kursk. By the summer and early fall of 1919, the Volunteer Army, under General Denikin's command, controlled large sections of southern Russia and the Ukraine, including the Kursk region. Four known accounts offer similar details of Plevitskaya's and Levitsky's fate: a detachment of mounted intelligence officers in the Second Kornilov Shock Regiment detained Plevitskaya and Levitsky, who were encamped with Levitsky's Red Army unit in the Kursk region.[32] Whatever the exact details were, and they cannot be ascertained, it appears that by September 1919, Plevitskaya and Levitsky were back with the Whites.

There is also evidence to suggest that Plevitskaya soon involved herself in an extramarital affair. According to an account of a White Army captain, the night after she and Levitsky were captured by the Whites, she improvised a concert for the officers.[33] The next morning, she was sent, together with Levitsky, to the rear. Captain Yakov Pashkevich, a commander in the Second Kornilov Shock Regiment, played a key role in pardoning the singer and immediately befriended her. For his part, Levitsky convinced Pashkevich and the other White officers that he was willing to change sides again. He became a lieutenant in the First Corps of the Volunteer Army, which occupied Kursk beginning in September 1919 and operated under the command of Lieutenant General Alexander Kutepov.[34]

Until November 1919, the Volunteer Army continued to win battles in the Ukraine and southern Russia, including around Kursk. In October, Denikin's AFSR forces came within two hundred miles of Moscow, the Bolsheviks' new capital, but that was the closest they ever came to capturing it. In late November, the tables turned for the last time. The Reds again took Kursk, and the Whites never again defeated the Reds in a sustained campaign.[35] By March 1920, White commanders had been forced to retreat into Crimea. General Denikin resigned his leadership post in April, and General Pyotr Wrangel replaced him.

For over a year after her capture by the Whites, Plevitskaya, now around forty years old, remained with Kornilov units and occasionally performed for them. She separated from Levitsky, who seems to have begun philandering, and took Pashkevich as her next lover. Plevitskaya performed for the Second Kornilov Shock regiment in Perekop, where the Crimean isthmus meets the European continent, around the time of Orthodox Easter, which fell on March 29 in 1920. At this time, she was recuperating from a bout of typhus in nearby Armiansky Bazar, which the Reds were bombarding daily.[36]

During an evening concert for the regiment, the sky was clear, and the moon shone brightly. Kerosene lamps lit up the stage while an orchestra accompanied Plevitskaya and a baritone. Then came a sudden barrage from Red Army units stationed a mile or so away. According to an official regimental account of the incident, Pashkevich yelled, "Everyone to your places!" when the bombardment began and then took Plevitskaya by the hand and led her to safety.[37] "Sitting out the siege," Plevitskaya remembered, "I was in the cozy dugout of Lieutenant Ivanov . . . and when returning to Kula [a nearby town] it was again quiet and clear on the steppe. I couldn't understand why tears were welling up in my throat, why peace is so wonderful, why there's so much evil in the world."[38] She was present in the staff quarters later that same evening, with Pashkevich presiding over the festivities and singing regimental songs.

Plevitskaya's second and last Perekop concert began more peacefully than the first. But then another artillery barrage ensued. Shock caused her to forget words to one of her standard hits, "The Moscow Fire." "I felt ashamed," she wrote. "At the front, you're not supposed to act afraid, but what can you do?—nature takes hold." Plevitskaya remembered these Perekop concerts as "the last ones on my native soil."[39]

From March until July, Plevitskaya remained close to Pashkevich's encampments. For Pashkevich and his fellow Whites, defeat was only a matter of time. After the Red seizure of southern Russia in the summer of 1920, little hope remained for a White victory. As for Plevitskaya's new romance, this came to an abrupt end with Pashkevich's death in mid-July, fighting in the south Ukrainian town of Bolshoi Tokmak. Laying her fallen lover to rest, Plevitskaya wept and sang loudly, like a peasant woman at a countryside funeral.[40] Alone again, she could not return to Vinnikovo due to intense fighting. Instead, she traveled to Crimea, the last White stronghold in the south.

Even here, though, safety was temporary. Pressed southward by the Reds, all General Wrangel could hope for after mid-1920 was to defend Crimea long enough to carry out an orderly evacuation of the Volunteer Army before the Bolsheviks swept to final victory. Plevitskaya was one of thousands of civilians who were trapped on the peninsula during these months. Sometime in the early autumn, she started volunteering in a hospital in Simferopol. It was probably here that she began her final romance, with a young major general in the Kornilov Shock Regiment named Nikolai Skoblin. Skoblin stood five feet, ten inches tall and had brown hair and deep-set, chestnut-colored eyes.[41] He was only twenty-seven, over a dozen years younger than Plevitskaya. Skoblin, who had been ill with typhoid earlier in the year, was in Simferopol to recover from battle wounds sustained on October 15.[42]

Neither Plevitskaya nor Skoblin ever wrote about their courtship. We cannot know for sure why they joined forces, so to speak, although there are a number of possible reasons. Those who suspected that Plevitskaya had begun serving the Soviets argue that, by rushing into affairs with Pashkevich and then Skoblin, the singer was attempting to set a "honey trap" for the most highly placed White officer she could ensnare.[43] More plausible is the simple notion that Plevitskaya—feeling lonely and vulnerable—may have been motivated to find another military officer who would protect her, and Skoblin was available. For his part, Skoblin may have been attracted by Plevitskaya's strong presence and celebrity. A man of modest means, he also may have believed that she would offer him financial security after the civil war. If so, he miscalculated, for he and Plevitskaya would be forced into exile before the fall was out. Whatever the case, a précis of Skoblin's biography to this date is in order, given his central role in Plevitskaya's life for the next two decades.

Nikolai Vladimirovich Skoblin was born on June 9, 1893, in Nezhin, approximately ninety miles northeast of Kiev. His father, Vladimir Alexan-

General Nikolai Skoblin, in Kornilov Shock Regiment uniform, circa 1919

drovich Skoblin, was a retired army colonel who later worked as a police officer; his mother died of tuberculosis when he was young.[44] Nikolai had four brothers and three sisters. Two brothers and one sister followed him into exile after the civil war.

During their childhood, the Skoblin children lived with their father, a strict disciplinarian who demanded that his children study hard in school. According to Marina Grey, daughter of General Denikin, "the Skoblin children were raised by a father who was so strict and domineering that the development of their personalities suffered from it. The habit to obey and conceal, and the compensatory desire to be made of good use, perhaps was more pronounced for Nikolai than for his brothers and sisters."[45] Nikolai did not disappoint his father. In 1914, he graduated from Chugevsk Junker School, a provincial military academy, at the age of nineteen.

Months afterward, Skoblin entered the Imperial Army, and World War I gave him ample opportunity to distinguish himself. He began at the rank of ensign in the 126th Rylsky Infantry Regiment and, right away, sustained the first of many battle wounds he would receive throughout his career. For valorous behavior in battle, he received the Orders of St. George and St. Vladimir. He finished World War I as a captain in one of

Russia's shock battalions, used in frontal assaults and surprise attacks against enemy defenses.

During the civil war, Skoblin fought with the Volunteer Army in southern Russia and continued his ascent up the military hierarchy. In early 1918, he was a staff captain in the Kornilov Shock Regiment; although Kornilov was killed in April 1918 by Red Army fire, his regiment remained intact. The regiment had been formed in 1917 and fought in 570 battles. Later in the war, Skoblin served under Generals Denikin and Wrangel. In November 1918, he was promoted to commander of the Kornilov Shock Regiment and fought the Reds in southern Russia's Kuban region. Under Skoblin's leadership, the Kornilovs took part in the temporary wresting of the Northern Caucasus from the Reds. He was with them when they fought the Reds in Stavropol, Orel, and finally Crimea. In early September 1919, a large contingent of the Volunteer Army, which included Skoblin's shock regiment, took control of Kursk. In March 1920, Skoblin was promoted to the rank of major general, becoming one of the youngest generals in the Volunteer Army. When Wrangel took supreme command in April 1920, he reorganized his troops into four units. One was the First Army Corps, led by General Kutepov. Skoblin served under Kutepov as a commander in the Kornilov division.

Opinions regarding Skoblin's civil war performance are mixed. Several accounts, including one from fellow general Anton Turkul, describe him as a courageous and talented young officer and an honorable brother-in-arms.[46] Skoblin's rapid promotions and many medals of distinction serve to reinforce this favorable impression. Other narratives, however, portray him as a kind of "young Turk," whose youth and arrogance caused him to make bold and sometimes brash decisions. Part of this came from belonging to a "lost generation" of young officers who fought for tsarist ideals and traditions but lacked a great longing for Imperial Russia due to their relative youth. In any event, many men in the Kornilov Regiment—and some of Skoblin's superior officers—were not overly fond of him, largely because of his careerism and occasional unscrupulousness.[47] Skoblin earned a reputation for treating captured Red Army soldiers cruelly. According to one witness, Skoblin "ruthlessly tortured and then hanged all captives."[48] In this, however, he conformed to the behavior modeled by his superiors. Kornilov once exclaimed to his soldiers, "The greater the terror, the greater our victories," and both Wrangel and Kutepov ordered the execution of hundreds of Red soldiers.[49]

Other criticisms of Skoblin's civil war behavior surfaced during the 1930s—more serious, but less provable. As with rumors about Plevits-

kaya's time in Odessa, many allegations of actual misconduct came long
after the fact as Skoblin fell under suspicion of being a Bolshevik spy.
For example, Colonel Dmitry Vozovik of the Kornilov Shock Regiment
claimed that Skoblin, during the Volunteer Army's retreat from Ekateri-
nodar (now Krasnodar), vanished near the village of Medvedovsk, at a
point when the Volunteer Army's situation was extremely dire.[50] Vozovik
added that General Kutepov had reprimanded Skoblin for this disappearance. The publisher Vladimir Burtsev, who, in emigration, investigated
Bolshevik infiltration of the White community in exile, insisted that
Plevitskaya had lured Skoblin into informing for the Bolsheviks as early
as 1920.[51]

I. F. Patronov, a colonel in the Volunteer Army's general staff, like-
wise assumed that Skoblin was already aiding the Reds during the civil
war. Patronov later averred that had General Miller known about Skoblin's
treacherous behavior during the civil war, he would not have trusted him
so much during their time in exile.[52] Patronov also complained that several
Kornilov commanders, including Skoblin, had lacked discipline and honor
during the campaign in southern Russia. In September 1919, Patronov was
supposedly informed by a group of officers about disorder and arbitrariness
in the Kornilov division. There was talk at this point of removing Skoblin,
Patronov said—but if so, nothing ever came of it.

As the fall of 1919 progressed, Patronov wrote, morale within the
regiment increasingly broke down. If he is correct, Skoblin went so far as
to argue for Denikin's arrest, on grounds of incompetence, although the
other officers opposed taking such drastic action. Patronov even suggested
that Skoblin's actions might have contributed to Pashkevich's killing by
the Reds in 1920. Whatever the truth of Patronov's many allegations, they
remain unsupported by tangible evidence, nor did Kutepov ever feel the
need to launch an inquiry into Skoblin's conduct.

In late October 1920, during a cold snap in southern Russia and Crimea,
bitter fighting ensued. The Whites were fatally outnumbered, with only
37,000 soldiers in contrast to 133,000 Red Army troops.[53] The Reds had
planned to break Wrangel's front and cut off his retreating troops before
they entered Crimea, but Kutepov's soldiers had managed to slow the Red
Army's advance. In the meantime, thousands of White officers and pro-
White civilians, many of whom had abandoned everything they owned,
boarded trains for the Crimean coast in an attempt to escape. Kutepov's
November stand allowed for the safe evacuation of 126 Russian, American, British, and French ships carrying a total of 145,693 White soldiers

and civilians, including nearly 27,000 women and children.[54] The last ship departed on November 16.

The refugees who boarded Wrangel's ships helped form the first wave of Soviet-era émigrés, amounting to more than one million Russians, destined to resettle in thirty countries.[55] Most left because they were tied to the Whites and feared the fate that would have awaited them under Bolshevik rule. Wrangel's refugees crossed the Black Sea and disembarked ten days later in Turkey, exhausted and starving. At this time, the French army controlled Constantinople, Turkey's capital, and had supported the Whites in Crimea.

Alexander Miakin, the journalist who had made Plevitskaya's acquaintance in Odessa in 1919, later claimed to have renewed contact with her in Simferopol, shortly before her evacuation. He was aware of her romantic attachment with Skoblin. In October, she dropped by the office of the newspaper *Vremya*, where Miakin and Konstantin Shumlevich were then working, to ask them to help sponsor a show of hers, and they agreed. Miakin noted that the show enjoyed a large turnout. (It bears mentioning that Miakin's anecdote contradicts Plevitskaya's recollection of having given her last concert on native soil in Perekop the previous spring.) In November, Miakin and Shumlevich met Plevitskaya at a restaurant, hoping to arrange for a second concert. But she appeared two hours late with the news that she would be leaving Crimea with Skoblin from the port of Sevastopol.[56]

In preparation for the voyage, Plevitskaya frantically grabbed some clothes, jewelry, photographs, and sheet music. She had lost her great wealth: the Bolsheviks had confiscated her properties in Moscow, Petrograd, and possibly Vinnikovo. Her savings had all been in now-worthless tsarist-era rubles. In an interview she gave in New York City in 1926, Plevitskaya revealed that, at the moment of her evacuation, she was still ill with typhus. Either on November 14 or 15, American admiral Newton McCully transferred her to one of the U.S. destroyers that were present during the evacuation. She remembered being on board the ship and weeping with grief at leaving her homeland, but gave no further detail.[57]

Assuming that Skoblin and Plevitskaya were not Bolshevik "sleeper" agents but genuinely sympathized with the Whites at this point, Skoblin would almost certainly have been killed had he remained in Russia and fallen into Bolshevik hands. With her recent ties to the Whites, Plevitskaya might have been imprisoned or killed as well. The Cheka had no compunction about executing even famous performers if they seemed to be counterrevolutionaries. In one of the more colorful episodes from the Red

Terror, Cheka assassins tracked down a beloved Moscow Circus clown named Bim-Bom, shooting him dead in front of a horrified audience.

Plevitskaya and Skoblin may have been comforted by the same false hope that thousands of other Whites had at the time—that the Reds would be overthrown with the help of the Whites' Western allies in a few years, if not months, allowing them to repatriate. Stripped of their citizenship, Plevitskaya, Skoblin, and hundreds of thousands of Russians were now forced to settle as stateless people in foreign countries. For White Army veterans, the successful evacuation and the first year of exile in Turkey served during the rough times ahead as important symbols of honor and collective identity. In exile, Plevitskaya became a unifying voice for Russian émigrés. Her music expressed a sense of nostalgia that many felt for their homeland. In her memoirs, Plevitskaya described her own longing for Russia:

> In a foreign land, feeling immense homesickness, one joy remained: my quiet thoughts about the past.
>
> About the dear past, when Mother Russia shined with countless riches and embraced us in her great expanses.
>
> My homeland is far away, and our happiness remains there.
>
> A menacing threat roared; a wild, dark wind rose up and scattered us all over the world. But each wanderer carried away with him a radiant image of Old Russia, of love for the faraway native land and a noble memory of the past.

4

EARLY YEARS IN EXILE

Plevitskaya was only one of many cultural luminaries who left Russia during the first wave of emigration, between 1917 and 1922. This list includes Marc Chagall, Feodor Chaliapin, opera singer Maria Kuznetsova, writer Irène Nemirovsky, Sergei Prokofiev, Sergei Rachmaninoff, and painter and mystic Nikolai Roerich, to name only a few. Many who left at this time failed to assimilate into the culture of their newly adopted countries. Chaliapin left Russia in 1921 and, like Plevitskaya, never stopped feeling homesick. "How could I give up that country," he later wrote, "where I had not only compassed all that one can see and touch, hear and feel, but where I had dreamed dreams and enshrined my deepest longings, especially in the years that preceded the revolution?"[1]

Unlike Chaliapin and most other Russian émigré artists, Plevitskaya tied her life to the remnants of the defeated White Army forces, through her relationship with Skoblin, who served as commanding officer of the Kornilov Shock Regiment in exile. The couple set up camp with the regiment for one year on the Gallipoli peninsula, where the Turks had routed British and Allied forces in 1915. Some White officers and soldiers, including many Cossacks, returned to Bolshevik Russia, but most settled in European countries and began looking for jobs to support themselves and their families. Plevitskaya and Skoblin's path would take them from Gallipoli to Bulgaria and finally to France.

Living conditions on Gallipoli were crude. White veterans and their families barely survived on rations donated by the French government, and humanitarian assistance from the International Red Cross and the Save the Children Fund went little further. Yet the Whites referred to this as the "Gallipoli miracle," when a sense of a "spiritual and moral resurrection" renewed their determination to fight the Bolsheviks.[2] The White commanders preserved what was left of their forces, which consisted of a twenty-three-thousand-man Don Cossack Corps under the command of Lieutenant General Fyodor Abramov, a twelve-thousand-man Kuban Cossack Corps under General M. Fostikov, and a twenty-nine-thousand-man First Army Corps under Kutepov (later renamed the Gallipoli Group). Wrangel relied for support on his chief of staff, General Pavel Shatilov, and General Alexander Kutepov, Skoblin's superior officer.

By the spring of 1921, White organizers had begun to provide entertainment for the troops as a way to boost morale and infuse their camp with Russian culture. Plevitskaya performed regularly for them. At one concert, the soldiers were so enthusiastic about her renditions of popular Russian folk songs that they hoisted her onto their shoulders as an informal form of salute.[3]

Still, however much the troops idolized Plevitskaya, she and Skoblin faced criticism from the senior staff, particularly Kutepov, for cohabiting out of wedlock. She shared Skoblin's tent, one of the best outfitted.[4] Kutepov asked one of his subordinates, an officer named Kotchkin, to give Skoblin an ultimatum: either expel Plevitskaya from the camp or marry her. (Kotchkin refused to deliver this message, and the task fell to someone else, a General Veselovsky.)[5] Skoblin chose marriage. Plevitskaya had already divorced Levitsky, who was also based in the Gallipoli camp. According to the émigré historian Tatiana Varsher, Plevitskaya spoke to her about Levitsky disapprovingly as "an empty person," who had lost some of her diamonds.[6] Plevitskaya and Levitsky did not maintain ties after their divorce, and he eventually settled in Romania.

Skoblin and Plevitskaya married in the Gallipoli camp in June 1921 in a modest ceremony attended by the top brass. General Kutepov officiated. One of the wedding guests, a Captain Konetsky, told Plevitskaya that "we accepted you into our regimental family. You are a mother-commander to us."[7] For years to come, the Kornilov soldiers continued to address Plevitskaya as "mother-commander." When it came time to leave Gallipoli, she cried because she had felt appreciated there and had been treated as a member of the regiment.[8]

Once married to Skoblin, Plevitskaya grew concerned about how to behave as an officer's wife in camp. She noticed that officers' wives often meddled in others' business, but as a condition of their marriage, Skoblin asked her to promise that she would avoid politics.[9] He hated for women to involve themselves in such matters, which was a widespread view in the socially conservative Russian émigré military culture. In her prison diary (1937–1938), Plevitskaya wrote that she herself was not interested in politics and cared only for using her art to raise the morale of her husband's men. (However, this part of her diary, written shortly before her trial, may have been produced with an audience in mind.)

Plevitskaya and Skoblin had significant worries beyond setting the ground rules for their marriage. These included failing health and finances. Plevitskaya had just recovered from typhus, and she also had to nurse Skoblin, who suffered from tuberculosis and other ailments while on Gallipoli.[10] Like the other thousands of Russian exiles stranded in Turkey, they survived on little. Female aristocrats waited tables in Russian restaurants, and Russian women of more modest backgrounds sold flowers or worked as maids.[11] Plevitskaya was forced to sell much of her valuable jewelry collection. This story is confirmed by Miakin, who had emigrated to Turkey shortly after Plevitskaya did. He claimed that he pawned a pair of earrings for her that may have been a gift from the tsar.[12] Reportedly, she later pawned more jewels.[13] While she and Skoblin were in Turkey, she also performed in Constantinople and may have done so outside the country.[14]

Despite their ambitions for returning to Russia to defeat the Bolsheviks, the White Army commanders soon faced major financial and logistical

General Nikolai Skoblin (standing at center), surrounded by other members of the Kornilov Regiment, Gallipoli, 1921

hurdles. In March 1921, the French government announced that it would not support them for much longer. This decision caused widespread and lasting resentment among the White military personnel, not only about the French government, but also about Western culture and values more generally.[15] The Turks also wanted the White Army veterans and their families to leave their country. The Volunteer Army's pride in their "Gallipoli miracle" partly rested on a mistaken belief that their unity had prevented the French from dissolving their units.[16] The reality was that their resurrection and sense of political and moral cohesion were myths. "Not only were émigrés remarkably fractious," historian Paul Robinson argues, "but even if they had succeeded in uniting it is unlikely they would have made any difference to the fate of Russia."[17]

Knowing that they would need to vacate Turkey by year's end, in the spring of 1921, Wrangel and other White leaders negotiated with the friendly governments of Serbia and Bulgaria to allow the remnants of the Volunteer Army to immigrate to their countries. Approximately twenty-five thousand soldiers moved to Yugoslavia, and nineteen thousand to Bulgaria. Some also relocated to Czechoslovakia, Romania, and Hungary.[18] On November 27, 1921, a fleet of ships transported the Skoblins and other White Army soldiers and their relatives to Bulgaria. Through decrees issued in November and December 1921, the Bolshevik government had stripped Russian refugees of their citizenship, and they were issued temporary travel documents by the new League of Nations shortly before leaving Turkey. These documents were called "Nansen passports," after the Norwegian humanitarian and explorer Fridtjof Nansen, whom the League of Nations appointed as high commissioner for refugees. Nansen helped coordinate the effort to assist Russian refugees through settlement in various countries, but they were ultimately dependent on the governments that accepted them.

As White Army veterans dispersed throughout Europe, their commanders tried to maintain organizational cohesion, in the quixotic hope of resuming their fight against the Bolsheviks. While most other officers and soldiers left to seek jobs, each major unit kept in place a small cadre and command staff. Unit leaders were responsible for keeping in contact with their men, helping them find jobs and shelter, and providing for other needs as they arose. By the mid-1920s, most veterans were working in civilian jobs—largely in mines and factories.

White military commanders insisted that they were the legitimate representatives of Russia and that their military organizations should be subsidized by Russian imperial assets. However, many civilian émigrés wanted funds to be distributed in the form of humanitarian assistance to those struggling financially. As a result, the émigré community as a whole became embroiled in long-standing leadership, financial, and identity conflicts. White military organizations never had sufficient funds to maintain an army and train new personnel.

In exile, Skoblin stayed involved in White military affairs. Bulgaria, his first posting after Gallipoli, was only a way station. Bulgaria, ruled by Tsar Boris III and his prime minister Alexander Stamboliyski, was politically and economically unstable. The military overthrew Stamboliyski in 1923, while Bulgarian communists attempted their own rising and battled White Army soldiers in 1923. When the Skoblins arrived in Bulgaria in late 1921, they moved—along with other Kornilovites and their families—into dilapidated army barracks in the isolated, hilly village of Gorno-Ponicherovo.[19] Later they resettled in a mining town near Sofia named Pernik, where Soviet intelligence agents monitored them. A Soviet agent reported to his Moscow superiors that the group numbered between 3,000 and 3,500 men and was led by Skoblin.[20]

While in Bulgaria, Skoblin trained his soldiers and helped provide for them. But for White military families, poor living conditions and lack of money made the situation in Bulgaria untenable. Skoblin urged his men to seek jobs, even though General Kutepov initially opposed the idea.[21] In 1922, the Bulgarian government arrested and then expelled Kutepov and several other Russian officers, who were increasingly seen as a threat to an already unstable regime.[22] Skoblin and Plevitskaya remained in Bulgaria for nearly two more years, although not without peril. From Crimea, Skoblin had brought with him an orderly named David. Several Bulgarian communists tried to persuade David to grant them access to the Skoblins' quarters, but the young orderly, suspecting a kidnapping plot, warned Skoblin, who took steps to protect the house.[23]

In Bulgaria, Plevitskaya sang for White Army veterans and in benefit concerts. For Orthodox Easter in 1922, she performed for the regiment and shared with them some memories of her father, who had served in the tsar's army.[24] In January 1924, she hosted a Christmas party for Russian children in Pernik, where nearly 1,500 Russians were employed in coal mines. She helped raise funds for gifts, food, and a tree. Grandfather Frost, the equivalent of Santa Claus, paid a visit, and an orchestra played as partygoers sang with Plevitskaya around the tree. In an article about the experience, Plevitskaya commented that the party had brought back memories of her childhood in Vinnikovo.[25] In general, though, she found life in Bulgaria unfulfilling and stressful, given all the deprivations that the exiled soldiers and their families suffered.

In 1922, with Skoblin accompanying her, Plevitskaya performed throughout Europe in cities with sizable Russian émigré populations, including Prague, Warsaw, Brussels, Paris, Berlin, and cities in Latvia and Estonia. Everywhere she sang, the audiences greeted her with warmth and enthusiasm. When she sang in Riga, she was accompanied by the Jewish-Latvian composer and pianist Oscar Strok. At one concert, Strok recalled, "she interpreted my song 'Simple Love'—about the life of a peasant woman who lost her husband in a war—so movingly that I was overcome by emotion and could not keep playing."[26]

In 1923, Plevitskaya sang to émigrés in sold-out concerts across Europe, often visiting Berlin, which hosted one of the continent's largest Russian émigré communities. She returned to the same cities as the year before and added more, including London, to her itinerary.[27] In January, she appeared in Warsaw and then returned to the Baltics. In February, she performed in Berlin and Prague. Émigré newspapers gushed about her singing.[28] On March 29, 1923, Plevitskaya performed to a packed audience in the Beethoven Hall in Berlin.[29] There she sang for the first time what would become her best-known tribute to Old Russia and the White community's anthem, "Russia, You're Frozen in Snow" (Zamelo tebia snegom, Rossiya). Its lyrics may have been written by Ivan Lukash, who edited Plevitskaya's memoirs. The melancholy chorus ran thus:

> Russia, you're frozen in snow,
> Holed up by a gray blizzard,
> And cold winds blow across the steppe,
> Requiems are sung over you.

Berlin audiences responded so enthusiastically that organizers booked additional concerts there in April. Later in the spring, she sang in Brussels and then again in Berlin.

In the summer of 1923, Plevitskaya performed in Belgrade, Sofia, and Stockholm. In the fall, she sang in Paris and Vienna. Reviewing one of her concerts in Sofia, a music critic wrote that "no artist living abroad evokes such reminiscences and feelings as N. V. Plevitskaya."[30] Plevitskaya's new impresario, Yuri Borkon, booked more concerts in Berlin, and she sang more frequently in Paris, including at the 1,020-seat Gaveau Hall. Another popular new song in her repertoire was "And Russia Will Be Again" (I budet Rossiya opiat'). In 1924, she made a series of recordings in Germany and received modest royalties from these for several years.[31]

Regrets, however, may have underpinned these successes. Plevitskaya reputedly tried to persuade her husband to return to Russia while they were in Bulgaria, and may even have tried to do so during their time on Gallipoli.[32] In November 1921, the Soviet government had issued an amnesty decree, meant to lure White Russian military personnel back to the USSR to serve in the Red Army. Also, in May 1922, a Union for Return to the Homeland was established to expedite the repatriation of Russian émigrés. Plevitskaya and Skoblin learned of how another former White Army officer, General Slashchev, had returned home with the approval of Cheka director Felix Dzerzhinsky, receiving amnesty and a job.[33] Skoblin apparently told Plevitskaya that he thought the Soviet government would not issue him a pardon.[34] If such discord indeed arose, it can be seen as an early manifestation of the deeper homesickness that caused the couple to shift allegiances later.

In late 1923 or early 1924, the commanding body of the White Army—under General Wrangel's leadership—issued Skoblin a reprimand, citing lack of attention to his troops and his frequent trips abroad with Plevitskaya. Skoblin seems to have already grown critical of his senior officers, who in his mind were not planning sufficiently for the overthrow of the Bolsheviks.[35] Soon afterward, Skoblin reportedly applied for permission to take a long business trip through Europe to assess the condition of the White Army, while Plevitskaya was performing in various cities. Plevitskaya had planned a flurry of concerts between February and May, including in Paris, Nice, Stockholm, Brussels, Prague, and Berlin. A review of an April 17 concert in Berlin noted that even Germans attended her performances and that her talent was "God-given."[36]

Finally, the Skoblins left Bulgaria for good in the spring of 1924, causing some members of the regiment to grumble that the young general had callously left them to their fate.[37] On May 30, he and Plevitskaya officially landed in France as immigrants, and French officials issued them residence permits.[38] While France was their country of residence from 1924 onward, they never gained French citizenship and continued to spend months at a time abroad. They obtained identity certificates whenever they left the country.[39] Whatever their exact agendas were, Plevitskaya and Skoblin were constantly on the move and expanding their circles of acquaintance.

Skoblin made the same choice that thousands of other White Army veterans had made—that is, to leave the less economically developed region of Eastern Europe for points west. Of all European countries during the 1920s, France was the most open to Russians. Some estimates place the number of Russians residing in France during the 1920s and early 1930s as high as 120,000.[40] Russians were drawn to Paris, although they settled as well in places like Nice, Cannes, Marseilles, and Lyon. Dozens of work groups of Russian soldiers were placed in factories across France due to the arrangements made by General Shatilov of Wrangel's general staff; the soldiers often lived in workers' barracks for many years.[41]

Ironically, as White Army veterans were moving to France in higher numbers, its government, led by Édouard Herriot's left-wing coalition, decided to recognize the USSR in 1924. French authorities began to curtail the number of visas they issued to émigrés and to weaken France's official ties to the White Army. It also became more difficult for immigrants to obtain French citizenship.

Four million people lived in Paris during the mid-1920s, 10 percent of whom were foreign-born. Between 1921 and 1926, the Russian émigré population in Paris more than doubled, reaching a total of thirty-five thousand, thus making it the epicenter of Russian emigration.[42] The Russian population in Paris was composed of four major groups: Soviet citizens such as diplomats, journalists, and trade representatives; those who had left Russia before World War I, including thousands of Russian Jews; military officers and soldiers; and nonmilitary émigrés, including political leaders, cultural figures, and businesspeople.[43] Many White Army veterans, including officers, still struggled to improve their living standards, as their jobs tended to be menial and low paying. Chauffeurs and taxi drivers were considered the elite of menial workers; Russian aristocrats, such as Prince Pyotr Dolgoruky, were known to drive cars for a living.[44] The more rank-and-file émigrés worked in factories in the Paris suburbs, such as the Renault automobile plant in Billancourt.

Those Russian émigrés who could afford it—including the Skoblins—lived in the upscale sixteenth arrondissement (district) on the Right Bank of the Seine, which featured luxury apartment buildings, hotels, and exclusive shops. During the 1930s, the Skoblins frequently rented a room in a hotel in the sixteenth arrondissement, although during the 1920s, they rented a flat in the first arrondissement, on rue de Richelieu, close to the Royal Palace.[45] Russians also congregated in other neighborhoods, including the seventeenth arrondissement, where St. Alexander Nevsky Cathedral is located, and Montparnasse on the Left Bank, in the fourteenth arrondissement, with its strong café culture. Other Russians chose to live in suburbs of Paris, such as Vincennes, Meudon, Billancourt, and Issy-les Moulineaux. In 1930, the Skoblins bought a home in the suburb of Ozoir-la-Ferrière, which also had a Russian presence.

Despite the Russian population's diversity, it still had a unifying mission, which was to preserve Russian culture.[46] Part of this sprang from an impulse to remain apart from the mainstream culture. Many Russian émigrés, including Plevitskaya, assumed that they would eventually return home, and so they did not bother to become fluent in the language of their adopted country or otherwise assimilate. Most émigré performers, especially those for whom nostalgia was their principal selling point—like Plevitskaya and other folk musicians—gave shows mainly for émigré audiences.

The cultural divide between the Russians and their French hosts was generally wide enough that the émigrés kept largely to themselves socially. As historian Robert Johnston puts it, a Russian exiled in France "was just 'le Russe' down the hall or further along the assembly line. His foreignness might be overlooked but was never forgotten and would be recalled in moments of stress."[47] Occasionally, formal gatherings brought Russian and French writers together to nurture mutual interests. In 1929 and 1930, such gatherings included Boris Zaitsev, Ivan Bunin, and Marina Tsvetaeva among the Russians, and Jacques Maritain, André Malraux, and André Maurois representing the French. According to Johnston, however, these meetings did little "to enhance the image of National Russia among the Paris literati."[48]

Famous American expatriates such as F. Scott and Zelda Fitzgerald, Ernest Hemingway, Gertrude Stein, and Alice B. Toklas had occasional contacts with Russian émigré artists and writers, although there is no evidence that they crossed paths with Plevitskaya. During the mid-1920s, Zelda Fitzgerald took dance lessons from Lubov Egorova (Princess Trubetskaya), who had been a top ballerina with the Russian Imperial Ballet and, once in exile, was affiliated with the Ballets Russes.[49] Stein and Toklas took an interest in the works of Russian surrealist painter Pavel Tchelitchew and in Diaghilev and the Ballets Russes.[50] Hemingway found the Russian émigré community an interesting topic on which to write. In 1922, in the *Toronto Star*, Hemingway noted that the Russians "are drifting along in Paris in a childish sort of hopefulness that things will somehow be all right, which is quite charming when you first encounter it and rather maddening after a few months. No one knows just how they live except it is by selling off jewels and gold ornaments and family heirlooms that they brought with them to France when they fled before the revolution."[51]

In Paris, the Russians in exile maintained their cultural ties by patronizing Russian restaurants, clubs, stores, theaters, and youth groups. They joined military associations and Orthodox churches and supported community events and Russian-language schools. The principal Russian Orthodox church in Paris was St. Alexander Nevsky Cathedral, where parishioners marked important holidays and anniversaries. They paid respect to deceased relatives and friends in the Sainte-Geneviève-des-Bois Cemetery south of Paris, where many famous émigrés are now buried, including Ivan Bunin and Rudolf Nureyev.

During the interwar period, émigrés obtained their news from various Russian-language sources. Two major Russian newspapers served different Russian readerships. More popular, with a daily circulation of forty thousand, was the liberal *Poslednie novosti* (*The Latest News*), edited by Pavel Miliukov, a former leader of the Constitutional Democratic (Cadet) Party who grew less critical of the Soviet regime with the passing years.[52] Its conservative rival, *Renaissance* (*Vozrozhdenie*), with a smaller circulation, was edited during the mid-1920s by Pyotr Struve, who had also been a Cadet but was now a moderate monarchist in exile. Later, the paper was run by an anti-Soviet reactionary named Yuly Semenov.

Members of the Russian emigration may have agreed that they needed to preserve their culture, but they disagreed on what its exact components were. Differences of opinion about what constituted culture were especially stark between liberal intellectuals and the more conservative military veterans. For example, Russian military officers such as Skoblin associated culture "not only with literature and other higher arts," but also with "service to the state, honour, duty, the traditions of the regiment, preserving the memory of Russian military victories, and so on." To intellectuals of a liberal stripe, such things were "almost universally anathema."[53] As a cultural celebrity married to a Russian officer, Plevitskaya stood between these two distinct worlds and served as a bridge between them.

In terms of political culture, the majority of Russian émigrés, including most military veterans, were conservatives who "ranged from moderate constitutional monarchists to antisemitic reactionaries and imitators of Italian and German Fascism."[54] Only a minority could be labeled liberal democrats; fewer still were on the far left. Due to the emigration's high concentration of former Russian political figures and military leaders, all still fighting old battles, intrigue and conspiracy flourished in Paris.[55] To them, la Ville Lumière "held out a front row seat in the spectacle of world politics, the best place to organize, propagandize and, it was devoutly hoped, influence decisions about the subject closest to their hearts, Russia's post-Bolshevik future."[56] Some émigrés formed new political movements in Paris during the 1920s, as in the case of the Eurasians. Eurasianism was a largely anti-Bolshevik and anti-Western ideology whose adherents, many of whom were young émigrés, viewed Russia as a part of a unique geographical and cultural space spanning from the Baltics to Asia.[57] (During the mid-1920s, Skoblin reportedly met several times with Pyotr Suvchinsky, one of the movement's leaders. The general made a poor impression on Suvchinsky, and they eventually lost contact.[58]) During the interwar era, all attempts to unify disparate émigré political factions, including during the Congress of Russia Abroad in 1926, failed, and no leader emerged who could foster such harmony.

On the whole, Russian émigrés during the 1920s did not greatly concern the French police, who were more troubled by Italian and North African immigrants. However, for surveillance purposes, the police divided the Russian émigré community into three groups: those who sympathized with the Soviet regime and wished to return to their homeland, those who were profascist, and those who were apolitical and planned to remain in France.[59] The security challenge was to identify and expel potential trouble-makers, and, to that end, French authorities increasingly monitored White Russian military veterans' organizations.

The organization on which the French most squarely fixed their attention, and the one most intertwined with Skoblin's and Plevitskaya's fate was the Russian General Military Union (Russkii Obshche-Voinskii Soiuz, or ROVS). General Wrangel founded ROVS in September 1924, one month before the French government established diplomatic ties with the Soviet Union. Two major decisions led to its creation. Already in 1921, Wrangel had instructed his officers to organize their soldiers into societies and unions. Wrangel now envisioned ROVS, with himself as commander in chief, as an umbrella organization capable of gathering those disparate groups together. Once functioning, ROVS would offer useful services to veterans, including employment assistance, hospital care, free dinners, and rail passes. The need for such enticements was acute: by 1924, several White officers had returned to Soviet Russia, potentially weakening the will of those who remained. Providing for the well-being of émigré veterans was an important way to persuade them to remain abroad. Beyond this, the primary goal of ROVS, which also trained young recruits as soldiers, was to return to Russia—and to overthrow the Soviet regime.

After 1928, the year of Wrangel's death, the organization was headquartered in Paris and was divided into six administrative departments based on geographical area. The First Department, for instance, represented France, Italy, Holland, North Africa, and the Middle East. All veterans were members of ROVS due to their membership in individual military organizations (including former army units and military academies), and they were required to pay membership dues. Operating funds and assistance to needy veterans were also raised through charity balls and concerts, many of which Plevitskaya performed in during the 1920s and 1930s. ROVS members still spent time with their unit organizations, such as the Society of Gallipoli Veterans (henceforth, the Society of Gallipolians) in Paris, which provided meals, entertainment, and other social activities to its members and their families. ROVS membership reached a peak of 35,214 in 1925, but plummeted as veterans passed away and were not replaced by new recruits.[60]

ROVS offered its members several benefits, but it failed in its mission to maintain a standing army capable of combating the Soviets. Instead, its weaknesses—infighting, lack of funds, poor communications—outweighed its strengths. ROVS's intelligence-related efforts, and those of other White Russian organizations, would prove equally ineffective.

Another reason ROVS leaders failed in their mission was that Soviet counterintelligence planners consistently outsmarted them and other anti-communist émigré organizations. The leaders of the nascent Soviet regime treated national security as a paramount concern. Their perceptions were framed by Marxist-Leninist ideology and paranoia about internal and external enemies—and not without reason. Western powers opposed the Bolshevik Revolution and sent troops in support of the Whites during the civil war. Throughout the 1920s, numerous foreign spies and White Russians, many of them captured or at least foiled by Soviet intelligence, conspired against the new regime.

Soviet leaders created a secret police state that targeted all enemies, real or imagined. The name of the agency changed through the interwar years, from the original Cheka to the GPU (State Political Department, 1922–1923), the OGPU (United State Political Department, 1923–1934), and the NKVD (People's Commissariat of Internal Affairs, 1934–1945). However, its fundamental purpose remained the same, as did its leaders' disregard for human life. By 1925, the Soviet security apparatus had killed an estimated 250,000 people.[61]

For pragmatic reasons, the Soviet government established diplomatic relations with Western states during the 1920s and early 1930s, but it still recruited hundreds of agents there. A primary counterintelligence objective was to undermine enemies in the Russian emigration. Most Soviet agents consciously avoided joining communist parties or taking part in the Soviet-backed Communist International (Comintern), which formed in 1919 to promote the worldwide spread of communism. They were instead trained to maintain their cover and deceive their main targets and the local authorities.

Soviet counterintelligence carried out three interrelated tasks aimed at the White Guardists, the collective label the Soviets gave their émigré foes. The most routine was monitoring their organizations in order to collect information, feed them false information, and weaken them from within. This was typically achieved by carefully positioned informants or agents provocateurs, émigrés who were willing to betray the White movement for ideological or personal reasons—or a combination of both. Secondly, Soviet counterintelligence kidnapped and executed leading White Guardists and agents who infiltrated the USSR on sabotage missions. The third task demanded the most long-term planning: the deception operation. Deception operations involved fabricating anti-Soviet organizations, persuading naive Whites to join them in plotting supposedly anti-Soviet operations, and thus luring them into the USSR for destruction or to turn them into double agents.[62] Deception campaigns allowed the Soviets to control enemy forces from within and expose, and ultimately undermine, their sabotage efforts.

To this purpose, on December 20, 1920, only a few weeks after Wrangel's ships left Crimea, Cheka head Felix Dzerzhinsky founded the agency's Foreign Department (Inostrannyi Otdel, or INO). Among other tasks, the INO concerned itself with exposing anti-Soviet conspiracies and disrupting anti-Soviet organizations. During the interwar period, the White Guardists of ROVS were among the INO's major targets, and indeed its primary target until the early 1930s, when Nazi Germany and Japan became of greater concern.[63] In addition, in 1926, Viacheslav Menzhinsky, Dzerzhinsky's successor, created the Administration for Special Tasks, which carried out sabotage operations, kidnappings, and assassinations abroad, including against ROVS members.[64] Soviet intelligence officials worked to ensure that ROVS would lack the capacity to wage war or execute sabotage operations against their regime. They viewed White Guardists as terrorists and knew that they regularly cooperated with foreign intelligence agencies and were supporting a White army in exile.[65]

It did not take long for INO officials and operatives to begin monitoring Wrangel, Kutepov, and even Skoblin. A Cheka report issued in November 1921 included a brief profile of Skoblin: "A young and capable officer. Without a military education. Good regimental commander, but no higher."[66] The Cheka assumed that Skoblin and other young leaders of the Volunteer Army had been promoted prematurely because the Whites were in such dire straits. A Cheka report of November 1922 contained two conclusions that came to hold particular importance for the Soviets. First, Kutepov had killed many communists and had personally assisted in their executions. Second, his First Army Group would disintegrate if he were no longer its leader.[67]

Soviet intelligence responded by launching a deception campaign called the Trust (TREST) operation, which functioned between 1921 and 1927.[68] As a result of this extended operation, the Soviets became even better acquainted with ROVS's sabotage plans and killed or turned some of its agents. Kutepov, who sent clandestine ROVS operations into the USSR across the Finnish border, doomed several of his agents by failing to understand how badly compromised his operations were. When the TREST deception was exposed to the West in 1927, it enormously embarrassed ROVS and the several European intelligence agencies that had fallen for it. The TREST catastrophe also heightened the level of paranoia among Russian émigrés, and accusations of spying among their ranks continued to increase.[69]

Even after the TREST failure, Kutepov did not back down but decided to plan even more ambitious anti-Soviet operations, including sabotage activities inside the USSR and the forming of centers of resistance there, with the assistance of French, Finnish, Polish, and Romanian intelligence officials. This clandestine work came to be called the "Outer Line," and Kutepov hoped it would convince Western governments and an increasingly skeptical émigré community that ROVS remained worthy of financial and institutional support. In fact, Outer Line activities allowed Soviet intelligence to infiltrate ROVS even more thoroughly. They may also have contributed to the brief but unnerving Anglo-Soviet war scare of 1927, and they likely served as a pretense for Stalin's crackdown on his domestic political enemies in the late 1920s.[70]

The Soviets also learned that ROVS had created a secret counterintelligence branch called the "Inner Line," organized and led by Captain Klavdy Foss, who served as General Abramov's assistant in Bulgaria. The Inner Line spread to other centers of the Russian emigration, including France, and it aimed to expose traitors in White military organizations and to monitor the émigré youth groups that preferred to operate independently. In the words of one historian, the Inner Line was "a logical extension of the concept of a knightly order acting as a moral centre in the midst of the Russian emigration. However, as befitted an organization that viewed itself as something of a special 'order,' the Inner Line began to take on a life of its own outside the proper chain of command, and tried to get all the strings of power in ROVS into its own hands."[71]

Both the Inner and Outer Lines were penetrated by the Soviets, with disastrous results for ROVS. Kutepov understood that his men were vulnerable to Soviet recruitment, but the Reds astutely judged him to be "curiously naïve about the danger of Soviet penetration of his entourage."[72]

The same would prove true for Kutepov's successor, Evgeny Miller. A key asset in undermining ROVS's goals was Skoblin, who eventually abandoned the Whites in favor of the Reds.

A perennial debate surrounds the question of when exactly Soviet intelligence recruited Skoblin and Plevitskaya. As noted in the previous chapter, some émigrés believed that the couple had been turned as early as the Russian Civil War. Among these was the spy hunter Vladimir Burtsev. It is true that the Cheka sent sleeper agents, such as master spy Dmitri Bystrolyotov, to Europe as the civil war ended.[73] These were awakened afterward, and their ranks may have included the Skoblins. Other émigrés assumed that the pair switched sides sometime during the 1920s.

One possibility involves the Jewish-Russian psychoanalyst Max Khaimovich Eitingon, best known for his close association with Sigmund Freud. Although Eitingon's family had immigrated to Germany during his boyhood, it had amassed a fortune by trading furs in Imperial Russia and maintained its wealth for decades by fostering business ties with the Soviets after the Bolshevik Revolution. In 1925, Eitingon became president of the International Psychoanalytic Association; his generosity sustained Freud, whom he regularly sent money and gifts of cigars and food.[74] For several years, Eitingon lived in Berlin with his wife Mirra, a fellow Jewish-Russian émigré. Before emigrating to Germany and marrying Max in 1913, Mirra (née Burovskaya) had acted in the Moscow Art Theater—using the stage name Mirra Birens—and may have been acquainted with Plevitskaya.

During the interwar era, the Eitingons extended patronage to artists and performers as well as to psychoanalysts. They offered Plevitskaya regular stipends and may have bankrolled her U.S. concert tour in 1926 and 1927.[75] When they visited Berlin, Plevitskaya and Skoblin sometimes guested with the Eitingons, who helped arrange some of her Berlin concerts and funded the publication of her memoirs. At their house outside Berlin, the Eitingons hosted a salon to which they often invited famous figures from the world of Russian arts and letters. Plevitskaya performed at some of these gatherings. Among the audience were Lou Andreas-Salomé, a Russian-born female psychoanalyst, and Lev Shestov, a religious existentialist from Kiev. The night she sang for Shestov, Plevitskaya kneeled at his feet in homage.[76] In 1933, Max and Mirra Eitingon emigrated to Palestine to escape Nazi persecution, but they continued to visit Europe, particularly over the summers between 1935 and 1938.[77] It was in Palestine that Max died in 1943.

Max Eitingon's life story is controversial, largely because of his ties to Plevitskaya and how they were framed during the police investigation of General Miller's kidnapping and her subsequent criminal trial. Police investigators and the Miller family's attorney claimed that Eitingon had passed money and secret codes to her and Skoblin from Soviet intelligence. Whenever Plevitskaya was questioned about Eitingon, she insisted that he was not a Soviet spy and was only her artistic benefactor.

Although scholars and journalists still dispute the issue, much circumstantial evidence points to Eitingon's involvement in Soviet intelligence.[78] According to biographer Mary-Kay Wilmers, an Eitingon descendant, Max was secretive enough to have been a spy and was sometimes absent for months.[79] It is an accepted fact that one of Max's distant relatives, Leonid Eitingon—also known by the first name Naum—worked for Soviet intelligence and played a central role in the assassination of Leon Trotsky.[80] (However, no proof has ever indicated that Max was at all acquainted with Leonid.) In addition, papers from Israel's state archive suggest that Max and Mirra both had ties to Soviet intelligence, and that Max likely served as "paymaster" to Soviet intelligence agents, including the Skoblins.[81]

Perhaps most intriguing is the information in the memoirs of former NKVD operative Alexander Orlov. According to Orlov, INO official Sergei Shpigelglas recruited Skoblin in the late 1920s, with Plevitskaya's help. Shpigelglas, Orlov claims, approached her through "a Russian millionaire whose hobby it was to befriend and support Russian artists in exile," which is a possible reference to Max Eitingon.[82] Still, Orlov's allegation is based on hearsay and therefore should not be taken at face value. Moreover, no declassified NKVD files have acknowledged the Eitingons' clandestine activities, so the matter remains unresolved.

Although the Eitingon spy rumor particularly intrigued Russian émigrés and French authorities, it settled no questions about the Skoblins' recruitment. During the mid-1920s, a second rumor circulated among Russian émigrés that Plevitskaya had returned to the USSR for a series of concerts, but it was soon revealed that she had been confused with another émigré singer with a similar-sounding name, Elena Polevitskaya.[83] Polevitskaya, who left Russia in 1920 and appeared in concerts and plays all over Europe, put on three musical tours in the USSR between 1923 and 1925. Despite enjoying a wider popular appeal in Europe than Plevitskaya ever did, Polevitskaya repatriated to the USSR in 1955.

A third rumor appears to clear the Skoblins of actually spying at this early date but does indicate a pro-Soviet turn of mind. In 1925 or 1926, one of Plevitskaya's former impresarios, Vasily Afanasiev, allegedly appealed for amnesty on her behalf to Felix Dzerzhinsky himself at the infamous Lubyanka, the Moscow headquarters of the secret police.[84] During the mid-1920s, the Soviet regime was keen to repatriate émigré artists and—falsely, as it turned out—promised those who returned that no political strings would be attached.[85] If the story is true, Afanasiev ventured to the Lubyanka several times but met with Dzerzhinsky only once. The date is not specified, but it would have to have been before July 1926, when Dzerzhinsky died. As the tale has it, Afanasiev approached Dzerzhinsky's desk, holding a tube with Plevitskaya's application for amnesty in it.

"Give it to me!" Dzerzhinsky exclaimed impatiently, extending his hand to Afanasiev. Dzerzhinsky quickly unrolled the paper and wrote something on the top corner of the form. Next, he rolled the application back up and thrust it across the table to Afanasiev. "Take it," he ordered. Startled by how swiftly Dzerzhinsky had read the application, with only a cursory glance, Afanasiev backed toward the door and uttered some quick words of gratitude. Then Dzerzhinsky barked, "Read it!" Afanasiev took out the application and saw the scribbled mark of refusal on it, presumably an X.

This narrative, if true, suggests that during the mid-1920s the Soviet regime did not trust Plevitskaya because of her marriage to Skoblin, and that neither was then on Dzerzhinsky's payroll. (Other would-be returnees were sometimes rebuffed by the Soviets. The painter Nikolai Roerich met this fate, and Maria Olenina-d'Alheim, another Russian émigré singer—one vocally sympathetic to the Bolsheviks—was rejected when she tried to repatriate during the early 1930s, presumably because the Soviets did not trust her.[86]) Artistic merits, or the lack of them, may also have contributed to Dzerzhinsky's rejection of Plevitskaya. In the early 1920s, the Soviet government's Main Administration for Literary and Publishing Affairs, or Glavlit, is said to have issued a negative verdict on Plevitskaya's legacy. Not only had she been promoted by monarchists and linked with the Black Hundreds, an ultraconservative nationalist group, the report supposedly said, but her musical output lacked artistic value.[87]

One last source seems to corroborate the theory that the Skoblins were already spying for the Soviets in the 1920s. Grigory Besedovsky, a chargé d'affaires at the USSR's Paris embassy during the 1920s (and possibly an OGPU operative stationed there under diplomatic cover), defected to France in 1929 and published his memoirs in 1931, *Revelations of a Soviet Diplomat*. He also testified at Plevitskaya's trial in 1938. On the stand, Besedovsky claimed that, during a card game in 1927, an OGPU operative named Yanovich (probably Vladimir Yanovich, the Soviet embassy's OGPU *rezident*) told him about a White Army officer who was a Soviet agent and whose wife was a famous singer.[88]

Undoubtedly, the Skoblins had motives to spy by the late 1920s. They faced mounting financial problems. Skoblin's resentment of several senior ROVS officials was hardening. Plevitskaya felt homesick. It had become more difficult for her to receive letters from her relatives in the Soviet Union, and several of them had already died from famine and other hardships. Plevitskaya and Skoblin both felt a powerful need to belong to something greater than themselves. For Skoblin, it was an army corps, while for Plevitskaya it was a close-knit family sharing kinship and cultural bonds. Soviet intelligence officials understood well how to exploit such needs in new recruits. However, anyone who writes about espionage knows not to trust the memoirs of defectors completely. Besedovsky's testimony is compelling but lacks detail. Soviet files on Skoblin that were briefly declassified during the late 1980s and early 1990s do not refer to any intelligence work done either by him or by Plevitskaya before the fall of 1930. At best, we can only say that the Skoblins may have been agents as early as 1927 and interpret some of their actions prior to the fall of 1930 in this light.

Having arrived in France, the Skoblins needed to make a living, and Plevitskaya was their main breadwinner. In June 1924, in one of her first concerts in France after immigrating there, Plevitskaya sang in Paris at Gaveau Hall with the Kedrov Quartet. She also performed with other artists in charity concerts in Paris and Meudon, where the Skoblins lived intermittently until 1930. The émigré scholar Tatiana Varsher was initially charmed by Plevitskaya, whom she met in 1924.[89] The singer struck her as friendly and dignified, and Varsher appreciated the singer's natural storytelling abilities. Before leaving Bulgaria for France, Plevitskaya had read Varsher's memoirs, *Things Seen and Suffered*, and complimented her on them in person. Varsher attended Plevitskaya's June 1924 Gaveau Hall concert and was favorably impressed with her performance and with the way she behaved with Grand Duchess Xenia Alexandrovna, without a trace of a servile tone. Eventually, though, Varsher began to suspect that Plevitskaya may have been using her as part of a broader strategy to cultivate a large number of acquaintances, perhaps for espionage purposes.

In July 1924, in Meudon, Plevitskaya completed her first volume of memoirs, *Dezhkin karagod*, which covered events of her childhood up to 1909. She drafted most of the manuscript in Berlin while staying with the Eitingons, and they helped pay for its publication.[90] Only a few thousand copies were produced, earning her about 10,000 francs.[91] Plevitskaya dedicated her second volume of memoirs, *Moi put' s pesnei* (*My Way with a*

Song), to Mirra Eitingon; it covered her life from late 1909 to 1915 and was published in 1930.[92] Sergei Rachmaninoff helped her publish both volumes under the Tair Publishing imprint and was among the first to encourage her to write them.[93] Unfortunately for Plevitskaya, the print runs of her memoirs were small—in the low thousands—so she did not earn sizable royalties.

Ivan Lukash, a writer of historical novels who worked for *Vozrozhdenie*, edited both volumes of Plevitskaya's memoirs, although some of her contemporaries suspected others of having acted as her ghost writers.[94] Avant-garde author Aleksei Remizov, who, like Plevitskaya, felt a deep attachment to the Russian countryside, wrote the preface to the first volume.

Dezhkin karagod was favorably reviewed in several émigré publications for depicting Russian peasant life authentically and in clear prose. A reviewer for a Bulgarian newspaper was reminded of the works of Maxim Gorky and pleased by Plevitskaya's portrait of her relatives as real people who embodied strong Russian values, not high-flown intellectual or political agendas.[95] *Vozrozhdenie* praised Plevitskaya's book for its rich, concise, and soulful descriptions of the Russian landscape.[96] Not all of the feedback was positive, though. The newspaper *Vremya* criticized Plevitskaya for failing to elaborate on what motivated her, instead merely providing scattered details of village life and her early career moves.[97]

Upon the release of each volume, Plevitskaya's authorship was questioned due to her peasant upbringing and lack of formal education. How could a barely literate woman produce such lyrical, sometimes literary prose? Despite her academic limitations, Plevitskaya very likely drafted most of her memoirs. She was an autodidact who quickly adapted to new social milieus, including the company of nobles, military officers, literati, and musicians. She wrote frequently to relatives and acquaintances. While awaiting trial in Paris in 1937–1938, she constantly used her diary to record her experiences and fears. Although the quality of her prose wavered, she was not untutored in the art of written expression. As harshly as Varsher later criticized Plevitskaya, she still assumed that the singer had largely written her memoirs, which were on the whole simply composed.

Meanwhile, in the fall of 1924, Plevitskaya performed across parts of Eastern Europe. In Riga, Latvia, she appeared before packed audiences who demanded several encores. The newspaper articles she collected from here and pasted into scrapbooks extolled her storytelling abilities and her charming intonation.[98] One writer called her "a daughter of the Russian people."[99] Another gushed, "When she sings, the entire hall sings. . . . She sings like she's a bird, a worker in the fields, unrehearsed in her joy and sorrow. . . . Her singing is eternal. . . . She's authentic, not methodical . . . an expression of the Russian people."[100]

Dezhkin karagod was released in time for Plevitskaya's January 3, 1925, Jubilee Concert at Berlin's Blüthner Hall, an event that celebrated fifteen years of her artistic achievements. She received accolades and good wishes from music and theater people throughout the Russian emigration. According to one of her French acquaintances, the tickets were expensive, and the performance was not well attended.[101] On January 7, though, she performed a second Jubilee Concert, this time in Gaveau Hall in Paris. This audience was enthusiastic, and one reviewer compared her to Chaliapin.[102]

These two concerts marked the start of one of Plevitskaya's busiest years as an émigré performer. Most of her Paris concerts did not generate revenue for her; they were fund-raisers for various émigré groups. These included a benefit concert sponsored by the Committee of Assistance to Russian Writers and Scholars and a literary-musical evening with Remizov, both later in January. Then, from February through May 1925, she performed again in Berlin, and then in Warsaw, Vilnius, Bratislava, and other cities in Eastern Europe, with fifteen concerts in Poland alone. Her September-to-December concert season was heavily booked with concerts in Paris. In October, she took part in a benefit concert for members of the Society of Gallipolians, which continued to regard her as their "mother-commander."

In November and December 1925, Plevitskaya performed several times at tenor Dmitry Smirnov's Dom Artista (Artist's House), a venue where Russian émigré artists' diverse talents were showcased. Here, Plevitskaya performed in some of the same programs as Nadezhda Teffi, a politically liberal humorist writer who satirized Russian émigré life in Paris as absurd and aimless. In early December, Plevitskaya gave a farewell concert at Dom Artista before leaving for a much-anticipated U.S. concert tour with Skoblin. *Vozrozhdenie* wrote of Plevitskaya's strong ability to express a sense of separation from the motherland, from its forests, fields, and sky.[103] At this point in her career, a Plevitskaya concert was not complete until she sang her torch song, "Russia, You're Frozen in Snow." On December 29, her final concert before sailing to America, Plevitskaya appeared with a French counterpart, the celebrated actress and singer Yvette Guilbert, who had her own repertoire of beloved French folk songs.

In a newspaper interview given three months before her departure for the United States, Plevitskaya revealed that she was afraid of crossing open water and of being attacked by sharks if her ship sank.[104] Still, she and Skoblin set sail as planned in January 1926 and did not return to Europe until

May 1927. Most of Plevitskaya's U.S. concerts took place in New York City, home to a large Russian émigré population. She also performed for enthusiastic audiences in Elizabeth (New Jersey), Springfield (Massachusetts), Philadelphia, and Detroit. Typically she received standing ovations and gave many encores. She sang at benefit performances for different segments of the Russian émigré population, in small and large concert halls, and in Russian Orthodox churches.

Plevitskaya earned accolades for her performance on February 16, 1926, at the Plaza Hotel in Manhattan, where she performed at a benefit concert for financially struggling Russian émigrés. The event was sponsored by Princess Xenia Georgievna, a member of the Romanov family who had settled in New York with her then husband William Bateman Leeds, and Helen Astor, the wife of multimillionaire Vincent Astor. Max Rabinowich, who often played for Chaliapin, accompanied Plevitskaya on piano for most of the concert, and Peter Biljo's Balalaika Orchestra added more old-world charm. But the showstopper was a new arrangement of "Powder and Paint" (Belilitsy, rumianitsy vy moi), which Sergei Rachmaninoff composed especially for her—and which he himself performed with her on this occasion, accompanying her on piano. Rachmaninoff at this time lived in New York City with his wife and daughter. Like Plevitskaya, he was homesick for the Russian countryside, and they shared an appreciation for folk music.[105] In addition to performing the piece together live, they recorded it at Victor Studios in New York City, although it was not released until 1952.[106]

Another émigré artist inspired by Plevitskaya's visit to America was the sculptor Sergei Konenkov, who had known her in Russia and shared her love for Russian folkways. In his New York studio, Konenkov sculpted a likeness of her in a peasant's costume, touching the side of her face with her right hand, a pose she sometimes affected in photographs. The bust is considered one of Konenkov's most famous works.[107] Konenkov attended Plevitskaya's concert at the Plaza Hotel and admired her pearl-studded peasant headdress and lively folk intonation. He noticed how several Russian émigrés cried openly at the concert. "To them," he wrote, "Plevitskaya's voice seemed like the lost motherland."[108] When the bust was completed, Rachmaninoff came to Konenkov's studio to see it for himself. To Konenkov's relief, the great composer judged that "the hand couldn't have been done any better."[109] The bust was publicly unveiled in 1927 at a New York exhibit of Konenkov's work and is now on display in a Moscow museum dedicated to Konenkov's works.

Enthralled by Plevitskaya's celebrity, peasant costumes, and uncanny ability to evoke the spirit of Russian village life during the prerevolutionary era, the émigré press and mainstream American media alike reported on her performances. This piece, by one émigré journalist, typifies much of what was published at the time: "There is no one among the Russian emigration who would not know Plevitskaya, would not have heard her songs, would not have remembered her singing. Now the old Russian colony, the peasantry and workers, are coming to hear their own 'Dezhka.'"[110] In addition to Russian-language newspapers such as *New Russian Word* (*Novoe russkoe slovo*) and *The Russian Voice* (*Russkii golos*), mainstream American papers—including the *New York Times*, *New York World*, and *Detroit Times*—reported on her successes. The *New York World* gushed,

> In Russia, Mme. Plevitzkaia was as popular as Al Jolson over here, which accounts for the fact that Aeolian Hall was packed to the doors last night with as many varieties of Russians as New York contains. Princes, middle class merchants and gawky peasants rubbed elbows as they leaned forward or to one side the better to catch Plevitzkaia's most delicate innuendo, though most of her innuendos were anything but delicate, for the Russian Yvonne Guilbert concerns herself chiefly with the peasant songs of her native land—not the familiar, slightly varnished product that has spread to Europe and America, but the juicy, raw legends of millions of people who have had their noses in the soil of Russia for many centuries.[111]

Russian émigrés were not her only fans. She also won over some Americans. Artist Harriet Blackstone painted her portrait, which now hangs in the Brooklyn Museum. Gloria Swanson, arguably America's most popular film star at the time, attended Plevitskaya's concert at Manhattan's Aeolian Hall on March 12, 1926. Swanson remarked, "I don't understand Russian, but I feel that the words of Plevitskaya's songs are so wondrous, so tender. Russians, I see, have lived through these native words together with her. I very much like her singing."[112] Similarly, Herman George Scheffauer, an American poet and a translator of Thomas Mann, commented after hearing her perform, "Such potent art deserves the ear, and the heart of the world, for it arises primarily from a great love. It was an unforgettable and unique experience."[113]

Perhaps Plevitskaya's most devoted admirer was the acclaimed German-American conductor and composer Kurt Schindler, who translated lyrics for some of her New York concert programs. Schindler had visited Russia in 1914 to collect folk songs. While there, he had been urged to see Plevitskaya in concert, but he never managed to do so. Years later, in 1926, upon arriving at a party in New York, he learned that Plevitskaya was in attendance:

When I entered the music room and saw her, I could hardly believe that this young and attractive woman was the same who had given pleasure in past years to millions of Russians and had become quite a national institution like Chaliapin and Pavlova. In her face, as it swayed and moved with the expression of each song that she sang, I saw like a compound picture, a synthesis of all that is dearest and deepest in the Russian people. And I was inclined to think that those who call her the greatest singer of Russian folk songs, do not say enough; that she is more: that she is herself the spirit, the pure soul of Russian folksong.[114]

In addition to attending parties and performing, Plevitskaya gave the occasional interview. She often professed a lack of interest in politics. To a reporter for *Novoe russkoe slovo*, Plevitskaya noted, "How can I belong to any [political] parties? I wouldn't be able to judge anyone, and I don't understand what's happening. . . . When I sing, immediately people listen, and I treat them like brothers; it feels like my heart is opening up."[115] She stressed her closer identification with Russia's common people than with its nobility.

Plevitskaya's final performance in America was held on April 12, 1927, in Town Hall, New York City, and featured V. F. Kibalchich's Russian Symphonic Choir. Sergei Rachmaninoff attended, and other audience members were heard to say that she was "Chaliapin in a skirt."[116] The *New York Times* reported that, "while most of her songs gave scope to her inimitable drollery and robust humor, there were others that gave opportunity for pathos and poignant dramatic effect."[117] A journalist who had seen Plevitskaya perform years before in Russia found that she still sang with the same vitality.[118] From these rave reviews, it appeared that Plevitskaya had conquered America. Her and Skoblin's financial prospects also improved, at least temporarily. Thanks to the proceeds from Plevitskaya's concerts, the couple was able to reimburse their associates approximately 30,000 francs.[119]

However, more than a few Russian émigrés construed some of the Skoblins' activities in New York as pro-Soviet. First, it was rumored that one of Plevitskaya's concerts, at the Engineer's Club, had been staged to raise funds for disadvantaged children in the Soviet Union. Reportedly, Plevitskaya sent some of this money to her relatives, including her brother Nikolai. Other sources claimed that she used the Amtorg, a Soviet trade organization with an office in New York City, to transfer the funds to the USSR.[120] She reportedly received $100 in donations at the concert, a handsome sum in those days. The Amtorg became known as a front organization for Soviet intelligence later in 1927, when it was implicated in a spy scandal in Great Britain. Eugene Somoff, Plevitskaya's New York–based impresario, who was also Rachmaninoff's secretary, may have helped her arrange this concert.[121] His office was located in the same building as the Amtorg, at 136 Liberty Street; moreover, Somoff was also employed by another Soviet-backed organization, the All-Russian Central Union of Consumer Societies, or Tsentrosoyuz. Whatever the details, even the hint that Plevitskaya might have had any dealings at all with a Soviet organization would have been repellent to White Army veterans back in France.

Russian émigrés were also disturbed to learn that the newspaper *Russkii golos*, assumed to have Bolshevik sympathies, described Plevitskaya as a "worker-peasant singer," a term with communist connotations.[122] Plevitskaya tried to calm growing fears about her supposed ties to the Soviets in an interview she gave to a New York reporter in March 1927. She reminded readers that she had sung both for the tsar and for Red Army soldiers. "I am outside of politics," she insisted. "I sing for the people."[123] She talked about her desire to aid poor Russian children whose childhoods were not unlike her own, and she also apparently asked Metropolitan Platon, primate of the Russian Orthodox Church in America, for his blessing in singing on their behalf. Years later, however, Platon complained that she had deceived him by not informing him that the children in question were Soviet.[124]

To make things worse, Skoblin angered members of the Russian émigré community in France by writing an open letter to General Denikin, dated December 28, 1926.[125] In it, Skoblin charged that Denikin's memoirs about the civil war years contained inaccuracies, including his accusation that members of the Kornilov Regiment had been involved in a plot to kill Denikin's former chief of staff, Ivan Romanovsky. Skoblin sent this letter to Pyotr Struve, the editor of *Vozrozhdenie*. Although Struve declined to publish it, the letter's contents soon became widely known.

Several former Volunteer Army officers, Generals Wrangel and Denikin first and foremost, were now convinced that the Skoblins had Soviet ties and that Skoblin had acted insubordinately. In 1923, Wrangel had issued an order prohibiting members of Russian military associations from engaging in political activities, and Skoblin had clearly violated it. On February 9, 1927, with the consent of Grand Duke Nikolai Nikolaevich Romanov, supreme commander of the Russian Army in exile and ROVS's titular head, Wrangel dismissed Skoblin from his regimental command. Skoblin petitioned to reverse this decision, but to no avail.[126] This episode marks the first time that Russian émigrés in Paris seriously began to consider that the Skoblins' political allegiances differed from their own. A decade later, at Plevitskaya's trial, Denikin testified that he had suspected Skoblin of being a Soviet agent since 1927.

The Skoblins returned to Paris in May 1927 and immediately set out to restore their tarnished reputations. Plevitskaya tried to win back émigrés' hearts through the power of her music.[127] Her first concert after her return was held on June 4, 1927, at Gaveau Hall and featured a balalaika orchestra. More Paris concerts were to follow, including one on July 2, in the hall of the Society of Gallipolians, where she sang Russian patriotic songs.

In July and part of August, Plevitskaya performed in the Baltics. Skoblin—who used the tour for his own ROVS business purposes—traveled with her. Nina Rauman, a Russian émigré who attended one of Plevitskaya's concerts in Estonia, noted that she was well received and engaged many of her fans in conversation.[128] In an interview with a newspaper in Kovno, Lithuania, Plevitskaya recalled her World War I days as a nurse in the city. Ever mindful of the need to repair her and Skoblin's images, she stressed, "I am not just a singer. I am a storyteller, and I convey the soul of the people. . . . I am only a simple Kursk peasant woman. I don't know any foreign languages, and I speak with foreigners through hand gestures."[129] In Riga, Latvia, where she performed on July 22, Plevitskaya and Skoblin visited with his brother Sergei, and also with Edmund Plevitsky and his second wife, a ballerina named Nikolaevna.[130]

After her Baltic concert tour, Plevitskaya returned to France in August to sing for émigrés in several provincial cities. To the Skoblins' relief, ROVS members there warmly received them. Back in Paris, on September 4, Plevitskaya performed at the tenth anniversary of the founding of the Kornilov Shock Regiment. It seemed that the negative rumors about Soviet contacts in New York City had largely been forgotten.

Key developments the following year, 1928, offered the Skoblins major relief. Whether he died naturally or, as some believe, at the hands of a Soviet poisoner, the passing of General Wrangel in Brussels, on April 25, 1928, represented a windfall for Skoblin. Wrangel's deputy and Skoblin's former commander, General Kutepov, became the president of ROVS and set up the Central Directorate, the organization's headquarters, in Paris. Moreover, Kutepov had not lost trust in Skoblin, and on July 8, 1928, he persuaded Grand Duke Nikolai Nikolaevich to reinstate Skoblin as commander of the Kornilov Shock Regiment. If Skoblin was already in fact a Soviet agent, he was now in a pivotal position to undermine ROVS's anti-Soviet operations. If not, he had at least attained the rehabilitation he felt he deserved.

However satisfying Skoblin's reinstatement must have felt, he and Plevitskaya still had much to resolve. For some time, Skoblin had been dealing with ridicule from his fellow veterans for not holding down a salaried job. Many disdained him for his subservience to Plevitskaya, and some even mocked him as "General Plevitsky" behind his back.[131] On a more practical level, Plevitskaya's U.S. concert tour had not earned enough to last as long as they had hoped. Worst of all was the couple's long-term outlook. Plevitskaya's star appeared to be fading. From this point forward, a dwindling number of her concerts generated income.

By the second half of the 1920s, many members of the émigré intelligentsia noticeably began to turn away from Plevitskaya, whose talents they viewed as beneath theirs in refinement.[132] A prime example is the polyglot writer Vladimir Nabokov, who knew Plevitskaya in Berlin and "admired her natural vocal gifts while recoiling from her vulgarity of taste."[133] Nabokov based the first short story he wrote in English, "The Assistant Producer" (1943), on the Skoblins' life in exile and Miller's kidnapping. Nabokov envisions their final years through the lens of a melodramatic film. He portrays "La Slavska," his nickname for Plevitskaya, as a mediocrity:

> Style: one-tenth *tzigane* [gypsy], one-seventh Russian peasant girl (she had been that herself originally), and five-ninths popular—and by popular I mean a hodgepodge of artificial folklore, military melodrama, and official patriotism. The fraction left unfilled seems sufficient to represent the physical splendor of her prodigious voice. . . . Her artistic taste was nowhere, her technique haphazard, her general style atrocious; but the kind of people for whom music and sentiment are one, or who like songs to be mediums for the spirits of circumstances under which they had been first apprehended in an individual past, gratefully found in the tremendous sonorities of her voice both a nostalgic solace and a patriotic kick.[134]

Anatoly Lunacharsky, the Soviet people's commissar for enlightenment, a post amounting to a combined ministership of culture and education, heard about Plevitskaya's situation while visiting Paris in the late 1920s. He learned that her status had fallen so low that she needed—again, as during her youth—to perform "between tables" in émigré cafes.[135]

During the second half of the 1920s, Plevitskaya and Skoblin pursued farming as a new way to earn income. Sometime within a year of their departure for America, they leased a farm, possibly including a vineyard, in the south of France.[136] One of Skoblin's close friends and a fellow Kornilov veteran, Colonel Karl Gordeenko, partnered with them and supervised operations in their absence, but the couple broke with him after returning from America. Next, they recruited Skoblin's older brother Feodosy and another veteran to help. Between 1928 and 1930, several of Plevitskaya's concerts took place in Nice, Juan-les-Pins, and Cannes, not far from their farm. Sometime in the first half of 1930, the Skoblins realized that the investment had become a financial boondoggle. They ended their lease and moved closer to Paris by the late summer. Fortunately, Plevitskaya had just signed a new performing contract.

Aleksei V. Ryzhikov, the proprietor of the Grand Moskovsky Ermitazh Restaurant in Paris and an acquaintance of Plevitskaya's since 1908, ran into her and Skoblin by chance while vacationing in the south of France that summer. The Skoblins invited him to their house, and he learned about their farm. Ryzhikov noticed that they lived modestly. Skoblin and his brother Feodosy worked in an aluminum factory and earned around 80 francs a day. Their car was old and rundown. Ryzhikov convinced Plevitskaya to sing at his restaurant that fall. They negotiated a contract whereby she would earn a monthly fee of 15,000 francs, plus a commission from any bottles of champagne sold.[137]

Finances continued to be one of the Skoblins' paramount concerns—but by the early 1930s, their acquaintances began noticing that the Skoblins seemed to be living beyond their means. As suspicions grew about their financial situation, their accusers found other reasons to think that Skoblin and Plevitskaya were working for the Soviets.

5

1930

The year 1930 started out routinely for Plevitskaya, now fifty years old. On January 14, she and other émigré musicians performed in a concert sponsored by the *Poslednie novosti* newspaper. Twelve days later, at the Hotel Lutetia, a luxury hotel on the Left Bank, she performed at a concert benefiting Russian émigré students in France and honoring the 175th anniversary of Moscow State University's founding. But this particular Sunday was not at all routine for her husband's superior, the head of ROVS, General Kutepov. Nor was it routine for the Soviet operatives in Paris who had a special task to fulfill that day.

By 1930, Joseph Stalin had consolidated his power as Soviet dictator. He feared that his regime was still under threat, both internally and externally, and took steps to eliminate his perceived enemies. According to his spy networks in Europe, White Russian military organizations, notably ROVS, were planning new sabotage operations within the USSR. Although in reality it lacked the resources to wage a successful war against the Soviet Union, in Stalin's mind ROVS—as the largest White Russian military organization—was a primary right-wing threat to his regime. As Christopher Andrew and Oleg Gordievsky have noted, "In the Stalin era the significance of all forms of counterrevolution was wildly exaggerated. Even Kutepov was perceived as such a potential menace at the head of the ROVS that he had to be liquidated."[1]

Soviet intelligence officials knew that Kutepov was planning sabotage operations inside the Soviet Union. In their minds, eliminating him would help neutralize a dangerous threat and perhaps precipitate the collapse of the White Russian military apparatus. OGPU rezident Vladimir Yanovich allegedly had once boasted to diplomat Grigory Besedovsky that he had "placed someone very near Kutepov. Soon they will be friends, and then it will be all up with Kutepov's activities."[2]

A former OGPU official and Soviet defector, Alexander Orlov, described in his memoir how the Kutepov operation was conceived. In Orlov's account, Stalin, sometime between 1927 and 1929, met in Moscow with Artur Artuzov, chief of Soviet counterintelligence, about the White Guardists. He told Artuzov, "We must liquidate every terrorist [Kutepov] sends to us and, if he insists on fighting us, we will bump him off right there, in France."[3] For his part, Artuzov feared that assassinating Kutepov in France would pose too high a political risk and thought that the OGPU had planted a sufficient number of informants in ROVS and in Kutepov's inner circle. For months, the issue remained unresolved. But in the winter of 1929, Stalin was almost assassinated by a man he thought Kutepov had sent. As a result, he ordered that Kutepov be abducted and sent to Moscow for a "final accounting."[4]

While not every detail of Orlov's narrative is corroborated, many sources verify that the operation was led by Yakov Serebriansky, head of the OGPU's Administration for Special Tasks.[5] The planning may have begun as early as the summer of 1929, and Serebriansky, along with other operatives from the USSR, reportedly arrived in Paris on January 1, 1930.[6] Serebriansky was likely assisted by Valentin Speransky, the OGPU rezident at the Soviet embassy in Paris who handled illegals, or agents not working under diplomatic cover.[7] The Soviets hoped that, to any random observer, Kutepov's abduction on a Paris street would look like a routine police arrest. Serebriansky knew from local informants that Kutepov had a memorial service to attend on Sunday, January 26, at 11:30 a.m. at the Gallipoli church in the seventh arrondissement, a twenty-minute walk from his apartment on rue Rousselet.[8]

Around 11:00 a.m. on January 26, an eyewitness named Auguste Steinmetz looked out from the window of his workplace and saw a middle-aged bearded man, who turned out to be Kutepov, walking down rue Rousselet. Suddenly, a large gray-green car pulled up, and two men dressed in yellow coats forced him into it.[9] Next, a man dressed as a French police officer jumped into the front seat of the car. A second car followed closely behind. Once in the car, Kutepov was either chloroformed or given a shot of morphine.[10] It is widely assumed that Kutepov died before reaching the USSR, with the drug overdose causing a fatal heart attack, but sources disagree whether he perished in the car or on board a Soviet ship.[11]

Hours passed. When Kutepov did not appear at the memorial service as planned, his family and ROVS associates began to feel uneasy. That morning, he had told his wife Lydia that he would return after the service to spend the afternoon with her and the children. Always punctual and conscientious, Kutepov would not neglect to inform his family about a change of plans. By the midafternoon, ROVS officials alerted the police of their leader's disappearance.[12] Soon, French authorities mobilized security units across the country to find him. They blocked land and sea frontiers and began surveillance of Soviet-occupied buildings and a counterespionage operation.[13] However, despite these measures, the police failed to gather clear evidence about Kutepov's disappearance or to arrest any of his abductors.

As news spread about Kutepov's disappearance, Russian émigrés and other concerned Paris residents demanded that the Soviet embassy and the Soviet trade delegation be searched, while conservative politicians called on the government to sever diplomatic ties with the Soviet Union.[14] French officials—wanting to maintain diplomatic ties with the Soviets for pragmatic reasons—took none of these actions. The French and émigré press covered the story only until late February, stopping for lack of anything further to report.

At the time of Kutepov's kidnapping, the Soviet government vehemently denied its involvement and suggested that the general had fled to South America with cash in hand.[15] "The Kutyepov operation was one of the best kept secrets in the OGPU," Orlov wrote. Apart from OGPU director Viacheslav Menzhinsky, Genrikh Yagoda (his successor), and a handful of other top officials, "nobody knew exactly how the kidnapping had been accomplished."[16] The Soviet regime formally acknowledged its role in the abduction only in 1965.[17] Although Kutepov died before the OGPU had a chance to interrogate him in Moscow, the operation was a triumph as far as the Soviet secret police were concerned: they had removed Kutepov from the ROVS leadership. According to Evgeny Primakov, who led Russia's KGB successor agency during the 1990s, "the White émigré community was shocked and negatively affected by Kutepov's kidnapping, so the OGPU considered it a success for destabilizing the population."[18] It also set an "important precedent," as Soviet intelligence officials would now place more emphasis on such "special tasks" than on mere intelligence gathering.[19]

Were Skoblin and Plevitskaya involved, directly or otherwise, in Kutepov's kidnapping? In 1938, the French government and a number of witnesses at her criminal trial assumed this to be a given. But we still do not know for sure, and no physical evidence in the Paris police file on the Kutepov kidnapping or in declassified OGPU files supports this theory. In fact, Pavel Sudoplatov, a top Soviet intelligence official during the 1930s and 1940s, maintained that Skoblin was not involved.[20] Some compelling circumstantial evidence exists, though, suggesting that Skoblin and Plevitskaya acted suspiciously.[21] The most revealing information about their actions in January 1930 comes from Lydia Kutepova. At Plevitskaya's trial, the judge read out a letter of December 7, 1938, from Kutepova, who then lived in Belgrade:

> I do not know whether Plevitskaya played any role in my husband's kidnapping, but during the years since it happened, I have come to think that she probably knew something. . . . Relations between my husband and Skoblin were formal. He treated Skoblin like a subordinate, and we rarely went over to their house. After my husband's kidnapping, Plevitskaya visited me almost daily and was updated on the investigation. During my visits to Paris, Nikolai Skoblin and Nadezhda Plevitskaya often told me that my husband was alive. When I asked what the evidence was, Plevitskaya said that she had a dream about it. My husband often told me that Plevitskaya "wore the general's stripes."[22]

There are three possible explanations for Plevitskaya's behavior. The first and most benign is that she was taking advantage of her access to Kutepova to help advance Skoblin's career. Skoblin, an ambitious and arrogant man resentful of his superior officers, was likely jockeying for a stronger leadership role in ROVS in the wake of Kutepov's disappearance. A second possible scenario is that in early 1930, Plevitskaya—not yet working for the OGPU, but plotting a return to her homeland—may have already begun collecting what she thought would be information of interest to Soviet intelligence to prove her commitment to their cause.

The last scenario assumes that Plevitskaya and Skoblin were already OGPU informants. Their task in this case would have been to glean information from Kutepova about the investigation and to insinuate Skoblin into the highest ranks of ROVS. According to two sources, a Paris restaurant owner named Tokareva, who was Plevitskaya's friend and a Soviet agent since 1925, sometimes accompanied Plevitskaya on visits with Kutepova.[23]

Whatever the case, General Kutepov had vanished forever, and Russian émigrés rightly assumed that the Soviets had killed him. Many ROVS members were now even more adamant about planning anti-Soviet sabotage operations. General Evgeny Karlovich Miller, Kutepov's deputy chief, reluctantly replaced him as ROVS leader. Sixty-two years old and in failing health when he took the reins of the ROVS leadership, Miller was of medium height and had piercing blue eyes and a prominent mustache. He was conscientious and courageous, felt a strong call to duty, and was a loyal friend and family man. Miller did not rush to judgment—normally a positive attribute that, in his case, would prove fatal.

Miller was born in Dvinsk, in present-day Latvia, on September 25, 1867, to Baltic-German parents. He attended the Nikolaevsk Military Academy and went on to distinguish himself in the Imperial Army, achieving the rank of major general in 1909. For several years, he worked as a military attaché at Russian embassies in Belgium, Holland, and Italy. In this capacity, he gained intelligence and diplomatic expertise that he later used in exile. During World War I, Miller became a lieutenant general and headed the Moscow District and the Russian Fifth Army. A monarchist and anticommunist, he commanded the White Army of the North during the civil war. In 1920, with his army defeated, he evacuated to Norway and settled in France.

During the early 1920s, Miller served for a time as General Wrangel's chief of staff. Miller and his wife Natalya met the Skoblins in Paris in 1927, but they did not grow friendlier until after Miller became chairman of ROVS.[24] In 1929, Kutepov appointed Miller first deputy chairman of ROVS, a post that required him to oversee the organization's administration and finances. As a result, before becoming the organization's head, Miller knew relatively little about its military plans and anti-Soviet operations. Other weaknesses handicapped him, and he himself doubted his own ability to lead ROVS after Kutepov's abduction. Indecisive and overcautious, he had a difficult time setting priorities and delegating duties; he tried but failed to instill a spirit of compromise among competing ROVS factions.[25] To his detriment, Miller never built a counterintelligence apparatus strong enough to defend ROVS and guard his safety.

Some of Miller's detractors criticized him for lacking Kutepov's drive and boldness in arranging anti-Soviet sabotage operations and planning eventual war against the USSR. In particular, Pavel Shatilov, whom Miller appointed as head of the important First Department of ROVS in May 1930, found Miller's plans inadequate and, until his dismissal in 1934, used his position as head of the secretive Inner Line to plot against Miller.[26] Under pressure, Miller worked more actively to build ROVS into the organizational core of a new White Russian army, and he endorsed more anti-Soviet sabotage operations. In the summer of 1930, Miller and King Alexander IV of Yugoslavia agreed in principle to form regulated forces among White Army veterans and new recruits. Miller also drew up plans to mobilize anti-Soviet cells in the Ukraine and the Caucasus regions of the USSR.[27] In this, he had to remain mindful of ROVS's limited financial means. The estimated cost of infiltrating a single agent into enemy territory was 5,200 francs, and ROVS's resources were shrinking.[28]

From the beginning of his leadership, though, Miller had to walk a fine line. In order to stay in office, he had to appease vocal members of ROVS like Shatilov, Skoblin, and younger members, who called for radical action. An August 1930 French intelligence report noted that ROVS members in Belgrade had already become discontent with Miller for not confronting the Bolsheviks and for his lack of energy and leadership.[29] But to prevent the French authorities from dismantling ROVS for violating public order, Miller needed to deny the existence of military planning and anti-Soviet operations. He also served as a Paris police informant, work that he was likely in no position to refuse, and had agreed to monitor Shatilov in 1930.[30] Paris's police department, the Préfecture de Police, closely monitored Miller, ROVS, and other White émigré military organizations. A September 1930 report mentioned that Miller, with a war chest of 7.5 million francs at his disposal, supported a return of the Russian monarchy and was doing little to bar Shatilov from pursuing his anti-Soviet agenda.[31]

For the Skoblins, life returned to normal soon after the Kutepov kidnapping. On February 9, Plevitskaya resumed her concert schedule, singing at Gaveau Hall with a women's balalaika orchestra. In late May, Skoblin saw an ad in *Poslednie novosti* about the sale of a two-story "villa" at 345 Marshal Pétain Street in Ozoir-la-Ferrière, a Paris suburb surrounded by forests. Ozoir-la-Ferrière had a small Russian émigré community and two Orthodox churches. The couple drove out in their Citroën to view the property one day. Skoblin toured the house quickly, according to the house agent, D. M. Shneider, while Plevitskaya waited in the car. They bought the house on credit for somewhere between 82,000 and 113,000 francs, with a down payment of somewhere between 1,000 and 10,000 francs. Their ten-year mortgage required monthly payments of 800 francs.[32]

The house was not considered expensive at the time, and French house agents were known to use "villa" as a euphemism for what was more often than not a modestly sized cottage.[33] However, few Russian émigrés owned homes of any kind. In fact, only a minority of French citizens, not to mention immigrants, could afford cars during the early 1930s, making the Skoblins' ownership of their Citroën as unusual as the ownership of their house.[34] Reportedly, they acquired loans from friends, including from Edmund Plevitsky, to help cover the down payment. Plevitsky and his second wife may even have been present on June 7, the day the contract was signed. The Skoblins moved into their house in the late summer, after vacating their rental near Cannes and selling their stake in the farm.

The Skoblins' villa in Ozoir-la-Ferrière, a Paris suburb, mid-1930s. Courtesy of Irina Raksha

Plevitskaya's last concert before moving north was held on July 15 at the Orpheum Theater in Juan-les-Pins.

The Skoblins' house had five large rooms. In the living room, Plevitskaya hung portraits of Chaliapin and Rachmaninoff. The latter signed his portrait, "Health, happiness, success to dear Nadezhda Vasilievna. S. Rakhmaninov." Skoblin allegedly stored in the attic the Kornilov Shock Regiment's archive, the subject of intense scrutiny later in the 1930s. In the yard, Plevitskaya tried to recreate her Vinnikovo childhood by planting birch trees and a garden and raising chickens, a dog, and several cats.

Surprised that the Skoblins could afford to own a house and furnish it on Plevitskaya's meager concert earnings, some Russian émigrés began to suspect that the couple had a secret funding source. Was it her mysterious benefactor, Dr. Max Eitingon, or possibly the OGPU? The couple's financial situation was hardly transparent, even to French investigators in 1937 and 1938.

It is important to recall that, right before moving to Ozoir-la-Ferrière, Plevitskaya had signed a contract with Aleksei Ryzhikov to perform at his Moskovsky Ermitazh Restaurant between late September and the end of December 1930. In addition, Plevitskaya earned supplemental income from impromptu concerts at Ryzhikov's restaurant. In total, Ryzhikov claimed to have given her close to 100,000 francs during this period, although Plevitskaya later claimed that she had earned only 34,000 francs.[35] He also noted that Skoblin—not Plevitskaya—received the checks from him in person, implying that the general controlled the family's finances. Given the high cost of Plevitskaya's costumes and cosmetics, the mortgage payments, and the car maintenance, whatever money she earned at the Ermitazh was probably depleted fairly quickly.

With their failed farming career now behind them, the Skoblins moved into their new home in July or August. They often entertained and hosted their acquaintances and friends, including the Millers, Edmund Plevitsky (at least in 1930 and 1936), and their banker, G. I. Shulman, who operated the Banque Internationale in Paris. When Shulman came to visit, he noticed that the couple seemed happy. Their political views struck him as monarchist.[36] Skoblin's brothers Sergei and Feodosy occasionally lived with them between 1930 and 1934.[37] Afterward, the Skoblins hired Russian neighbors to watch their house and care for their animals in their absence.

They frequently drove to Paris, a journey of sixteen miles, where Skoblin had his meetings and Plevitskaya her concerts, hairdressers, and dressmakers. On August 31, 1930, in the auditorium of the Society of Gallipolians in Paris, they took part in the annual celebration of Skoblin's regiment. Plevitskaya, their "mother-commander," sang military-patriotic songs. Miller gave introductory remarks, and Shatilov acted as keynote speaker. To the casual observer, the Skoblins were like any other ROVS supporters. They seemed to have become reconciled to settling in France for the time being. They appeared to support the White movement's increasingly unattainable goal of returning Russia to its prerevolutionary state of affairs with the help of its Western allies. But the Skoblins would soon lead a double life, forcing them to betray the very Russian émigrés who attended the celebration that day.

On January 30, 1930, only four days after Kutepov's kidnapping, Artur Artuzov, OGPU head Viacheslav Menzhinsky, and Mikhail Trilisser (head of the OGPU's Foreign Department, the INO) met in Moscow with Stalin and other members of his Politburo. All agreed to place more emphasis on creating and maintaining networks of illegals.[38] Stalin praised the OGPU for its successes against the White Guardists and for gathering useful political intelligence. Artuzov returned to the Lubyanka to start planning in earnest for the expansion of illegal networks. The Soviets' renewed effort to recruit more illegals was aided by domestic case officers, who recruited agents, and was supervised by OGPU rezidents in charge of illegals and posted in Soviet embassies worldwide.

Before 1930, the OGPU had already recruited agents in the White émigré community. They included Sergei Tretyakov, who became an agent in 1929.[39] Tretyakov, a member of a wealthy and influential Moscow family, had served in Russia's Provisional Government and, in exile, was the deputy chair of a six-hundred-member Russian business association.[40] He was a significant catch: to White émigrés in Paris, his credentials were impeccable. Many of the White émigrés whom Soviet intelligence recruited in the 1930s have yet to be identified, but among those known to us are Nikolai Abramov, the son of former White general Feodor Abramov; Leonid Linitsky, a former Russian army officer, who settled in Belgrade; and Sergei Efron, the husband of poet Marina Tsvetaeva. Himself a poet, Efron—like Skoblin—did his work for the Soviets in France, and also like Skoblin, he had once been a White Army officer.[41]

The OGPU's most desired targets for recruitment were members of White military organizations, and agency officials in Moscow composed a list of potential candidates during the winter and spring of 1930.[42] The OGPU's Ukrainian branch identified one of its employees, Pyotr Kovalsky, as a potential recruiter of White Army veterans. Born around 1897 in the Ukraine, Kovalsky served with distinction in the Russian Imperial Army during World War I and became a staff captain. During the civil war, he served in the Kornilov Regiment in southern Russia, where he fought under Skoblin. The two became friends, and Skoblin invited Kovalsky to rest at his residence in Debaltsev, Russia, after a battle injury. But Kovalsky did not evacuate with Skoblin and his other men in 1920. He landed in Poland at the end of the civil war and, in late 1921, successfully petitioned the Soviet embassy in Warsaw for amnesty. After working for the Cheka abroad, Kovalsky returned in 1924 to the USSR.

Ordered in 1930 to create a list for the OGPU of White Army veterans living in exile, Kovalsky naturally put Skoblin's name on it. Skoblin's status as leader of the Kornilov Regiment and his close ties to ROVS's Paris headquarters made him an ideal target for possible recruitment; he was well positioned to influence ROVS's operations and identify additional targets for recruitment. Moreover, Skoblin's psychological state made him ripe for recruitment. By the late 1920s, he had become disillusioned by the White movement. A number of senior officers, namely Wrangel and Denikin, had not placed their trust in him, and he felt demoralized and betrayed. During the civil war he had been a wunderkind, one of the youngest generals in the White Army, and in exile, he felt he deserved better treatment from his elders. To his way of thinking, he was not rising through ROVS's ranks fast enough. Could he be persuaded to return to Russia and serve again as an officer in the army of his homeland?

The OGPU also knew that Plevitskaya yearned to return home. In her memoirs, Plevitskaya appeared to express survivor's guilt: "Who thought then [as a child] that my dear country would be extinguished, that my sisters and brothers would die from hunger, that free-wheeling song would cease?"[43] She wanted to reunite with her relatives and hoped to revive her singing career; the Stalin regime tolerated Russian folk music, considering it easily consumable mass entertainment. She was not alone in her thinking. For career and personal reasons, composer Sergei Prokofiev repatriated in 1936, admitting that "foreign air does not suit my inspiration, because I'm Russian, and that is to say the least suited of men to be an exile, to remain myself in a psychological climate that isn't that of my race."[44] In the meantime, Plevitskaya and Skoblin needed the extra money that could be earned through espionage.

Kovalsky's OGPU bosses agreed that he should target Skoblin. He was instructed to tell Skoblin that he would be working for the Red Army, although he would actually be on the OGPU's payroll. As added incentives, he and Plevitskaya would be promised personal amnesties. But there was a catch: they would first need to prove their devotion to Stalin and his regime before returning home.

OGPU officials in Moscow assigned Kovalsky a code name, Sylvestrov, and a code number, Ezh/10, to be used in secret communiqués. They sent him to Berlin in late May, and then to Vienna. Once in the Austrian capital, he met regularly over the summer with "Vatsek," the rezident in charge of illegals at the Soviet embassy. They decided that Kovalsky would first visit the Skoblins in September, in Ozoir-la-Ferrière. He left Vienna by train and arrived in Paris at 11:45 p.m. on Tuesday, September 2, and then checked into a hotel.

The next day, Kovalsky took a train to Ozoir-la-Ferrière, arriving there around 5:00 p.m. When he reached the Skoblins' house, no one was home. After waiting for fifteen minutes, Kovalsky watched as a car drove up and a man in a light gray suit climbed out.

"Nadiusha," Skoblin exclaimed upon seeing Kovalsky, "it's Petya, whom I've told you so much about!" Plevitskaya and Kovalsky were introduced, and the former staff captain kissed her hand. Kovalsky and Skoblin addressed each other on a first-name, informal basis. Skoblin asked his former brother-in-arms how he had managed to escape the Soviets, and Kovalsky had a ready, if suspect, answer: he had bought a fake Iranian passport in Leningrad and was traveling on it.

The Skoblins invited Kovalsky into their home for the night, despite already having other guests to entertain. One source claims that Edmund Plevitsky was one of the guests and that the whole group reminisced about Russia.[45] Kovalsky stayed overnight with the Skoblins and returned to Paris the following morning. He must have reckoned that this was not the right time to recruit new assets, with the guests around, so he and the Skoblins arranged to meet later.

On Friday, September 5, the Skoblins drove to Paris to join Kovalsky at his hotel and took him to lunch. After lunch, Skoblin and Kovalsky went to a barbershop for a shave. While there, Kovalsky handed Skoblin a letter from one of his brothers who remained in the Soviet Union and may have been working in intelligence. Skoblin looked stunned but seemed to understand the implications of the letter. They picked up Plevitskaya and returned to Ozoir-la-Ferrière. Back in the village, Skoblin and Kovalsky walked alone down a quiet street.

At that point, Kovalsky turned to Skoblin and asked whether he wanted to return to his homeland. "What do you mean?" Skoblin inquired nervously.

Kovalsky reassured him: "We want to offer every White Army veteran the chance to return home and work in the new Russian army."

"Who is 'we'?" Skoblin asked.

"The General Staff of the Red Army," answered Kovalsky.

"If I return, they'll prosecute me or simply shoot me!"

Kovalsky reassured Skoblin that the Soviet regime did not consider him a political figure but a military expert, so he would not be prosecuted. He asked, "Are you with us or against us?"

With a shaking voice and tears in his eyes, Skoblin expressed his concern about betraying the men he was leading in exile. He also worried about Plevitskaya's reaction. Kovalsky told him that he would be working for the good of the people and not a monarch as before, and that the Red Army would treat him honorably. But it was clear to both men that the matter would not be resolved right then, and the conversation ended abruptly.

Later that day, Kovalsky approached Plevitskaya while Skoblin was out running an errand. He appealed to her sense of vanity, hinting that if she repatriated, she could revive her singing career. He also figured that, if he could convince her first, she in turn might be able to persuade her husband that working for Soviet intelligence was in their best interests. Kovalsky pointed out that her audiences in Europe were steadily shrinking and intimated that she would be better treated in the Soviet Union. Plevitskaya agreed that her humble upbringing and her celebrity would help her adapt quickly to Soviet life, but she still feared that, if they returned, Skoblin might be shot. Before Kovalsky returned to Paris, Plevitskaya took him aside and asked that he be allowed to visit with them again in two days.[46]

Kovalsky returned on Sunday, September 7, and intuited that the couple had discussed the matter of recruitment in his absence. Not wasting time, he turned to Skoblin and demanded an answer to his question. Skoblin expressed doubt that he would be allowed to serve as an officer in the Red Army. "What's important is that I receive an agreement in principle from you that you'll work with us," Kovalsky offered. "Whatever remains can be decided later." Kovalsky claimed that the matter could be resolved in no less than six months. He told Skoblin that he would have to prove his loyalty to the regime first and that, in the immediate future, he would be more useful to the Soviets in Europe than in the USSR. He also assured Skoblin that his intelligence functions would fall somewhere between the General Staff of the Red Army and the OGPU.

"I want to hear your direct answer: Are you with us or not?" Kovalsky insisted.

Skoblin hesitated for two agonizing minutes. Then he answered, "I've spoken with Nadiusha and . . . I agree. If anyone other than you, Petya, had come here, I would have thrown him out of the house."

The next day, Monday, September 8, Skoblin met Kovalsky at his hotel to discuss future arrangements and monthly payments. Skoblin signed a statement renouncing his work with the Whites, promising never to actively or passively work against Soviet power, and requesting a personal amnesty from the Central Executive Committee of the USSR.[47] Soon afterward, the rezident at the Soviet embassy in Vienna telegrammed Moscow Center—OGPU headquarters in the Lubyanka building—with the news:

> Ezh/10 returned to Vienna from Paris. The general's wife agreed to work for us. The general agreed to everything and even has written the Central Executive Committee with a request for personal amnesty. In my opinion, he will work well. The general's signed statement is written in [a kind of special ink]. His business card will serve as a password. The general will speak with anyone sent from us who presents him with such a business card. The general desires a monthly payment of 200 American dollars. Vatsek[48]

To sweeten the deal, the Soviets reportedly offered Skoblin an additional one-time lump sum of 5,000 francs and yet another payment in American dollars.[49] On September 10, Artuzov, now head of the OGPU's Foreign Department in Moscow, sent the Vienna rezident a brief telegram confirming that Skoblin's code name and number would be *"Fermer* [Farmer]— Ezh/13.*"* Shortly after the telegram was sent, one of Artuzov's subordinates followed up with a longer communiqué:

> We consider the general's recruitment a valuable achievement in our office. Henceforth, we will call him "Fermer" and his wife "Fermersha." For payment, we have agreed to give the general 200 American dollars monthly. . . . First and foremost, you will receive from him a full review of his connections and possibilities for his work. Let him give detailed instructions about people whom he considers potential targets for recruitment. . . . Take from him a review of the situation in ROVS and leave before him the task of penetrating the heights of ROVS. While negotiating with Ezh/10 (Sylvestrov), "Fermer" spoke about how General Miller one time proposed his working in intelligence for ROVS. Is there any possibility that he could return to this conversation? Inquire through Ezh/10 whether it is possible for "Fermer" to travel to another country for a meeting with our people. Andrei[50]

The couple's pseudonyms were the OGPU's way of poking fun at their failed farming venture. But their recruitment was no laughing matter: The OGPU considered Skoblin to be a top asset, especially because he was the commander of a White Army regiment. But before they could return home, the Skoblins first had to prove their usefulness and unwavering devotion to the Soviet cause.

After signing his life away to the OGPU in September, Skoblin endured a months-long adjustment and training period. He did not earn Moscow's trust quickly, and neither did Plevitskaya. After all, they did not appear to be ideologically driven to spy for the Soviets, as others were during the interwar period, including the notorious Cambridge Five (Anthony Blunt, Guy Burgess, John Cairncross, Donald Maclean, and Kim Philby). The Skoblins' motives were self-interested, and therefore inherently suspect.

OGPU officials in Moscow, as well as Kovalsky and Vatsek at the Soviet embassy in Vienna, grew concerned that Skoblin was not holding up his end of the bargain. In darker moments, they suspected that he could be a double agent, still primarily serving the White Guardists. Soviet intelligence officials would sooner suspect their agents of treachery than assume they could be fully trusted. In fact, there is evidence that Skoblin was a triple agent, on the Germans' payroll in addition to ROVS's and the Soviets'. If true, then Skoblin was no different than several other White émigrés during the interwar era whose loyalty was mainly to themselves.[51] However, Skoblin and Plevitskaya's first priority was to ensure that their work satisfied the Soviets, not the Germans. Vatsek assumed that Skoblin had not yet learned Soviet tradecraft and needed more exact instructions. Another operative (named Nikolai) suspected that Skoblin had quickly figured out that Kovalsky was low in the OGPU hierarchy and wanted to engage more directly with OGPU officials in Moscow.[52] Whatever the case, Skoblin's handlers had a hard time at first assessing his character and determining how best to mold him into the agent they wanted him to be.

After his September 1930 recruitment, Skoblin frequently sent letters to Kovalsky—whom he continued to address affectionately as "Petya"—informing him of ROVS's activities, such as the military training courses it was arranging, and his difficulties enciphering messages and reading messages written in invisible ink. Sometime in mid-November, Skoblin wrote that Miller was planning to hold a meeting in Bulgaria later that month about executing Kutepov's anti-Soviet operations. He proposed that General Anton Turkul, who lived in Bulgaria at the time, might be a good candidate for OGPU recruitment.[53]

As Skoblin established regular contact with his OGPU handlers, Plevitskaya was keeping busy, covering for her husband and performing regularly at the Ermitazh Restaurant. Alexander Vertinsky, a renowned Russian émigré singer who also performed at the Ermitazh and at night clubs in Montmartre at the time, recalled that, "Every night, [Plevitskaya's] small husband dropped her off and picked her up in his small car. He did not do anything worth noting, but was quite humble and even shy. He rather looked like a forgotten husband up against such an energic and strong-willed wife as Plevitskaya."[54] In addition to her Ermitazh engagements, Plevitskaya had several other Paris concerts in November: one in Gaveau Hall, a concert ball with other artists to raise money for disabled Russian veterans, a charity concert for Russian youth, and performances for White Army veterans.

In early December, Skoblin planned to travel by train with Plevitskaya to Latvia for a brief concert tour. They went there via Berlin, where they met with Kovalsky and an operative named Vsevolod. Skoblin outlined his strategy for climbing the ROVS leadership ladder and explained ROVS's organizational structure.[55] A few days later, on December 19 in Vienna, Kovalsky met with Skoblin and Plevitskaya in the Hotel Continental. The meeting centered on Skoblin's main duties and required that he answer specific questions.[56] Skoblin offered to expose ROVS's anti-Soviet intelligence operations. However, at least one OGPU official, code-named Zigmund, suspected that the White general was really a double agent for Miller and General Abram Dragomirov, who supervised ROVS's anti-Soviet operations between 1930 and 1935. Skoblin took notes about his meeting with General Aleksei von Lampe, a profascist ROVS leader in Berlin. According to Kovalsky, the Skoblins did not act, while in Vienna, like they trusted the Soviet side.[57]

Kovalsky spoke alone with Plevitskaya, who described her earlier ties with Russia's royal family and stressed how dedicated she now was to serving her own people, the common folk. She begged Kovalsky not to force her husband to report on matters that were outside his immediate purview, noting that he was only a soldier and not a political figure by nature. This conversation made Kovalsky nervous, and he decided to run a check on Skoblin.[58]

Three days later, the two men met at the Skoblins' hotel, then took a taxi to an empty café.[59] Kovalsky flustered Skoblin by warning him that they would have a difficult conversation. The former subordinate confronted his former commander about his shortcomings: Skoblin's refusal to travel to Vienna immediately to meet at the Soviet embassy and his failure to inform the OGPU about important ROVS events. His eyes welling up with tears, Skoblin explained that he was trying his best but that intelligence work was new to him. He requested more specific instructions.

"You need to understand correctly, Kolya," Kovalsky said. "We approached you with the deepest caution, because we consider you not a simple informant, but a valuable employee of the General Staff [of the Red Army] who is fulfilling a special mission abroad. This means we've placed a special trust in you. But, naturally, we need to be sure of your faithfulness." They ended their conversation for the time being, and Kovalsky gave Skoblin a folder with a payment inside. Skoblin thanked him as Plevitskaya approached, looking coldly at Kovalsky.

Plevitskaya sat down and told Kovalsky that she and Skoblin were committed to their intelligence work. "You should explain to us about your friends," she suggested. "All our sympathies are with the Russian people, so we are with you. And I ask you to be very cautious. Kolya's downfall [in ROVS, if he were to be exposed as a Soviet spy] would mean his life."

"No, no, Nadiusha, I well understand Moscow's distrust of me," Skoblin scolded. "I was in the Volunteer Army, for years I fought against the

Bolsheviks, and suddenly I transfer to the Red Army? I believe you, Petya. Hundreds of letters from my two brothers [in the USSR] couldn't have done what you did. I believe you as a friend, soldier, and former comrade. And from your side, I ask that you treat me the same way. . . . Now I know what you need, what you demand from me, and I'll try to fulfill it."

Despite Skoblin's assurances, Kovalsky described him in a report to the OGPU as "a weak-willed man," subordinated to the hysterical and pampered Plevitskaya. The OGPU operative understood that he had recruited the pair at an opportune time, when they were in need of a life change and more money.[60] A return to Russia offered Plevitskaya the hope for a reawakening of her former glory. Kovalsky proposed to his OGPU superiors that the couple be separated: Plevitskaya could return first to the USSR for concerts, while Skoblin remained behind in Europe to fulfill his duties under the watchful eyes of his OGPU controllers. OGPU headquarters in Moscow quickly dismissed Kovalsky's proposal. Plevitskaya and Skoblin would remain together in Europe as a *komplekt*: a complete set, two for the price of one. Skoblin was the principal agent, she his accomplice. Rumors spread that a USSR concert tour may have been in the works in 1931 or 1932, although it never transpired.[61]

The Skoblins' decisions in 1930 transformed their lives. Their new "opportunities" gave them a slice of comfort on top of a thick layer of anxiety. The Soviets had great ambitions for Skoblin, who they hoped might lead ROVS someday. In the meantime, he was tasked with providing the secret police with a list of potential targets for recruitment and sensitive documents about ROVS's anti-Soviet operations and military plans. In general, as a Soviet agent provocateur, Skoblin was expected to provoke further disharmony within ROVS, which was already dividing into factions over the question of how best to pursue the anti-Soviet struggle. Miller and other older members called for more caution, while younger members were often more militant and demanded Miller's resignation. Skoblin adroitly exploited these internal weaknesses to his and the Soviets' advantage. He would soon become involved in planning ROVS's anti-Soviet activities; as a leader of clandestine counterintelligence operations aimed at the Soviet Union, he was ideally positioned to sabotage those very operations. If the declassified files on Skoblin reveal the totality of his work for Stalin's secret police, then he was not a spy handler, a job generally reserved for full-time intelligence officers. Nor has any evidence from the archive of the ultrasecret GRU (Soviet military intelligence agency) indicated that Skoblin was an agent of military intelligence, despite having been told that he was working for the Red Army.

One of the early communiqués from Moscow defining Skoblin's duties included remarks about Plevitskaya: "She can work independently. Ask about her contacts and acquaintances, in what circles she moves in, whom and what she can report on. Our decision on how to use her in the long run will be based on these factors."[62] Plevitskaya's European concert tours served as a pretense for Skoblin's frequent absences from Paris, when he would have the opportunity to meet with his handlers in person and furnish them with copies of sensitive ROVS documents. Plevitskaya was tasked with creating a good name for herself and Skoblin by means of her performances at ROVS banquets and other émigré gatherings. She was to report on major developments in White émigré circles.[63] She and Skoblin had much work ahead of them.

6

DOUBLE LIFE

By the early 1930s, living conditions in France had become less hospitable to immigrants. The onset of political instability and xenophobia exacerbated their plight. French citizens also worried about growing economic problems, as unemployment levels, inflation, and the cost of living rose and average income fell, especially once the Great Depression struck France in 1932. Immigrants became scapegoats for economic malaise, and crimes perpetuated by them stoked growing resentments. The Kutepov kidnapping and the assassinations of French president Paul Doumer in May 1932 by a deranged Russian émigré named Paul Gorgulov and of King Alexander of Yugoslavia and French foreign minister Louis Barthou in October 1934 in Marseille by a Croatian terrorist gripped the headlines. Politicians across the political spectrum responded by ordering police to crack down on immigrant populations and by passing anti-immigration laws, including more restrictive quotas on foreign workers. Nor did growing fears of war improve the French public's outlook toward immigrants.

Most immigrants were preoccupied with their daily lives, but those who engaged in internecine conflict increasingly commanded the police's attention. Paris police reported that more than a quarter of crimes were caused by immigrants, who made up 10 percent of the population.[1] As they policed foreigners, authorities tended to focus more on communist activists than fascist ones, considering the former to be more subversive. During the 1930s, the French came to view Russian émigrés as a criminally and politically suspect immigrant population in need of more policing.

In 1930, approximately 43,350 Russian émigrés lived in Paris and 9,500 more in its suburbs.[2] Officials of the nationwide Sûreté Générale (renamed the Sûreté Nationale in 1934) and the Prefecture of Police placed

known communists and anti–Bolshevik White Russian military personnel alike under surveillance. French officials increased their monitoring
of ROVS's activities beginning in 1931. That January, the French police
issued reports about comments Miller had made in an interview in the
Sunday Times of London in which he described how ROVS was organizing a struggle against the Soviet regime. Miller's statement contradicted
subsequent, and false, comments he made to Russian émigré publications,
in which he characterized ROVS's activities as strictly commemorative and
humanitarian.[3]

In March 1931, the Ministry of the Interior and the Ministry of Foreign Affairs instructed the Paris police to begin collecting intelligence on
Skoblin and Plevitskaya, and to treat it as an urgent matter.[4] An early report
resulting from this endeavor, in April 1931, concluded—wrongly, as it
turned out—that there was nothing suspicious about the couple's activities.[5]

In fact, the Skoblins were acting as any well-trained spies would,
masking their clandestine activities under a law-abiding facade. It was not
always in France that they reported on their spying to their OGPU case
officers. Instead, they often traveled abroad to meet with them, using
Plevitskaya's concert tours as cover. As 1931 began, she toured Yugoslavia and Bulgaria; Berlin was a convenient layover and the location of the
Skoblins' first meeting with an OGPU official from Moscow. On January
21, Plevitskaya and Skoblin met in the German capital with an OGPU operative named Vsevolod, who reported back to Moscow that the Skoblins
were both extremely well informed about everything concerning White
Russian circles and had made a positive overall impression on him. Most
importantly, they each signed two duplicate handwritten statements in the
presence of an official from the OGPU's Foreign Department in Moscow,
Semyon Kostrov.[6] These reconfirmed the statement that Skoblin had signed
in Pyotr Kovalsky's presence in September 1930. The first statement was
a request to the Central Executive Committee of the USSR, the leading
organ of the Soviet government at the time, for personal amnesty and citizenship. They also agreed to keep the instructions they received secret.[7]

Skoblin and Plevitskaya also signed a second statement, pledging that
they would work for the Red Army. This was essentially an acknowledge-
ment of their recruitment as intelligence agents. However, OGPU officials
never revealed to the Skoblins that they would be working exclusively for
their agency, as opposed to military intelligence (the GRU).[8]

In Austria, Kovalsky had planned to rendezvous with the Skoblins
in Berlin, but he was apprehended by the Vienna police the day before
and interrogated.[9] The police confiscated potentially compromising notes

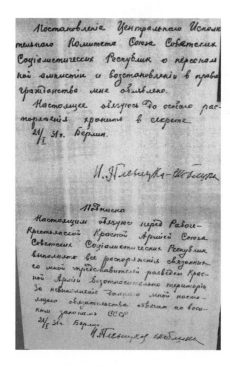

A photocopy of Nadezhda Plevitskaya's two signed statements to the Soviets, Berlin, January 21, 1931. In the top statement, addressed to the Central Executive Committee of the USSR, Plevitskaya is requesting personal amnesty and Soviet citizenship. In the bottom statement, she is pledging to provide military intelligence services to the Red Army, although, in reality, she and Skoblin worked for the OGPU/NKVD. Courtesy of the Museum of N. V. Plevitskaya, Vinnikovo

from Skoblin. Kovalsky was released after managing to fool the police into thinking that the notes were related to his work with Skoblin's Kornilov Regiment. But Kovalsky knew his cover was blown, as the Austrians would soon try to verify his story with ROVS and the Czech government (he was carrying a fake Czech passport) and would discover that it was false. In a matter of days, the OGPU whisked him back to the USSR, where he worked in local OGPU offices. In 1937, he was executed as a traitor during Stalin's Great Terror.

As 1931 progressed, the Skoblins' OGPU handlers began to consider them more useful.[10] Skoblin was strengthening ties with ROVS officials and people from other White Guardist organizations across Europe, while Plevitskaya provided cover by organizing gala concerts and gatherings with White acquaintances and collected information on them in the process.

Once back in France, the Skoblins needed to decide what to do with their new windfall. Curiously, instead of hiding it at home, Skoblin opened an account with US$2,000 at Banque Internationale, where their acquaintance G. I. Shulman was the director.[11] (As a woman, Plevitskaya could not open her own French bank account.) For years, the couple dropped by the bank to exchange currency, such as U.S. dollars or British pounds sterling, into francs or vice versa, and it seemed to Shulman that they had considerable financial means.

Most of Plevitskaya's time was filled with charity concerts and visits with friends. Her performances between May and July included galas, a concert at a school named for Rudolph Steiner (founder of the Waldorf movement), and several benefit concerts at hotels and major auditoriums in Paris.[12] During the autumn of 1931, Plevitskaya performed in at least seven concerts in the Paris area, chiefly with other Russian émigré musicians and artists. Several of the performances were charity balls for veterans' groups, and many were sponsored by Russian aristocrats, including Prince Sergei Volkonsky, who had directed the Imperial Theaters in Russia and was now a theater critic.

Skoblin continued to remain active in White Russian émigré military associations. By the early 1930s, due to years of financial deprivation and failed hopes, these and other émigré groups "split into ever smaller fragments as personal animosities and ambitions grew ever greater."[13] As an agent provocateur, Skoblin focused on how he could advance the Soviet cause by exploiting these rifts. He increasingly focused on undermining Miller's leadership in ROVS. He may have leaked news of general dissent against Miller to the newspaper *Poslednie novosti*.[14] In an even bolder move, he persuaded Major General Anton Turkul, the young and popular commander of the Drozhdovsky Infantry Regiment, to move to Paris from Bulgaria in November 1931. Once in Paris, Turkul unknowingly acted in the Soviets' interests by serving as Skoblin's cat's-paw against Miller.[15] Turkul, like General Pavel Shatilov, personally felt that Miller was a weak leader, and, by fanning the flames of internecine conflict, he unwittingly furthered Skoblin's aims. Miller himself suspected that Soviet provocateurs were manipulating Turkul, but he remained unaware of the threat posed by Skoblin.[16]

In July 1931, in the midst of this confusing intrigue, Skoblin hosted an anniversary banquet for his Kornilov Regiment. Miller spoke at the event, referring to the struggle to free Russia from the grips of the Communist International. ROVS, he stressed, was at the helm of the White movement, directing it toward this goal. Trying to mend bridges among the movement's factions, Miller called for unity and a universal admission of guilt for failing to defeat the Bolsheviks.[17] That summer, Skoblin, Turkul, and other ROVS officers urged Miller to intensify these efforts immediately or face further scrutiny. Skoblin knew that the Soviets wanted him to inform them about such plans, as well as about any ROVS initiatives to infiltrate agents into the USSR. The sooner he could tell his handlers, the better.

Nadezhda Plevitskaya and Nikolai Skoblin, circa 1930s. Courtesy of the Museum of N. V. Plevitskaya, Vinnikovo

    The Soviets ordered Skoblin to remain "independent" of any factions within ROVS.[18] In this way, Skoblin could more effectively invite confidences from ROVS comrades. Skoblin's OGPU handlers also worried that he might attract suspicion if the ROVS sabotage operations he devised were routinely compromised. Concerning the Soviets further was Skoblin's request for a brief respite from his duties, probably in the summer of 1931, so he could relax, and to allow Plevitskaya to recover from an unspecified surgery.[19] Was he feeling burned out or, worse, regretting his Soviet ties?

    Fortunately for Skoblin, sometime between the end of 1931 and early 1932, A. P. Fedorov, the head of the Fifth Branch (on White emigration) of the OGPU's Foreign Department, gave him a positive assessment.[20] Skoblin came to be seen as one of OGPU's best assets in Europe, accurately informing the Soviets about developments in the upper echelons of ROVS, including Miller's movements in France and abroad. He also warned the Soviets about Dmitry Slonovsky, a former White Army commander who had recently crossed into the USSR on a ROVS intelligence mission and returned to Europe to report about it. Skoblin had provoked dissent in the ranks of ROVS, using an unsuspecting Turkul to lead the attack against Miller. In addition, Skoblin's handler pointed out, Skoblin had exposed a former tsarist-era captain named Igor Zavadsky-Krasnopolsky as a French police informant; helped prevent the assassination of the Soviet commissar for foreign affairs, Maxim Litvinov; and stymied a ROVS sabotage mission from Romania into the USSR.[21] Before too long, Skoblin's efforts would aid the Soviets in trapping nearly twenty ROVS agents who tried to infiltrate the USSR, and they thwarted ROVS's attempts to build anticommunist cells inside the country.

Plevitskaya also favorably impressed her handlers. As expected, her concert tours gave Skoblin the opportunity to carry out inspections of ROVS's provincial branches and to collect information of operational significance for the OGPU. In one instance, a handler named Oleg reported from Paris that Skoblin and Plevitskaya stayed up all night to copy by hand three lengthy reports about plans that Shatilov had devised for ROVS's war preparations.[22] Shatilov had lent Skoblin the reports for one evening and insisted that he return them the next day.

In 1932, the Skoblins continued to produce more of the same fruitful results for their Soviet masters. Through her concerts in France, Plevitskaya came into contact with a wide variety of Russian émigrés. She performed in at least seventeen concerts, mainly in the Paris area. Plevitskaya had become a fixture at these events, and she continued to lean on her strengths: her ability to dazzle émigré audiences through her sentimental interpretation of folk songs and her conversational and listening skills.

Skoblin's job, of course, was more complex and critical to Soviet strategy. In 1932, he introduced some new methods. One was to encourage all émigré military groups in Europe, including the National Labor Union of the New Generation (NTSNP), to unite in their anti-Soviet struggle. In reality, he was trying to keep tabs on everyone, to limit the number of infiltration operations against the Soviets, and to sideline ROVS officials who argued for different approaches. That year, Skoblin convened a general assembly of all these groups to obtain his objectives.[23]

His campaign was only partly successful. Skoblin was not universally liked or trusted in ROVS, and this weakness continued to plague him. When an unknown assailant detonated a bomb in ROVS headquarters sometime in the mid-1930s, some Russian émigrés suspected that Skoblin was involved. His detractors, the vast majority of whom were right-wing conservatives, increasingly assumed that his politics were more liberal than fascist and were bothered by the fact that he and Plevitskaya owned a house and cars.[24] Some simply disliked Skoblin's demeanor. General Fyodor Abramov, head of ROVS's Third Department (with jurisdiction over Bulgaria and Turkey) later stated that Skoblin gave him the impression of insincerity and never even looked him in the eye.[25] If he wanted to lead ROVS someday, Skoblin needed to gain the trust of more White Army officers and stand above the fray. He failed at both, but he was gifted at undermining White Guardists' secret operations, and this kept him in business with the Soviets. Skoblin and his Soviet handlers were correct to assume that ROVS's political activism only served to weaken the organization by heightening factional conflicts and making its most radical and vocal members advocate for increasingly unrealistic goals.

In May 1933, six senior White Army officers—including Skoblin—sent Miller a memorandum criticizing his passivity and called for terrorist activities inside the USSR. Shortly afterward, Miller received individual protests and jotted down summaries of each for his personal files. He noted that Skoblin recommended the use of terrorist acts for the purpose of provoking mass panic.[26] Miller spent the remainder of 1933 reassuring his ROVS peers that he would back anticommunist activity inside the USSR.[27] However, in the autumn of 1933, a Romania-based operation that would have required sailing a ship to the southern USSR was canceled due to widespread fears of its being too high risk.[28]

The ascendance to power of the Nazi Party in Germany offered new opportunities for ROVS. Miller was not an avowed fascist, but he acknowledged an affinity between the White movement and fascism, and he even instructed ROVS members to study it.[29] On the other hand, Miller's long-term loyalties appeared to be more with the French. During World War I, the Russian Imperial Army had fought on the same side as France, and Miller was grateful that its government had accepted so many White Russian refugees during the 1920s. Out of a sense of pragmatism, though, he agreed to open discussions with members of Germany's new Nazi government about possible cooperation. His ROVS representative in Germany, General von Lampe, was sympathetic to fascism and had already established contacts with Nazi officials, including the ideologue and racial theorist Alfred Rosenberg.[30] Negotiations centered on future joint operations against the Bolsheviks.[31] But ROVS first had to overcome the Nazis' early mistrust. The Nazi regime even imprisoned von Lampe for a few months in 1933 on suspicions that he was a French spy.[32]

Skoblin did not discourage Miller's efforts to strengthen ROVS's contacts with the Nazis and increasingly portrayed himself as a German sympathizer. He met regularly with a group of émigré activists led by the pro-German Alexander Guchkov, the 1917 Provisional Government's first war minister.[33] Skoblin had reportedly spoken with Miller about cultivating closer ties with the Nazis, and Skoblin's pro-Nazi stance was likely a tactic to keep Miller convinced that his sympathies were not with the Bolsheviks.[34] However, some have argued that Skoblin was also a German agent, largely because of his ties to Guchkov and, as described below, his alleged involvement in Stalin's framing of Soviet marshal Mikhail Tukhachevsky in 1937.[35]

The OGPU quickly learned of ROVS's pro-German strategy. One of Skoblin's handlers in Paris, code-named Oleg, reported on how Ivan Lukash, the journalist who had edited Plevitskaya's memoirs, promoted the idea of sending young White Russian generals to Germany to help Hitler suppress the communists there.[36] Stalin and his henchmen well understood that the USSR would almost certainly fight Nazi Germany someday, and knowing that ROVS was building a rapport with the Germans stoked Stalin's existing paranoia about the group.

For the moment, the most direct threat ROVS posed to the USSR came in the form of infiltration operations run out of Finland. These gave Miller another way to appease his detractors within ROVS. Miller's point man in Finland was White Army general Severin Dobrovolsky (code-named Severov), who placed his old comrade-in-arms in contact with Colonel Lauri Malmberg of the Second Bureau, Finland's military intelligence agency.[37] The Finns agreed to help Miller, but wisely refused to divulge the names of their own agents in the USSR.[38] Miller, or "Ivan Ivanovich" in correspondence, appointed Skoblin (code-named Pyotr Petrovich or N. Skii) as his liaison in Finland and asked him to facilitate the travel of ROVS agents into the USSR.[39] This, of course, allowed Stalin and the OGPU to monitor the operations and apprehend ROVS agents as they crossed over from Finland. Operations did not actually commence until the spring of 1934 because Miller and Skoblin needed to confirm details with their contacts in Finland and recruit "emissaries," as they called their agents. As a cautionary measure, they coded their correspondence in business language, making it appear to outsiders that they were engaged in economic trade instead of anti-Soviet activity. The Finns refused to aid ROVS agents directly because they did not wish to harm their already strained relations with the Soviets.

Evidence of Miller's misplaced trust in Skoblin included his September 1933 appointment of the younger man as head of the Society of Gallipolians in Paris.[40] Later that month, the first Congress of National White Russian Groups took place at the Society of Gallipolians' headquarters and was sponsored by émigré publications, student groups, and émigré groups from the French provinces. Lasting a week, the Congress was run by about two dozen leaders of the Inner Line from the French provinces. ROVS officials, including Miller, attended the opening, and Miller spoke to the Congress's central theme of opportunities for émigré youth.

In theory, the Inner Line was supposed to have identified Soviet provocateurs within ROVS; clearly it failed in this task. In practice, Shatilov, Skoblin, and other principal Inner Line leaders used it to discredit Miller.[41] Skoblin—as a real Soviet provocateur—was perfectly situated to manipulate Shatilov and others into plotting against Miller and fueling conflict within the organization.

The historical record sheds little light on Plevitskaya's activities in 1933, apart from a sporadic concert schedule. In January and February, she—with Skoblin in tow—performed in Bulgaria. She appeared in at least five concerts per month in France in March and April, and fewer in May and June. At one of these performances, a gathering to mark the fifteenth anniversary of General Kornilov's death, Skoblin spoke about his belief in the impending rebirth of Russia and how Kornilov's memory would be honored there.[42] Plevitskaya seems to have taken a break from performing between July and September, after which she appeared in a few concerts from late October through early December. Most of these would have earned her little to no income because they were charity fund-raisers or balls marking White Army anniversaries.

One source that reveals more about how the wider White community viewed the Skoblins and their personal lives is Viktor Larionov, a former captain in the White Army.[43] Larionov gained notoriety in 1927 by leading a ROVS operation that bombed the Leningrad Communist Party headquarters and then escaped back to France. In 1930, he formed a right-wing group in Paris called the "White Idea," which arranged its own anti-Bolshevik operations. As a ROVS member, Larionov became acquainted with the Skoblins. His assessment of them was largely negative. Skoblin, he recalled, was scheming, ill bred, and boastful. Plevitskaya came across to Larionov as an uncultured *baba* whose education, such as it was, had been gained in taverns and low-class dives. Such experiences, Larionov felt, had corrupted her, leaving her vain, cunning, and greedy.

The Skoblins invited Larionov to their home several times. Despite his criticisms of them, he found them generous hosts. The first floor was Plevitskaya's domain, a temple to her artistic glory, filled with portraits of Russian artists and performers. She treated Skoblin affectionately, calling him "Kolya." He called her "Vasily," in reference to her father's name. She did not allow him out of her sight for long and disliked being alone. Larionov noted how, when she and Skoblin motored to Paris, she often accompanied him to meetings and waited for him in the car for hours.

Skoblin's office was on the second floor of the house, and it contained an archive of Volunteer Army documents and memorabilia. Mementos of the Kornilov Regiment hung on his office walls. During one visit to the Skoblins' house, Larionov was warned by Skoblin that a split within ROVS was imminent and that the leadership's authority was lost. Still, Skoblin insisted, it was not too late to save the organization, and he urged Larionov to plan other terrorist operations in Russia.

Along with Larionov, the Millers, and other White Army veterans, the Skoblins hosted relatives as well. Skoblin's brothers Sergei and Feodosy lived with them between 1930 and 1934, but they clashed with Plevitskaya, whom they regarded as bossy and unwelcoming. Sergei, the youngest brother, recalled that "Nikolai dreamed of seeing his family together, his close relations gathered around him, but his wife always tried to break us up."[44] Feodosy complained that he had been treated like "my sister-in-law's domestic servant." Fed up, he moved to Paris in the fall of 1934.

Plevitskaya and Skoblin sometimes hosted his sister, Tamara, her husband Colonel Vorobiev, and their two daughters.[45] Vorobiev later complained that Plevitskaya had treated him and his wife like servants. When Plevitskaya and Skoblin drove to Paris for a few days, they left the Vorobievs with little food. According to Vorobiev, "Nikolai always preached economy, but he did not give me the impression of being short of money." Skoblin's sister and brother-in-law both observed that Plevitskaya treated Nikolai like an imbecile and that he tended to obey her orders. In June 1937, the couples had a falling-out, and Vorobiev found work as a night guard and garage attendant in Paris. On the other hand, Helene, Tamara's older child, who was an adolescent in the mid-1930s, professed affection for her aunt and uncle. She recalled that Plevitskaya did not know French and would sometimes ask her to translate. Helene remembered her fondly as exhibiting both a sense of dignity and grandeur.

By 1934, everyone in Europe—not just paranoid White Guardists—was preparing for the eventual outbreak of war. Even the Soviets had pragmatically adopted a foreign policy of collective security and joined the League of Nations. Collective security involved an active effort by the Soviet diplomatic community to become friendlier with the Western democracies and convince them to form an alliance against Germany. As a result, the French were less inclined to sympathize with the anticommunist White movement, especially as Comintern propaganda had convinced many that anticommunist sentiment was profascist.[46]

To complicate matters further, in February, Paris experienced weeks of riots and political turmoil in response to an enormous financial scandal and news of widespread political corruption. The figure at the center of the scandal was a Russian embezzler and pawnshop operator in Bayonne, France, named Alexandre Stavisky. Stavisky, who had counseled government officials, sold thousands of people valueless bonds and ended up killing himself in January when news of his fraudulence broke. The Radical Socialist prime minister, Camille Chautemps, fell, to be replaced by his fellow Radical Socialist, Édouard Daladier; the profascist head of the Prefecture of Police, Jean Chiappe, was also dismissed. As French politics became more unstable, the police were under increased pressure to restore public order and fight crime. Their efforts were not always effective, and the Soviets understood this well. Léopold Trepper, a Soviet operative, once noted that in France at this time, legality "always had vague limits that could easily be transgressed."[47]

Despite its official policy of collective security, Stalin's regime had no intention to squander the intelligence opportunities afforded by France's political upheaval. Behind the scenes in the OGPU (renamed the NKVD in June 1934), Yakov Serebriansky and his Administration for Special Tasks relied on illegals—such as the Skoblins and Sergei Tretyakov—to gather information and act as agents provocateurs. Although he was not a ROVS member, Tretyakov was uniquely positioned to spy on its leaders. Once Miller became head of ROVS, he moved its headquarters to the first floor (the second floor in American usage) of the building at 29 rue du Colisée, a one-way street in the eighth arrondissement, beginning at the Champs-Élysées and ending at rue du Faubourg-Saint-Honoré. Conveniently for the Soviets, Tretyakov owned the building. In 1933, the OGPU ordered Tretyakov to install listening devices in Miller's office, as well as the offices of Shatilov and General Pavel Kussonsky, Miller's assistant. The recording equipment was housed in Tretyakov's second-floor apartment, right above ROVS headquarters, and he began surveillance operations in January 1934.[48]

The Skoblins were acquainted with Tretyakov, and it is likely that they knew he was an NKVD agent. However, they would not have been aware of all the Soviet agents operating in Paris, because a key part of spy tradecraft anywhere is compartmentalization. For instance, there is no evidence that the Skoblins knew that Mireille Abbiate (code name Aviatorsha, or "aviatrix") or her brother Roland (pseudonym Vladimir Pravdin) were NKVD agents. Mireille was also spying on General Miller; the OGPU recruited her in 1931, shortly after the Skoblins agreed to spy for Stalin.[49]

Soviet agent Leonid Linitsky, a former White Army officer based in Belgrade, betrayed ROVS agents to the Soviets before local police unmasked him in 1935, but it is unknown whether he and Skoblin coordinated their espionage work.[50]

The Skoblins must have felt relieved not to have collaborated with Robert Gordon Switz, an American who worked for the Soviet military intelligence agency (GRU). In December 1933, the Paris police arrested Switz, along with his wife Marjorie, on charges of espionage.[51] The Switzes—and at least fifty other GRU agents in France and Finland—were gathering classified documents about French and Finnish weapons and military plans. In return for exposing several other agents in their ring and detailing which secrets they had handed to the Soviets, the couple were freed after sixteen months and never convicted. However, in April 1935, twenty-three Red agents were convicted of espionage in Paris and given sentences of up to five years in prison. One of these agents was Lydia Stahl. Born Lydia Chkalova in Rostov in 1890, Stahl worked as a Soviet operative in the United States before transferring to France, and at the April 1935 trial, she was widely viewed as one of the spies' ringleaders. In behavior that mirrored Plevitskaya's emotional performance in 1938, Stahl broke down in sobs upon hearing her sentence, which was shortened to four years that July.[52] After her release, Stahl reportedly worked for Germany's military intelligence agency, the Abwehr, and then fled to South America after World War II.[53] This 1935 trial was the first Soviet spy scandal in France, and French authorities and newspapers gave it serious attention.

Undoubtedly aware of the Switz affair, General Miller must have felt a need for even greater vigilance. He continued to hatch a ROVS-led plan to defeat the Red Army, all the while reassuring French authorities that he was doing no such thing. In a speech to other ROV officials, Miller warned, "There is no time to lose. It is time to work toward a general mobilization and training against the Soviet government in Moscow, the supreme headquarters of international communism, which uses our former Russia as the staging ground for world revolution and civil war worldwide."[54]

Miller dedicated much of his time to the above-mentioned Finnish operations. He dispatched Skoblin to Finland in January 1934 to make contact with General Malmberg and the Finnish military General Staff and to hand a letter to Dobrovolsky. In the letter, Miller told Dobrovolsky that Skoblin had remained in France longer than intended in order to care for Plevitskaya, who had had to postpone her concert tour due to illness.[55] Plevitskaya, now recovered, went with Skoblin to Finland, where she performed in several concerts. A month later, on February 19, 1934, Dobrovolsky informed Miller and Skoblin that the Finns would be prepared in the spring to help send ROVS agents into the USSR.[56]

In May 1934, the Skoblins visited Larionov and his wife at their home outside Paris.[57] Plevitskaya sat down with Larionov's wife while Skoblin and the captain walked along the Seine. Skoblin urged Larionov to take part in the Finnish operations, given Larionov's previous experience and his ties to Russian émigré youth who might be able to serve as ROVS agents. "But there is only one condition," Skoblin said: "General Miller must not know that you will be aware of these affairs." Larionov suggested to Skoblin that a friend of his, an émigré with ambitions to create anti-Bolshevik cells within the USSR, might be interested in taking part in the mission. Larionov soon spoke with his friend about the opportunity, and he agreed to participate. They also found a second person to serve as a ROVS agent. Both agents were young members of Larionov's anti-Bolshevik White Idea.[58] In June 1934, they met with Skoblin to plan their infiltration into the USSR via Finland.

The operation took place sometime in July. Its mission was to form a group of supporters in Leningrad and then regroup in Finland for future operations. Immediately after crossing into the USSR, the two agents were spotted by Soviet border guards, but they managed to escape back into Finland before they could be apprehended.[59] Upon hearing the news, Skoblin flew into a fit of rage and cut off support to the two ROVS agents, which Larionov found insensitive. Still, Larionov and the agents did not suspect Skoblin of anything except poor leadership skills and egotistical careerism. In reality, Skoblin had tipped off the NKVD. The Finns, who were then prosecuting Soviet agents involved in the Switz ring, soon suspected that Skoblin was working for the Soviets and warned Miller. The general stubbornly rejected their conclusions.

The added stress of the anti-Soviet operations, coupled with widespread criticism from various White factions, took a toll on Miller's health. He took an extended holiday in the summer of 1934 and appointed General Abramov as interim head of ROVS. Miller also suffered personal misfortune in July when his apartment was broken into and some documents were stolen.[60] The police noticed that the door had been damaged from the inside, which made them suspect that the thieves were feigning a breaking and entering. Miller told the police that the stolen documents were relatively important and wondered whether the thieves were Bolsheviks. The Skoblins had spent some of the summer in the Millers' apartment, where Plevitskaya had recuperated from another bout of illness.[61] However, the thief was actually NKVD agent Mireille Abbiate, who lived next door to the Millers.[62] She also planted a hidden microphone in his apartment for surveillance purposes.

Plevitskaya's 1934 schedule was not packed with concerts. Nonetheless, she claimed to have earned 130,000 francs in concert revenues that year—enough to pay off the mortgage on her and Skoblin's house.[63] The best explanation is that most of this money had been given to Skoblin by the NKVD but was disguised as income from Plevitskaya's concerts.

If 1934 marked a time of decline for Plevitskaya's health and career, the following year brought her even more distress—as it did for Skoblin. Skoblin was forced to go on the defensive to keep from being exposed. The year began like any other, with a concert tour. In January 1935, the couple traveled abroad, including to Kishinev, Moldova, for concerts. Despite her flagging health, Plevitskaya had not yet completely lost her allure to émigré audiences. One newspaper remarked that she "compels us to depart with her from the reality of the present day to the wonderful, intoxicating world of Russian song."[64] By mid-January, she and Skoblin were back in Paris, where she sang with other artists at a concert sponsored by the Union of Russian Sisters of Mercy. Then, from late January to mid-February, they vacationed at a resort in Serbia.[65]

Such placid normality would not last. Back in 1932, Colonel Boris Fedoseenko, a fellow White Army veteran, had confessed to Miller that he had been recruited by the OGPU in 1932 and that he knew Skoblin was a spy. Miller told Fedoseenko to cease his contacts with the OGPU, but he dismissed the accusation of Skoblin's spying.[66] For the time being, Skoblin and Plevitskaya were spared being exposed. However, on January 27, 1935, Fedoseenko, under the pseudonym Alibaba, published his allegations in the conservative Paris émigré newspaper *Vozrozhdenie*. A few days later, he sent a report to General Ivan Erdely, the new head of ROVS's First Department, detailing what he knew about Soviet infiltration of ROVS, including Skoblin's recruitment.[67] Erdely, who already suspected Skoblin, ordered an investigation.[68]

Skoblin, upon returning from Serbia with Plevitskaya on February 17 and hearing the news of Fedoseenko's report, urged Miller to convene a court of honor to determine the validity of Fedoseenko's charges.[69] A key method of enforcing discipline, courts of honor were composed of White Army generals who ruled on the behavior of ROVS members. If a court of honor found someone's behavior objectionable, he could be expelled. At this point, Miller refused to convene such a court against Skoblin. He—like a majority of ROVS members at the time—suspected that Fedoseenko's report was really a Soviet provocation and slandered Skoblin without credible evidence.

Skoblin's Soviet handlers followed the story closely and grew worried.[70] (The Switz scandal, which damaged the USSR's reputation, also fueled Moscow's fears, causing it to suspend intelligence operations in Paris for a few months.[71]) Skoblin's handlers characterized the Fedoseenko affair as a struggle to the death between Erdely and Skoblin. They knew that the French authorities were aware of Fedoseenko's report and were now keeping even closer tabs on Skoblin. Nor was it a secret that amateur spy hunter Vladimir Burtsev was conducting his own investigation of Skoblin and Plevitskaya. At this point, Burtsev viewed Plevitskaya as the couple's mastermind, based on rumors that she had worked for the Soviets as early as the civil war. In addition, an increasing number of émigrés were questioning how the Skoblins could afford a house on Plevitskaya's meager earnings. On the other hand, NKVD officials were relieved to learn from Skoblin that Miller and Shatilov continued to trust him and that only a minority of ROVS officers believed Fedoseenko's story.[72]

With Burtsev's crusade, the Switz case, and other irritants in mind, NKVD officials in Moscow urged Skoblin to meet less often with Oleg, his Paris contact, for the time being.[73] Moscow ordered Oleg to tell Skoblin to lie low for one to two months, but to meet with him on occasion to pass him money and calm him down. Skoblin's Soviet handlers devised methods for shielding his payments. For instance, they asked him to show Miller the funds that Plevitskaya allegedly earned from her recent concerts—8,000 francs actually supplied by the NKVD. They also had Skoblin place 25,000 francs in a bank safe.

Fortunately for Skoblin, another ROVS scandal detracted attention from the espionage allegations he faced. On February 23, shortly after announcing the need to cut ROVS's budget drastically, Miller was presented with an ultimatum by fourteen unit commanders of the First Army Corps (including Skoblin): make ROVS more financially viable and operationally effective or resign.[74] This event came to be called the Generals' Revolt. Skoblin may have leaked the news of the revolt to *Poslednie novosti*, which was already predisposed to view ROVS and Miller negatively.[75] The Generals' Revolt did not lead to Miller's resignation or prompt him to adopt their proposed reforms, but it further undermined his authority, which could only benefit Skoblin's and the Soviets' interests.

In the midst of the internal attack on Miller and the controversy over Fedoseenko's allegations, Plevitskaya and Skoblin were injured in a car accident at around 10:00 p.m. on February 27. They were returning to Ozoir-la-Ferrière from Paris in their Peugeot, with Skoblin in the driver's seat as usual, when they collided with a truck near the Vincennes Forest. The truck was operated by a driver named Fassiola. The Peugeot was damaged beyond repair, and Plevitskaya and Skoblin were both thrown from the car and briefly knocked unconscious.[76]

For eighteen days, the couple recovered in the Mirabeau Clinic in Paris, the same facility where Trotsky's son, Lev Sedov, would die—likely at the hands of the Soviets—in 1938. Plevitskaya sustained deep gashes near her left eye and on her left leg, and multiple bruises on her left side and right shoulder blade. She complained of headaches, restlessness, and insomnia. Skoblin broke his right shoulder blade and suffered other injuries. According to an NKVD report, Skoblin suffered from spells of anemia and had been treated for the condition around that same time, so this may have slowed his recovery from the accident.[77] Plevitskaya told journalists that she and her husband had survived thanks to an icon that always hung from the inside wall of their automobile.[78] Although it was not fatal, the accident left a lasting impact on Plevitskaya's health, including recurring headaches.

A nurse who treated the Skoblins in Mirabeau was questioned by Paris investigators in Plevitskaya's criminal case two years later.[79] The nurse claimed that she had observed suspicious behavior, particularly when Turkul came to visit them. They asked her to leave the room whenever he arrived, leading her to think that they were involved in conspiratorial activities. In her defense, Plevitskaya retorted that they did not know the nurse personally and simply did not want her in the room when they held private conversations.

The Skoblins sued Fassiola and two businesses connected to the truck and its maintenance, Willeme and Bonnet, to recover the cost of their medical treatment and Plevitskaya's lost concert earnings. They hired Russian émigré attorney Maximilian Filonenko to represent them. Filonenko, who had been commissar of the Eighth Army in the ill-fated Russian Provisional Government in 1917, was now a law professor at the Free University in Brussels and one of the few Russian émigrés who belonged to the Paris bar. Plevitskaya claimed that the accident, by causing her to cancel her concert engagements in the spring of 1935, had cost her close to 30,000 francs. Miller testified about the Skoblins' suffering, including Plevitskaya's inability to perform. Plevitskaya's piano accompanist also spoke on her behalf. The Skoblins gave testimony as well, but the driver did not appear in court. A witness to the accident, a man named Romano, said the driver was to blame.

Filonenko asked the court to appoint a medical expert and to award the Skoblins 65,000 francs to be paid by the business's insurance company, Lloyd's of London. The attorney for the defense claimed that Plevitskaya was not a real singer but merely spoke her songs, and so had not suffered any significant harm to her performance quality. Filonenko, in rebuttal, said that the court could listen to her recordings to prove how she sang. The court assigned blame to the driver but took longer to rule on the monetary settlement. In February 1936, the Skoblins were awarded 60,000 francs, only 5,000 less than they had requested.[80] It would not be long before Plevitskaya required Filonenko's services again—although the outcome in that case would be far less favorable.

In March 1935, while the Skoblins were still recuperating in the hospital, members of Skoblin's regiment wrote a letter to the Russian émigré publication *Chasovoi* (*Sentinel*) professing their complete trust in Skoblin. They had also met at a gathering of First Army Corps officers in Paris to urge support of Skoblin.[81] Skoblin thought that the best way to clear his name and vanquish his enemies within the émigré community was for a court of honor to exonerate him. On April 22, he sent a letter to Miller again requesting a court of honor. Miller spent two months mulling over this decision. At that point, he was initiating a new series of clandestine operations, this time based in Romania, and ordered Skoblin to help organize them.[82]

In the meantime, on April 28, the Skoblins appeared at the White Army's celebration of Orthodox Easter, which took place at the Society of Gallipolians. Plevitskaya sat on Miller's right, holding her own place of honor as mother-commander of the Kornilov Regiment. Larionov was present for the event and recalled how the Skoblins were invited later that evening to a closed meeting of the veterans of the Markov Artillery Division, two floors above the hall where the celebration was being held.[83] They all met with a handful of young men who belonged to Larionov's White Idea group. The Skoblins attended for nearly four hours. Skoblin spoke to the young men about old Russia, and Larionov observed how Plevitskaya teared up. "Stop, Vasily," an embarrassed Skoblin told Plevitskaya, using his nickname for her. It appears from Larionov's vignette that the Skoblins were doing their duty for the Soviets by collecting information about the White Idea group and insinuating themselves into it.

On May 2, only a mere five days after the Easter celebration, the news broke of a new French–Soviet mutual assistance pact, negotiated by Stalin and French prime minister Pierre Laval. Miller was distraught about the pact, as it signaled that the French government would now be less tolerant of ROVS's military plans against the Soviets. Such dreaded news served to strengthen Miller's resolve about seeking ways—sooner rather than later—for ROVS to cooperate with the Germans. Skoblin knew this to be the case and kept Miller's concerns in mind for future reference.[84]

Also in May 1935, Miller decided to appoint Skoblin to serve as his rapporteur with the Inner Line.[85] This move seemed extremely ill advised, especially at a time when some ROVS members suspected Skoblin of treachery. But Miller assumed that Skoblin was one of his most loyal officers and thought that he would do his bidding with the Inner Line. According to one of Miller's contemporaries, Miller did not want Skoblin to serve as head of the First Department, which the Society of Gallipolians' membership had nominated him for, so the ROVS leader awarded him the rapporteur position as a consolation prize.[86] Miller appointed himself head of the First Department, taking Erdely's place. So, within a matter of days, Miller had further guaranteed his own demise by granting Skoblin another power base within ROVS to exploit—and by disempowering Erdely, whose chief mission as head of the First Department had been to expose Skoblin as a Soviet agent provocateur.

While Miller was still digesting the disturbing news about the French-Soviet pact, he finally decided on June 11 to convene a court of honor to investigate Fedoseenko's allegations against Skoblin. The court consisted of four ROVS generals and a chairman, Major General Nikolai Stogov, who had headed ROVS's central directorate. Skoblin was not called to testify when the court met on July 6. They ruled quickly: Fedoseenko's allegations lacked proof, and the case was dismissed. A few days later, Miller wrote Skoblin a congratulatory note: "I convey to you greetings, coming at the end of this unhappy event for you and Nadezhda Vasilievna."[87]

For Skoblin, the court of honor had achieved exactly what he had intended it to—the majority of members of the military émigré community would see him as a target of Soviet provocation, and such a pleasant result would limit the chances of his being accused of treachery in the future.[88] However, the decision did not convince everyone that Skoblin was innocent. Fedoseenko, Burtsev, and members of the NTSNP émigré youth group who had accused him of past treachery were still keeping a watchful eye on him and Plevitskaya.[89] They urged Miller to be cautious, although he heeded none of their warnings. A top-secret Paris police report of August 31, 1935, claimed that evidence existed that Skoblin was a Soviet agent, so the Fedoseenko affair soon became known to French authorities as well, as the NKVD had predicted.[90]

During the second half of 1935, Miller and Dobrovolsky renewed their correspondence about the Finnish operations. Their letters reveal the Finns' growing concern that a ROVS officer was on the Soviet payroll, and the Finns called for a suspension of operations. In an August 26 letter, Dobrovolsky told Miller that the top military brass in Finland wanted to end ties with "Pyotr Petrovich" (Skoblin), suspecting that even if Skoblin himself was not a Soviet agent, someone in his circle surely was.[91] In fact, in 1935, the Finnish authorities discovered that the Soviet military attaché in Finland had received some information from someone in Paris about the sending of emissaries into the USSR.[92]

By November 1935, the Finns were convinced that Miller had a traitor in his midst and that he was in denial about Skoblin. In response, Miller insisted that Skoblin was the object of calumny and constant intrigue. Miller used the Fedoseenko story to explain how Fedoseenko, a Soviet agent, had tried to entrap Skoblin. Miller also considered the February car accident to have been an attempted murder against Plevitskaya and Skoblin, perpetrated by the Soviets.[93] If Miller had come to his senses in late 1935 and called on French and Finnish authorities to investigate Skoblin further, his kidnapping in 1937 might have been averted. But Miller's strong sense of honor and fairness precluded him from doing so.

After all, how could Miller possibly accuse Skoblin and Plevitskaya of treachery when they were such outstanding citizens—at least on the surface—in the Russian émigré community? At every special military or church event, the Skoblins were front and center, doing their bit. On September 1, 1935, they hosted events marking Kornilov Regiment Day in Paris. First came a prayer service at the Gallipoli church, followed by a breakfast at the Society of Gallipolians. Skoblin spoke at the breakfast about his pride in the close ties between the Kornilov Regiment and ROVS. Miller contributed some remarks, and then Skoblin's deputy in the Society of Gallipolians, Regiment Adjutant Staff Captain Pyotr Grigul, thanked Plevitskaya for providing musical entertainment, which he described as "the healing balm of the Russian soul, known to the world from region to region."[94]

The following month, in October 1935, the Skoblins appeared for the consecration of a new Russian Orthodox church in Ozoir-la-Ferrière.[95] Father Alexander Tchékan, who happened to be Miller's son-in-law, was appointed rector. As the top financial donors to the church, the Skoblins were given special treatment at the consecration. That day, October 20, Plevitskaya arrived with Miller in the head car, followed by Father Tchékan in the second car. She sang briefly at a reception after the consecration, and then Skoblin drove Miller to the train station. Nothing seemed untoward between the two men.

In mid-November, Skoblin, Miller, and other top White Army officers gathered again at the Society of Gallipolians to mark the eighteenth anniversary of the founding of the Volunteer Army. In his remarks, Skoblin spoke about the "clean and peaceful conscience of the participants of the White Movement and their preparedness for the decisive struggle against Bolshevism."[96]

Early in December, Skoblin and his Soviet handlers could not have missed the news that the Yugoslav police had arrested three members of the Belgrade branch of the Society of Gallipolians: Dr. Linitsky, whom the Russians later admitted had been a Soviet spy; Captain Shklarev; and a man named Drakin. The Yugoslav police caught the trio breaking into the home of V. M. Baidalakov, the president of the NTSNP. Also taken into custody was the secretary of the ROVS Fourth Department, Squadron Commander A. N. Komorovsky. The four arrestees were accused of being NKVD agents, and all but Komorovsky were convicted of spying.[97] Miller opened an inquiry in Belgrade, which found evidence of even more Soviet infiltration of ROVS's Inner Line. Instead of clearing the air, the inquiry commission "greatly antagonized ROVS members and made it harder for the more correct elements of their accusations to be treated seriously."[98] Worst of all for ROVS, the inquiry did not connect the incident to the Soviets' most dangerous agents, namely Skoblin and Tretyakov.

Miller responded to the disturbing events of 1935 by ordering Inner Line operatives to strengthen their counterintelligence methods. Of course, Miller remained unaware of one insurmountable obstacle: his agent of change was a Soviet asset—Skoblin. As Miller's rapporteur with the Inner Line branches throughout Europe, Skoblin was tasked with compiling a list of members. Unbeknownst to Miller, Skoblin produced only a partial list, excluding the most active members in Paris, who tended to disapprove of the old general's leadership.[99]

In 1936, while Skoblin, Miller, and other ROVS officials plotted new and dangerous operations, Plevitskaya continued to play the parts of honored folk singer to the White émigré community in Europe and mother-commander to the Kornilov Regiment. However, this would be her last full year as a performer. Other than a February cabaret at the Society of Gallipolians and a June charity concert at Gaveau Hall for disabled veterans of the Kornilov Regiment, her concert schedule in the first half of 1936 was sparse. During the summer of 1936, she sang before audiences in the Baltics, Germany, Finland, and Britain.

Meanwhile, French intelligence officials continued to monitor Skoblin and, by extension, Plevitskaya, but they did not collect sufficient evidence to justify bringing charges against them or expelling them from France. According to Paul Paillole, a top official in France's special intelligence services during the interwar period, French authorities "had already observed Skoblin's curious contacts with the Germans" by 1936 and had planned to increase their surveillance of him.[100] French intelligence officials were well aware of Miller's established relations with the German ambassador in Paris and had concluded that Skoblin was his main envoy with the Germans. The French also suspected by now that Skoblin had ties with the Soviets, not only after learning about Fedoseenko's accusations against him, but also because they assumed that Plevitskaya "had long been on good terms with the Soviets, without a doubt with the OGPU."[101] A counterespionage expert with the Paris police assumed that the Skoblins' house in Ozoir-la-Ferrière was paid for with funds they had received from both the Soviets and the Germans.[102]

In 1936, Miller focused his mind on more than ROVS's internal problems. He was disappointed by the electoral victory in May of the Popular Front coalition—socialists, communists, and members of the Radical Party—that formed France's next government. In Miller's mind, France's right-wing forces were losing political ground, and so it was time for ROVS to work more closely with Germany's Nazis. He may have traveled to Berlin for discussions, including with Gestapo director Reinhard Heydrich. Miller reportedly secured an agreement to share secret information about the Red Army, although this arrangement did not satisfy him; he was already disappointed that Hitler had never responded to any of his correspondence.[103] Unfortunately, no other source verifies this account. However, French intelligence officers had gathered enough evidence of Russian émigrés' affinities for Hitler's regime to convince the French Ministry of the Interior in March 1936 to step up its surveillance of this immigrant group.[104]

Another disappointment for Miller concerned the Finnish operations. In the summer of 1936, the Finnish government informed ROVS that it would no longer be cooperating with the organization or allowing its agents to infiltrate the USSR via Finland.[105] But the foreign policy matter that most occupied Miller and ROVS in the second half of 1936 turned out to be the Spanish Civil War, which began in July. Lasting until 1939, this conflict proved to be a dress rehearsal for World War II, with the Germans and Soviets arming and training their allies in Spain and trying out new weapons and tactics. Starting in the late summer of 1936, the Soviets sent matériel and advisers—including NKVD operatives—to aid the Republican government. Pro-German activists in ROVS quickly lobbied Miller to recruit some of their men to fight for the German-backed Nationalist rebels under the leadership of Francisco Franco. Although he feigned support for sending ROVS volunteers to Spain to fight on Franco's side, Skoblin's true intentions were to serve the Soviets' interests by ensuring that as few ROVS volunteers as possible even reached Spain.

Ever the diplomat, Miller was reluctant to support a ROVS operation in Spain. The French government, despite the fact that a majority of its members supported the Soviet-backed Republicans, chose to remain neutral for reasons tied largely to domestic politics. Miller knew that it was illegal for ROVS to send its men en masse to fight in Spain for Franco's forces. Once the war started, Miller had to contend with widespread discontent regarding his passivity, opposition that Skoblin fomented behind the scenes. In keeping with his image as an anti-Soviet firebrand, Skoblin quickly gave his consent to allow men from the Kornilov Regiment to take part in a future pro-Franco operation.[106]

By the autumn of 1936, caving in to pressure from his most vocal critics, especially Shatilov, Miller began planning to involve ROVS's volunteers in Spain. On September 20, Plevitskaya hosted and performed at an event honoring the Kornilovs, held at the Society of Gallipolians. Skoblin spoke about the Kornilov veterans' love of Russia, the army, and their regiment and about the need for military solidarity. He wished Miller good health, strength, and success. Miller spoke as well, anticipating a stellar contribution from ROVS to Franco's military campaign. ROVS, Miller declared, had become a force to reckon with, and he had faith that White Russian military personnel would carry out their duty to the end.[107]

In November, ROVS contacted Franco's staff. For the next few weeks, little happened beyond the usual round of military balls and charity functions. On November 26, Plevitskaya performed at a gathering at the Society of Gallipolians to mark the publication of a book about the Kornilov Shock Regiment that Skoblin had authored.[108]

In December 1936, Franco's staff approved ROVS's proposal to send a group of its soldiers to fight for the Nationalists as volunteers in the Spanish Foreign Legion. Miller chose Skoblin to serve as one of his envoys, but Skoblin announced that he could not travel to Spain due to Plevitskaya's ill health. His NKVD handlers had ordered him to stay in France, where he would prove more useful.[109] Another ROVS officer and a friend of

Skoblin's, Captain Pyotr Savin, was tasked with planning and executing the journey of the ROVS detachment across the Pyrenees into Spain, eight men at a time. Despite the meticulous planning, no more than thirty-two volunteers, a smaller group than expected, crossed the Spanish border that January.[110] Many did not see fighting. At least three of them were killed, including General Anatoly Fok.

Skoblin most likely tipped off the French and alerted the Soviets in Spain about ROVS's impending arrival.[111] Miller chose not to expand the Spanish operation, partly because of this initial failure, but also because news about the illegal crossing leaked to the émigré press in Paris and to the French government. To worsen matters, the Soviets confiscated Fok's suitcase in Spain, and propagandists used the documents and letters inside it to paint the Whites in Europe as fascist spies.[112] The lackluster performance of ROVS volunteers in Spain weakened Miller's reputation, thus bolstering Skoblin's value as an NKVD asset.

There is strong evidence that Miller finally began to question Skoblin's loyalty to him in the second half of 1936. A combination of factors might have influenced his thinking: Skoblin's suspicious behavior around the Spanish operation, fallout from the Fedoseenko affair, the Finns' and Dobrovolsky's suspicions about a Soviet spy in Miller's circles, and negative assessments of Skoblin by a growing number of ROVS officers and other émigrés. As early as February 1936, the chair of NTSNP's branch in France, V. D. Poremsky, met with Miller about Skoblin's role in the Inner Line's shady activity. Miller told Poremsky that he lacked a basis for accusing Skoblin at the time.[113] But Miller now seemed less trusting of Skoblin. ROVS officials took note of Miller's changing attitude.[114] For instance, Shatilov claimed that several ROVS high commanders did not trust Skoblin by this point and that Miller had come to see him as disloyal and shifty. Even Skoblin himself admitted to Shatilov that his relations with Miller were deteriorating. Prince Sergei Trubetskoi considered Skoblin two-faced and untrustworthy and warned Miller of how he had provoked Miller and Turkul into conflict.[115] Other ROVS officers spread rumors about how the Skoblins were spending more money than they were earning, insinuating that they were on the Soviets' payroll.[116]

Whether Miller was more influenced by others' comments about Skoblin or by his direct contact with him, he took steps to weaken Skoblin's authority within ROVS. In December 1936, Miller dismissed him as his rapporteur with the Inner Line and told Vice Admiral Mikhail Kedrov that he might have been wrong to have trusted him.[117] In a December 28 letter to a ROVS official named Lieutenant Mishutushkin, Miller said that all questions related to the Inner Line needed to be addressed to him directly.[118] Miller took it upon himself to appoint two new officers to head the Kornilov unit stationed in Finland. Learning of Miller's abrupt move, Skoblin, the regiment's actual commander, wrote Dobrovolsky in January 1937 to instruct his soldiers not to subordinate themselves to Miller and to transfer back under Skoblin's direct command.[119]

With all this brewing in Western Europe, Skoblin may also have embroiled himself in one of the most notorious episodes in the history of Stalinist repression. In the USSR, the Great Terror, which began in 1936, reached its peak in 1937. Stalin, who had long been jealous and resentful of Red Army marshal Mikhail Tukhachevsky's military expertise and authority, targeted him and other top Red Army officers at this time for several reasons, but one in particular stands out: the dictator's goal to eliminate all potential political rivals in the lead-up to a seemingly inevitable war with Germany.[120] There is a scholarly near consensus that Tukhachevsky was not plotting against Stalin in any way, and certainly not working with fellow officers to overthrow him. However, as early as the summer of 1936, Stalin began using his henchmen in the NKVD to build such a case against him.

Skoblin may have played a minor role in Stalin's anti-Tukhachevsky plot, although this has not been fully substantiated. The primary evidence of Skoblin's involvement originates from an article in the October 27, 1938, issue of the Nazi newspaper *Deutsche Wehr* (*The German Army*), supplemented by the 1939 memoirs of Soviet intelligence officer and defector Walter Krivitsky and the memoirs of two German foreign intelligence officials, Wilhelm Höttl and Walter Schellenberg.[121] Unfortunately, no corroborating proof has been unearthed from Soviet or German archives. In discussing this vast and complex subject, this chapter will confine itself to what can most plausibly be said about Skoblin's alleged role in it.[122]

Several accounts claim that, in December 1936 or January 1937, Skoblin traveled to Berlin, where he secretly met with Reinhard Heydrich, head of the Nazi Party's intelligence and security service, the Sicherheitsdienst (SD). Skoblin is said to have given Heydrich information indicating that Tukhachevsky and other Red Army generals were planning a coup against Stalin, in conjunction with members of the German High Command. If Skoblin was an SD agent, as some authors have assumed, or was simply viewed as a Russian émigré with proven German sympathies (because of his close ties to the Guchkov circle), then he would have had some credibility with Heydrich, who viewed the German High Command as one of the SD's organizational rivals and tended to suspect the worst from its members. Kurt Jahnke, an SD intelligence analyst, warned Heydrich that Skoblin was likely an NKVD agent whose task was to plant disinformation in order to harm the reputation of the German High Command or to encourage Nazi intelligence to fabricate its own evidence against Tukhachevsky and other Soviet Red Army generals.[123] Heydrich did not trust Jahnke, though, and passed on Skoblin's information to Heinrich Himmler, head of the Schutzstaffel (SS), and directly to Hitler.

Sometime before March, Hitler—apparently deciding that it was in Germany's interest to discredit Tukhachevsky, regardless of what Stalin intended—reportedly authorized Heydrich to fabricate documents to support the theory that Tukhachevsky and German army leaders were participating in an anti-Stalin coup. Several authors assume that Skoblin helped in the fabrication process in March or April 1937, but this part seems unlikely; the SD had its own expert forgers and a copy of Tukhachevsky's genuine signature.[124] The fake dossier, sometimes called "the Red File," was reportedly completed within a week. Its contents have never been officially unveiled, if they existed at all.[125] Some authors assume that Skoblin played a role in transferring the file to the Soviets; but, again, we have no evidence of this beyond Krivitsky's word, and it seems unlikely.[126] According to some authors, including Krivitsky, General Miller knew about Skoblin's participation in the Tukhachevsky affair and the existence of the Red File, although there is nothing to support this claim.

In another version of the Tukhachevsky affair, this one involving French authorities, Skoblin also appears to have played a role.[127] In March 1937, the Soviet ambassador to France, Vladimir Potemkin, sent a telegram to Stalin and other top Soviet officials in Moscow, describing a recent meeting with French war minister Édouard Daladier, a center-left politician. Daladier told Potemkin that he had received word from the War Ministry about an impending German-backed military coup by top Red Army personnel against Stalin's regime. The sources included someone from "Russian émigré circles," a potential reference to Skoblin.

What is undoubtedly true is that Stalin and his new NKVD chief, Nikolai Yezhov, had independently amassed what they assumed was enough false evidence—from the torture of witnesses and the accused themselves—to substantiate their grounds for convicting Tukhachevsky and seven other generals of treason. The purpose of the alleged Red File, then, may have been as a kind of fallback, in case Stalin ever felt the need to explain the convictions to Western governments that were, for the moment, allied to the USSR. There is no evidence that the Red File's contents were used at the June 11 Tukhachevsky trial, which was closed to the public and amounted to summary justice at its worst. Between 1937 and 1939, thousands more officers died in Stalin's purge of the Red Army. Among the victims was Skoblin's oldest brother, Vladimir.[128]

★ ★ ★

In early 1937, while Skoblin was preoccupied with his provocateur duties inside ROVS and—if the above account is to be believed—the unfolding Tukhachevsky affair, Plevitskaya was busy arranging concerts and performing in them. On February 6, she and other artists performed at a ball sponsored by the Union of Russian Pilots. Later that month, she invited writer Ivan Bunin to take part in a celebration of the Kornilov Regiment.[129] Bunin, an opponent of Bolshevism, left Russia in 1920 and settled in Paris, winning the Nobel Prize for Literature in 1933. Although they were not friends, Plevitskaya and Bunin shared a love for the Russian countryside and saw each other on occasion in Paris. On February 21, he joined her in celebrating the Kornilov Regiment at the Society of Gallipolians, together with Miller, Skoblin, and other White Army veterans.

At events like the February 21 Kornilov ball, conflicts within ROVS were kept out of sight. But in letters from around this time, they were kept fully in view, with the focus largely on Miller and Skoblin. On February 14, in a letter to General Kussonsky in Paris, General von Lampe, writing from Berlin, spoke of a growing schism between Miller and Skoblin, largely provoked by Skoblin's Inner Line maneuverings.[130] Four days later, Kussonsky wrote Dobrovolsky to inform him that there had not been a complete break between the two men. He did admit, however, that Skoblin felt let down by some of Miller's personnel decisions. Skoblin also opposed General Vladimir Vitkovsky's leadership of the First Department and seemed to be forming a new faction with Turkul.[131] (In 1936, Turkul was expelled from ROVS after forming a profascist organization, the Russian National Union of War Veterans. The NKVD instructed Skoblin to seek Turkul's readmission to ROVS in an effort to sow more division within the group; his efforts on Turkul's behalf, though, caused senior officers to resent him even more.[132])

Did Skoblin intentionally publicize his disagreements with Miller in late 1936 and the first half of 1937 to provoke just this kind of response from other ROVS members—and if so, why, especially when his NKVD handlers had ordered him to continue cultivating Miller's trust? Perhaps Skoblin was maneuvering to gain favor with more ROVS members and to persuade them that Miller should step down and let him—or possibly Shatilov—take over. It appears from another letter that Colonel Gregory Troshin, one of Skoblin's close confidants, thought Miller should resign.[133] Since the Generals' Revolt in 1934, ROVS members who did not like Miller's governing style felt increasingly freer to express their opposition to him, and Skoblin capitalized on this vulnerability.

Despite Miller's recent decisions to curtail Skoblin's official capacities within ROVS, he still relied on Skoblin to carry out secret operations. In April 1937, he authorized Skoblin to plan more infiltrations of ROVS agents into the USSR via Finland.[134] Miller may have regretted his decision, however. In a letter to Abramov, Miller criticized Skoblin for organizing the infiltrations his way rather than following Miller's suggestions and those made by ROVS's Finnish contacts.[135]

By mid-1937, more ROVS officers were expressing concerns about Skoblin. In a June 4 letter from Colonel Sergei Matsylev, secretary of ROVS's First Department and commander of the Paris detachment of the Alexeevsky Infantry Regiment, to Major General Mikhail Zinkevich, commander of the Alexeevsky Infantry Regiment, the former complained how hard it was to decipher Skoblin's behavior. He also noted that Miller was viewing Skoblin more critically.[136] In late June 1937, even Turkul voiced his growing suspicions, mentioning to a Berlin acquaintance that Skoblin might have intrigued against him. Skoblin had recently invited Turkul and his wife on a drive to Finland to see the Valaam Russian Orthodox Monastery, but Turkul, feeling threatened, declined. Turkul later claimed that, even earlier in 1937, he had begun to assume that Skoblin was serving the Bolsheviks and maneuvering a takeover of the ROVS leadership on their behalf.[137]

French authorities continued to monitor the Skoblins in the summer of 1937. One informant reported that the Skoblins visited Vichy in the second half of July and stayed in the Hôtel des Lilas.[138] Two other Russian émigrés, Count Aleksei Ignatieff, an ex-general in the Russian Imperial Army, and his wife, former ballerina Natalya Ignatieff-Troukhanova, happened to be staying there at the same time. Ignatieff-Troukhanova and Plevitskaya were known acquaintances.[139] The couples met in Vichy to talk business, and Ignatieff may have even taken part in Miller's kidnapping plot.[140] Ignatieff had been living in France since before the Bolshevik Revolution, first as a representative of the Imperial Army, but by the 1920s as a trade representative for the Soviets. He and Ignatieff-Troukhanova returned to the USSR for good later in 1937.

Edmund Plevitsky and his second wife stayed with the Skoblins at their Ozoir house during the summer of 1937.[141] In an interview he gave days after the Miller kidnapping, Plevitsky swore that he did not think that Plevitskaya was tied to Miller's disappearance or that rumored plans for a concert tour of the USSR were true. But Plevitsky did suspect that Skoblin had been involved in some kind of clandestine activity. He often joined the Skoblins during their drives into Paris, and he had noticed how Skoblin met with people who were not White Russian veterans. Plevitsky and Plevitskaya would wait for him in cafés and cinemas, and he never heard Plevitskaya question Skoblin about his work. Plevitskaya, however, did tell Plevitsky that she feared for Skoblin's life and that, if something terrible ever happened to him, her desire for life would die with him.

Also during the summer of 1937, it appears that Plevitskaya and Skoblin intensified their effort to discredit senior members of ROVS, including Miller.[142] Plevitskaya discussed with members of the Society of Gallipolians how she wanted to see Miller replaced as head of ROVS by a more activist leader.[143] She allegedly told some of them, "Kolenka thinks the same way I do. And if you prefer to watch ROVS turn into an old folks' home, then don't complain."[144] She was also overheard saying at a Society of Gallipolians banquet that Shatilov should replace Miller as the head of ROVS.[145]

During Plevitskaya's trial, the prosecution made good use of such witness testimony and letters to tie her to Miller's kidnapping circumstantially. Evidence of this sort demonstrated that Plevitskaya was aware of Skoblin's ROVS work, was almost always at his side, had exerted a strong influence over him, and sometimes publicly expressed her political opinions. In other words, she was politically aware and involved in Skoblin's business, despite her protestations that she was ignorant of politics and knew little about her husband's work. In an undated letter, Miller told Plevitskaya in plain terms that "it is time to end the intrigues and dedicate ourselves to the struggle against the Bolsheviks."[146] In a letter to Plevitskaya on January 5, 1937, General Abramov spoke of her and Skoblin's open opposition to Miller's rule: "We agree that he has many faults, but who would do better than he does?" he asked.[147]

Even more intriguing are two letters from Boris Solonevich to Plevitskaya, written during the first half of September 1937. Boris Solonevich and his brother Ivan were profascist émigré journalists who advocated for more anti-Soviet activism; they allegedly escaped from a Soviet prison to Finland in 1934 and then moved to Bulgaria. Many ROVS members, including Generals Abramov and Zinkevich, suspected them of being Soviet provocateurs because of their strong criticisms of the ROVS leadership.[148] French and Finnish intelligence also suspected that Boris was a Soviet agent. The language in Boris's letters to Plevitskaya was cryptic. His final words to her included a reference to Caesar's crossing of the Rubicon and his joyful anticipation of Plevitskaya's visit to Brussels, where he was then residing, later that month.[149] But she would never travel there again. Her and Skoblin's plans, which had seemed so well crafted, would soon collapse—and their double life together unraveled within hours.

7

THE KIDNAPPING
OF GENERAL MILLER

In 1937, during the height of the Great Terror, the NKVD targeted certain Russian émigrés for special operations. Given his stature among White officers, Evgeny Miller was an obvious candidate. The NKVD's chief of operations in Spain at the time, Alexander Orlov, who defected to the West in 1938, claimed that Miller's kidnapping was the idea of NKVD head Nikolai Yezhov. Yezhov wanted to show Stalin that, contrary to what had happened during the Kutepov operation, his team could capture a White Russian general and bring him back to Moscow alive.[1]

By now, Skoblin, Plevitskaya, and others had passed the NKVD enough information to convince Stalin that Miller and ROVS were planning new anti-Soviet plots and were conspiring to work with the Nazis in an eventual war with the USSR. The NKVD learned through Skoblin and other operatives that ROVS had sent volunteers to fight alongside General Franco, the USSR's enemy in the Spanish Civil War. The Soviets also knew that Miller had initiated the training of cadres for partisan fighting in the rear of the Red Army in the event of war with the USSR.[2] A June 1937 NKVD report outlining how ROVS and the Japanese intelligence service had aided an underground anti-Soviet cell in a failed attempt to seize power in Western Siberia may have further convinced Yezhov and Stalin that the time was right to kidnap Miller.[3]

There is some evidence that part of the reason for the kidnapping was to replace Miller with Skoblin as head of ROVS. However, the Soviets must have known that eliminating Ded—"Grandpa," the NKVD's code name for Miller in secret documents—would not guarantee their man's appointment.[4] Miller did not consider Skoblin his heir apparent, and other senior ROVS officials already suspected Skoblin of treachery.

General Evgeny Miller, circa 1934

As it turned out, Skoblin's cover was blown only hours after completing his task in the Miller kidnapping, so he never had the opportunity to replace Miller, and Plevitskaya's subsequent arrest and prosecution were unexpected blows to the Soviets as well. But the plot succeeded in two major ways: the NKVD apprehended its target and brought him back alive, and Miller's capture shattered ROVS and the White movement. As NKVD official Pavel Sudoplatov wrote, "eliminating Miller disrupted his organization of czarist officers and effectively prevented them from collaborating with the Germans against us."[5]

Information about the earliest days of the planning process comes from two sources: the NKVD operatives and defectors Alexander Orlov and Walter Krivitsky. As with all intelligence-related memoirs, their accounts must be read with skepticism, and neither man informs us fully as to what actually happened. Orlov claimed to have learned that Yezhov and Sergei Shpigelglas, deputy head of the NKVD's Foreign Department (the INO) and the plan's chief executor, argued beforehand over details, such as where Miller should be abducted. Yezhov's proposal prevailed: Miller was to be lured into a building in a quiet neighborhood on the outskirts of Paris, drugged, and shipped to the USSR.[6]

Krivitsky wrote that, in December 1936, while stationed in Holland, he received a message on microfilm from Abram Slutsky, Artur Artuzov's successor as head of the INO, ordering him to choose two agents who could impersonate German officers. In this same message, Slutsky required Krivitsky to meet him in Paris two days later.[7] At the meeting, Krivitsky balked at having to sacrifice two of his operatives for a job in Paris whose purpose remained a mystery to him, but Slutsky reassured him that the new case was of "colossal importance."[8] Krivitsky claimed to have met with Shpigelglas in July in Paris to finalize arrangements. Even so, the purpose of the operation remained unknown to him until he, like nearly everyone else, read about it in newspapers the day after the kidnapping.[9]

The principal operatives on Shpigelglas's team included Georgy Kosenko (alias Kislov)—the NKVD resident in the Soviet embassy in Paris, serving under diplomatic cover as vice counsel general—and two INO operatives, Mikhail Grigoriev (alias Alexandrov) and Veniamin Grazhul (alias Beletsky).[10] Stanislav Glinsky, an INO officer in Paris working under the name of V. V. Smirnov, may have helped with early planning, but he was recalled to Moscow in August 1937 and executed in December 1937.[11] According to Orlov, Kosenko and Shpigelglas jointly ran the operation, and Grazhul (Beletsky) and an embassy chauffeur named Dolgorukov took part, as did the Skoblins.[12] Mireille Abbiate, who had bugged Miller's apartment in 1934, was also assigned to the kidnapping.[13] Lastly, Yakov Serebriansky, the longtime head of the Administration for Special Tasks, had a hand in the planning.[14]

Shpigelglas probably informed Skoblin about his role in the operation—to lure Miller to the place of his abduction—a few weeks in advance and coached his every move. Skoblin was instructed to speak with Miller sometime earlier in September, proposing to schedule—on the 22nd—a secret meeting, supposedly with two representatives of the German government. This was to be the bait. Skoblin assured Miller that the meeting stood a good chance of leading to cooperation between ROVS and the German General Staff, and he extracted Miller's promise to tell no one else about the meeting.[15] Miller had no security guard at the time, and Skoblin offered to accompany him.[16] Recall that Skoblin, ostensibly on Miller's behalf, had spent several years cultivating closer ties with the Nazis, so it is not surprising that Miller chose to attend the meeting, despite receiving few details about it.

How much, in fact, did Plevitskaya know in advance about the plan to abduct Miller? The available sources give no clear answer, but the most logical assumption is that she knew at a minimum that a major operation would unfold on the 22nd.[17] While it is conceivable that Skoblin was ordered to shield his full purpose from Plevitskaya in order to keep security as tight as possible, the two were a well-established team, and she was likely aware not just of the plot's existence and date, but also its target.

Few Paris participants would have been fully apprised of every detail due to the time-honored practice of compartmentalization, according to which intelligence handlers protect complex operations by telling individual agents no more than what they specifically need to know to play their part. Plevitskaya had a supporting role in the Miller operation, so she did not need to know everything. Moreover, the kidnapping was a highly sensitive matter, politically speaking. The Soviets and the French had been formally allied since 1935, and the Stalin regime did not want even the slightest hint about the operation leaking out. Still stung by the Kutepov abduction, French officials, according to one source, "had warned Moscow that they would break off diplomatic relations with the USSR if Soviet agents perpetrated another murder on French soil."[18] Stalin preferred to keep French attention fixed on the USSR's great public relations coup that year: the immense popularity of the Soviet Pavilion at the 1937 Paris International Exhibition.[19] The Soviets wanted the French to admire their achievements in industrialization, aviation, and literacy—not to learn of their plot to kidnap another White Russian general. In any event, Plevitskaya can safely be considered complicit in the Miller abduction, but also ignorant of many of its details.

In the weeks before the kidnapping, Shpigelglas worked with Skoblin to craft his alibi in case police ever suspected him of involvement. He also briefed Plevitskaya on her role in supporting it.[20] According to Orlov, Shpigelglas advised the couple "to see as many people as possible during that day and to try to narrow down the fateful hour and ten or twenty minutes required to drive General Miller to the villa and to return back to downtown Paris."[21] The places that Skoblin and Plevitskaya visited that day were chosen precisely so they would be noticed and therefore have people to vouch for their whereabouts.

Along with coordinating his activities for the day with Plevitskaya, Skoblin prepared his alibi in at least one other way. He insisted that General Kornilov's daughter, Natalya Kornilov-Chaperon, who came from Brussels to attend the September 20 celebration of her deceased father's regiment, return home on the 2:15 p.m. train on September 22, instead of on a later train, as she had originally planned.[22] Skoblin would bid farewell to her at the station.

As the days counted down, Skoblin and Plevitskaya strove to act as if everything was normal. They took their final trip abroad, to Yugoslavia, in early September. Russian journalist Alexander Miakin met Plevitskaya for lunch in a Belgrade restaurant at this time and noticed that she was nervous.[23] The singer reminisced about Russia, waxing nostalgic about her years of prosperity and fame. She mentioned to Miakin that someone in Prague had recently proposed that she return to the USSR. Then Skoblin entered the restaurant and interrupted her, saying that they needed to board their train. She bid farewell to Miakin and vowed to return soon to Belgrade. Shortly after returning to Paris, Skoblin dropped by the Banque Internationale, where he had accounts; G. I. Shulman, the bank manager, recalled Skoblin's conspicuously telling him that Hitler would save Russia.[24]

With the 22nd drawing nearer, Skoblin and Plevitskaya attended various gatherings with Miller and other ROVS officers in Paris. The Skoblins' plan called for them to stay in Paris from Sunday, September 19, to Wednesday, September 22.[25] On September 18, the Skoblins were seen in a café with Miller and two other men. Waiters later testified that they had heard Skoblin speaking of preparations for a leave of absence. He referred to the sale of his house and his possessions.[26] This may indicate that the NKVD had instructed the Skoblins to leave for the USSR shortly after Miller's kidnapping and that they were making the necessary arrangements.

Despite mounting evidence of Skoblin's perfidy, Miller remained skeptical about his associates' criticism of the younger general. Shortly before the kidnapping, at a late-night gathering at the Society of Gallipolians, Colonel Sergei Matsylev, secretary of ROVS's First Department, overheard a conversation between Skoblin and other veterans. Skoblin was excoriating Miller and other older generals for concentrating power in their own hands. Matsylev reported to Miller what Skoblin had said, but Miller dismissed it as drunken talk not worthy of scrutiny. Still, Miller admitted that Skoblin should be observed more closely, and he recalled General Dobrovolsky's warning from Finland about a possible Soviet spy in his circle.[27] Also, a delegation of émigré youth from the NSNP (the former NTSNP) had recently warned Miller that Skoblin and Plevitskaya were Soviet spies. Miller may have suspected Skoblin of treachery by this point but wished to make no formal accusation against his friend until he had sufficient evidence—and so, yet again, he dismissed all assertions of wrongdoing on Skoblin's part.[28]

September 19 would mark the last time Skoblin attended a White Russian military event—and the last time Plevitskaya performed in a concert. In the morning, the couple attended a service at the Alexander Nevsky Cathedral. In the afternoon, at the Society of Gallipolians, Skoblin hosted a jubilee banquet in honor of the twentieth anniversary of the Kornilov Regiment. Generals Miller, Denikin, and Skoblin spoke. Skoblin drove the

Millers back to their apartment after the banquet. Natalya, Miller's wife, later noted that Skoblin seemed uncharacteristically nervous that day and even forgot his coat.[29] But she did not suspect anything was amiss and still regarded the Skoblins as her and her husband's close friends. "In the days leading up to the Kornilov Regiment celebration," she recalled, General Miller "read much about the civil war in southern Russia, and he fully admired Skoblin's exceptional courage there."[30]

At around 6:00 a.m. on Monday, September 20, the Skoblins saw Max and Mirra Eitingon off at the Lyon train station, from which the Eitingons were traveling to Florence. Between February and September, Mirra had been staying with her sister and brother-in-law, Leonid Raigorodsky, in their Paris apartment. Then, in September, Mirra moved to be with Max in the George V Hotel on rue Georges Sands—suspiciously close to the building where Miller would soon be kidnapped.[31] At around 4:00 p.m. on September 20, Skoblin met alone with General Turkul, who later testified that they spoke about events in the USSR and the state of the Red Army.[32]

On the morning of Wednesday, September 22, General Miller did not tell Natalya about the meeting he had scheduled with Skoblin. This was not out of the ordinary. Miller and his family did not normally talk about his work schedule. He told her only that he planned to order train tickets to

Headquarters of the Russian General Military Union, Rue du Colisée, Paris, 1937. Courtesy of Roger-Viollet/The Image Works

Yugoslavia that morning for his daughter-in-law and granddaughter.[33] He was not expected home for lunch, as he typically dined in his office.[34] At approximately 9:15 a.m., Miller left his residence on Avenue Jean-Baptiste Clément in Boulogne-Billancourt, a southwestern suburb of Paris. He caught a bus, arriving at ROVS headquarters on rue du Colisée at around 10:30 a.m.[35] Close to 11:30 a.m., Miller met with a journalist named Bormann from the newspaper *Vozrozhdenie.*

At around noon, Miller told ROVS vice president Pavel Kussonsky that he had a meeting at 12:30 p.m. "Don't think I'm crazy," he added, "but right now I'm giving you a note in a sealed envelope. I ask that you open it only in the event that you don't see me again. I'll return to rue du Colisée after lunch."[36] Miller smiled when he said this, and his tone was not somber, so Kussonsky did not interpret it as a serious threat to his boss's security. Kussonsky placed the envelope in a box on his desk and locked it. French investigator André Roches later maintained that this was the first time Miller had left behind a note as a precautionary measure.[37] However, a historian of Soviet intelligence posits that, ever aware of Kutepov's tragic fate, Miller had consistently written notes of this kind before conspiratorial meetings, burning them upon his safe return.[38] This theory is borne out by a Russian émigré who averred that Miller had once warned Kussonsky, "If you go to a suspicious meeting, always leave behind a note; this is what Kutepov should have done."[39]

Whatever the case, at around 12:10 p.m., Miller announced to his staff that he would not be returning to ROVS until 3:00 or 4:00 p.m. At 8:00 p.m., Miller was scheduled to chair a meeting of the Society of Northerners—veterans who had fought under him on the civil war's Arctic front—at the ROVS headquarters.[40] After that, he planned to return home.

On that same Wednesday morning, the Skoblins woke up in room 2 in the Hotel Pax at 143 rue Victor Hugo. The timing of everything that followed is crucial to understanding how Plevitskaya later tried but failed to use the couple's alibi to avoid prosecution. Sometime between 10:15 and 11:00 a.m., Captain Pyotr Grigul, concierge at the Society of Gallipolians and a close associate of Skoblin, spoke by phone with Skoblin about buying train tickets for Kornilov-Chaperon. Skoblin advised him to order the tickets directly from the station and to tell her that he would be there by 2:00 p.m. to escort her to the platform. Skoblin told Grigul that at 1:30 p.m. he would be at the society building's gates waiting to take him and his wife, Maria Kondratieva, to the station to see off Kornilov's daughter.[41]

At approximately 11:00 a.m., Skoblin left the hotel to retrieve his car, a Peugeot 302, from a nearby parking garage and returned to the hotel to pick up Plevitskaya. The Skoblins planned to have lunch at the Serdechny, a popular restaurant for Russian émigrés in their neighborhood, at 64 rue de Longchamp. The Skoblins arrived at the Serdechny around 11:30 a.m., finding it nearly empty.[42] They sat at the bar and ordered sandwiches. Plevitskaya sipped wine. They stayed no more than twenty minutes and carried out a bag with a sandwich and croissants.[43]

After leaving the Serdechny, Skoblin dropped off Plevitskaya at the Caroline dress shop located less than a mile away, at 3 avenue Victor Hugo. According to Nocin Epstein, the store manager, Plevitskaya entered Caroline's between 11:45 and 11:50 a.m.[44] Plevitskaya constantly reminded him that her husband was waiting for her in their car outside the shop. Epstein asked if she wanted to invite Skoblin in, but she demurred. The plan was for Plevitskaya to stay at Caroline's while Skoblin drove to his rendezvous point with Miller, about 2.5 miles from the dress shop, or perhaps a ten-minute drive depending on traffic. After conveying Miller to the abduction site, Skoblin was to proceed back to Caroline's. At this point came a fatal deviation from the plan. At 1:40 p.m., Plevitskaya left the shop after paying a deposit for a dress and a suit she had ordered, but she failed to find Skoblin, who was running late.[45] This would prove to be a catastrophic glitch. Epstein noticed that Plevitskaya, after leaving the shop, did not walk to Skoblin's car, but instead stayed on the sidewalk to flag down a taxi.[46]

In the meantime, Miller left his office at around 12:15 p.m., taking the metro to the Jasmin stop. This, like the Hotel Pax, the Serdechny, and Caroline's, was located in the sixteenth arrondissement, on the more residential western edge of the city, near the Bois de Boulonge. Numerous Russian émigrés, Soviet diplomats, and NKVD operatives lived in this neighborhood.[47] According to some reports, Miller, after reaching street level, walked approximately five minutes to the corner of Jasmin and Raffet Streets, his rendezvous point with Skoblin. However, a witness named Leon Pik claimed to have seen two men, both speaking Russian, near the exit to the Jasmin metro at 12:53 p.m. Pik later identified Skoblin from a photo, but not the other man, whose back had been turned to him.[48] The Paris police found no witnesses to place Miller on the corner of Raffet and Jasmin any earlier than 12:55 p.m., which means he was running late.[49] Whether Skoblin met Miller at the metro station or on the corner of Jasmin and Raffet, he drove the general to 41 Montmorency Boulevard, arriving at the site of Miller's abduction at close to 1:00 p.m.

The Soviet government had rented the building in question in March 1936 for 30,000 francs a year. Apart from its use for special Soviet intelligence operations, the building also housed a school for the children of

Soviet embassy personnel, although the school was on break at this time.[50] On the Raffet Street side, a tall stone wall with barbed wire on top ran alongside the building; a high gate at the Montmorency Boulevard entrance to the building obstructed the view of the courtyard and the main door.[51] It was an ideal place for an abduction.

There is now no doubt that the Soviets arranged and carried out Miller's kidnapping. An official history of Soviet intelligence, edited by Evgeny Primakov—a former head of the Russian Federation's Federal Security Service and prime minister during the 1990s—openly acknowledges the deed. The book tersely states that "on September 22, 1937, on Nikolai Skoblin's invitation, Miller went with him to a building in St. Cloud, outside Paris, where they were supposed to have met with German representatives. Inside the villa, an operative group of Chekists met [Miller]. The group seized him and placed him on a ship that left from Le Havre to the USSR."[52] Orlov presented a fuller account of Miller's abduction. According to Orlov's memoirs, Skoblin and Miller were greeted by the "Germans" (most likely Kosenko and Shpigelglas) immediately upon entering the building. Miller sat down in an armchair. Then,

> at that moment, General Skoblin stepped out of the room, while the embassy chauffeur Dolgorukov, a strong fellow of about thirty-five, and the little Dr. Beletsky [Grazhul] entered. Suddenly, without saying a single word, Kislov [Kosenko], Dolgorukov and Shpigelglas pounced on General Miller and, holding him fast, rolled up his sleeve and pinned his arm against the armchair, while Dr. Beletsky slipped a needle into the General's vein. General Skoblin later told his wife that, when a few minutes after he had stepped out of the living room he passed by the door which was left ajar, he caught sight of General Miller lying motionless on the floor.[53]

Close to twenty minutes elapsed between the moment Miller entered the building and when he left it. Miller's abductors put him in a crate and then placed it inside a Ford truck with Soviet embassy license plates. Witnesses passing over a nearby bridge saw the truck leave the compound at around 1:30 p.m.[54] The truck, with Kosenko, Dolgorukov, and Shpigelglas also on board, left Montmorency Boulevard and drove about 140 miles northwest to Le Havre. The time of its arrival was contested during Plevitskaya's trial; some said it was 3:00 p.m., while others, probably correctly, claimed that it reached the port closer to 4:00 p.m.[55] A Soviet ship was waiting for the truck and its valuable cargo. The *Maria Ulyanova*, named in honor of Vladimir Lenin's sister, left the dock early that evening, carrying

Miller and bound for Leningrad. With the exception of Dolgorukov, who drove the truck back to Paris, everyone who delivered Miller to Le Havre boarded the ship.

The *Maria Ulyanova* reached Leningrad on September 29, after taking a new route that avoided passing through Germany's Kiel Canal, where the Soviets worried that the Nazi authorities might board and search the ship. From Leningrad, Miller was transported overland to Moscow. He was imprisoned for nearly nineteen months in cell number 110 in an NKVD facility near the Lubyanka and given the pseudonym "Pyotr Vasilievich Ivanov" to maintain secrecy.[56] Many of the stories that circulated among Russian émigrés in Paris were false, but the chilling rumor that Miller had arrived in the USSR and was being interrogated by the NKVD turned out to be true.[57] Still, uncertainty about the details prevailed for a long time. Until the NKVD file containing materials about Miller was declassified in 1989, no one besides the top Soviet leadership and a handful of NKVD officers knew exactly what had become of him.

From his cell, Miller wrote Natalya, a number of his ROVS associates, and the Moscow head of the Russian Orthodox Church, but his letters were never posted. To Kussonsky, shortly after arriving in Moscow, Miller commented on his ordeal and on Skoblin:

> Today marks almost a week since I, saying goodbye just past noon, handed you a letter asking you to read it if I did not come back in a couple of hours. I had some subconscious premonition that N. V. S[koblin] was dragging me into something possibly dangerous. But of course nothing of what happened could I either envision or even imagine. I can't, of course, describe to you what happened . . . or how it happened, or where I am now, for a letter so written would doubtless have not been sent to you. I have not the slightest idea what happened in Paris and how it happened after I "was made unserviceable." I would like only to write you regarding some internal and personal matters, which have to do with other people entirely uninvolved in any sort of politics.[58]

In December 1937, the NKVD chief himself, Nikolai Yezhov, entered Miller's cell to interrogate the general. Otherwise, Miller saw only his immediate jailers. He desperately longed for news from his family and was particularly worried about Natalya's health. In July 1938, Miller, frustrated at being kept in complete ignorance about the outside world and his own impending fate, wrote Yezhov directly: "I earnestly ask you to examine my request in the given case from the perspective of humaneness and to end my moral torments, which become more intolerable with each passing day." Yezhov never replied. In November 1938, Yezhov ceded his position to Lavrenty Beria and soon suffered the same fate—execution by the secret police—that he had visited on so many thousands.

The NKVD may have been holding Miller in case an opportunity arose to use him as a pawn in the USSR's negotiations with Western powers or for potential propaganda purposes. It would have been a publicity coup for the Soviet Union to produce a signed statement from someone of Miller's stature in support of Stalin's regime.[59] However, a man of his convictions, Miller refused to the end to betray his beliefs or to succumb to the NKVD's pressure to perjure himself.

War preparations in Europe seem to have played a pivotal role in the general's fate. On May 4, 1939, Stalin appointed Vyacheslav Molotov as foreign minister in place of Maxim Litvinov, who was not only Jewish but was the principal architect of the USSR's policy of collective security against Nazism. This move is generally read as a signal of Stalin's emerging willingness to negotiate a nonaggression pact with Germany—which he did in the late summer. With this shift all but decided on in May, keeping Miller alive no longer served any purpose.

Therefore, on May 11, in a perfunctory secret trial, the Military Collegium of the Supreme Court of the USSR, under the chairmanship of Vasily Ulrikh, found Miller guilty of treason and sentenced him to death. The grounds for conviction included Miller's supposed involvement in civil war atrocities, his responsibility for pillaging carried out by White Guardists under his command in Northern Russia, and his organization of diversionary and terrorist acts against the USSR during the 1930s.[60] Stalin and other members of the Politburo had approved Miller's execution in advance, and the Military Collegium, which had already sentenced tens of thousands to death, blithely fulfilled these latest orders.[61]

The NKVD lost no time carrying out the sentence. That evening, Miller was escorted to an execution chamber—perhaps in the cellar of the Military Collegium building—and shot at 11:05 p.m. by NKVD commandant Vasily Blokhin, the executioner of thousands of Stalin's victims. The general's remains were cremated at 11:30 p.m.

To return to September 22, 1937, and the scene immediately following Miller's abduction, Skoblin left 41 Montmorency Boulevard at around 1:30 p.m. He had completed his main task but now needed to resume his "routine" day. He drove back to Caroline's to retrieve Plevitskaya, but discovered that she had left there only minutes before.[62] Figuring that she had made her own way to North Station, he drove there next, arriving a bit after 2:00 p.m.

Another crimp in Skoblin's supposedly seamless plan was that, due to his running late after Miller's kidnapping, he neglected to drive Grigul and Kondratieva to North Station as promised. The Griguls ended up taking a taxi. When they reached the platform, they found that the Skoblins were already standing there with Kornilov-Chaperon, her son Lavrik, and more of her friends.[63] Witnesses swore that the Skoblins had arrived five to ten minutes apart, with Plevitskaya getting there first.

To maintain Skoblin's alibi, the couple needed to pretend that they had arrived together in their car, and Skoblin wished in particular to avoid any impression that he had been with Miller. Plevitskaya claimed that their car had overheated and that she had gone ahead to the platform while her husband tinkered with the engine.[64] At this point, no one had any inkling yet that Miller had gone missing, but Skoblin could not be sure of this. ROVS officials went about their business without worrying about Miller's schedule—that is, until the evening.

Soon after the train for Brussels departed at 2:15 p.m., the Griguls and Skoblins headed to the Society of Gallipolians for tea, but they first dropped by Caroline's to search for a pair of gloves Plevitskaya had purposefully left behind.[65] The Society of Gallipolians was located at 81 rue de la Faisande-rie, less than a mile from the Hotel Pax. Plevitskaya was in no mood to linger over tea and complained of being tired. Skoblin's brother, Sergei, was there and quarreled with her. Exhausted and anxious, Plevitskaya told Skoblin, "I'm growing weary. Take me to the Pax."[66] The Skoblins left the Society of Gallipolians around 3:30 p.m. and returned to the hotel.

Sometime in the late afternoon, at home, Kussonsky thought about phoning ROVS to see whether Miller had returned between 3:00 and 4:00 p.m., as the general had intended. But he decided against it.[67] Nor had he opened Miller's note yet. Kussonsky's lack of concern worked in the Soviets' and the Skoblins' favor. It would also prompt French investigators and others with knowledge of the case to suspect that Kussonsky was a Soviet agent.[68]

Shortly after 4:00 p.m., Skoblin returned to the Society of Gallipolians. His next step now was to ask Grigul and Colonel Gregory Troshin to accompany him on an outing, ostensibly to drop by General Denikin's and General Miller's apartments to thank them personally for participating in the Kornilov Regiment celebrations on September 19.[69] The three men visited Denikin at his residence in Sèvres, a southwestern suburb of Paris, around 5:00 p.m., and Skoblin offered to accompany him to Brussels the following week.[70] Troshin later noted that Skoblin behaved in no way un-characteristically during their call on Denikin.[71]

When it came to visiting Miller in Boulogne-Billancourt, though, Grigul noticed hesitation on the part of Skoblin, who agreed to go only after Grigul and Troshin insisted.[72] According to Troshin, when the trio arrived, Natalya told them, "As always, he's not here yet."[73] Grigul, how-ever, recalled her saying that she was beginning to worry that her husband had not phoned, which he usually did when he was running late.[74] Also present, the Millers' daughter-in-law Olga thought Skoblin seemed unusu-ally nervous.[75] She mentioned that she and her daughter were leaving for Yugoslavia the next day. Skoblin, seated in an armchair, asked her, "You're still going to go anyway?" Olga, thinking this an odd thing to say, told him yes, that her father-in-law had bought them tickets. Skoblin cast his gaze downward to avoid looking Olga in the eye, then got up to leave and wished her a safe journey. Skoblin, Troshin, and Grigul returned to the Society of Gallipolians at around 5:30 p.m., and then Skoblin and Troshin drove to the Hotel Pax, arriving at 6:00 p.m.[76]

At the hotel, Skoblin suggested that he, Troshin, and Plevitskaya drive to Ozoir-la-Ferrière to check on their dogs and cats. At first, Plevitskaya refused, due to the late hour and her fatigue.[77] But Skoblin managed to convince her that the Russian monk who was supposed to be caring for their pets might have been too absorbed in prayer to carry out his duty. Troshin and the Skoblins stayed at the house for around a half hour. Marie Czhor, also helping to feed the animals, recalled the group arriving around 7:30 p.m. Czhor saw the Skoblins pack some clothes in a small suitcase before leaving.[78]

Skoblin, Plevitskaya, and Troshin drove back to Paris, where all three dined in the restaurant of the Society of Gallipolians. They discussed the Skoblins' search for a Paris apartment, as well as the doctor's appointment Plevitskaya had scheduled for the following afternoon.[79] Troshin returned home by around 9:30 p.m., where he remained for the night, while the Skoblins returned to their hotel.[80]

At the Hotel Pax, the Skoblins changed for bed and had two visitors. Skoblin's ex-brother-in-law Davydov, who had been staying at the same hotel, came by to pick up a cat that Plevitskaya was giving him and to say good-bye before taking a train to Brussels. Skoblin's brother Sergei was ac-companying Davydov to the train station and talked with his brother—as fate would have it, for the last time.[81]

Meanwhile, Vasily Asmolov, the caretaker of ROVS headquarters, was beginning to worry about Miller, who had not returned for the 8:00

p.m. meeting of the Society of Northerners.[82] At 8:30 p.m., Asmolov phoned Miller's apartment and found out that he had not come home for dinner and had not contacted his family at any point after leaving the apartment that morning.[83] Half an hour later, Natalya Miller, now panicking, phoned Grigul at the Society of Gallipolians to inquire about her husband; she then called Asmolov, urging him to contact the police. Instead, Asmolov—whom Kussonsky had not told about Miller's note—waited until 10:00 p.m. before sending a messenger, I. N. Popov, with a note to Kussonsky about Miller's absence. He also delayed phoning Admiral Kedrov, whom Natalya had already alerted.[84] Kussonsky opened Asmolov's note at 10:30 p.m., discussed its contents with three friends who were guests in his apartment, and then left for ROVS headquarters. When Kussonsky arrived, Asmolov, Popov, and Captain Pavel Sergeyev were waiting. Minutes later, Kussonsky finally opened Miller's note. It read,

> I have a meeting at 12:30 p.m. with General Skoblin on the corner of Jasmin and Raffet Streets. He is to accompany me to a meeting with a German officer, Colonel Strohman, a military attaché in the Baltics, and with Werner, who is posted here at the German embassy. Both speak Russian well. The meeting was arranged on Skoblin's initiative. It may be a trap. To be on the safe side, I am leaving this note.
>
> General E. Miller
> 22 September 1937[85]

Miller's family, Kedrov, and French investigators later confirmed that the note was in Miller's handwriting, and although Plevitskaya's defense attorneys argued otherwise, the note was likely written by him, albeit in haste.[86] However, a serious question remains, particularly with respect to Kussonsky: why did he take so long to open Miller's note? Could he have planted it on the NKVD's behalf? If this were the case, then the Soviets would have intended for the note to persuade people that the meeting and the kidnapping that followed had been organized by the Germans and that Skoblin was a German spy. Was it a matter of convenient "forgetfulness" that caused Kussonsky not to open the note until later that night, when the *Maria Ulyanova* was far out to sea? According to a police witness and acquaintance, Kussonsky was widely known to abuse alcohol and, during the civil war, acquired the nickname "Zakusonsky," a play on *zakuski*, the Russian word for hors-d'oeuvres.[87] Perhaps he was home drinking that afternoon. Another theory, posed by Russian archivist Yuri Bugrov, was that Kussonsky (or General Shatilov) wrote the note on his own initiative to frame Skoblin, a rival for the ROVS leadership.[88] If Bugrov's theory is correct, then Kussonsky would have to have known in advance about Miller's 12:30 meeting, making him a Soviet collaborator. Purposeful or not, Kussonsky's neglect postponed the start of the French investigation for several crucial hours.

Whatever the case, Kussonsky acted distraught in the presence of his ROVS associates, including Kedrov, who arrived shortly after 11:00 p.m. with his wife. Kussonsky asked that Skoblin be sent for at once. Some thought that Skoblin might have left for Brussels by train that evening with other members of the Kornilov Regiment.[89] Sergeyev went to the station to confirm that he had not gone. Kussonsky now assumed that Skoblin was in Ozoir-la-Ferrière and ordered Asmolov to bring him back for questioning.[90] Of course, this was a fool's errand, as the couple was settling into bed at the hotel, less than two miles from ROVS headquarters. As of 11:00 p.m., Asmolov later said, he did not yet know about Miller's note.[91]

Grigul confirmed that Skoblin was at the Hotel Pax, and Sergei Matsylev was sent there to retrieve him. Matsylev arrived there at approximately 1:30 a.m. and knocked on the Skoblins' door.

Skoblin opened it halfway and asked, "Who's there?"

Matsylev identified himself and could tell that Skoblin was in his bedclothes and had apparently been sleeping. He told Skoblin that he needed to come to ROVS headquarters quickly and that they were concerned about General Miller.[92]

Skoblin answered, "Wait for me downstairs. I'll get dressed and come down."[93]

On the other side of the door, Plevitskaya overheard some of this conversation. Did she hear Matsylev mention Miller's disappearance? If not, she may have assumed this was the reason Skoblin was being summoned. She later reported to investigators that Skoblin, in his rush, did not ask Matsylev any questions at the time. "My husband barely responded to me because Mr. Matsylev pressured him to get dressed quickly," she said.[94] Plevitskaya also told investigators that Skoblin left that night without taking much money, but she did not know whether he had a passport on him. In addition, she told investigators that Skoblin changed into a gray suit and walked out of the room without taking his wallet.[95] Clearly, Skoblin did not know he was leaving the hotel for good.

Matsylev waited downstairs for five minutes before Skoblin appeared carrying a black coat.[96] They took a taxi to ROVS. According to Matsylev, Skoblin, once in the taxi, asked what had happened. Not knowing about Miller's note yet, Matsylev had little to add and noticed that Skoblin did not appear shaken.[97] At around 2:00 a.m., Matsylev returned to ROVS with Skoblin. When they entered the building, the staircase was dark.[98] The light bulb had burned out—or had been removed.

Skoblin entered Kussonsky's office where Kedrov was waiting, while Matsylev sat down in the adjoining room.[99] "What happened?" Skoblin inquired.

"We're worried about General Miller's whereabouts," answered Kedrov. "But before we report the matter to the police, we decided to clarify first what you know, given our information that you should have seen him around noon today." Kussonsky and Kedrov proceeded to ask Skoblin questions related to Miller's whereabouts, and Skoblin became increasingly irritated. In response to their question about when he saw Miller earlier in the day, Skoblin answered quietly and calmly, "Today I did not see General Miller. I saw him last yesterday."

"Think hard," urged Kedrov, "about the rendezvous you had with General Miller on the corner of Raffet and Jasmin streets at 12:30 p.m."

"Raffet Street, Jasmin Street, what strange names," Skoblin said. "I don't know these streets." Kedrov was surprised that Skoblin had not heard of these streets, for the latter often drove around Paris.

Then, placing a hand on his forehead, as if struggling to recall the events of the past afternoon, Skoblin said, "Yes, at 12:30 p.m. I was with my wife at the Serdechny, and at 4:00 p.m. I was at General Denikin's thanking him for attending our Kornilov celebration."

Kussonsky asked, "So you confirm that you had no meeting today with General Miller and that you did not arrange to meet him at 12:30 p.m. on the corner of Jasmin and Raffet Streets?"

"Nothing of the kind happened," Skoblin snapped.

It was now around 2:15 a.m. Kedrov realized that they were losing time questioning Skoblin. "Well," he proposed, "let's go to the police and give them what we know about General Miller's disappearance." Skoblin seemed to acquiesce.

According to Matsylev, who had not yet learned of Miller's note or witnessed Skoblin's conversation with Kussonsky and Kedrov, his associates were not rushing to judge Skoblin a traitor. They still thought it possible that he had set up the meeting with Miller and the Germans but that he had not intended to go to the meeting and so did not know that it was a trap.[100]

However, what followed next soon changed their minds and sealed Skoblin's and Plevitskaya's fate.

8

SKOBLIN'S EXIT

The plan now was for Kedrov, Kussonsky, Matsylev, and Skoblin to report Miller's disappearance to the Paris police. Kedrov and Skoblin left Kussonsky's office and waited in the corridor while Kussonsky grabbed his coat. Then Kussonsky motioned to Kedrov to speak with him "for a minute" in his office. Kussonsky whispered to him nervously, "Didn't you find Skoblin's behavior strange?"[1] Kedrov agreed.

"Probably only a few seconds passed," Kedrov said, "but when Kussonsky and I walked out into the corridor, Skoblin wasn't there. I had a sinking feeling he'd fled."[2]

From his seat outside Kussonsky's office, Matsylev saw Skoblin open the door leading into the hallway and go down the stairs. "I was sure that he'd be waiting for us outside on the sidewalk, and the three of us [Kussonsky, Kedrov, and Matsylev] went down the unlit stairs," he said. "We were stunned when we looked on the street and didn't see Skoblin."[3]

Kedrov said what everyone now feared: "He ran away." But Matsylev, who still did not know yet about Miller's note, held out hope that Skoblin was standing on a nearby corner. He was disappointed within seconds when he saw only a deserted street veiled in fog.

Kedrov urged the group to go to the police station. But when Kussonsky showed Miller's note to Matsylev, the latter insisted that they first hunt for Skoblin at the Hotel Pax, where Matsylev believed the general might have gone to collect Plevitskaya and his wallet.[4] Kedrov was convinced that Skoblin had run off, but he agreed to accompany Matsylev to the hotel.

Sometime around 2:30 a.m., Matsylev appeared at the Hotel Pax to inquire after Skoblin. To his great distress, only Plevitskaya was there. Matsylev told her that Miller had disappeared and that he did not know where Skoblin was, since he had left without saying a word. "I thought first of all that my husband would go with the other Russian officers to look for General Miller," she later told the police.[5] She asked a barrage of questions and grew hysterical.

"What happened?" Plevitskaya inquired. "Where's Kolya? Where's General Miller? You should tell me everything. You took my husband, you know. What did you do with him? Do you suspect him of something? Answer me!" She was in such a panic she began stumbling over her words. "Tell me," she cried. "He's a proud man, capable of shooting himself."[6]

Matsylev tried to calm her. "Nadezhda Vasilievna," he said reassuringly, "I came for your husband in the hope that he was here, and it was completely unexpected when he abandoned us at the office and vanished. There's nothing more I can tell you, except that Admiral Kedrov and General Kussonsky are waiting for me downstairs, and we're going to the police to inform them of General Miller's disappearance."[7]

Matsylev told Plevitskaya that if Skoblin did return to the hotel, she should tell him to go to the police. Then Matsylev and his group headed for the police station, where they finally reported Miller's disappearance and the contents of his note. It was 3:15 a.m., fourteen hours after Miller's abduction.[8] Within a few hours, the Sûreté Nationale—France's national security police—alerted all frontier posts, ports, train stations, and airports to search for Miller. Skoblin was identified as a suspect. The police informed ROVS officials that they would begin questioning witnesses that morning. Plevitskaya, Natalya Miller, Troshin, Grigul, and others were on the list.[9]

When Kussonsky and Kedrov said that Skoblin should go with them to the police, he must have feared that they would surely detain and even arrest him. So, the second he could, he fled ROVS headquarters and, in the process, exposed himself as a traitor. Where did Skoblin go next? We know that he was carrying little to no money and that his car was not parked near the ROVS building. Trained in intelligence tradecraft, he should have designed escape routes ahead of time. Did he actually run down the stairs, as Matsylev, Kedrov, and Kussonsky had assumed, or did he escape somewhere else in the building first? The evidence points in two directions, but there is a strong likelihood that Skoblin first climbed up, not down.

At the time, most people assumed that Skoblin had immediately run outside and contacted his Soviet handlers.[10] The police began piecing together information from other witnesses about Skoblin's whereabouts on the early morning of September 23. According to these reports, after leaving ROVS headquarters at around 2:15 a.m., he headed for a garage on Pershing Boulevard, where his brother-in-law, Colonel Vorobiev, worked. The garage was approximately 1.5 miles from rue du Colisée.[11] He may have wanted Vorobiev to give him money and a lift somewhere. Not finding him, Skoblin went next to the apartment of an acquaintance, a former White Army captain named Alexander Krivosheev, who ran Kama Bookstore at 27 avenue de Villiers in the neighborhood of Neuilly-sur-Seine.[12] This was a journey of approximately 1.5 miles. Krivosheev was out, but his wife Maria was home.

According to Maria's testimony, Skoblin arrived at the Krivosheevs' door at around 2:45 a.m., looking pale and acting distraught. He told Maria that he had lost his wallet and asked her for 100 francs. She offered him 200 francs, which he accepted, along with a glass of water. After gulping down his drink, he left in haste. This was the last trace the French police ever caught of him—assuming, of course, that Krivosheeva spoke truthfully.

There is, in fact, room for doubt concerning Krivosheeva's account. According to Marina Grey, who interviewed her several decades after her encounter with Skoblin, the NKVD may have pressured her to fabricate this story.[13] Krivosheeva was a child when she and her mother left Russia, and it was rumored that her mother was connected to the Soviet secret police. Grey assumed that it was the NKVD, not Skoblin, who came knocking on her door that fateful morning, ordering her to report to the police that Skoblin had dropped by. This would have persuaded the police not to bother searching the building or interviewing the tenants at 29 rue du Colisée for more evidence about Skoblin. They would assume, as Skoblin's associates did, that he had sprinted down the stairs and outside the building at 2:15 a.m.

What makes Grey's theory about Krivosheeva compelling is the high probability that, instead of going downstairs, Skoblin dashed up one floor to Sergei Tretyakov's apartment. Recall that Tretyakov, a Soviet agent since 1929 and the owner of the building at 29 rue du Colisée, had been bugging ROVS headquarters since 1934. His apartment contained recording devices, and he transmitted the recordings to the Soviet embassy in Paris. His clandestine activities were unknown to French authorities during the Miller investigation. Only in August 1942, as reported in a German newspaper and the *New York Times*, did the story about Tretyakov become public knowledge.[14]

Tretyakov's cover was blown by a revelation from the other side of Europe. Shortly after their 1941 invasion of the USSR, the Germans learned from pilfered Soviet intelligence archives either in Smolensk or in Minsk that Tretyakov opposed the tsarist regime and had Bolshevik ties. In June 1942, while under interrogation—and likely torture—at Gestapo headquarters in German-occupied Paris, Tretyakov confessed to being a

Soviet spy. The Gestapo transferred him to Germany, where he was shot the following year. According to the *New York Times*, the Gestapo uncovered evidence that Tretyakov hid Skoblin in his apartment after Miller went missing.

While this may have been the case, there is nothing to say how long Skoblin might have been at Tretyakov's. His goal was not to return to the Hotel Pax, where Plevitskaya was a sitting duck, but to connect with his NKVD handlers. At this stage, the narrative branches in various possible directions.

NKVD defector Alexander Orlov, who did not mention Tretyakov's role, claimed that Skoblin visited the garage and the Krivosheevs' apartment first, and then called the Soviet embassy from a pay phone in a café.[15] In this version of the story, an NKVD operative named Sokolov met him at a metro station and drove him to the Soviet embassy on rue de Grenelle, where he remained in the secure NKVD headquarters for a month. Orlov noted that hiding an agent—particularly one fleeing from the police—in an embassy building countered Stalin's order not to involve Soviet diplomats in the Miller operation, and Yezhov wisely kept this information from the Soviet dictator. Before leaving the embassy, Orlov recalled, Skoblin was "asked to write a number of short undated letters for his wife containing a few encouraging words and expressions of love and devotion. Some of these letters must have been sent to her later when her case began to look bleak, in order to bolster up her morale and keep her from telling the truth about the role of Moscow in the kidnapping."[16]

Alternatively, Skoblin might have phoned his Soviet handlers from Tretyakov's apartment and been whisked off to rue de Grenelle or a safe house. No matter what the exact details of his exit from ROVS, Skoblin left the building at 29 rue du Colisée within hours, if not minutes, and NKVD operatives arranged for his departure from France.

Unsubstantiated rumors about Skoblin's fate flew wildly around Europe. He had been killed, his body thrown into the Seine, some said, although his body was never found.[17] According to a French weekly called *Gringoire*, the NKVD exfiltrated Skoblin on October 4, 1937, to Barcelona, a Soviet-controlled front in the Spanish Civil War, where he was stationed at an NKVD prison; the article's informants speculated that he had been liquidated there within days.[18] Others insisted that he was living in Leningrad under a pseudonym.[19] Elisabeth Poretsky, the widow of murdered NKVD defector Ignace Reiss, wrote that "Soviet ships were standing by in the harbour of Barcelona to take those who were needed to Moscow or to dispose at sea of those who were not."[20] In the opinion of émigré writer Victor Alexandrov, Skoblin left Spain for Odessa on board the Soviet ship *Kuban* and vanished.[21] Alexandrov even refers to a novel by revolutionary Marxist Victor Serge, *The Case of Comrade Tulayev*, which features a man like Skoblin (under the name Stern) who was poisoned on board a ship to Odessa and whose skeleton ended up on display in a Soviet anatomy laboratory.[22]

Although no one knows for certain, Skoblin was most likely killed by the NKVD less than a year after Miller's kidnapping. Skoblin had become a liability for the NKVD, and his many accomplishments for the agency could not compensate. His identity had been unexpectedly compromised by Miller's note and his decision to flee the scene, and his conduct had given the French authorities more reason to suspect the NKVD of organizing Miller's abduction. The Stalin regime and their allies abroad, including communist parties and media outlets, blamed the kidnapping on fascists and members of ROVS. The contents of Miller's note, ROVS's profascist reputation, ROVS's aid to Franco's Nationalists in Spain, and rumors of Skoblin's Nazi sympathies gave the Soviets ammunition. *Pravda*, the Soviet Communist Party's main newspaper, theorized on September 29 and September 30 that fascists had kidnapped Miller due to the general's lukewarm support for the Nazis and fascism in general. The Soviets particularly singled out Anton Turkul and Skoblin as possible plotters.[23] Their portrayal of Skoblin as a German agent would now prevent him from fulfilling his own goal of returning home and serving as an officer in the Red Army. It also signaled that his days were numbered.

The Great Terror engulfed even NKVD personnel, including agents and officers posted abroad. Stalin did not trust his secret police and assumed that many Soviet assets were double agents bent on treachery.[24] Nearly 6,000 out of 24,500 members of the NKVD's staff were purged during the Great Terror, although fewer than 200 were actually executed.[25] In the NKVD's Foreign Intelligence Department (the INO) alone, 60 percent of personnel were repressed in 1937 and 1938, including several illegals.[26] The INO's former head, Artur Artuzov, was arrested in May and executed in August 1937. The Soviets liquidated defectors, including Ignace Reiss in Switzerland in early September 1937, only a couple of weeks before Miller was kidnapped. At least four of those involved in the Miller operation—Abram Slutsky, Sergei Shpigelglas, Georgy Kosenko, and Mikhail Grigoriev—were arrested in 1938 and later killed.[27] Yezhov himself was arrested in 1939 and shot the following year.

Stalin used Spain's civil war as an occasion to eliminate his enemies on the right as well as the left, including illegals like Skoblin who were compromised.[28] The version of Skoblin's demise that appears in the official history of the Soviet secret police is that he reached Spain alive, only to die in Barcelona during a bombing raid by Franco's forces in late October 1937.[29] The assumption here is that the NKVD assigned Skoblin work in Spain, where he became just another casualty of war. Given the misfortune of other participants in the Miller kidnapping plot and Skoblin's exposure as a Soviet agent, however, this cut-and-dried explanation seems inadequate. As outlined below, the most likely scenario is that he was taken to Spain by the NKVD and killed there.

Several sources report that the NKVD evacuated Skoblin from France in a plane chartered by Alexander Orlov, the NKVD's chief of operations in Spain at the time.[30] Some Russian researchers have argued that Orlov, Pavel Sudoplatov, and Naum Eitingon killed Skoblin during the flight and then pushed his body out of the plane, presumably over a secluded, mountainous part of France or Spain.[31] Russian political scientist Nikolai Petrov bases this scenario on an NKVD telegram dated September 28, 1937, from Slutsky (alias Aleksei), the head of the INO, to Orlov (alias Schwed) and Yakov Serebriansky (alias Yasha), the head of the NKVD's Administration for Special Tasks. The telegram reads,

> Your plan is changing. The boss [Yezhov or Stalin] asks to make everything possible so that it goes cleanly. The operation should not have any traces. His wife [Plevitskaya] should remain certain that number 13 [Skoblin] is alive and is home [the USSR]. Aleksei.[32]

However, the telegram could just as easily have referred to a plan to kill Skoblin in Spain. According to Orlov's biographer, Boris Volodarsky, a former Soviet military intelligence officer, Orlov was tasked with eliminating Skoblin after he arrived in Spain.[33] Before completing his mission, Orlov first sequestered Skoblin in a mansion in Barcelona that housed the NKVD's station. There is no proof of exactly when or how Skoblin was murdered, but there is evidence that he was dead before mid-1938 and that Orlov had a hand in his murder. In a letter to Yezhov in July 1938, Orlov mentioned that he had FARMER's engraved ring.[34] "Possession of a man's ring," Volodarsky argues, "is a classic symbol of its former owner's untimely death" and is immediately understood by organized criminals and Chekists alike to represent a secret murder.[35] The cryptic reference to Skoblin's ring may have been Orlov's confirmation to Yezhov that his order had been carried out.

The final clue we have about Skoblin's fate provides no clear answer about his final disposition. It is a handwritten letter signed by Skoblin, dated

November 11, 1937. It was found in the Soviet secret police archives in the 1990s attached to documents concerning Miller.[36] The letter is addressed to an NKVD officer named Stakh and contains an appeal to help Plevitskaya:

Dear Comrade Stakh!

I take this opportunity to send you a letter and ask you to accept belated but most heartfelt congratulations on the twentieth anniversary of our Soviet Union.[37]

My heart is now filled with special pride, for at this juncture I belong, wholly and entirely, to the Soviet Union, and no longer do I feel the ambivalence that had artificially existed prior to September 22nd. Now I am perfectly free to tell everyone about my Great Leader Comrade Stalin and my Motherland—the Soviet Union.

Recently I had a chance here to leaf through some old magazines, and I came across this year's first issue of the *Bolshevik* monthly. It was with much interest that I read it all, but the article "Bolsheviks on the North Pole" made a particular impression upon me. At the end of that article they quote the Hero of the Soviet Union Vodopianov. When, before his flight, they asked him, "How will you fly over to the Pole, how will you land there? What if you crash—it's a long way back on foot!"—he answered: "If I crash, I will not walk on foot, because behind me I feel a force, a might: Comrade Stalin will not abandon a man!"

These words, said quietly but with an unbending faith, have had a strong influence on me, too. At present I remain firm, strong, and at peace, and I, too, believe that Comrade Stalin will not abandon a man. There was only one thing that made me sad, which was that on November 7, when all our multi-million-strong country celebrated the day, I could not have Vasenka [a diminutive form of Plevitskaya's patronymic] share my feeling about the great holiday.

Before I knew it, two more weeks had passed since your last visit. Nothing new has happened in my personal life. Being idle and bored, I have taken up Spanish, but knowing nothing about my Vasenka, I cannot give it my undivided attention.

Do you think that Georgy Nikolaevich [possibly Kosenko] should visit me now and work out certain steps concerning Vasenka directly?

I could have offered a number of suggestions of a psychological nature, which could be of enormous moral significance, given the almost two-month long imprisonment and the need to encourage her and, above all, to calm her down. I shake your hand firmly.

Yours sincerely—

[Skoblin's signature]

Assuming that this letter was actually written by Skoblin in November 1937, his comment that he was studying Spanish suggests that he was still in Spain. However, his reference to taking part in the recent national celebration of the twentieth anniversary of the Bolshevik Revolution suggests that he might have been in the USSR. It is plausible that the NKVD told Skoblin that he would be trained in Moscow and returned to Spain for operational work, which would have explained why he was learning Spanish. In addition, the "Georgy Nikolaevich" Skoblin referred to could have been Georgy Kosenko, who had reportedly boarded the *Maria Ulyanova* en route to Leningrad. Kosenko may have kept a low profile in Moscow for a few months before returning to his NKVD post in Paris, and Skoblin may have had occasional contact with him.

If Skoblin was living in the Moscow area, the NKVD would have kept him under close surveillance.[38] Most likely, he would have been confined to an NKVD-controlled facility in a Moscow suburb, as was the case with another NKVD agent, Sergei Efron, at around the same time. In several ways, Efron's and Skoblin's lives ran parallel to each other. Both were former White Army officers who emigrated to France after the Russian Civil War. Both were married to prominent artistic figures—Efron's wife was the poet Marina Tsvetaeva—and both were recruited by Soviet intelligence in 1930. They were both involved in NKVD operations in September 1937—the killing of Ignace Reiss, in Efron's case—that led to their untimely demise. A November 10, 1937, report by Slutsky and addressed to Yezhov acknowledged that several NKVD operatives would be awarded commendations for their participation in the recent Reiss and Miller operations: Orlov, Eitingon, Sudoplatov, Shpigelglas, Grigoriev, Kosenko, Grazhul, V. S. Pravdin (Roland Abiate, Mireille's brother), B. M. Afanasiev, A. L. Dolgorukov, and M. S. Arseniev.[39] Skoblin's and Efron's names were notably absent. The official Soviet version of Efron's fate mirrors that of Skoblin's: both were said to have disappeared in Spain sometime after September 1937.[40] And why award commendations to agents who had officially "disappeared"?

In actuality, Efron's final years were quite different. After arriving in the USSR by ship in October 1937, Efron was housed in an NKVD dacha in Bolshevo, a town outside of Moscow.[41] The NKVD arrested Efron in October 1939 and charged him with conspiring with Trotskyites against the Soviet regime; after being convicted by a Soviet military tribunal, Efron was shot and buried in October 1941 at an NKVD facility south of Moscow called Kommunarka.[42] The details of Efron's fate lend some support to the theory that Skoblin himself was brought to the USSR and murdered by the NKVD there.

Skoblin's November 1937 letter suggests that he felt confident and secure enough to ask his superiors to help Plevitskaya—his Vasenka—and to offer advice about how best to approach the matter and calm her nerves. It seems that at this point he had not yet discerned that Yezhov no longer valued him as an NKVD asset. The sentiments he expressed in his letter intimate that he still loved Plevitskaya, although he may also have worried that she might lose her resolve and start "singing" to the French authorities about her NKVD contacts in return for leniency.

On December 20, 1937, a ceremony in the Bolshoi Theater in Moscow marked the twentieth anniversary of the founding of the Soviet secret police. Stalin, Yezhov, and other top Soviet officials attended. Keynote speaker Anastas Mikoyan, people's commissar of the food industry, praised NKVD personnel for their hard work. "Their work is very onerous and strenuous, very strenuous," Mikoyan sympathized, "but I believe that, on the twentieth anniversary of their struggles, the members of the NKVD can be satisfied with their victories and with the fact that the nation they serve rewards them with its overwhelming love."[43]

This festive occasion, however, did not mark the end of the persecution of NKVD employees and Stalin's other enemies. An internal order issued shortly before the celebration noted that it was meant to "mobilize all Chekist members of the NKVD . . . for the struggle against all enemies of the Soviet nation. It should sharpen their gaze and increase the vigilance and dedication of all personnel of the Soviet intelligence service!"[44] A banner exclaiming "Long Live the NKVD!" hung over the crowd like the sword of Damocles.

Most likely, Skoblin was not present. With Skoblin out of commission, the NKVD still had plenty of other productive agents. Everyone was expendable. Which leads us back to the still unanswerable question of how he died. Seconds before Skoblin was murdered—whether it was in a plane, in Spain, or at an NKVD shooting range near Moscow—did he regret having fled ROVS headquarters? Did he feel guilty for having abandoned his wife? Plevitskaya never learned his fate. In her prison diary, she expressed her wish to be reunited with him. If she revealed her true sentiments in her diary, she continued to love and miss her husband, despite his having exited her life so abruptly.

9

CAGED NIGHTINGALE

On Thursday, September 23, French authorities were just beginning to investigate Miller's disappearance. The chief police investigator assigned to the case was André Roches. Roches created a special brigade and instructed main inspector Piguet to commence a preliminary inquiry, the initial phase of the investigation before a charge is laid against a suspect.[1] In France, special brigades are used in criminal cases of particular concern and complexity. In such an inquiry, police first prepare the ground for the interrogation of a potential suspect by collecting witness statements and evidence.

Anticipating that the inquiry would proceed to a full investigation of Miller's kidnapping, French authorities appointed an examining magistrate, responsible for supervising the investigation of the most serious felonies. Pierre Marchat, a forty-one-year-old former attorney, was chosen for this important role. Marchat was authorized to review the inquiry's findings, examine any suspects, and decide whether there were sufficient grounds to charge and detain anyone. Once the full "judicial" investigation began, he could call witnesses, issue arrest warrants, keep an accused person in police custody, appoint experts, and order searches and seizures of evidence.[2] After the testimonial and documentary evidence was compiled and placed in a dossier, Marchat's final task would be to write a report recommending whether or not the case should proceed to trial.

Meanwhile, at 5:00 a.m. on September 23, Plevitskaya was still alone in room 2 in the Hotel Pax, trying to devise her own strategy. She and Skoblin had carelessly neglected to plan for a worst-case scenario. Where was her husband? Because she did not know about Miller's note yet, she had no idea that Skoblin was the main suspect, although she knew that he had fled ROVS headquarters instead of going with his associates to the police. Plevitskaya must have assumed by now that Skoblin had contacted his NKVD handlers and that they might be trying to reach her. She had enough cash to flee Paris by train, but where could she go? She would have known that neither Skoblin nor the NKVD would come to the Hotel Pax, so she decided to set out for the Society of Gallipolians in search of news.

Before Plevitskaya left the hotel, though, police inspectors arrived at around 5:15 a.m.—together with Kedrov, Kussonsky, and Matsylev—to question her briefly. Matsylev served as her translator. The officers wanted to know her and Skoblin's whereabouts in the early afternoon of September 22 and whether she knew where he was now. This was the first time Plevitskaya used her prearranged alibi—offering times that conflicted with witness testimony. She and Skoblin, she said, had been at the Serdechny Restaurant between 12:15 and 12:45 p.m., had gone to Caroline's dress shop around 1:00 p.m., and had arrived *together* at North Station around 2:00 p.m. She expressed concern that her husband might be the target of a second attack. This seems like an attempt to persuade the police that Skoblin's decision to flee was motivated by a fear of becoming the next victim, not of being arrested as a conspirator. Kedrov found Plevitskaya's behavior suspicious and begged the police to follow her, but they were not authorized to do so at the time.[3] Plevitskaya was not yet a suspect.

Next, the inspectors went to the garage where Skoblin's car was parked and impounded it. They ran into Grigul there and questioned him. Matsylev saw Plevitskaya across the street from the garage, heading in the direction of the Society of Gallipolians, and noticed that she was constantly glancing around. Matsylev and Kedrov reported this to a police inspector, but according to Matsylev, "he obviously didn't see any significance in this, and Plevitskaya turned the corner and vanished from sight."[4] She was carrying a purse and dressed in a black skirt, a brown-and-black overcoat, a black hat, and black pumps. Her choice of pumps, which—as any woman knows—are uncomfortable to wear for long periods, suggests that she initially was not planning to walk very far. Perhaps she was hoping to find Skoblin or her NKVD contact within an hour or two. Before leaving the hotel, she had spoken with manager Jean Boyer, who noticed that she was crying and very distressed. She told him that Miller and Skoblin had vanished and that she was heading to the Society of Gallipolians.[5]

Plevitskaya intended to meet with Grigul at the Society. Around 8:00 a.m., she ended up speaking only with his wife, telling her that Skoblin had left the night before and had not returned.[6] Kondratieva told Plevitskaya that Grigul would be returning soon, but Plevitskaya said that she needed to see a doctor. This was Ivan Chekunov, who resided at 122 Murat Boulevard, around 2.5 miles from the Society of Gallipolians on rue de la Faisanderie.[7] At the Society of Gallipolians, Plevitskaya may also have learned that Skoblin was being viewed as a suspect in Miller's kidnapping.[8] If true, she would have panicked and felt even more desperate to locate her husband.

As it turned out, Plevitskaya did not reach Chekunov's apartment until that evening.[9] During the afternoon, some witnesses saw her on the balcony of a café near the Tuileries Garden, looking around, as though she were waiting for someone.[10] According to one account, she tried that afternoon to phone an NKVD contact several times, but failed.[11] (The NKVD clearly did not consider Plevitskaya a top priority, but she did not know this at the time.[12]) In a revealing sign of her guilt, Plevitskaya neglected to contact Natalya Miller, who had equal reason to feel distraught.

"I roamed around all day," Plevitskaya later told the police. "I don't know where exactly—the Champs-Élysées and nearby streets. I entered some cafés, but I don't know precisely which ones, just ones I passed by chance. That evening around 8:00 p.m., I felt very weak and went to see Dr. Chekunov. I stayed there an hour, and he gave me some medicine."[13]

When Plevitskaya arrived at Chekunov's apartment, she was crying and highly agitated. She asked if she could stay with him that night, but he refused and telephoned Leonid Raigorodsky, Mirra Eitingon's brother-in-law.[14] Chekunov's wife drove Plevitskaya to Raigorodsky's apartment at 6 Henri Paté Square, in the Passy-Auteuil neighborhood located between the Seine and the Bois de Boulogne. When Plevitskaya arrived, she cried out to Raigorodsky, "Someone's going to kill my husband."[15] Unbeknownst to them, sometime later on September 23, investigators decided they needed to question her further about Skoblin and ordered police officers to begin searching for her.

Raigorodsky told the police that, on the morning of September 24, he dropped off Plevitskaya at the Society of Gallipolians. However, he apparently neglected to let them know everything about his activities with Plevitskaya that morning. According to two accounts, Raigorodsky actually took Plevitskaya to see her NKVD contacts.[16] It is impossible to prove the accuracy of either story, but their implications are quite interesting. If true, it appears that the NKVD tried to assuage Plevitskaya's fears and give her hope that she would be cared for and would perhaps see Skoblin again. It is then possible that the Soviets persuaded Plevitskaya to resurface and go to the police, as a tactic meant to confuse the press and police into thinking that she and her husband were dupes.

After this alleged meeting with the NKVD, Plevitskaya arrived at the Society of Gallipolians at around 10:00 a.m. and located Grigul.[17] She told him that she had read in the paper that the police were searching for her. "What tie could my husband possibly have to this dark affair?" she asked.

"Nadezhda Vasilievna," Grigul answered, "you understand that General Miller's life and your husband's honor are at stake, and you were running off somewhere, missing all night."

Wiping away tears, Plevitskaya replied defensively, "You told the papers that I didn't stay anywhere, but roamed the streets all night!" She explained to him about going to see Dr. Chekunov and staying overnight with Raigorodsky and his wife, and stressed that they had urged her to go to the Society of Gallipolians and contact the police from there.

Next, Grigul phoned the nearest police station to tell them that Plevitskaya was there and to ask them for guidance. While he was on the phone, others gathered around Plevitskaya, including Skoblin's sister, Tamara Vorobieva. Vorobieva reproached Grigul and others for turning Plevitskaya away the day before, when she arrived there for news. "That's not true!" Plevitskaya interrupted her sister-in-law. "No one could turn me away. I left of my own accord."

This time, though, she could not escape. News about Miller's note and Skoblin's flight from ROVS had spread quickly throughout the émigré community. By September 24, a large number of Russians were already assuming that the Soviets had orchestrated Miller's abduction with Skoblin's help.[18] When Natalya Miller was first questioned by police, on the morning of September 23, she was shocked to learn that Skoblin was a suspect.[19] Once she found out more about the case, though, she changed her mind and lost her sympathy for the Skoblins. ROVS members accepted that Miller was either dead or outside France for good and quickly appointed Admiral Kedrov as acting ROVS president until General Abramov, Miller's chosen heir, could take command.

Within minutes of receiving Grigul's phone call, two police inspectors arrived and asked Plevitskaya to come with them to a police station for questioning "just" as a witness. Plevitskaya began to feel faint and grabbed Grigul by the hand. "Pyotr Yakovlevich, don't leave me. Take me there," she pleaded. Vorobieva and Grigul accompanied Plevitskaya in a police car to the station, which was located in the regional directorate of Paris's judicial police, at 36 Quai des Orfèvres, near Notre-Dame Cathedral.[20] Vorobieva's husband and Grigul's eighteen-year-old daughter Liuba followed in a second car. The police found that Plevitskaya had in her possession 7,500 francs, 50 U.S. dollars, and 50 British pounds, which was the equivalent of around 600 U.S. dollars at the time and not a small sum. At around noon, Marchat and the head of the police's criminal division, a man named Meyer, accompanied Plevitskaya to another building, where she was questioned at length by them and Roches. Liuba served as her translator.

When Plevitskaya first appeared at the police station, she acted with self-assurance and delivered what seemed to be a prepared statement about her and Skoblin's whereabouts on September 22. It ended with, "There, that's all."[21] Then she got up as if she had already received permission to leave. Roches informed her that they had not finished with her yet, and by 7:00 p.m., he and a prosecutor decided to hold her overnight for further examination. When their questions became more pointed, she began crying. The investigators suspected that she had prepared her statement, which consisted of ten or so stock phrases, and her timeline—and that she had received help.

Roches asked, "Why did Skoblin drop you off at the dress shop?" She answered, "He wanted to read the paper and didn't like the noise from the street, so he moved to a different spot."[22] Roches observed how Plevitskaya "did not think of referring to her loss of memory or to her lack of concern for the passage of time in her daily life."[23] Instead, she was intent on giving exact times of her and Skoblin's comings and goings that day. She said that it was typical for them to be together all day and for one to wait nearby while the other was in a shop or elsewhere.

For much of the day and into the night, and without a defense attorney present, Plevitskaya answered questions about her and Skoblin's whereabouts on September 22. She also responded to queries about their finances.[24] Plevitskaya said that her husband did not have salaried employment and that his main role was to act as her concert tour organizer. Each tour, she claimed, earned her 20,000 to 25,000 francs (her last tour, to Riga, actually netted her 15,000 francs), and she gave three or four of them a year. Plevitskaya told the police that she had a benefactor, Dr. Max Eitingon, who had last given her money in October 1936; her mention of Eitingon led the police and Russian émigrés to suspect that he was a Soviet operative. She also mentioned that she and Skoblin had received compensation for their 1935 car accident and that she had been paid for acting in a film.[25]

Sometime on the afternoon of September 24, Plevitskaya was required to confront two witnesses, Alexander Zarubin, a server at the Serdechny, and Nocin Epstein, the manager of Caroline's. Her alibi unraveled as the times she attested to clashed with those provided by the witnesses. Whereas Plevitskaya swore that she and Skoblin had left the restaurant at 12:30 p.m., Zarubin vowed that they had arrived around 11:00 a.m. and left before noon; he claimed to have remembered because no other customers had been in the restaurant when the Skoblins were there. Plevitskaya insisted that she could not have arrived at the Serdechny at 11:00 a.m., because Grigul had phoned her husband around that time, before the Skoblins had even left the hotel.[26]

Plevitskaya's testimony conflicted with Epstein's both chronologically and in terms of Skoblin's afternoon whereabouts. She stressed that Skoblin could not have met Miller at 12:30 p.m. because she and Skoblin were at that moment at the Serdechny, after which Skoblin waited for her outside the dress shop.[27] It is important to note that Plevitskaya signed a statement which affirmed that Skoblin, while driving his car, had found her walking down the street toward the Hotel Pax and then drove her to North Station, arriving there around 2:00 p.m. According to the shop manager and his assistant, Plevitskaya had remained in Caroline's without Skoblin between around 11:45 a.m. and 1:45 p.m., so her husband could have been free to do whatever he liked during that period.[28] Epstein never saw Skoblin waiting outside his store.

Something else happened the afternoon of September 24 to persuade the investigators that Plevitskaya was covering for Skoblin. Earlier in the day, during a break in the questioning, Plevitskaya had asked Liuba to take care of some of her things, because her purse was very heavy and full. Liuba agreed but did not realize that she should have reported this incident to the investigators. Three days later, Liuba showed her father what Plevitskaya had given her: old photos (one of which was signed, "To my dearest husband until death"), some bandages, a key to the hotel room, and a wallet. The wallet was empty except for a small red notebook. Grigul glanced through it and noticed Skoblin's handwriting. He had seen Skoblin write in it more than once. Grigul handed it to the investigators, figuring that it would be of interest to them. His instincts were right.

Plevitskaya's interrogation with Roches resumed around 10:00 a.m. on Friday, September 25, and yielded nothing new. She largely repeated what she had already said the day before, using the same stock phrases to declare her ignorance of anything related to Miller's disappearance.[29] By the end of the interrogation, she was exhausted, and her voice had hoarsened. She lashed out verbally at her interrogators for having detained her overnight in a cell, where she had to sleep on a small iron cot, comforted only by mild sedatives.[30] After several hours of testimony and fitful sleep, she became desperate. She wept and claimed that she had a bad memory and poor eyesight, and that she had relied on imprecise clocks in establishing her timeline.

By this point, the police had interviewed dozens of witnesses. Roches, Marchat, and Meyer were convinced that they had enough information to support their theory that Plevitskaya was being used to provide an alibi for Skoblin's whereabouts between 12:00 and 2:00 p.m. on September 22. They designated Skoblin as the principal perpetrator of the crime and Plevitskaya as his accomplice. In his office, Marchat arrested and charged Plevitskaya with violating Article 60 (serving as a knowing accomplice in the commission of a crime) and Article 341 (illegal confinement of and violent acts against a person) of the French Criminal Code.[31] Plevitskaya was never charged with espionage, very likely because the French government did not want to single out the Soviet Union—its ally against Germany—as the responsible party guiding her actions.

News of Plevitskaya's arrest spread quickly throughout Paris and beyond. The majority of journalists, witnesses, and Russian émigrés found it all too easy to believe that Plevitskaya and Skoblin had been involved in one way or another in Miller's kidnapping. Paris newspapers reported on every aspect of the Miller case, although the conclusions they reached depended on their ideological slant. Politically centrist and right-wing French newspapers, such as *Le Figaro*, *Le Jour*, *Le Matin*, *Le Petit Journal*, *Le Temps*, and *L'Action Française*, assumed that the NKVD had kidnapped Miller. Newspapers more sympathetic to the Soviets (*L'Humanité*, *L'Oeuvre*, and *Le Populaire*) blamed Hitler's agents and other fascist actors.

Meanwhile, the French authorities pressed on. They now hoped to prove not just that Plevitskaya had known about the crime, but that she had actively helped her husband to carry it out. If they could prove that Miller had died as a result, Plevitskaya could possibly face the death penalty—and even if they could not, prosecutors could still threaten her with life imprisonment.[32] In addition to arresting and charging Plevitskaya, Marchat issued an order for Skoblin's arrest, charging him with kidnapping, the committing of violent acts, and complicity in carrying out a crime. But unless Skoblin reappeared, which everyone knew was unlikely, French authorities had no one else to prosecute except his wife. Obviously, they could not indict Yezhov, Stalin, or the USSR. Strangely, no real effort was made to track down and arrest the drivers of the Soviet embassy truck.

Horrified to learn of her arrest, Plevitskaya demanded that she be freed immediately and declared that she had had nothing to do with Miller's disappearance. The investigator asked her whether she wanted to complete the interrogation then or to wait for a defense attorney to join her. She said that she would prefer to answer any remaining questions in the presence of an attorney and requested that she be given time to summon one. Marchat next signed an order for Plevitskaya to be detained until further notice in Paris's La Petite-Roquette women's prison.[33]

Also on September 25, the family of General Miller filed a lawsuit against Skoblin and Plevitskaya as a *partie civile* and retained Maurice Ribet and Alexander Strelnikov to serve as their counsel. In France, civil cases can be adjudicated concurrently with criminal ones, and the counsel of the plaintiffs can be present at police interrogations and during confrontations between witnesses and the accused. The plaintiffs' counsel can also speak at trial and call witnesses, although the plaintiffs themselves are barred from testifying in court as witnesses. Ribet, an experienced advocate, took full advantage of his powers. In an undated memorandum to Marchat, he urged the magistrate not to release Plevitskaya from detention and argued that she was clearly guilty of point 3 of Article 60 of the French Criminal Code, which defined an accomplice as someone who knowingly aids or assists the perpetrator or perpetrators of a crime in preparing or facilitating it. "Plevits-kaya was intimately tied to her husband and had knowledge of his affairs," Ribet insisted. "By covering for him, she facilitated his crime."[34] Ribet and Strelnikov, a former White Army officer, would be thorns in Plevitskaya's side throughout her legal ordeal.

The prison of La Petite-Roquette stood adjacent to the famed Père La-chaise cemetery.[35] It was housed in an imposing six-story building sur-rounded by high stone walls and towers on each corner. It had been built to hold juvenile delinquents in the 1830s and became a women's jail a century later. In 1932, with the closing of the Saint-Lazare women's prison—where Mata Hari had been incarcerated in 1917—the female inmates needed to be relocated, and the Petite-Roquette was chosen for this purpose. An interior circular courtyard with archways made the place feel more like a monastery than a prison, an impression reinforced by the fact that Catholic nuns managed the facility.

Ironically, after rejecting a life of constraint in the Kursk convent four decades before, Plevitskaya was now penned up in an environment that resembled the convent more than a little. At first she could not even receive newspapers in jail, although she was allowed occasional correspondence and visits from her attorneys.[36] It is possible she made contact with the NKVD while incarcerated. In December 1937, the Paris police received a report from a man alleging to be the husband or lover of Theodoria Timofeev-Peters, a former inmate in the Petite-Roquette who had met Plevitskaya while imprisoned there. According to this informant, Timofeev-Peters acted as an intermediary with Plevitskaya's "friends" in Paris, a reference to her NKVD contacts.[37]

The principal, albeit imperfect source of information about Plevitskaya's impressions of her experiences in jail is her diary, which she kept from early October 1937 to December 1938. In her diary, written in pencil in flimsy notebooks, Plevitskaya described her financial concerns, her declining health, her anguish over being tarred as a criminal by her husband's former ROVS associates, and her deep longing for "Kolechka," as she affectionately called Skoblin. However, it is important to note that, like any autobiographical source, its contents should not be viewed as completely accurate. Plevitskaya may have been writing it with an audience in mind, as a tool for gaining sympathy or even with the objective of selling it, as some reports indicate. Despite its drawbacks as a source, the diary still offers us glimpses into her mind during a time of great tragedy and loss.

Plevitskaya kept a running tally of how her remaining cash was spent. Initially, she had enough for larger meals and coffee and even offered to buy food for other inmates. But her money quickly dwindled, and the French government had confiscated most of her and Skoblin's bank holdings. In an early, unnumbered page of her diary, Plevitskaya seems to have written a rough draft of a note to her attorney about potential financial support from Tretyakov: "It's possible to obtain money with Tretyakov's help! Contact him right away." Her mention of Tretyakov suggests not only that she and Skoblin were his acquaintances, but that she knew of his assistance to Skoblin in the early hours of September 23.

Plevitskaya lost more than thirty pounds awaiting trial. She slept and ate poorly and complained in her diary of heart pain and other bodily ailments.[38] She mentioned at times that French inmates treated her poorly because she was a foreigner. She also expressed her anger at the ROVS officials who testified against her.

Plevitskaya's diary reveals her deep familiarity with ROVS politics, particularly regarding quarrels among Skoblin's associates and Miller, and also about internal financial problems. Her knowledge is on clearest display in a lengthy section of her diary, near the beginning, possibly written for her defense team or in preparation for a future newspaper article. She critiqued the relations of key ROVS officials with Miller, devoting attention to Matsylev, Turkul, Kedrov, Kussonsky, Denikin, and Erdely. She insisted repeatedly that she was not a political actor. At one point, she recalled a confrontation she had with Turkul in the presence of French investigators. When Turkul accused Skoblin of being a Bolshevik agent, Plevitskaya scornfully asked the investigators, "If he was so sure of that, then why did he take money from us?" She expressed her dismay at how several of Skoblin's ROVS associates were now calling her the "Red Mother." Above all, she felt betrayed by Grigul, whom she had considered a friend. "Grigul knows how modestly we lived," Plevitskaya reminisced. "He knows that I didn't get wrapped up in my husband's politics. He knows that I never argued with my husband or dominated him. . . . My husband did what he wanted." She wrote, "No one liked General Miller!" and referred to him as "deaf and dumb" to the 1934 Generals' Plot against him.

Also in her diary, Plevitskaya wrote about people other than Skoblin's associates. She described Max Eitingon as a well-known psychoanalyst and the son of a wealthy furrier. "He's not concerned with politics," she noted. "He is a scholar and rich. His wife is a former artist at the Moscow Art Theater. She and Max helped me and my husband financially and were our friends." She expressed her disgust at Marchat for inquiring whether she and Eitingon were lovers. A little later on, she insisted, "We lived modestly in France, quietly, not violating order . . . we didn't smoke, didn't play cards, no French people said we violated the peace. Why would I begin to be involved in politics? For money, but who says that I was for money? I only know that I can't figure out who's right and who's wrong." She sat in the car while Skoblin attended his meetings, she claimed. "I never had any enemies." Were these reflections written to help clear her head, or did she have an audience in mind?

In subsequent parts of her diary, Plevitskaya discussed the testimony of her accusers and sometimes viciously attacked them. In her October 20 entry, she wrote that she was not surprised by the accusations lodged against her and Skoblin by Matsylev, because Matsylev was "such a Jew." There is no evidence of pronounced anti-Semitism in Plevitskaya's earlier writings or actions, but anti-Jewish sentiment was so rampant in turn-of-the-century Russia that it would have been not at all unusual for someone of Plevitskaya's upbringing to fall back on such a commonly held prejudice in a moment of pique and desperation. Such outbursts as the one provoked by Matsylev's testimony indicate her growing anger and feelings of martyrdom with each passing month in custody.

Plevitskaya increasingly described herself as sick and mentally fragile. In her diary entry of January 18, 1938, she wrote that she was exhausted from the day's confrontations with witnesses, which "convinced me that I'm going insane and that it's impossible to escape. . . . Can no one understand my grief?" Perhaps as a method for coping with her own fears, she often recounted her dreams, especially those in which Skoblin appeared.

As a child, she had believed that dreams held important truths and foretold her future—and she still felt that way.

Despite the anguish she expressed on nearly every page of her diary, Plevitskaya accustomed herself to the Petite-Roquette, due largely to her close relationships with some of the nuns and to her confidence that she would, in the end, be freed. Plevitskaya wrote warmly of her nun friends and their reassurances that she would be exonerated. She also found solace in friendships with some of her fellow inmates and in attending services in the prison chapel and singing in its choir. Based on her diary, Plevitskaya seems to have felt compassion for several other prisoners. In May 1938, she expressed relief at the fact that so many foreigners like herself were entering the jail: "An Englishwoman, a Pole, a Jew, a Belgian, a French woman, an Arab, a Spaniard, an Italian, a Danish woman!" By October 1938, she had become used to living in captivity and no longer felt uncomfortable around women who had been accused of violent crimes.

Plevitskaya also seemed to gain strength from her own presumption of innocence and from her Russian Orthodox faith—or at least this is how she portrayed herself in her diary, which contained prayers and excerpts from the New Testament. A Russian Orthodox priest, Father Dmitry from her church in Ozoir, gave her an icon, which she kept in her cell. Father Dmitry became a target of some controversy as a possible cutout between Plevitskaya and the NKVD, although investigators did not consider him a suspect.[39] Some of her later diary entries suggest that she held out hope for an eventual rescue by her Soviet contacts. She was sadly mistaken. According to Moscow investigative reporter Arkady Vaksberg, "Soviet authorities always denied any links with Plevitskaya, whereas as soon as General Skoblin was brought to Moscow, the press called him a rogue in the pay of German intelligence. So Plevitskaya could not count on any helping hand from the new bosses who had unashamedly exploited her greed and lack of scruples."[40]

Certain aspects of prison life continued to unnerve her. As she grew increasingly pessimistic about her own chances of being freed, she admitted that her depression worsened whenever she learned that one of her fellow inmates was being released. On August 20, 1938, she reported that she enjoyed speaking with a new inmate from Poland, but she complained at the same time about the low level of culture among her fellow prisoners, next to whom she felt comparatively well educated. Sometimes inmates grew hysterical at night, screaming loudly and hurling objects to the floor of their cells.

As months passed and Plevitskaya became more depressed and exhausted, the handwriting, spelling, and grammar in her diary became noticeably sloppier. She lamented her failing health and felt abandoned. In a photo taken after one of her interrogations with Marchat, she stands with her eyes closed and arms folded across her chest; her left foot, which would give her problems later, appears to have been bandaged. Twenty-eight years before in Yalta, when Plevitskaya had thought of her heart as "young and winged," she had stood on the brink of stardom and imagined herself free as a bird and full of promise. Now, alone, vilified by her fellow Russian exiles—many of whom had once been her admirers—and facing prosecution in a foreign land, Plevitskaya had indeed become a caged nightingale.

10

THE INVESTIGATION

The Miller case was politically sensitive for both domestic and diplomatic reasons. France's political scene was volatile in the waning years of the Third Republic, and governments toppled on average every nine months. French voters demanded that the authorities tackle the high immigrant crime rate and were further alarmed by Miller's kidnapping.[1] In January 1937, Dmitry Navashin, a Russian émigré economist who openly criticized Stalin's show trials, was killed in broad daylight in the Bois de Boulogne. The police never found his killer, although many assumed it was an NKVD operative. Within hours of Miller's abduction, police investigators and Russian émigrés had already begun to suspect the NKVD.[2] However, France's government, controlled in late 1937 by a center-left Popular Front coalition led by Prime Minister Camille Chautemps, needed to remain on friendly terms with the Soviets due to national security concerns regarding Nazi Germany.[3]

French officials ordered investigators to gather evidence without provoking the ire of the Soviet government.[4] Nowhere else was their approach clearer than in how they investigated the building at 41 Montmorency Boulevard, the truck's route from Paris to Le Havre, and the Soviet ship's departure from France. The Miller family's attorneys, Maurice Ribet and Alexander Strelnikov, knew of the Soviet-owned buildings at numbers 41 and 43 Montmorency; after hearing from an eyewitness, they informed Marchat on September 27 that the building was a possible kidnapping site.[5]

At issue was diplomatic immunity. Soviet government representatives occupied the building, and so it was considered Soviet territory, an extension of the Soviet embassy. Marchat contacted the French Ministry of Foreign Affairs, led at the time by Yvon Delbos, to inquire about the possibility of obtaining a search warrant but received no response. Natalya Miller, with her attorneys' assistance, appealed to President Albert Lebrun for access to the building.[6] To gain sympathy for her own plight, Plevitskaya sent Lebrun a letter in support of Miller's appeal, writing "I quickly joined this appeal, for, with all my soul, I want disclosed the real perpetrators of the crime committed against General Miller and, I am convinced, my own husband."[7] Finally, nearly a month after Miller's abduction, investigators and Miller's attorneys gained entry. To no one's surprise, the Soviets, by this point, had removed all traces of evidence.

The matter involving the truck's progress from Paris to Le Havre and the Soviet ship's departure from Le Havre was even more controversial. This portion of the case was supervised by the Sûreté Nationale because it occurred largely outside of Paris. On the afternoon of September 22, in Le Havre, an inspector named Chauvineau reported to the Ministry of the Interior headquarters in Paris that at around 3:00 p.m., he had seen a truck with Soviet diplomatic plates pull up to the dock next to the *Maria Ulyanova*. Chauvineau spoke with a witness who had seen a crate loaded on board, and Chauvineau himself watched as the ship left hastily in the early evening before unloading all its cargo.

Chauvineau's supervisors in the Ministry of the Interior were concerned that his report, if leaked to the press, could disastrously affect France's relations with the Soviet Union. According to NKVD operative Sudoplatov, "Our ambassador vigorously denied any Soviet involvement and warned the French they would be held responsible if a peaceful Soviet vessel was halted and searched in international waters. General Miller would not be found, the ambassador insisted."[8] Fearing Soviet reprisals, French officials failed to send a naval vessel to shadow the ship. Chauvineau was transferred as a result of his report, and the Sûreté Nationale sent Commissaire Papin and Inspector Verrier to Le Havre to investigate further.[9] Contradicting Chauvineau's report, Papin concluded that the crate supposedly containing Miller could not have been brought on board as early as 3:00 p.m. and that the vessel had not departed with any great speed, as Chauvineau had claimed.[10]

Observers critical of the French government questioned why it let the Soviet ship leave French waters without stopping and inspecting it, and Interior Minister Marx Dormoy, a vehemently anti-Nazi socialist, particularly came under fire in the right-wing press for his handling of the matter. The most plausible explanation is the following: On the evening of September 23, French Minister of War Édouard Daladier summoned the Soviet ambassador to his office to speak about the strong public reaction to the Miller kidnapping. Daladier then proposed that the *Maria Ulyanova* return post-haste to a French port for inspection.[11] However, the Soviet ambassador, Yakov Surits, had already made his own arrangements.[12] Convinced by the ambassador that France's diplomatic ties with the USSR might be severed if the French government ordered the Soviets to return their ship, other members of the cabinet—Dormoy and Minister of Justice Vincent Auriol, it is said—had already agreed to allow it to pass out of French territorial waters without incident. Dormoy and Auriol then tried to seal Chauvineau's testimony, or at least deny its validity.[13] Because of these political considerations, the investigators were compelled to remain quiet about the Soviet embassy's participation in the Miller kidnapping and to focus instead on the Skoblins as the perpetrators of the crime.

Moreover, the investigators well understood that, in lieu of finding Miller and Skoblin, they had to collect compelling witness testimony and material evidence. They also needed to keep their initial findings secret to avoid discouraging witnesses from coming forward with potentially valuable information.[14] In one early break, police learned from the German government that Strohman and Werner were not their employees. But many more questions remained unanswered.

Marchat ordered a search of the Skoblins' hotel room. The investigators seized their belongings, including a typewriter. They impounded Skoblin's car and removed documents from ROVS headquarters, Miller's apartment, the Skoblins' house in Ozoir-la-Ferrière, and the Society of Gallipolians. They then hired a team of translators. Some documents were written in code but were later deciphered and translated. By the end of the investigation, in late August 1938, the police had collected over 1,300 pounds of documents, and the investigation dossier contained 2,500 pages.[15]

Under the circumstances, it is not surprising that the Plevitskaya investigation was strongly shaped by the politics of the time. The indictment against her did not even name the Soviets as the organizers of the Miller kidnapping for fear of injuring France's relations with the USSR. Long before Plevitskaya's trial opened, a majority of newspaper reporters, witnesses, and Russian émigrés were convinced that Skoblin and Plevitskaya had been involved one way or another in the plot. Despite the lack of formal proof, the circumstantial evidence indicating Plevitskaya's support for Skoblin's alibi was compelling. This includes the discrepancies between her testimony and that of witnesses in the Serdechny Restaurant and Caroline's dress shop, and at North Station; the correspondence revealing her knowledge of Skoblin's affairs; and her handing over of Skoblin's notebook, with its incriminating information, to Liuba Grigul.

However, in their rush to paint her as an evil vixen, Plevitskaya's critics exaggerated her role in the kidnapping and her influence over the way it unfolded. Many suspected—wrongly, as we now know—that Plevitskaya had even masterminded it. Although one can blame sheer sensationalism and the simple desire to generate exciting news copy, this distorted view of Plevitskaya's character and her role in the plot was also heavily colored by gender stereotypes. In interwar France, women still could not vote or serve on juries. This antiquated understanding of women was reflected in the criminal justice system, as shown by this description of female criminals taken from a 1931 book by a Paris police officer:

> Women always tend more than men to conform their actions according to their desires or passions. When changing their ideas into actions, they are less restrained than men by any thought of the criminal character of their deed. . . . Women do not trouble to think carefully of their desires; they do not trouble to plan their future with realization of the consequence of their actions—they act blindly and passionately and are therefore more disposed to have recourse to assassination than are men . . . though women more easily entertain the idea of a criminal attempt they are as a general rule less capable of carrying out their plans to a successful finish. . . . Naturally, the crime of a woman attracts so much more attention, the journalist is given so much more scope for his flaring pen and vivid imagination.[16]

Given these sexist attitudes, women were usually treated differently by the French legal system, sometimes to their advantage. Juries acquitted female criminal defendants at higher rates than male ones and gave them lighter sentences. Women could not be sentenced to beheading, which was the standard form of execution at the time.[17] According to American expatriate Janet Flanner, who lived in Paris during the interwar period, "six years [was] a normal clement 'stretch' for French female killers."[18]

There were exceptions to this rule in the 1930s, especially when crimes like aggravated murder attracted the press's attention. For instance, Christine and Lea Papin, sisters who worked as servants for the same family, were accused and found guilty of murdering their employers in 1933. They received a death sentence (commuted to life imprisonment) and a ten-year prison sentence, respectively. In another high-profile case, nineteen-year-old Violette Noziére, described as a nymphomaniac who schemed to steal her parents' life savings, was given a death sentence in 1934 for murdering her father, who allegedly attempted to force incestuous relations upon her. (Her sentence was later reduced to twelve years' hard labor.)

Female defendants sometimes walked free if they had ties to powerful men or were involved in crimes of passion. For example, in 1908,
Marguerite-Jeanne Steinheil—mistress of French president Félix Faure—
was acquitted of murdering her husband and mother-in-law due to a lack
of physical evidence. In another notorious case, Henriette Caillaux, the
wife of France's finance minister, was acquitted in 1914 of murdering a
newspaper editor who had criticized her husband. The jury concluded that
the murder was not premeditated but was instead the product of strong,
sudden emotion.

Unlike Caillaux and Steinheil, Plevitskaya had no influential protec-
tors, and her crime was not considered one of passion. Instead, her case,
with its ties to dangerous foreigners and secret agents, evoked a darker gender stereotype, that of the femme fatale. In the minds of most Frenchmen,
the shady profession of espionage was taken up only by women who were
conniving and controlling. Xenophobia and fear of war were widespread
in France at this time, fostering an anti-immigrant atmosphere that further
hindered Plevitskaya's chances for acquittal. After all, the public most likely
still remembered the 1935 trial of Soviet female spy Lydia Stahl. Plevitskaya
was portrayed by the European press, by ROVS witnesses, and by French
investigators as a Red seductress who had manipulated her husband into
becoming a Soviet spy.

The archetypal femme fatale preys on men's inherent weaknesses. She
is sexually driven, alluring, childless, estranged from family, marginal to society, and dangerous. In any country, she is readily associated with intrigue
and espionage. From the days of Mata Hari onward, stories about femmes
fatales sold newspapers and primed the public to support the prosecution in
spy-related cases, regardless of the strength of the evidence.

Plevitskaya's profession as a stage performer was another mark against
her, just as exotic dancing had counted against Mata Hari. In a revealing
passage from a December 1937 investigative report released by the Paris
police, a translator and analyst named Tastevin (Tsatskin in Russian) wrote,
"It is a constant rule in all countries that spies are recruited among women
in theater, dancers, singers, stars, or semi-stars. It's true that Troukhanova,
a dancer celebrity and wife of Count Ignatieff (who sided with the Soviets),
was a Bolshevik spy herself and was friends with Nadezhda Plevitskaya."[19]

Because the investigators lacked physical evidence of Plevitskaya's
involvement in Miller's kidnapping, they needed proof that she had lied
to them and that she had been generally aware of, and even involved in,
Skoblin's skulduggery. Indeed, prosecutors could show that Plevitskaya had
changed her testimony on a number of points. Thanks to correspondence

seized from the Skoblins' house, and to testimony given by past and current ROVS officials, investigators also found evidence that Plevitskaya knew about, and had connections to, some of her husband's activities.

An overwhelming majority of Skoblin's closest comrades made similar observations about Plevitskaya. For instance, Colonel Levitov of the Kornilov Regiment said that Plevitskaya acted as if she headed the regiment, and Captain Vosovik claimed that she never left Skoblin alone and must have known all about his operations. For his part, General Turkul commented, "When I came to Paris in 1931, I stayed at the Skoblins. I often observed that, when he was outside washing the car, she was opening business letters. She's more intelligent than Skoblin, who is good at executing orders, but not an intelligent man." General Erdely remarked that before meeting Plevitskaya, Skoblin had been an admirable soldier who was not overly concerned with politics. "But under her influence," Erdely continued, "Skoblin became the traitor we unmasked today."[20] The consistency of such remarks lends them some weight, and they proved influential as testimony. But even if they had a degree of accuracy to them, they were highly subjective and reflected the male chauvinist attitudes prevalent among this conservative and militaristic group. Also, not all of these witnesses agreed that Skoblin had informed Plevitskaya about his final act of treachery.

If investigators tended to trust most ROVS officials, they usually did not believe Plevitskaya's defenders. Her ex-husband stepped forward as one of her few supporters. Shortly after her arrest, Edmund Plevitsky insisted to a Russian émigré newspaper that Plevitskaya had no tie to Miller's disappearance and no knowledge of Skoblin's clandestine activities. Plevitsky portrayed his former wife as a victim of circumstance, but because he was living outside France, he was not called as a defense witness.[21] Similarly, Boris Solonevich, who was convinced that the Soviets had kidnapped Miller, expressed his doubts that the Skoblins were capable of such a thing. He described Plevitskaya as a "profoundly thoughtful woman," implying that she in particular would not have become involved.[22] However, enough people suspected Solonevich himself of being a Soviet agent that he lacked credibility. Colonel Gregory Troshin told the police that he thought the Gestapo had kidnapped Miller. But because he was Skoblin's assistant and the police had already decided that the Gestapo was not involved, his testimony was dismissed.[23]

Another important factor influencing the outcome of Plevitskaya's case was France's civil law–based, inquisitorial criminal justice system. In inquisitorial criminal justice systems—as opposed to the common-law adversarial systems found in countries like the United States and Great Britain—there is often a stronger accusatorial bias, and more emphasis is placed on the longer investigatory phase. In the French criminal justice system, the suspect is expected to play a more active role in the investigation than in adversarial systems, by contributing to the search for the truth.[24] In addition, investigators, prosecutors, and judges do not gather evidence exclusively about the suspect's alleged criminal actions in a particular case; instead, they also scrutinize her entire biography.[25] However, such information is not supposed to determine a suspect's culpability so much as help the examining magistrate decide whether or not to recommend that a case proceed to trial.[26] In Plevitskaya's case, this meant that Marchat as the examining magistrate could evaluate evidence and "hearsay" statements about her character, her relations with Skoblin and other ROVS members, and her rumored service to the Cheka during the Russian Civil War.

In inquisitorial systems, defense attorneys (*avocats*, or advocates) serving in serious felony cases can advise their clients, identify inappropriate procedures, take part in interrogations and hearings, and request supplemental investigations. However, their influence on the investigation is restricted by examining magistrates, who ultimately decide what evidence is added to the case file.[27] On the other side, victims (or their families, in cases of murder or disappearance) are given a more formal role to play in inquisitorial systems, and they can initiate a civil case alongside the criminal one. As it happened, Plevitskaya's defense team and the Miller family's attorneys were both reportedly unable to gain immediate access to all gathered documents for their own investigations. They typically were allowed to see only the official dossier, which contained summaries of evidence collected, witness statements, and formal court documents.[28] In an inquisitorial system, once a suspect is indicted, it is difficult for her case to be dropped—even more so when it has political ramifications.

Plevitskaya's lead defense attorney was Maximilian Filonenko, who had represented the Skoblins in their 1936 lawsuit against the Lloyd's of London insurance company, in which they were awarded close to 60,000 francs for damages related to their car accident. Plevitskaya probably chose Filonenko because of this earlier success. Some Russian émigrés suspected that Filonenko himself was on the Soviets' payroll, but while this is possible, the evidence is anecdotal at best.[29] Now detained, Plevitskaya was comforted by Filonenko's assurances that the police had not amassed enough evidence to proceed to trial and would be forced to release her.

During their first meeting, Filonenko asked Plevitskaya to tell him the truth about her knowledge of the Miller case. Before outlining to him what she had essentially told the police, she insisted, "I didn't know anything and I don't know anything now. . . . You'd think that if I had taken part in Miller's kidnapping, they would have taught me what to do, where to hide. They wouldn't have thrown me away like this, to the arbitrariness of fate. . . . My husband promised me he would never involve me [in his affairs]. . . . But now, after Miller's note, I'm beginning to have my doubts."[30] Whether or not Filonenko was convinced that Plevitskaya had somehow fallen prey to Skoblin's machinations and crimes, he at least thought that a story to this effect could be used as a defense strategy.

Filonenko's initial confidence that the case against Plevitskaya would be dropped before it came to trial had some basis in reality: in 1937 and 1938, the French police lacked tangible evidence of Plevitskaya's direct involvement in the kidnapping, and even of her and Skoblin's recruitment by Soviet intelligence. In fact, police commissionaire Jean Belin, who worked on the investigation, later admitted, "We did not have any formal proof of Nadezhda Plevitskaya's complicity in this affair."[31]

Filonenko employed a variety of defense tactics. First, he tried casting doubt on the authorship of Miller's note. In a letter to Marchat early in the investigation, Filonenko questioned why Miller would suspect a trap and yet still run the risk of death by attending the secret meeting. "It seems not to be in keeping with his cautious nature," Filonenko wrote.[32] Filonenko ventured his own theory that this note had been written by Kussonsky to frame Skoblin. This was perhaps Filonenko's strongest argument, but it did not gain any traction. Filonenko also pointed out that "Kedrov told police that Miller had no doubts against Skoblin, but Miller mentioned his doubt of Skoblin in the letter." Filonenko's arguments about the note upset the Miller family, who had authenticated the general's handwriting. In December 1937, the family's attorneys filed a protest with Marchat against the way Plevitskaya's defense team had used the press to cast doubt on the authenticity of Miller's note, but this complaint did not result in any court action.[33]

More generally, Filonenko tried to convince investigators that there was no proof that the NKVD had planned Miller's kidnapping. He offered alternative theories, capitalizing, for instance, on the testimony of Skoblin's friend Pyotr Savin and General Shatilov that the abduction had been masterminded by a mysterious pro-Soviet Spanish aristocrat named Marquis Mendez de Sevilla.[34]

Filonenko also questioned the accuracy of the timelines sketched out by the witnesses in the Serdechny and the dress shop. Filonenko claimed that Plevitskaya had not had a timepiece in her hotel room and that the

Palace of Justice, Paris. Courtesy of Pamela A. Jordan

clock at the restaurant had been running fifteen to thirty minutes fast.[35] In some of his pleadings, he referenced earlier legal decisions that had taken narrower interpretations of what constituted admissible evidence. It was not clear from the evidence that Miller had been abducted, he maintained. It could not be shown that Plevitskaya had been intimately involved in Skoblin's political activities, or that she had lied to investigators. As a result, Filonenko insisted, the evidence did not justify an indictment under Article 60 of the Criminal Code.[36]

The imposing Palais de Justice (Palace of Justice) is the home of Paris's law courts. Designed by civic planner Baron Georges-Eugène Haussmann, the massive neoclassical complex was built during the 1860s and sits on the east end of the Île de la Cité, the cradle of Paris's history. Pierre Marchat's office was housed on the third floor of the building, where most of the interrogations and witness confrontations in the Miller investigation took place. On October 1 and 2, 1937, he interrogated Plevitskaya there.[37] Exhausted after a week in an uncomfortable jail cell, the singer had difficulty breathing as she ascended the stairs to the magistrate's office.[38]

On October 1, Natalya Miller and her son Nikolai were present—in addition to Plevitskaya, Marchat, Filonenko, Ribet, and Strelnikov. Plevitskaya answered questions relating to her last moments with Skoblin.

She stated that, in Skoblin's haste to accompany Matsylev to ROVS head-quarters in the early morning hours of September 23, he had left behind two wallets containing around 20,000 francs. She could not explain why he had left the money there or why he had fled. Plevitskaya emphatically told Miller's wife, "I could not have participated in your husband's kidnap-ping," to which the latter replied, "If you're such a good friend, then why didn't you drop by my house or phone me?" Plevitskaya explained, "I was out roaming around, lost in my head."[39]

Marchat also questioned Plevitskaya about her husband's red note-book, which she had given to Liuba Grigul at the police station before her arrest. Plevitskaya became visibly nervous when the notebook was men-tioned. On one page, Skoblin had apparently written, "Extend EK [Evgeny Karlovich Miller] an invitation about a meeting tomorrow at 12 h. 30 m. —1:00 h. We will speak." Plevitskaya swore that she had no idea what this note meant, and her attorneys argued that it was ambiguously written.[40] French investigators, however, interpreted it as evidence of Skoblin's role in Miller's abduction and as a confirmation of the meeting that Miller had mentioned in his note.

After three hours of questioning, Plevitskaya turned to Natalya Miller and pleaded, "Save me!" to which Natalya replied, "Pray to God."[41] Near the end of the day, after six hours of questioning, Marchat allowed Plevitskaya and Miller to meet alone for forty-five minutes in Marchat's office, hoping that the former might confess. Miller reported that Plevitskaya showed no remorse and tearfully asked her to advocate for her release. Needless to say, Miller demurred. According to Ribet, this episode illustrated Plevitskaya's "brutal egoism" and even jealousy of Natalya Miller, whose husband had been abducted, whereas Plevitskaya's had fled without her.[42] In a diary entry about the October 1 confronta-tion, Plevitskaya noted with distress that Natalya Miller had looked at her judgmentally and had fixated on her failure to visit her after General Miller's disappearance.

On October 2, Plevitskaya seemed calmer, sometimes smiling and laughing. Marchat and Ribet questioned her about her and Skoblin's savings, which she said amounted to around 76,000 francs. She claimed that her revenues came to thousands of francs, thanks to concert tours, individual concerts, and royalties. However, she insisted that Skoblin had been in charge of their finances and that she lacked detailed knowledge of them. Filonenko reminded everyone of Natalya Miller's testimony that her husband had never spoken about business with her, pointedly implying that the same was likely true for Plevitskaya and Skoblin.

Marchat then showed Plevitskaya two anonymous postcards and a letter, all addressed to her and mailed after her arrest. One of the postcards had been sent from the Baltics, the other from Yugoslavia; both contained cryptic messages. The first postcard sent anonymously from the Baltics read, "Be healthy, have hope. We are praying for you," and Plevitskaya's eyes reportedly brightened when she read it. (Investigators theorized that the postcards might have come from NKVD contacts, and they could have been written by Skoblin when he was hiding at the Soviet embassy.) The second postcard, of an unknown author, was mailed from Yugoslavia and reassured Plevitskaya, "We know that in this accursed country, troubling things are happening to you." The letter was from Grand Duchess Olga Alexandrovna, Tsar Nicholas II's sister. Olga Alexandrovna, then residing in Denmark, believed that Plevitskaya was innocent. Plevitskaya cried and kissed the letter. Overcome with emotions, she requested that someone bring her some sedatives.[43]

Also in October, Marchat showed Plevitskaya a letter from Tallinn, Estonia, addressed to her that had arrived at the Society of Gallipolians. This purportedly came from a female admirer named Valentina Malakhova, who wrote that she had seen Plevitskaya perform once and that her singing had brought her great pleasure.[44] Inside the envelope, investigators found a small ivory cross similar to one that Plevitskaya was said to have given Skoblin. According to several of the Skoblins' acquaintances, Plevitskaya had bought the cross as a memento of a visit to the Valaam Monastery in Finland, probably in 1934, and gave it to Skoblin, who always wore it. When Plevitskaya read Malakhova's letter and saw the cross, Marchat noticed, she smiled and grew calmer. He and other investigators came to suspect that the letter and cross were from Skoblin himself, a conclusion soon supported by government handwriting experts. Claiming that the investigation needed to keep the letter and cross, Marchat demanded them back. In a diary entry in mid-October, Plevitskaya mentioned that the cross "raised some suspicions. [The jailers] don't let me keep my letters, and I feel such anguish."

Sometime during Plevitskaya's October 2 interrogation, Filonenko handed Marchat a plea that demanded her immediate release from detention.[45] Filonenko argued that the police had no proof that Plevitskaya had *knowingly* aided and abetted a criminal conspiracy, as required under Article 60 of the French Criminal Code. He also discussed Article 212 of the Civil Code, which concerned how spouses were expected to show mutual fidelity by coming to one another's aid, but did not presume that they were acquainted with, or even had knowledge of, each other's affairs. At this point, it seems that Filonenko was gradually accepting the possibility that Skoblin had participated in Miller's kidnapping plot, but he remained steadfast in his strategy of insisting that Plevitskaya had no prior knowledge of it and was therefore oblivious on the afternoon of September 22 of the need to uphold Skoblin's alibi.

Marchat was unconvinced and did not grant Filonenko's request. So Plevitskaya returned to the Petite-Roquette, feeling defeated. In her diary entry for October 2, she wrote, "How can I be a criminal? . . . I am all alone." Despite her confrontations with Natalya Miller and ROVS officials, Plevitskaya still supported Skoblin's alibi and remained loyal to him. "Others consider him a criminal, but for me he is an honorable soldier," she wrote in her October 20 diary entry. She continued to worry about Natalya Miller's disposition toward her, noting on December 7 that she "does not believe I am innocent."

In October, investigators focused not only on obtaining testimony from witnesses. They also needed to collect more physical evidence. On October 5, Plevitskaya, Filonenko, and the Millers' attorneys were present at the Skoblins' home in Ozoir-la-Ferrière as investigators seized documents. When Plevitskaya arrived, she greeted her dog and cats. Before the cameras, she was playing the role of a typical Russian *baba*, or peasant woman, uninterested in politics, smiling and greeting her beloved pets.[46] According to a newspaper account, she searched for a green Bible for "spiritual reading in prison."[47] She did not find it. While Plevitskaya claimed that her Bible was valuable for religious and sentimental reasons, the newspaper noted the investigators' opinion that it might contain the key to one of the ciphers that Skoblin used in his conspiratorial work. Indeed, Plevitskaya's obsessive searching for the Bible raised Ribet's and Strelnikov's suspicions, and they alerted Marchat and the investigators about its potential significance. This first visit to her house clearly took a toll on Plevitskaya. On October 6, she wrote in her diary about depression, heart pains, and fear so intense that it caused her to shake. "Where is my dear one?" she wondered.

Plevitskaya appeared at her house at least two other times in October, as investigators confiscated documents and other evidence, including three typewriters and the controversial green Bible on October 27.[48] She found family photos and held them to her chest and cried. She also wept when a police inspector seized Skoblin's Kornilov Regiment flags. "My husband was a great hero," she exclaimed. "One of Russia's great heroes. He can't be guilty, can't be a traitor. He's a victim!" Every time a police officer reached for a document, she knit her brows and became nervous: "These are people I don't trust. I don't want this man reading my letters!" The investigators ignored her protests.[49] The green Bible was found in Skoblin's locked study upstairs. Plevitskaya asked if she could take it, but the police refused.

During a search of the Skoblins' hotel room, investigators found an address book belonging to Skoblin. One of the pages contained this notation: "Cipher—green Bible, page 20, Gospel of St. John."[50] Newspapers duly reported that the team of translators found an enciphering key and instructions for its use.[51] Ribet, Strelnikov, and the investigators concluded that Skoblin had used this key for communicating with the Soviets, but the defense team vehemently contested this notion, proposing instead that Skoblin and other ROVS operatives had used the cipher to coordinate actions with their anti-Soviet counterparts in Finland.

In a memorandum to Marchat in early December, Filonenko noted that another attorney on his defense team had learned that investigators were no longer considering the Bible important, although this news might have been premature. "It is already an avowed lie that the Bible contains a key in invisible ink," he wrote.[52] In a subsequent note to Marchat about the Bible, Filonenko criticized the court system for releasing information to the press first before giving the defense team access to it.[53] He argued that the press's stories about the Bible amounted to a public campaign against his client. Filonenko mentioned that he had learned from a source that French authorities were investigating a lead about how Captain Klavdy Foss, a ROVS member based in Bulgaria, had inserted the cipher and key information into the green Bible as a way of corresponding with Skoblin.

Investigators and journalists were also sifting through documents about the Skoblins' finances for clues about who might have employed them clandestinely. In a newspaper interview, D. M. Schneider, the house agent who handled the Skoblins' deal on their Ozoir-la-Ferrière house, noted that, from 1934 onward, Skoblin's mortgage payments became more sporadic.[54] Schneider assumed that the couple had financial problems, although they owned four cars during the time he knew them, from 1930 to 1937, and the cost of their upkeep was very expensive. Given that the Soviets were paying Skoblin at least US$200 a month and that Plevitskaya had earned some concert income, they should not have been in such dire financial straits, but they may well have been camouflaging their financial situation and purposely convincing Schneider that they were short on money.

Other than attending interrogations and occasionally confronting witnesses, Plevitskaya had little to do apart from writing in her diary, meeting with Filonenko, speaking with the nuns and her fellow inmates, and attending church services. So when something extraordinary happened, such as receiving a letter from relatives in the USSR, her spirits lifted. On October

21, Plevitskaya received a letter from her sister Masha, who relayed news of her son, who had started university, and her daughter and granddaughter, who were in good health. Although nothing can be proven, Plevitskaya may have received this letter thanks to official Soviet assistance. By this point, Soviet censors rarely allowed average citizens to mail letters to exiled relatives, and Soviet citizens often preferred not to even admit the existence of family members abroad. On December 3, Plevitskaya noted pensively, "Filonenko read the case file, and what's there against me? The 'good, clean' people tried to throw dirt and lies at me." The next day, she rehearsed songs with the prison choir, receiving a solo in a setting of "Kyrie eleison."

On December 7, Filonenko and Plevitskaya appeared at a court hearing, along with Advocate General Demangeot, a magistrate representing the prosecutor's office. The hearing's purpose was to determine whether the investigation should proceed and whether Plevitskaya should remain at the Petite-Roquette. Demangeot reproached Plevitskaya on several counts: for not contacting the police before September 24, for handing Skoblin's notebook over to Liuba Grigul the same day, and for establishing a rapport during Russia's civil war with Bolsheviks as their so-called Red Mother.[55] Demangeot maintained that the public interest would be best served by Plevitskaya's long-term detention. Back on November 26, after all, Marchat had warned the court that there was a strong likelihood that Plevitskaya would flee France if released. In response, Filonenko argued that Plevitskaya's health was worsening in the Petite-Roquette. She still suffered from the injuries sustained in her car accident, and separation from Skoblin depressed her. He criticized Demangeot for not questioning the police's interpretation of Skoblin's message in his notebook, and he took Marchat to task for neglecting to fully outline the reasons for her detainment. Nonetheless, the court decided to keep Plevitskaya in jail.

Having endured another interrogation, and facing the prospect of Christmas in jail, Plevitskaya exclaimed on December 21, "I am the world's unhappiest woman!" In mid-December, a confidential police report by the translator Tastevin summarized the investigators' key evidence and conclusions up to that point.[56] In his estimation, investigators, after considering alternative scenarios that involved ROVS members and Italian or Nazi agents, had reached a consensus that the NKVD had organized Miller's kidnapping. The investigators clearly felt they had gathered sufficient evidence to support their claim that Skoblin and Plevitskaya were knowing coconspirators and Soviet agents. Their proof included the breakdown of Skoblin's alibi, Miller's note, the message in Skoblin's notebook, the testimony of over 150 witnesses, and correspondence found in various locations.

On Christmas Day, Plevitskaya attended mass and ate a pastry that Filonenko had brought her. She spent time with an inmate named Yvonne, and they both realized with sadness that they had already been in the Petite-Roquette longer than most of their fellow detainees.

It was now January 1938. Once the holidays passed, the investigators resumed their interrogations, which Filonenko and Plevitskaya attended. She often challenged ROVS members who claimed she had been Skoblin's chief adviser. On January 4, investigators were still treating the green Bible as evidence. The newspaper *Poslednie novosti* published what it claimed were the full notes that Skoblin had written in his address book about using invisible ink and keeping the cipher to John 6.[57] "Nothing is in the Bible," Plevitskaya wrote in her diary that day. In a January 13 report, Marchat took special note of Plevitskaya's testimony from January 10, when she finally had admitted awareness of Skoblin's anti-Bolshevik activities.[58]

Despite his failure so far to win her freedom, Filonenko still reassured Plevitskaya about her impending release. Her January 19 diary entry noted, "Soon it'll be all over and I'll have my liberty; don't be worried, have patience." Filonenko also humored her at times. During a visit to the Petite-Roquette, he told her, "You're an intelligent woman, although sometimes you have a bicycle going around in your head." "What do you mean by a bicycle?" she asked. Filonenko motioned with his hands how her mind kept spinning round.

On January 28, she appeared at an interrogation of General Shatilov, Admiral Kedrov, Colonel Matsylev, and other White Army veterans who knew Skoblin.[59] Each argued that Plevitskaya knew all about her husband's activities. In her own defense, she remarked that Shatilov had rarely observed her together with Skoblin. "We were barely even acquainted," she said. "I saw him all of three or four times, not counting official ceremonies." (Her diary conveys even deeper contempt for Shatilov, whom she called a liar and "a most unkind, small-minded, and ignoble man. I very much regret defending this liar earlier." In contrast to this criticism, she praised Troshin, who maintained that it was the Nazis who had kidnapped Miller.) Trying to deflect attention from herself, Plevitskaya accused a White Army veteran named Igor Zavadsky-Krasnopolsky of attempting to murder Skoblin when he was hospitalized for tuberculosis. "They gave him an injection and from this one jab, made by a woman whose last name began with P, he nearly died," Plevitskaya declared. "I am sure that it was an attempt by Zavadsky-Krasnopolsky's group, which my husband and I suspected had ties to the Bolsheviks." (Zavadsky-Krasnopolsky was actually a French police informant and probably not a Soviet spy.) Concerning Colonel Fedoseenko's accusations in 1932 and 1935 that Skoblin was a Soviet agent, Plevitskaya said that "of course it was slander. A court of honor, appointed by Miller, rejected this slander."

By the end of January 1938, nearly all the key witnesses had testified more than once, as Marchat tried to strengthen his case for bringing Plevitskaya to trial. Witness testimony uniformly reflected the opinion that Plevitskaya knew all about her husband's conspiratorial affairs. Plevitskaya was seen as strongly defending her own interests in confrontations with her foes. Her mantra had become, "I am not guilty of anything. My husband did not inform me of his business dealings. . . . I knew nothing, and know nothing now!" She said that if she had had influence over Skoblin, then "sooner than not I would have forced him to cease his political activities. That he continued with politics shows how little he followed my suggestions."[60]

The investigation argued that Skoblin had used the Bible and a novel by White general Pyotr Krasnov, *Beyond the Thistle*, to encipher messages. Plevitskaya had asked to have both books in jail with her. Marchat said it was a strange coincidence that she had requested these particular reading materials. In response, Plevitskaya said, "Listen, I'm a half-literate woman. I don't know grammar or syntax. My writing is filled with errors. I'm well known as a singer, but you would not believe I could make out even a note. I understand things by hearing them. How would I understand a cipher?" She said she knew only generally about Skoblin's anti-Bolshevik activity but was not interested in the details: "I was occupied with housework in Ozoir-la-Ferrière and sang in concerts."[61]

An article appearing in the January 29 issue of *Poslednie novosti* infuriated Plevitskaya, who wrote a rebuttal three days later to its editor, the eminent liberal Pavel Miliukov.[62] She was particularly irked by how the article stated that she had taken the entire defense into her own hands, when she was still being represented by Filonenko. She also stressed that the so-called consensus among witnesses that she possessed full knowledge of Skoblin's conspiratorial activities was not grounded in fact but based on vague impressions. She asserted that she had no control over her husband's activities or thinking and that the green Bible was immaterial to her case. "I am anti-Bolshevik," she avowed, "and I confirm that all the documents in the court investigation show no ties between the Bolsheviks and my husband [Skoblin] or me." She claimed to have saved two of Matsylev's brothers from the Bolsheviks when they were serving in the White Army in the Don region in 1918. (Her claim, in fact, was verified by Matsylev, at his January 28 interrogation, although neither he nor Plevitskaya provided any more details.[63]) In addition, Plevitskaya reminded Miliukov that Max Eitingon was a scholar-doctor and not, as the article had said, a London furrier.

Plevitskaya's emotional defense did not move the investigators. According to a major progress report filed by Roches in early February 1938, they had studied the contents of many seized documents and interviewed over 150 witnesses.[64] They had also interrogated Plevitskaya several more times. The documents did not contain any smoking guns about Miller's kidnapping or its possible ties to the Reiss killing in Switzerland in early September 1937, but they did expose Skoblin's and Miller's clandestine anti-Soviet ROVS operations, including the infiltration of ROVS agents into the USSR via Finland. Moreover, the investigators knew that Dobrovolsky and the Finns had warned Miller about a possible traitor in his midst.

Investigators also concluded that they had sufficient evidence to prove Plevitskaya's knowledge of Skoblin's political activities. Key items included the notorious green Bible that Eitingon had given her and various letters addressed to Plevitskaya from ROVS officials. Roches noted that, at the January 10 interrogation, Plevitskaya had at last admitted that she had been cognizant of Skoblin's anti-Soviet activities—although she continued to deny advance knowledge of the kidnapping plot or Skoblin's alleged role in it. Roches concluded that one reason Miller was kidnapped was his participation in secret anti-Soviet activities. In Roches's opinion, Skoblin's culpability extended to both the preparation and execution of Miller's kidnapping. Roches also believed that investigators now had reason to assume that Plevitskaya had conspired with the kidnappers. By this point, the investigators were confident that the Soviets had organized Miller's abduction.

Some Russian émigrés mounted their own investigations and drew conflicting conclusions. For instance, Paris émigré spy hunter Vladimir Burtsev and several White veterans insisted that General Turkul and Captain Savin were also involved in Miller's abduction, but the French police chose not to treat them as suspects.[65] For his part, Savin told investigators that he thought Skoblin was innocent and that Marquis Mendez de Sevilla, with General Shatilov's involvement, had kidnapped General Miller.[66] Savin's allegations were dismissed, although when investigators sought to question him in late February 1938, he had already fled to Italy.[67] Leaders of the NTSNP youth group assumed that the leaders of ROVS's Inner Line had orchestrated Miller's kidnapping and that the Inner Line was a Soviet provocation similar to the USSR's TREST operation of the 1920s.[68] Under the chairmanship of General Erdely, a special ROVS commission issued a report in March 1938 about the Miller kidnapping.[69] This outlined several findings, based on internal documents and witness testimony. Erdely's commission concluded that Miller's note was the main piece of evidence in the case, and Kussonsky admitted his error for having waited so long to open it. The commission also decided that the NKVD had orchestrated Miller's kidnapping. Skoblin had lured Miller to the meeting and had managed to keep the general's trust because of Plevitskaya's collaboration and leadership. No one else in ROVS was involved in the plot, the commission averred, and the Inner Line as an organization had not taken part in the kidnapping, although it had harmed ROVS more generally and needed to be abolished.

Having shown courage in January, Plevitskaya plunged into depression the following month. On February 21, she wrote, "I don't want to think, don't want to even live. When witnesses lie, I feel like laughing, but Filonenko forbids it. How could I not laugh, when seeing everyone I've known a long time and having thought they were better, they turn out to be exactly like children who lie out of fear, for money, or because they are mean?" The next day, she recorded a chance interchange with a Russian émigré unknown to her:

> A Russian chauffeur drove up to the gates of the Petite Roquette and yelled, "Nadezhda Vasilievna, is that you?"
> "Yes, it is!" I replied.
> "Your fate! You've been abandoned! You're all alone!"
> My tears flowed because of this stranger's sympathy for me. I pointed to the sky—"God's with me. He wouldn't abandon a woman who never did anything bad!"
> The chauffeur's eyes teared up. He said to the police inspectors in French, "This woman never forgot the unfortunate!" [Turning back to me, he said,] "Stay strong, Nadezhda Vasilievna, and pray!"
> "Pray for me," I told him. He answered that his wife always prays for me. He told me that he was a Don Cossack, then he shook my hand, glanced at me, and drove off.

Did Plevitskaya fabricate this poignant story in an attempt to gain sympathy from her future readers, or to cheer herself up? Could the Russian chauffeur have been an NKVD contact, or was he a genuine admirer? We will never know.

Over two days, on March 1 and 2, Plevitskaya was questioned by Ribet, Strelnikov, Natalya Miller, and her brother-in-law, Karl Miller, in fulfillment of the legal requirements of the Miller family's civil lawsuit.[70] Also present were two investigators and Filonenko. During the first day, the focus was on the Skoblins' finances. Plevitskaya noted that most of her concert income came from her foreign concert tours and that she had earned no more than 3,000 francs in book royalties. In 1928, she added, Max Eitingon had given her and Skoblin US$2,000.

During the second round of questioning, on March 2, Plevitskaya slightly modified her story about what had happened immediately after her exit from the Caroline dress shop. Earlier, she had insisted that Skoblin had waited outside the shop, or at least across the street, and that they had driven to the train station together after she left the store. Now she claimed that, after leaving the store and reaching the sidewalk, she had noticed that Skoblin was gone. As she walked down Victor Hugo Avenue, he spotted her and caught up with her in his car, after which they drove to North Station.

"He could, of course, have absented himself" while she was in the store, Plevitskaya admitted to Ribet and the others present. "But if he left, I don't know where he went." Still, as in previous interrogations, she insisted that it was engine failure that had delayed Skoblin and caused her to run alone to the platform to meet Natalya Kornilov-Chaperon before her train left.

Ribet challenged Plevitskaya's revised account. "We know this isn't true," he replied. "We know your husband appeared at Caroline's ten minutes after you had left. We know you arrived alone at the station. You explained to people there that your husband was dealing with the car. To us, it is well known that you did not find your husband and arrived at the station alone. At the time when you were alone in Caroline's, Skoblin was involved in Miller's abduction. You know this full well! You not only know, you assisted Skoblin!"

Plevitskaya grabbed the arms of her chair and, gasping for breath, yelled, "No, no! I swear before God and the people. I know nothing!"

Strelnikov, with disgust, added, "Each of your words is a lie!"

Plevitskaya was crying loudly. "I'm not lying!" Someone ran to get her a glass of water, as she seemed on the verge of collapsing.

Filonenko asked those present if they would agree to limit Plevitskaya's punishment if she told "the whole truth." The Millers and their attorneys nodded their heads, while Marchat and the investigators said that they would recommend the least severe punishment. Turning to his client, Filonenko said, "If fear of punishment has prevented you from admitting everything you know, then now you can speak the whole truth."

Plevitskaya hesitated and replied to Filonenko, "And if I don't say anything, if I refuse?" In that case, Filonenko told her, nothing would change.

Strelnikov again accused Plevitskaya of muddying the facts.

Furious, Plevitskaya retorted, "Don't say this. I'm not muddying any-thing." Then, addressing Natalya Miller, she said, "I have some thoughts about Evgeny Karlovich, but I can say them only to Natalya Nikolaevna." Marchat agreed to allow Plevitskaya to confer with Miller privately in his chambers. His hope was that Plevitskaya might confess if made to feel suf-ficiently guilty.

Once the doors were closed, Plevitskaya tried to win Miller over with sympathy and praise. "You know how much I love you and Evgeny Kar-lovich. How could I have done this? How could Nikolai Vladimirovich? I would be the first person to denounce him [if I knew he had been involved in General Miller's kidnapping]. Do you believe me?" Miller remained silent.

Plevitskaya continued, "You haven't spoken to them. You haven't done anything that would lead them to release me."

"What will you do?" Miller responded.

"I'll go to Russia, where my husband is . . ."

"How will you find him there?"

"I know how to find him. He has two brothers . . ."

Miller was bewildered by Plevitskaya's words. "If you did find him, you wouldn't find out anything, because [the NKVD] will shoot him if he divulges anything, and you'd be all alone."

Plevitskaya disagreed. "No, he will tell me. I believe him. He will answer, and I will let you know where Evgeny Karlovich is."

"It's impossible," Miller replied. She was shocked by the implications of Plevitskaya's words as well as her naive assumption that she could go to the Soviet Union, find Skoblin, and demand that he tell her General Miller's whereabouts without suffering any consequences.

"Listen," Plevitskaya hastily said, "if you don't believe me, then let's go to the inspector." And with those words, their tête-à-tête ended. Again, Miller refused to promise Plevitskaya that she would advocate for her release. Marchat formally concluded the session without having obtained Plevitskaya's confession.

What Plevitskaya's words to Natalya Miller suggest is that Plevitskaya had probably heard from the NKVD—either via correspondence or an intermediary (Father Dmitry? Filonenko? Timofeev-Peters?)—that Skoblin was in the Soviet Union. Also, Plevitskaya's words imply confidence on her part in her ability to travel to the USSR, locate Skoblin, and uncover information about General Miller, all goals that could be achieved only if Plevitskaya had a connection with the NKVD, or at least thought that NKVD officials would cooperate with her.

Returning to the Petite-Roquette after the interrogation, Plevitskaya lashed out in her diary at her accusers for tormenting her. "What kind of people dream of tormenting me? These people think they're honorable!" On March 3, Plevitskaya mentioned how a newspaper had quoted Natalya Miller as saying that Plevitskaya hated Skoblin. "What a lie!" Plevitskaya wrote. "I adore my husband! My actual words were 'You know that I couldn't live without him, but there are minutes when I don't think about him.' This doesn't mean that I hate him."

After Plevitskaya's interrogation in early March, Filonenko submitted another memorandum to Marchat objecting to the prosecution of Plevitskaya.[71] He reiterated his argument that the evidence collected by the investigators thus far did not support a conviction and noted that Article 248 of the French Criminal Code recognized familial bonds as sacred and outside the bounds of automatic criminal liability. "The essential component of complicity," he wrote, "is that the person must have aided or assisted the author or authors of the criminal action. The ancillary element is the knowledge of the role that the complicity played." He focused further on a section in Article 60 of the Criminal Code that defined an accomplice as someone who used a gift, promise, threat, order, or abuse of authority in committing a crime or gave instructions on committing it. He referred to a case from 1897 about a man who had passively witnessed a crime and nevertheless was acquitted. But Filonenko also mentioned that, at the March interrogation, he had "begged Plevitskaya to tell all of what she knew about Miller's abduction"—an apparent admission that Skoblin had been involved in the kidnapping and that Plevitskaya was withholding something important from investigators. "We don't know where her husband was," Filonenko acknowledged. "Perhaps he was at the rendezvous with Miller. But she wasn't. Thus, this is proof that she had no direct participation in Miller's kidnapping. There's a profound difference between the husband's and the wife's situations."

"Madame Skoblin did not flee. She is here," Filonenko continued. "She could have fled after the police questioned her in her hotel room the morning of September 23, but she did not, although she had sufficient cash on her to flee the city. She went to the Society of Gallipolians; she was not hiding somewhere. . . . If she was a Bolshevik agent, she would have been assisted. The Soviets rescue their agents without any difficulty."

Filonenko maintained that there was no proof that the spouses had discussed the alibi beforehand. He also saw as useless Ribet's and Strelnikov's attempts to establish whether Plevitskaya had taken a taxi to North Station or had gone in her and Skoblin's car. "Everything that occurred before the crime was committed is immaterial," he asserted. Filonenko insisted that the charges against Plevitskaya lacked legal grounds, as did the investigation and the detention of his client. Filonenko's final remarks in his March pleading to Marchat accused the press and investigators of placing too much attention on Plevitskaya to the exclusion of everyone else.

Throughout the remainder of March, Plevitskaya's trust in Filonenko began to erode, particularly on days when she suffered from depression, insomnia, or heart pains. She doubted whether she would ever see Skoblin again. "Where is my husband? Where is he? Do you know how I'm suffering?" she wrote plaintively. Plevitskaya noted on March 21 that Filonenko grew angry when she wrote him letters with more demands. On March 31, she was moved to another cell and complained of its poor conditions. All she could do to calm herself was to stare at the passing clouds outside her window.

April brought Plevitskaya a series of disappointments. The beauty of springtime in Paris—the budding trees and flowers outside her window—only served to heighten her sense of melancholy and loneliness. On April 1 she wrote that Filonenko had visited and "promised me freedom soon, as always. I've stopped believing him and am unhappy." On April 8, she told Filonenko that she wanted to kill herself. She held out hope of being freed from custody by Russian Orthodox Easter, which fell on April 24 that year. But that very week, Marchat denied her request.[72] April indeed felt like the cruelest month to "La général Skobline," as investigators referred to Plevitskaya in some of their internal reports.

In May, Plevitskaya dreamed about Skoblin and the chance to go outside, if only to see the fragrant lily-of-the-valley blooms that were so common in Paris at that time of year. Filonenko dropped by on May 2, still with no news. She impressed on him the fact that she had now been incarcerated for eight months, despite her innocence. On May 5, Filonenko informed her that Marchat was now warning that she would have to "answer morally" for her crimes. In her diary that day, she asked, "Morally? What, is Skoblin now my son? And who saw my husband kidnap General Miller?" Filonenko reported to the doctor at the Petite-Roquette that Plevitskaya was complaining about heart and kidney problems.[73] But Dr. Paul examined her and ruled that prison did not endanger her life. She accused the doctor of wanting to kill her.

For Plevitskaya, the only encouraging moment that month came when Marchat returned the green Bible to her at a meeting on May 9.[74] On May 13, *Poslednie novosti* published Filonenko's letter to the editor informing readers that Marchat had given the Bible back to Plevitskaya. He stressed that no secret messages had been found in it, meaning that it was no longer useful to the investigation.[75] On May 29, Plevitskaya wrote a brief poem encapsulating her feelings of isolation and loss:

> For me the green maple stirs
> And for me the pigeon coos
> And the swallow circles on high—
> I languish behind a barred window
>   such a long time alone
> And my dreams are flying off in the distance
> And I am always thinking, where are you?

Throughout June, investigators were still following leads and translating and analyzing documents they had seized. On June 2, they issued an internal memorandum reporting that Soviet sources were spreading false rumors around Paris about how the Gestapo, not the NKVD, had kidnapped Miller with the help of Shatilov.[76] This was yet another sign to investigators that Skoblin and the NKVD had had a hand in the kidnapping.

Back in the Petite-Roquette, Plevitskaya suffered from sleeplessness and headaches. She recorded in her diary how Filonenko visited her infrequently now and, on June 17, sent a female assistant (probably Isabelle Goskind), who was "kind but knew nothing." She was transferred to yet another cell on June 16 and, on June 20, the jail doctor called her a scoundrel. Filonenko sent an angry letter about this matter to the jail director.

Plevitskaya's final interrogation with Marchat occurred in his chambers on June 22. She noted in her diary that day how she had grown used to him and felt he treated her decently. In reality, Marchat was not sympathetic to Plevitskaya's plight and ultimately agreed with the prosecution about her culpability. After this point, Plevitskaya's case file was transferred to the court for evaluation and a decision on how to proceed.[77] Also around this time, Plevitskaya had only 200 to 300 francs left in cash, down from the 20,000 francs she had arrived with the previous September. She had spent her money on food in the jail canteen and on taxis. At least one newspaper reported that Plevitskaya planned to sell parts of her diary for 30,000 francs, although such a transaction apparently never occurred.[78]

In late June, Plevitskaya seemed preoccupied with receiving word from "home," presumably meaning the Soviet Union. She referred more than once in her diary to having written, but without reply, to someone called Liubushka—the diminutive of the woman's name Liubov, which is also the word for "love" in Russian. Could Liubushka have been a female friend or acquaintance who she assumed knew of Skoblin's fate? (Plevitskaya used feminine pronouns in describing Liubushka, but she might have done so in case the police somehow acquired and read her diary). On June 25, Plevitskaya wrote, "No letters from Liubushka. I'm feeling very distressed. I wrote her and she hasn't answered me. My poor darling, is what's happening there making it worse for him?" Was Plevitskaya growing concerned about the ongoing Great Terror and its possible effects on Skoblin?

July brought Plevitskaya renewed hope that her case might be dropped. She looked forward to July 19, when Filonenko, returning to Paris from a trip to Brussels, was supposed to receive word about the investigation's next step. On a sadder note, she learned that her compatriot and fellow star Feodor Chaliapin had died in Paris on April 12. She wrote in her diary that Chaliapin had been a "famous son of the Russian people" and yet had been criticized by the Bolsheviks for leaving Russia. To escape her reality, she daydreamed about what she would do if she were released. This included simplifying her life and becoming a farmer, or Fermersha, the same code name chosen for her in 1930 by Soviet intelligence. After a priest came to visit her in mid-July, she wrote in Russian the text to 1 Corinthians 13:4–8, "Love is patient, love is kind."

Growing restless for news about her case, Plevitskaya decided to take matters into her own hands and contacted a new and younger advocate named Jean Schwab. How she found and paid him is unknown, although it is possible the Soviets had recommended him and footed the bill. Plevitskaya told Filonenko about her decision to add Schwab to her defense team, and the older advocate visited her on July 30. According to Plevitskaya, he "came to yell at me and pounded his fist on the table. He's angry that I invited another advocate, a Frenchman." Before leaving, Filonenko urged her to rethink her move. "I'm so alone and without any help!" Plevitskaya sighed. On August 2, Plevitskaya relented and wrote Schwab to withdraw her request for his services. "It wasn't pleasant to do, but Filonenko was happy," she wrote in her diary.

Despite his growing frustration with Plevitskaya, Filonenko remained on her case. He wrote the prosecutor's office on August 4.[79] In his correspondence, he repeated what he had said to Marchat, including key arguments that Plevitskaya had known nothing in advance about the Miller kidnapping plot, especially her husband's specific role in it. He also stressed that she had been deemed a Soviet agent without any proof and that *Poslednie novosti* correspondents were reporting that investigators had not found any direct evidence implicating her in Miller's kidnapping. Filonenko even went to the effort of meeting briefly with Minister of Justice Paul Reynaud, a center-right, anti-Nazi politician, as Plevitskaya reported in her diary on August 10.

With the Sudeten crisis brewing, Plevitskaya worried, like everyone else in Europe, about an impending war. She wrote about it in her diary, including on August 11: "Will this mean bloodshed again?" The next day, after reading articles in the conservative Russian émigré newspaper *Voz-rozhdenie*, she remarked that its editor, Yuly Semenov, had "gone insane" because he had expressed joy upon hearing that Germany and Japan were preparing to invade the USSR. In a later entry, Plevitskaya worried about rumors that Germany was preparing to invade Czechoslovakia. The combined stress she felt from the war scare and her own situation took a heavy toll on her health. She wrote Filonenko on August 16 that her heart was giving her problems again.

Plevitskaya wrestled constantly with conflicting feelings of despair and hope. The former seemed to gain the upper hand and intensified with each passing day. On August 23, during a choir rehearsal in the Petite-Roquette's chapel, she saw a dead bird: "It did not find an exit or escape to freedom. My poor one, I can't look at your sad head—you are like my soul." Plevitskaya was filled with so much grief about Skoblin that she could no longer bear to look at the portrait of him she had pasted in her Bible. On the other hand, she felt enough hope to take her own action in Filonenko's absence. So she decided to write Schwab's secretary to request an appointment with him. "I know that [Filonenko] will get angry," she noted on August 27.

In late August, Judge Marchat concluded that there was sufficient evidence to indict Plevitskaya. On August 28, he sent his summary of the case and the dossier to the prosecutor's office. The prosecutor's office quickly forwarded these materials to the Chamber of Accusation, a panel of three judges empowered to rule on whether to transfer a case to trial. In examining Marchat's *acte d'accusation* and the dossier, the judges needed to assess whether there was enough evidence to support the charges against Plevitskaya and whether the investigation had been thorough and lawful. Marchat recommended that Skoblin, in absentia, and Plevitskaya be tried by a jury for the crimes related to Miller's kidnapping.[80]

While on holiday in late August, Filonenko delegated to his junior attorney Isabelle Goskind the work of drafting a forty-page pleading to the Chamber of Accusation.[81] Signed by Filonenko, this appears to be the last document that Plevitskaya's defense team submitted before a decision was made in September 1938. It recommended that the police investigate leads other than those concerning Skoblin's and Plevitskaya's participation in the Miller kidnapping. The defense questioned Marchat's conclusion that any explanation of Miller's abduction must necessarily involve the Skoblins.

In the pleading, Filonenko pursued the defense attorney's standard strategy of finding fault with each of the prosecution's main conclusions so as to raise doubt later, during the trial, about their viability. In general, Filonenko argued that the witnesses who claimed that Plevitskaya played an active role in Skoblin's activities and remained in particularly close proximity to him in the ten days leading up to Miller's abduction were in no position to observe every moment of the couple's time together. He restated his arguments that the witnesses in the Serdechny and in Caroline's might have erred about the time, that Plevitskaya might not have known that her husband was not waiting outside of the dress shop, and that Skoblin's car might really have malfunctioned. Filonenko also challenged the investigators' assumption that the message Skoblin wrote in his red notebook clearly stated that there would be a meeting with Miller at 12:30–1:00 p.m. on September 22. The disagreement here hinged on a word that, if spelled only slightly differently, could mean either "tomorrow" or "lunch." The message, Filonenko argued, could easily have been a reminder about a lunch the Skoblins attended with Miller at the Moskva Restaurant on September 20. As for Plevitskaya's handing the notebook to Liuba Grigul, Filonenko asked, if it was so important, why had Plevitskaya not dispensed with the notebook the day before? As for another controversy, the Skoblins' finances, there was no mystery as far as Filonenko was concerned. Plevitskaya continued to earn income as a performer, and Skoblin occasionally pocketed ROVS funds earmarked for secret anti-Soviet activities.

The last section of the pleading focused on the prosecution's lack of legal grounds for indicting Plevitskaya on charges of complicity, elaborating on the same arguments outlined in earlier pleadings. In this case, the judges decided that, in order to prove that a crime had been committed, the prosecution needed to show that the alleged accomplice had committed a positive act. Plevitskaya's indictment singled out the Skoblins' finances, their mutual political activity, Plevitskaya's dominant role in the relationship, and evidence that the couple had formulated an alibi before Miller's kidnapping. But, the defense argued, there was no proof of Plevitskaya's intention to facilitate Miller's abduction: "It is a mistake to identify as a positive act Madame Skoblin's participation in a crime her husband had perpetrated," Filonenko declared. "Thus it is false to charge her with having specific knowledge of his intention." Filonenko concluded that prosecutors would be forced to use weak deductive reasoning in arguing their case that Plevitskaya's alleged involvement in Skoblin's past activities proved her active involvement in Miller's kidnapping.

On September 6, the chamber of judges concluded its review of the Miller case file.[82] Plevitskaya awaited its pronouncement in her jail cell. The decision confirmed her worst nightmares. She would be prosecuted for complicity in the illegal confinement of, and violent acts against, Miller. The chamber of judges also announced that Skoblin would be tried in absentia at some later date. On September 9, the court issued a statement that Plevitskaya's case would be decided by a jury. Plevitskaya could have asked for a trial before judges alone, but she and her attorneys opted for a jury trial.

In her September 8 diary entry, Plevitskaya responded matter-of-factly to the decision, simply writing, "They're transferring me to court." But in a subsequent passage, she recounted a dream that revealed her real fears: "I threw myself on [Kolechka's] chest and exclaimed, 'Where have you been?' He answered, 'There!' And suddenly his head disappeared. I shouted, 'Where is your head?' 'In the other world,' he answered. A bird was shrieking, an owl. And for a long time after that shriek my heart ached."[83]

Although he wrote Plevitskaya occasionally, Filonenko did not see her until late September. Plevitskaya felt lonely and wrote in her diary about growing thinner, feeling constantly hungry, worrying about the outbreak of war, and catching the flu, which was spreading throughout the facility. On September 14, she noted that an advocate named Vincent de Moro-Giafferri came by to see her and was "very nice."

Moro-Giafferri, who was born and raised in Corsica, was an acclaimed criminal lawyer and orator who had served as a Radical Socialist deputy in the Chamber of Deputies and as minister of education. Politically left wing and fervently antifascist, Moro-Giafferri had appealed to Prime Minister Chautemps in 1934 to allow German anti-Nazis—largely Jews—to seek asylum in France.[84] He would soon represent Herschel Grynszpan after the seventeen-year-old Jewish refugee shot and killed Nazi diplomat Ernst vom Rath in Paris on November 7, 1938, the event used by the Nazis as the pretext for Kristallnacht. "So great was the fiery barrister's reputation among members of the bar," the *New York Times* wrote of Moro-Giafferri, "that they often crowded into courtrooms to hear him to the exclusion of the public."[85] Plevitskaya may have come in contact with him through an acquaintance in the Petite-Roquette.

As September wore on, Plevitskaya's mind-set became more fatalistic, and on September 19 she wrote that her remaining wish was to see Skoblin's family and then die. This, she said, "would be my final happiness!" On September 28, she appeared in court to confirm that her case was proceeding to a jury trial and returned to the Petite-Roquette feeling utterly defeated. Sister Edith brought her a cup of hot chocolate as a special treat. Plevitskaya wrote in her diary, "I won't forget your mercy!" On September 30, Plevitskaya noted that it was her fifty-third birthday, which matches her claim to have been born in 1885, not 1879, as church records indicate. She also recalled her wedding day to Skoblin in June 1921 as "my favorite day ever." Both Filonenko and Schwab came to visit her, presumably at separate times.

For the remainder of the autumn, Plevitskaya had little else to do apart from meeting with Filonenko and other attorneys to prepare for her case. In early October, she suffered a panic attack in church; her heart beat uncontrollably and her legs became weak. She commented in her diary on developments in Europe and her difficulties in trying to understand émigré allegiances to Hitler, who had claimed diplomatic victory at the Munich Conference in late September. She took an interest in an inmate whose nationality was Georgian and who had seen her perform in Tiflis many decades before. When she learned that the Georgian woman had just received a telegram from her husband, Plevitskaya remarked in her diary on October 10 that she would be happy to receive correspondence in which the text simply read, "Alive!" Two days later, an inmate recommended that Plevitskaya arrange for Moro-Giafferri to be her defense attorney because he would be able to secure her a comparatively light ten-year prison sentence. Plevitskaya remarked, "What an idiot! Why would they jail me for even a month!"

To pass the time before her trial started, Plevitskaya socialized with her Georgian friend and a new Russian inmate, Vera Guchkova (married name Traill). Guchkova was the daughter of the now deceased Provisional Government minister Alexander Guchkov, in whose pro-German circle Skoblin was rumored to have traveled. According to Plevitskaya's diary entries, Guchkova was incarcerated in the Petite-Roquette for five days, during which time she was interrogated by the police. The police apparently suspected that she was somehow involved in the NKVD murder of Ignace Reiss.[86] If Guchkova and Plevitskaya confided in each other about their NKVD connections, such information is not revealed in Plevitskaya's diary. The Georgian woman and Guchkova were released by the end of October, leaving Plevitskaya feeling lonely again.

At some point in October, Filonenko finally agreed to allow Schwab to join the defense team. "I told him a long time ago that I wouldn't go alone with him to court," she wrote. She also recognized that the Millers had comparatively more money than she did and could use it to bolster their own side. Filonenko was no doubt frustrated by Plevitskaya's criticism of him, yet he continued to bring her money for food and coffee at the canteen.

Plevitskaya's letters to Filonenko from around this time reveal not only the tension in their relationship, but also her worries. In late October, she thanked him for giving her 100 francs and inquired about her remaining assets: "What's to be done with the house? Where are the Americans who bought my diary?" she asked him. (Apparently the Americans declined this offer because Filonenko later acquired the diary.) She mentioned that a woman had bought their car and asked Filonenko to return to Caroline's to retrieve the clothes she had bought there on September 22 so that she could sell them. In a letter from November 29, she demanded that Filonenko arrange for a priest to see her, and also that he bring her buttons, silk stockings, and money. More than anything, she begged, Filonenko must hire a taxi to drive her to the Palace of Justice because the prison van was uncomfortable. She told him not to worry about providing the funds out of his own pocket because "I don't doubt I'll be able to get money from friends." (Plevitskaya asked Filonenko to destroy this letter after reading it, but he kept it for his records.)

Before Plevitskaya's trial began in early December, she appeared one last time before Marchat to answer questions about her acquaintance with Max Eitingon. The Miller family and their attorneys had accused Eitingon of serving as the Skoblins' spy handler. In November, they reported to the court that they had evidence of Eitingon's presence in Paris days before Miller's kidnapping; they also pointed out that Eitingon and his wife had stayed in a hotel close to where Miller had been kidnapped. When asked about whether she had met with Eitingon in September 1937, Plevitskaya insisted that she had not and that she had last seen him in July 1936. She also continued to deny that Eitingon was anything other than a friend and benefactor.[87]

Anticipating further questions about Eitingon at trial, Filonenko contacted people who could provide positive character references for the psychoanalyst. One contact was a great-grandniece of Napoléon and the wife of Prince George of Denmark: Princess Marie Bonaparte, a psychoanalyst and a friend of both Eitingon and Freud. Residing at the time in Paris, the wealthy aristocrat agreed to write a letter on Eitingon's behalf, describing his renown as a psychoanalyst and his generous donations to worthy causes. The princess, who had helped Freud escape Nazi repression in Vienna earlier that year, also mentioned that she had hosted Eitingon at her apartment in August 1938, when he was in Paris to attend the fifteenth annual International Conference of Psychoanalysts.[88] Similarly, Filonenko received a letter from Dr. R. Loewenstein, a member of the Psychoanalytic Society of Paris, who also spoke highly of Eitingon.

Given Plevitskaya's boast in her diary—"Why would they jail me even for a month?"—she likely felt confident that the jury would agree that her prosecutors lacked the evidence necessary to prove her complicity in Miller's kidnapping. While her attorneys drafted their statements for trial, the performer prepared for the role of her life.

11

"LA PLEVITZKAÏA" ON TRIAL

Plevitskaya's nine-day trial took place between December 5 and 14, 1938, in the Palace of Justice's Assizes Court, where the most serious criminal cases in Paris were heard.[1] At this time, war was looming, and politics in France remained extremely volatile. Édouard Daladier, prime minister since April 1938, led a government leaning increasingly to the right. On December 6 in Paris, French foreign minister Georges Bonnet and his German counterpart, Joachim von Ribbentrop, signed a declaration recognizing their existing borders and calling for joint consultation. To complicate matters further, the 1935 Franco-Soviet mutual assistance pact was still in force, even after the Anglo-French appeasement of Germany at Munich that September. Given this stormy foreign-affairs climate, Daladier's government did not want Plevitskaya's trial to become a forum for investigating whether the Soviets or the fascists had masterminded Miller's kidnapping. Where French officials were concerned, the more narrowly the proceedings focused on Plevitskaya, the better.

Plevitskaya's trial was divided into two parts. The first and longer part was the court examination, in which over fifty witnesses testified. Thirty-one prosecution witnesses, sixteen civil party witnesses (who were de facto prosecution witnesses), and eleven defense witnesses were scheduled to appear. Judge Albert Delegorgue, the *président de chambre*, dominated the court examination, flanked by two court assessors, who spoke infrequently. Imposing, rotund, and witty, Delegorgue had presided over the famous 1898 jury trial of writer Émile Zola, who was convicted of criminal libel after publicly accusing French army officers of obstruction of justice and anti-Semitism in the explosive case of Captain Alfred Dreyfus. In French courtrooms, judges typically did not act as neutral arbiters between two opposing sides and enjoyed wide discretion in deciding the admissibility of questions posed to witnesses during cross-examinations. Furthermore, the public prosecutor, *l'avocat général* Flach, did not need to prove his case beyond a reasonable doubt, as in American criminal trials. He needed only to persuade the twelve jurors that there was sufficient evidence to convict the defendant. This approach carried a weaker burden of proof and allowed jurors more subjectivity in reaching their decision. The Ministry of Justice randomly chose jurors who came from diverse socioeconomic backgrounds and who were required to base their decision on "moral proof" rather than on specific legal grounds.[2]

The second part of the trial, spanning its two final days, featured closing arguments by the attorneys on both sides. As the accused, Plevitskaya had the right to the final word. All parties directed their remarks to the jurors, who would decide the verdict. The judge and the two assessors would join the jury in determining the punishment, if at least two-thirds of the jurors (at least eight, in this case) voted to convict the accused. Given the charges, Plevitskaya's punishment could be as severe as life imprisonment or as lenient as six days in jail.

In the early afternoon of Monday, December 5, the trial of "La Plevitzkaïa," as the French press dubbed her, began. A carnivalesque atmosphere prevailed in the large courtroom, which was overflowing with reporters, photographers, and sketch artists, as well as dozens of Russian émigrés. Some proclaimed it "the trial of the century," and it was the last time that Russian émigré affairs drew so much of the French public's attention.[3]

Maximilian Filonenko and Jean Schwab, dressed in formal robes like the judges and other attorneys, sat in front of the defendant's box. They assumed from the start that they had only three or four days to prove their case, so they needed to act quickly in planting doubt in the jurors' minds.

Plevitskaya entered the courtroom flanked by two guards. The right-wing newspaper *Action Française* described her as a black sphinx guarding horrendous secrets.[4] She indeed had her secrets, but the demeanor she attempted to project was more modest: wearing a black dress, hat, gloves, and veil, she cast herself as a grieving widow. Her face was pale and haggard, but she held her head high and smiled weakly. Calling herself "Nadya," Plevitskaya wanted the jurors to view her also as a guileless and illiterate Russian peasant, incapable of participating in her husband's intrigues. She claimed not to know French and was appointed a translator.

Plevitskaya avoided making eye contact with Natalya Miller, who was also dressed in black. Natalya and Nadya—both with good reason to don the veil of widowhood and to feel victimized by circumstance—were

Trial of Nadezhda Plevitskaya, Palace of Justice, Paris, December 1938. Sitting below Plevitskaya, who is standing in the defendant's box, is (left to right) Maximilian Filonenko, Jean Schwab, and Isabelle Goskind. Courtesy of Roger-Viollet/The Image Works

viewed by the public as each other's foil: the former to be pitied, the latter reviled. Attorneys Maurice Ribet and Alexander Strelnikov sat with the Miller family and reinforced this popular understanding of the dueling widows in their remarks.

The courtroom grew silent as the clerk read the indictment, which drew parallels between the Kutepov and Miller kidnappings and retraced Skoblin's activities in Russian émigré organizations and his movements on the day of Miller's kidnapping. While listening, Plevitskaya at first closed her eyes, then gazed out a window.

During most of the day's hearing, Judge Delegorgue led the *interrogatoire*, the first part of the court examination, in which Plevitskaya was questioned about her life prior to September 1937 and her alleged involvement in Miller's kidnapping. Her face grew tense as she listened to the judge's remarks and questions, struggling to maintain her composure. She admitted to having had three husbands, but lied when she said she had never left Russia until 1920. (In her memoirs, she had openly detailed her visits to France, Monaco, and Switzerland before World War I.) When Delegorgue asked her about Levitsky's service to the Reds during the civil war, she falsely claimed that her second husband had been a lowly "Red soldier" for only two weeks before returning to the Whites. "We were always Whites," she stressed, even though Levitsky had served the Reds as an officer for a number of months, possibly a year. When the judge inquired about a civil war poster in Red-controlled Kursk, said to have described Plevitskaya as "Our Red Mother," the singer retorted, "This is a lie. I was never depicted as a 'Red Mother.' This [name] was given to Lenin's wife or Trotsky's wife. I merely lived for a time under the Reds, as many Russian women did who remained behind." In her defense, Filonenko told the judge that the poster's existence was only a rumor.

Not only did Judge Delegorgue play the role of grand inquisitor at trial; he also acted as court jester when exchanges became heated. In response to Plevitskaya's claims about her activities during the civil war, he joked, "In a word, you earned applause in both tsarist and Soviet Russia." The courtroom erupted into laughter, with the exception of Plevitskaya and her defense attorneys, who looked annoyed.

The presiding judge now presented grounds for assuming Plevitskaya's participation in Miller's kidnapping. "Witness testimony confirms that Nadezhda Plevitskaya is a smart woman who is powerful and drawn to intrigue, and who had a large influence on her husband," he informed the jurors. Plevitskaya listened to Delegorgue's statement as it was being translated and asked her translator to thank him "for making me out to be a state minister. But I never was a minister, and I have no influence over my husband."

Judge Delegorgue summarized the evidence that the investigators had gathered about Miller's disappearance. He informed the jurors that, because they did not know whether Miller was dead or alive, they would try Plevitskaya only for her involvement in a crime involving sequestration, not murder. He also mentioned the note that the ill-fated general had left for Kussonsky. Plevitskaya, undeterred, contested the note's authenticity. Filonenko interjected that its wording suggested that Miller was actually concerned about the Germans' setting a trap. He also excoriated Kussonsky for having waited so long to read the note. In a rare moment of agreement with the defense, Delegorgue concurred that Miller's assistant should have read it earlier.

The judge revealed his own bias when he signaled to the jurors that the role of foreign governments was immaterial to the case. "Who kidnapped Miller?" he asked rhetorically. "The OGPU? The Gestapo? The Spanish? A ROVS group? No matter what, Nikolai Skoblin took an actual part in it. You jurors must decide whether Nadezhda Plevitskaya was her husband's accomplice."

Delegorgue identified the flawed alibi as a key piece of evidence against Plevitskaya. He referred to witness testimony at the Hotel Pax, the Serdechny Restaurant, and Caroline's dress shop. Taking up this thread, Ribet argued that the crux of the alibi came down to time—in other words, to Plevitskaya's supposed arrival at Caroline's at approximately 11:50 a.m. and her departure at around 1:45 p.m. Conversely, Plevitskaya claimed not to recall the precise time of each event between the morning and the midafternoon of September 22. The alibi's existence, she said, had been the investigators' idea, not hers. Why, Ribet wondered, had Plevitskaya not asked Skoblin to accompany her into the dress shop? "Rags didn't interest him," she replied breezily. She had simply ignored what Skoblin was doing. She also asserted once more that she and Skoblin had arrived together at the train station.

Turning to the events on the night of September 22 and the early morning of September 23, Judge Delegorgue described to the jurors how Skoblin had fled ROVS headquarters and then disappeared. He asked Plevitskaya to recount what Skoblin had said when Matsylev woke him up, and she replied that she could not recall exactly.

"Don't you think it's strange that he didn't ask why he was being roused from his bed?"

"Ah, it was so unexpected!" answered Plevitskaya.

The judge then asked, "You knew nothing about the preparations for Miller's abduction?"

Plevitskaya raised her hand and answered, "I swear!"

Turning back to the jurors, Judge Delegorgue noted, "All witnesses mentioned her great influence over her husband. She knew everything about his affairs. In letters, her name was mentioned. They asked her sometimes to pass along information to her husband."

Plevitskaya looked frustrated. "My husband, when I married him, made me promise that I'd never interfere in his regimental business or political matters," she remarked. "I never engaged in politics because I couldn't. [Skoblin's assistant] Troshin can confirm this." She stressed that they had loved each other very much.

"Why, if he loved you," the judge prodded, "did your husband run out on you?" Delegorgue called Skoblin a coward for allowing his wife to stand trial alone.

Defense attorney Schwab answered, "And what if he's dead?"

"It's terrible to leave a beloved wife at such a moment. How can you explain this?" the judge asked Plevitskaya, ignoring Schwab.

Plevitskaya's emotions gave way. Her lips trembling, she began to weep. "I do not know" was all she could muster in Skoblin's defense. Seeing her emotional vulnerability and sensing an opportunity, Ribet inquired about the letters from Skoblin's ROVS associates that had been addressed to her over the years. Were they encrypted? Did she have the key?

Wiping away her tears, Plevitskaya responded, "I had no understanding of such a key. I received no such letters. And if my husband used my name, then I know nothing of it." She was shaken but had not reached a breaking point. She would not confess to spying for the Soviets, as Robert and Marjorie Switz had done in 1934 in return for their freedom.

After a brief recess, the judge informed the jury about the truck with Soviet diplomatic plates that had left the building on Montmorency Boulevard and traveled to Le Havre, where the *Maria Ulyanova* had been docked. This "Le Havre trail" theory, as it was called, assumed that the Soviets had organized Miller's kidnapping. "Was Miller's body inside the crate? We can only guess that it was," he admitted. Tabling this topic for now, the judge returned to questioning Plevitskaya, focusing on her and Skoblin's finances and their acquaintance with Max Eitingon. "Experts examined the Skoblins' financial records," Delegorgue told the jurors, "and determined that they were living beyond their means between 1931 and 1935."

"My husband handled our finances," Plevitskaya insisted.

"Who's Eitingon?" Judge Delegorgue inquired.

Plevitskaya had a ready-made answer to this question. "He's a very good friend, a scholar and psychologist; his wife was an actor in the Moscow Art Theater." Responding to the judge's earlier remark about Eitingon's having given her money, she said, "I never sold myself. I received gifts from both of them."

The judge, trying to goad Plevitskaya into offering more information, exclaimed, "I don't know Russian tastes. But it seems strange that some other man would dress a general's wife." Dozens of men around the courtroom snickered.

"On my honor as a woman," she swore, "I did not soil my reputation by having intimate relations with him in exchange for gifts." The judge's questions about Eitingon's "gifts" to Plevitskaya were misleading. Financial auditors assigned to investigate the funds that Eitingon had allegedly given the Skoblins proved unable to trace any such monies.[5]

When Ribet accused Plevitskaya of lying about her final meeting with Eitingon, he stood on sturdier ground. During the preliminary investigation, Plevitskaya said that she had last seen Eitingon in July 1936. But investigators later acquired records of phone calls between the Skoblins and the Eitingons in September 1937 (copies of which Ribet showed the court in a subsequent hearing) and collected witness testimony confirming that the Skoblins had accompanied the Eitingons to a Paris train station on the morning of September 20, two days before Miller's kidnapping. It also became known that the Eitingons had been staying in a building near the corner of Jasmin and Raffet Streets, close to Miller's and Skoblin's meeting point. Ribet asked Plevitskaya why she had denied seeing the Eitingons then.

Caught red-handed, Plevitskaya gave a less than credible response. "Maybe I didn't understand the question before," she replied, "or maybe I forgot. But now it's true, I remember that we were with them early that morning to take them to the train station. There's nothing for me to hide."

"This is unarguably a contradiction of the testimony," Judge Delegorgue noted.

"She's explaining that being detained in prison naturally weakened her memory," Schwab intervened. The judge did not view this explanation as credible. Soon after this exchange, and in an apparent moment of desperation, Plevitskaya tilted her head to one side and made a sign of the cross.

Judge Delegorgue became increasingly frustrated with her. "You're accused of aiding your husband in completing a crime," he charged. "Your act of conspiracy is demonstrated by how you, together with your husband, had worked out an alibi beforehand, for the purpose of preventing him from later falling under suspicion."

"Never!" Plevitskaya shouted dramatically. "My husband never discussed his affairs with me! He was an honorable and valorous general, and I knew him to be only that way."

Ribet spoke next. "You spent the night of September 23 with Eitingon's brother-in-law?" he asked. "Why didn't you stay in the hotel?"

"I couldn't stay in the room where he was taken from. I couldn't even look at the street," she cried. "And where I went, I don't know." Filonenko stressed that Plevitskaya had been questioned by a police officer on the morning of September 23 in her hotel room and had not immediately gone into hiding.

"Is Natalya Miller your friend?" Ribet continued.

"Yes, my good friend," Plevitskaya answered, looking in Miller's direction for the first time.

"Why didn't you go to her then?"

Plevitskaya was sounding incoherent now. "A ROVS lieutenant . . . was it Matsylev? . . . told me that the general had disappeared. But so had my husband."

"Nonetheless," said Ribet, "why didn't you visit her?"

"I'm only human. . . . My husband spoiled me. I loved him," she insisted. "I went crazy, forgot everything, even where they lived." Her voice broke off, and she began to cry again.

Ribet did not comfort her. "Why didn't you phone?"

"I couldn't talk on the telephone. I didn't know where one was," she replied. "I'm completely helpless in Paris."

A juror asked about Skoblin's notebook, which Plevitskaya had handed to Liuba Grigul at the police station on September 24. At this point, the judge decided to halt his examination of the defendant, who had refused to answer candidly.

The press and the public had lost none of their interest when Plevitskaya's trial resumed on December 6 and various police officers who had been involved in the investigation testified. Plevitskaya, still wearing her widow's weeds, began the hearing looking calm and self-composed. On this second day, it became even clearer that the trial was not simply about the alleged criminal activities of an aging Russian singer. Witness testimony was punctuated by aggressive exchanges between the opposing sides as the subjects at hand strayed from the charges against Plevitskaya to other potential conspirators and the possibility of the USSR's involvement in Miller's abduction.

For the jury's benefit, Investigator André Roches, who was credited with identifying the discrepancies in Plevitskaya's alibi during his initial interrogations, outlined the investigation's definition of the timeline on September 22 and contrasted it with Skoblin's and Plevitskaya's story. Skoblin had told his ROVS colleagues that he and Plevitskaya were dining at 12:30 p.m. at the Serdechny, meaning that he could not have accompanied Miller to any meeting at that time. Similarly, in her initial statement, Plevitskaya claimed that she and Skoblin had left their hotel room at around 12:10 p.m. and remained at the nearby restaurant for forty-five minutes, leaving there closer to 1:00 p.m. She later claimed that she could not recall the exact times.

Using witness testimony, Roches described what in the investigation's view had actually happened: The Skoblins had left the hotel at around 11:00 a.m. and had stayed at the Serdechny until approximately 11:40 a.m. Plevitskaya had arrived at Caroline's at around 11:50 a.m. and had left there at around 1:40 p.m. Skoblin had never entered the shop during her time there, and she had repeatedly told the shopkeeper that he was waiting for her out in his car near the front of the store. During the final interrogations of Plevitskaya, she insisted that, upon leaving the shop, she had not seen Skoblin or their car and had begun walking down the street in search of him. He had been waiting on a side street, "where the noise did not distract him from reading his newspaper." She also claimed that he had quickly found her and that they had driven together to the train station, arriving around 2:00 p.m. She added that Skoblin had arrived at the platform later than she because he had been fixing the car. By contrast, investigators learned that Skoblin had entered the dress shop shortly after his wife's departure and had arrived at the station five minutes after she had. Plevitskaya had presumably taken a taxi, although the police never found the driver. Roches also remarked that documents seized at the Skoblins' house and elsewhere revealed the couple's involvement in espionage.

Judge Delegorgue now asked Plevitskaya, "For the sake of his wife, son, and brother, do you know whether Miller is alive or dead? I'm sure you know where Miller and Skoblin are."

Filonenko replied, "How would anyone know whether Skoblin's alive?"

The judge angrily exclaimed, "I order her to speak the truth! Translator, ask her, does she know where Miller is?"

Plevitskaya listened to the translation, holding a handkerchief to her face. "To all honorable French people and to the French court," she answered, "I can look you in the eyes honorably and with a clear conscience. I'm suffering more than the others. I can look everyone in the eye. God is my main witness, and he sees that I'm not guilty!"

Judge Delegorgue raised his hands in exasperation. "Alas! We have not moved forward even a single step!" To make matters worse for the judge, Schwab and Ribet traded verbal blows, while Roches waited patiently for his next question.

Schwab wanted jurors to doubt that the Soviets had organized and carried out the Miller kidnapping. He stressed that the civil party's attorneys were "trying to convince the court that the Soviets completed the crime, but there's no evidence of this!" To which Ribet replied, "I didn't know that you're the Soviet government's advocate!" Plevitskaya raised her eyebrows in response to the heated exchange and covered her face with her hand. Roches remarked that he did not think that any ROVS members other than Skoblin were involved in Miller's kidnapping.

Schwab and Filonenko inquired about Roches's statement. Schwab asked whether General Anton Turkul, known to be pro-German, had played any role in the plot, and Roches answered no. Filonenko asked Roches, "Did you consider it normal that a Frenchman or a foreigner arranged a meeting in Paris with official agents of Germany in September 1937, when these agents could any day become enemies of France?" The courtroom stirred, and an anonymous spectator yelled, "And von Ribbentrop?" who had signed an agreement with his counterpart in Paris that very day. Filonenko added, "I have in mind the secret meeting [between Miller and the so-called Germans]. Do you consider such a meeting to have been normal?"

Roches replied, "Yes, General Miller was involved in espionage!" This statement caused some Russian émigrés in the courtroom to protest.

"Against France?" asked Ribet.

"Oh, no, no!" answered Roches.

"Never call this espionage," Ribet corrected him. "General Miller was gathering information necessary for his political activity."

Next, Investigator Piguet, who had led initial inquiries in the Miller case, addressed questions from Schwab. Schwab commented on how one police report accused Kussonsky of holding Kedrov back in the ROVS building with the intention of letting Skoblin escape; Piguet admitted that Kussonsky had left an odd impression on him. Schwab also raised the names of General Shatilov and other ROVS members who had acted suspiciously at one point or another. Schwab was trying to confuse jurors into thinking that Plevitskaya had been used as a patsy.

Ribet asked Plevitskaya whether she approved of Schwab's defense tactics. She smiled at Schwab and answered, "He's my advocate and knows how to defend me." Schwab added, "In a word, the jurors see what kind of people were around Miller," causing spectators to grumble. In a somewhat bigoted aside, Judge Delegorgue noted that the Russian community was "known for its abnormal behavior."

The judge then shifted his questioning of Piguet to the topic of the truck with Soviet diplomatic plates. The judge's words indicate that he assumed the Soviets had transported Miller to the *Maria Ulyanova*, and Piguet answered that, while the investigators had examined a number of theories, the most plausible assumed that the Soviets had abducted Miller.

Schwab interrupted Piguet, exclaiming, "This is just an attempt to muddle the case. The Soviet government has nothing to do with it!"

As the courtroom erupted and Judge Delegorgue wielded his gavel, Ribet yelled, "And you are its advocate!" His associate Strelnikov added, "Go to Moscow!"

Schwab, looking bemused, replied, "Why to Moscow? I was born in Paris!" Many Russian émigrés in Paris suspected that Schwab was pro-

Soviet, as did right-wing French commentators, including the journalist and future Nazi collaborator Maurice-Ivan Sicard, who attended Plevits-kaya's trial.[6]

Moments passed, and the courtroom settled down again. Now Filonenko took up the questioning of Piguet, this time about the notorious green Bible. Piguet replied that investigators had failed to detect any hand-writing made with invisible ink but still assumed that the Bible had served as a key for deciphering correspondence.

"Isn't that why Nadezhda Plevitskaya wanted to have it with her in jail?" asked Prosecutor Flach. Plevitskaya shrugged.

Many spectators guffawed as they heard her reply, "This is the first I've heard of the green Bible. I had a Bible that I wanted to take . . . but it wasn't green. . . . It was yellow!" In any case, Filonenko interjected, the so-called green Bible had not been used as a key for encrypting or deci-phering secret messages.

Inspector Chauvineau next appeared as a witness, followed by two other inspectors appointed to the case after the minister of the interior had transferred him. Chauvineau recounted the information in his re-port, which he had telephoned to the Ministry of the Interior in Paris on the evening of September 22. His report stated that the *Maria Ulyanova*'s crew had been in such a hurry to leave after receiving a message from the USSR that morning and after taking a crate on board that afternoon that they had not even bothered to unload all their cargo before leaving port. Chauvineau added that he had met about his report with Pierre Mondanel, inspector general of the Sûreté Nationale, at the time. Chauvineau told the courtroom that the Ministry of the Interior's leadership had been distressed by the attention he had given the Soviet ship, as it was assumed that, if news leaked out, his report would heighten tensions with the Soviets.

During the discussion about the Le Havre trail, Plevitskaya seemed bored. She occasionally glanced around the courtroom, smiling and ac-knowledging her acquaintances. For a moment, she turned away and blot-ted her temples with a handkerchief she had wetted with eau de cologne from her purse.

Judge Delegorgue listened more attentively and interjected his belief that the eight-cylinder truck could have traveled the approximately 220-kilometer route within two and a half hours, in time to load the crate onto the Soviet ship. An investigation report confirmed that the same truck that had left the building on Montmorency Boulevard had appeared in Le Havre later on September 22. One of the other inspectors, named Papin, attested that he had seen nothing suspicious either about the truck or the box, which he described as more like a suitcase. Ribet asked Chauvineau about the role played by then Minister of the Interior Marx Dormoy, who after hearing Chauvineau's report did not want the French navy chasing after the Soviet ship. Judge Delegorgue then agreed to call Mondanel as a witness and adjourned the trial until the next day.

On December 7, the third day of the trial, Plevitskaya entered the room with a sure step, knowing exactly where she needed to sit. Natalya Miller reappeared, seated on the bench alongside her attorneys. Ribet demanded that Dormoy be called as a witness. Although the third day lacked fiery confrontations between the opposing sides, it drew strong interest because three key witnesses were scheduled to testify, all of whom believed that the Soviets had organized Miller's kidnapping and that Skoblin had been involved: General Kussonsky, Admiral Kedrov, and Colonel Matsylev. Kussonsky appeared first and conceded that he was guilty of negligence for not having opened Miller's note sooner.

"Why didn't you open it earlier?" Judge Delegorgue asked.

Kussonsky, whose testimony seemed to implicate, rather than exonerate, him, lacked a straightforward answer. "My conscience is clear. If I'd opened it earlier," he offered, "it wouldn't have changed Miller's fate or prevented Skoblin from fleeing." His words created a sensation. Kussonsky proceeded to describe his and Kedrov's fateful 2:00 a.m. meeting with Skoblin, adding an account of how Skoblin fled from ROVS headquarters.

"For a Russian general," Judge Delegorgue noted, "you committed a number of strategic blunders!" The spectators laughed.

Kussonsky then changed his testimony about what Miller had told him on the morning of September 22. Earlier Kussonsky had insisted that his boss had said he would be returning to his ROVS office later in the day. Now he said that Miller had not mentioned this and had put away his papers, suggesting to Kussonsky that he would not return to the office. Again, Kussonsky seemed keen to convince the jurors that he had waited to open Miller's note because he had not been particularly worried about the general's safety and had had no reason for concern when Miller failed to return to ROVS later in the day.

Judge Delegorgue was puzzled that Kussonsky had not insisted that Skoblin be detained and sent to the police. "You made a major error," he said.

"The French police also made a major mistake when they let Plevitskaya roam free an entire day," Ribet interjected.

Schwab saw an opportunity. "Would she really have fled?" he asked. "She went to the police voluntarily!" The questions that Schwab and

Filonenko put to Kussonsky show how they hoped to persuade jurors to think of his—and not Plevitskaya's—involvement in the kidnapping. These questions included why Kussonsky had assumed that Miller would not return to his office that afternoon and why he had detained Kedrov instead of Skoblin, allowing the latter to flee.

In his own defense, a flabbergasted Kussonsky said, "I can't recall all the details fourteen months after the fact!"

In contrast to Kussonsky, Kedrov appeared a credible witness. It was Kedrov who had quickly concluded that "the moment Skoblin ran off, it meant he was guilty." It was Kedrov who had insisted that he, Kussonsky, and Matsylev go immediately to the police, instead of returning to the Hotel Pax in search of Skoblin. One point that the two men agreed on was that Plevitskaya knew everything about Skoblin's business affairs.

Plevitskaya turned to the judge and asked, "Why does [Kedrov] think this was so? Did he hear it from me? Did he hear it from my husband?" Kedrov's argument was that he had closely observed the people around him. However, he did not give the court any specific details about how he knew Plevitskaya was knowledgeable of and engaged in Skoblin's intrigues.

Filonenko asked Kedrov, "You're sure, Admiral, of Skoblin's guilt because he fled. But Plevitskaya did not run. Shouldn't this convince you of her innocence?"

"Not a bit!" Kedrov replied. "Skoblin and Plevitskaya were inseparable." Kedrov noted how Investigator Roches had told him that he did not think it possible for the crate to have been placed on board the *Maria Ulyanova* in time for its departure. Ribet argued that this indicated that the police did not want to fully investigate the Le Havre route and instead aimed to conceal how French officials had allowed the Soviet ship to escape with Miller on board.

Matsylev's testimony about his conversation with Plevitskaya in the early morning of September 23 was a point of interest. His account of what Plevitskaya had said—especially her allegedly having asked him whether he had suspected Skoblin of something—was widely interpreted to indicate her knowledge of Skoblin's role in Miller's kidnapping.

"Were these your actual words?" Judge Delegorgue asked her.

"I don't recall," Plevitskaya answered, spreading her hands in a gesture of helplessness.

Turning to Matsylev, Schwab asked, "Is it true that Nadezhda Plevitskaya saved two of your brothers when they were White officers in Russia during the civil war?"

"It is true," Matsylev admitted. Ribet told the judge that Matsylev was compromised as a witness for the prosecution, because he likely could not sustain hostile feelings toward Plevitskaya due to her having saved his brothers.

Filonenko tried to build on this positive momentum for his client. He asked Kedrov whether he knew an Admiral Fridkin, who had written a letter praising Plevitskaya for defending Tsar Nicholas II in 1917. Kedrov said he had not seen Fridkin in twenty-five years. Undeterred, Filonenko mentioned that, during this time in Russia, Plevitskaya had written an article supporting the tsar. Judge Delegorgue asked Plevitskaya to comment.

Smiling, she answered, "It wasn't an article, but an interview I gave at the time of the Bolshevik Revolution." She tossed back her head and extended her hands toward the judge. "Reporters asked me whether I had often met with the tsar. 'Yes, yes!' I replied. But they wanted me to tell them that I saw him when he was drunk." At the time, she recalled, journalists were trying to collect dirt on the tsar and his family, but she had refused to aid their calumny. "Everything I had to say favored the tsar, whom I knew was wonderful! Everything I said about him was positive, because it was all I ever saw or knew!" Most spectators were not swayed by Plevitskaya's display of loyalty to the slain tsar. Instead, they laughed at her.

Ribet looked at her defense attorneys and asked, "Do you think that someone who supported the tsar twenty-five years ago couldn't be a Soviet agent now? The case of Aleksei Ignatieff [a Russian nobleman turned Soviet agent] is well known to us."

"Plevitskaya twice displayed high moral courage, risking her life for the sake of others," Filonenko replied, referring to her intercession with the Red Army on behalf of Matsylev's brothers. "Her feelings for the tsar and her homeland have not changed."

"Alas!" Ribet continued. "She lacked the courage to appear before Natalya Miller after her husband was kidnapped!"

Deciding that the quality of the examination had deteriorated beyond repair and that the witnesses had been adequately questioned, Judge Delegorgue ended the day's hearing.

On Thursday, December 8—the fourth day of the trial—Judge Delegorgue publicly scolded the attorneys. "Do not impede the court examination or digress," he said. "You need to move quickly in questioning witnesses. The trial should have concluded yesterday. But, given the way it's been going so far, we'll be here until next Monday or Tuesday."

Schwab ignored the judge's instructions and called Kedrov back to the witness stand. "Is it true," Schwab inquired, "that during a break yesterday, you told General Kussonsky that 'in this case we must give testimony not based on honesty but the circumstances'?" The spectators stirred.

Kedrov turned to address the jurors. "Never!" he replied. "I never spoke such words. During the break, Kussonsky approached me and said, 'It seems I said too much.' I answered jokingly, 'You should never try too hard, but should know when to stop.'" Schwab's diversionary tactic to discredit Kedrov backfired: the spectators viewed Schwab with disdain, and Judge Delegorgue dismissed Kedrov from the stand. What did Plevitskaya think? She sat silently, in an apparent attempt to remain calm and composed.

Next to take the witness stand was Pierre Mondanel, who stressed that he had carried out his duties on September 23 without any political interference. After receiving Chauvineau's report, which seemed inconsistent on the question of whether the truck supposedly carrying Miller had arrived in Le Havre before or after 3:00 p.m., Mondanel sent Commissaire Papin to the port to investigate. Ribet and the judge grilled Mondanel about why Chauvineau had been transferred from Le Havre and about his alleged meeting with Chauvineau shortly after September 23. Mondanel claimed not to recall this meeting and insisted that he had never threatened his subordinate in any way. Chauvineau proposed that an office worker he had spoken with outside of Mondanel's office moments after the supposed meeting be called as a witness.

The judge grew impatient with Mondanel. "We need to know the truth," he scolded. "I will do everything within my power to obtain it." But Mondanel was not swayed by the judge's authority, as he worked for an even higher body in the French government.

Ribet's next move was meant to strike a blow against the defense. He asked Mondanel whether he was aware of how Schwab was planning to speak on December 9 on "The Case of Skoblin: Conspiracy of Russian Fascists" at a meeting of the Paris branch of a Russian Masonic organization called the Grand Orient of the Peoples of Russia. In planning his speech, Ribet argued, Schwab was serving the interests of his Soviet masters.

"This is unconscionable!" Schwab stood up and exclaimed. He reminded the court that the judge had planned to conclude the trial before December 9. "I didn't intend to speak outside the court until the end of the trial. . . . I have the right to speak wherever I want, and Monsieur Ribet can't prevent me from doing so!" Schwab wiped drops of sweat from his pale face and sat down. Schwab may have had a reasonable explanation for why he had scheduled his talk on December 9, but his choice of subject—painting Skoblin as a fascist agent—raised suspicions in the courtroom that Schwab was on the Soviets' payroll. A furious Schwab struck back at Ribet by asking him where he had found a list of names of Soviet agents. "Investigators have no such documents," he said.

Ribet was ready for his rebuttal. "They're in materials that Marchat placed in the dossier!"

"These materials are not known to the defense," Schwab claimed. "You stole them from Marchat's office!"

Ribet spoke calmly, "Don't make such accusations, young colleague! If those materials are unknown to you, then that's because you were not curious enough about Skoblin's archive," referring to the documents Skoblin had stored in his home office.

Filonenko explained to the jurors that Skoblin had compiled the list during the years when he helped run ROVS's Inner Line, whose main job was to expose Soviet agents. "It's unknown whether the French authorities even knew about these people. The list was Skoblin's private information!"

Judge Delegorgue, struggling to advance the proceedings, ordered Captain Pyotr Grigul to the stand. A valuable prosecution witness, Grigul had spent years observing Skoblin and Plevitskaya and had seen them on September 22. Grigul did not pull his punches against Plevitskaya. He noted how she "came to us as a prisoner during the civil war, and within a week had already befriended the commander of our regiment"—presumably Yakov Pashkevich.

"Do you agree with Admiral Kedrov that Nadezhda Plevitskaya was the 'leading force' in the Skoblin household?" Judge Delegorgue asked.

"Yes," Grigul answered, "she was the leading force." In a gesture of incredulity, Plevitskaya smiled, covering her eyes with one hand.

The judge turned to address Plevitskaya. "Why did you go to Ozoir-la-Ferrière the night of September 22?"

"We hadn't been home for three days," she answered. "Our pets were hungry. We had to feed them."

Ribet asked, "Why did you return to Paris that night instead of staying home?"

Plevitskaya shrugged her shoulders. "I don't remember. Why do I need to give Ribet a detailed account of this?"

Prosecutor Flach spoke next to Plevitskaya. "What was in the suitcase that you took to Ozoir-la-Ferrière with you?"

Plevitskaya smiled. "Well, things . . . I don't recall."

Filonenko contested Grigul's statements about Plevitskaya's relations with Skoblin. "Answer exactly, does [Grigul] know for certain whether Nadezhda Plevitskaya was involved in preparations for Miller's kidnapping?"

"Now it seems as though those preparations were made," Grigul answered, "but at the time, who could have known about them?"

"Did she really know?" Filonenko continued.

"Nadezhda Vasilievna always knew about her husband," Grigul shot back. "She knew every step he took."

Filonenko brought to the jurors' attention the point that Grigul's comments about Plevitskaya were "not facts, but impressions." Clearly, Filonenko thought that this argument was his client's best defense. Maybe the jurors would see it this way as well and would exonerate Plevitskaya.

After all, there was no direct evidence at the time that Plevitskaya knew beforehand about the plot to kidnap Miller. Even if Skoblin had normally kept his wife informed on every facet of his life, how could the court prove that she had known about the Miller plan in advance and while it was happening? It was entirely possible that Skoblin might only have told her back at the hotel, hours after Miller had been drugged and forced into the crate. Viewed with hindsight, and especially considering that Russian intelligence sources have identified the Skoblins as Soviet agents, the circumstantial evidence against Plevitskaya now seems strong. Back in 1938, however, there was still some room for doubt.

Also with the benefit of hindsight, it appears that the jurors focused on Judge Delegorgue's and Prosecutor Flach's questions and comments. At this point, with Grigul still on the stand, they returned to the subject of Skoblin's notebook. Delegorgue and Flach wanted to clarify exactly what Skoblin had scribbled on one page. Investigators assumed that it was a reminder to inform Miller about a meeting happening between 12:30 and 1:00 p.m. *zavtra* (Russian for "tomorrow"), meaning September 22. Flach was certain that Skoblin had written *zavtra*. He reminded the jurors that "Plevitskaya had wanted to hide the notebook from French authorities," because she knew there was incriminating evidence in it.

Conversely, the defense argued that the contested word was not *zavtra* but *zavtrak*, meaning "breakfast"—and not on September 22, but on the morning of Monday, September 20, when Miller could be shown to have met Skoblin and other Kornilov veterans in the Moskva Restaurant. "Would Nadezhda Plevitskaya really have handed over the notebook had she been a Soviet agent?" Filonenko asked the jurors, implying that she would have known to destroy it instead of keeping it in her purse.

The judge ordered that the jurors be shown the page in Skoblin's notebook so they could decide for themselves whether there was an extra *k* or not, and tabled the matter for the time being. He thought it was more important to question the next witness, Antonin Collin, a maritime broker at Le Havre. Collin told the court that he had boarded the *Maria Ulyanova* at 3:40 p.m. on the afternoon of September 22, at which point the Soviet truck was not visible from the dock. He had disembarked at 4:15 p.m., when it was visible.

"You definitely recall the time?" Judge Delegorgue asked.

"Very much so," Collin answered. He was certain because he had been in the captain's quarters when a sailor walked in and spoke in Russian to the captain. The captain then immediately left his quarters, with Collin following closely behind. The latter watched as the captain gave orders to his crew. "I had the impression that something had happened on board the ship," Collin noted. "I asked the captain what it was, and he brushed me off, saying, 'Oh, no, nothing.'" The courtroom erupted in laughter. "It's possible that this is when they reported to the captain about the truck's arrival, before I'd disembarked," Collin continued. Collin confirmed that the *Maria Ulyanova* had left port at around 8:00 p.m. without unloading all its cargo.

"Could the *Maria Ulyanova* have left earlier?" one juror inquired.

"No, it couldn't have," Collin answered. "The water level was too low." This meant that the tide had gone out, and the ship would have gotten stuck had it tried leaving the harbor. Next on the witness stand, two customs officers confirmed Collin's testimony that the truck had arrived in Le Havre between 3:00 and 4:00 p.m. and that men had unloaded a crate from a truck with Soviet diplomatic license plates and taken it on board the *Maria Ulyanova*. The Le Havre trail theory seemed to be gaining more traction.

The court's examination of other witnesses that day, including Leonid Raigorodsky and witnesses at the Serdechny Restaurant and the Hotel Pax, mainly strengthened the prosecution's case. Although Raigorodsky defended his brother-in-law, Max Eitingon, as a reputable man, he admitted on the stand that he knew that the Skoblins had accompanied the Eitingons to the Lyon train station on the morning of September 20. His comment gave Ribet and the judge another chance to remind the jurors about Plevitskaya's contradictory testimony. "Two weeks ago, Plevitskaya said she had not seen the Eitingons in two years!" the judge interjected. "What does she say now?"

"I myself know well now," she answered. "Without any cunning or craftiness involved, I simply forgot. I am rather sick in the head. . . . Oh, my God, who finds this important? Of course I saw them, accompanied them to the train."

"The attorneys for the civil suit insist that Eitingon is a Soviet agent!" Filonenko tried to convey humorously.

"We can prove it!" Ribet insisted.

Filonenko proposed calling Princess Marie Bonaparte as a witness, which prompted widespread laughter in the courtroom. Apparently some spectators had a prurient interest in her psychoanalytical research on sexual frigidity. Needless to say, Judge Delegorgue chose not to accept Filonenko's proposal, and the princess never appeared.

The joking atmosphere in the courtroom soon dissipated when two servers from the Serdechny took the witness stand. Their recollection of the time that the Skoblins arrived at the restaurant on the morning of September 22 contrasted sharply with Plevitskaya's. The servers agreed that the Skoblins had arrived around 11:00 a.m. and left well before 12:15 p.m., whereas Plevitskaya insisted that she and Skoblin had arrived after 12:00 p.m. and left later than 12:30 p.m.

"Why all the rush?" Plevitskaya asked rhetorically. "Because we had to eat, I had to pick out clothes, and we had to go to the train station." In terms of the time discrepancy, all she could do was shrug her shoulders and say, "I wasn't keeping track of the time."

"At your first interrogation, why were you so exact about the time, then?" Judge Delegorgue asked.

"Yes, I saw on the wall clocks that it was after 12:00 p.m.," she replied. "Maybe I was mistaken. I have poor eyesight!"

"Ah, poor eyesight!" the judge guffawed, and the spectators laughed along with him.

Jean Boyer, manager of the Hotel Pax, was the final witness that day. He offered information about how the Skoblins had stayed occasionally at the hotel since 1932 and noted that Plevitskaya had always treated him kindly. On September 22, he had not observed her acting strangely. However, he recalled that the Skoblins had left the hotel at around 11:00 a.m., a full hour later than the time Plevitskaya reported.

Addressing Plevitskaya, the judge asked, "Why didn't you return to your hotel at night?"

"I already said that I couldn't," she answered. "I was afraid of being in the room. My husband left there and did not return. I'm afraid of going there alone."

"And yet she roamed around Paris all day!" Ribet said dismissively.

★   ★   ★

Friday, December 9, marked the fifth day of the trial and its halfway point. Witness after witness had accused Plevitskaya of being a diabolical genius. Experts had refuted her testimony. Despite the growing pressure to do so, Plevitskaya still refused to admit any wrongdoing and remained stubbornly committed to asserting her innocence.

On this day Judge Delegorgue used the testimony of an automobile expert named Hérard to convince jurors that Plevitskaya was lying about how events at the North Station had unfolded. Plevitskaya had told the court that, before rushing to the train platform to meet their friends, she had first watched Skoblin open the hood of their car and work on the engine. Hérard later found the car in full working order. "The engine couldn't have been banging on one day and then corrected itself on another," he argued. "When an engine fails, it doesn't heal itself without a doctor's intervention."

"Well, it means that my husband repaired it himself," Plevitskaya suggested. "But, in general, I didn't pay any attention. I don't know whether or not the engine was banging. I don't understand anything about it." Filonenko suggested that all car motors were noisy and maybe Plevitskaya had just not been bothered by it.

"This is the first I've heard of a car's behaving this way," quipped Hérard.

Juror 4 directed the discussion to the Soviet truck's route to Le Havre. "Is there a significant difference in speed between a truck and a car?" he asked. Hérard pointed out that this depended on the vehicle's weight and engine type. "The truck was an eight-cylinder Ford," he answered. "Normally, this Ford ought to average 120 to 125 kilometers per hour. If it's heavy, then 90 to 100 kilometers per hour."

Ribet inquired how much time it would have taken the truck to drive from Paris to Le Havre. Hérard estimated "no more than two and a half hours, in dry weather and on good roads."

"Could the truck that left Montmorency Boulevard at 1:00 p.m. have reached Le Havre by 3:30 p.m.?" asked Ribet.

"Absolutely!"

Trying to instill a sense of doubt in the jurors, Schwab introduced into evidence a letter from another automobile expert. This individual concluded that a truck such as this Ford model could not have taken less than four hours and fifteen minutes to drive the route. There was a loud reaction in the courtroom.

"The letter was written by someone who doesn't understand," Hérard commented.

"It's written by one of your colleagues, an auto expert working for the court!" Schwab responded.

Hérard laughed and said that his colleague "probably had in mind either a shoddy vehicle or a poor driver."

General Shatilov, one of Plevitskaya's avowed nemeses, now took the stand. He called Plevitskaya Skoblin's eminence grise, insisting that she had influenced his thinking on politics and regimental affairs. She had taken part in all the political debates among White Army officers, he claimed. Shatilov was sure that Skoblin and Plevitskaya were Soviet agents, although he lacked details; it was more of a hunch.

Ribet raised the point that, after Kutepov's kidnapping in 1930, Plevitskaya had visited the kidnapped general's wife several times, reportedly to gather information about the investigation into his abduction.

"Did she alone go to Madame Kutepova's?" Schwab wondered.

"No, many women did," Shatilov admitted.

"But she was the only one who had committed a betrayal!" Schwab sarcastically replied.

Plevitskaya added, "Misfortune follows me wherever I go." Turning to the jurors, she continued, "No, it wasn't like that. We found out about Kutepov's kidnapping after dinner at Ozoir-la-Ferrière. I was never friends with Lydia Kutepova, and I had rarely visited her."

"Before the kidnapping, you rarely visited her, but afterward you never left her apartment!" Shatilov exclaimed.

Plevitskaya recounted to the court how she had first met Shatilov outside the Kutepovs' apartment building and had had a negative impression of him. Apparently, Kutepova felt similarly put off by him and scolded him in front of Plevitskaya. After that, Plevitskaya claimed, "Madame Kutepova asked me to visit her more often."

Judge Delegorgue asked Plevitskaya to comment on Shatilov's characterization of her as Skoblin's eminence grise. With a restrained smile, Plevitskaya asked, "How would he have known that? I almost never saw him."

"The witness also called you a *cabotine*," Delegorgue added, meaning a show-off or poseur. Plevitskaya's translator struggled to find an appropriate definition in Russian, but Plevitskaya seemed to understand what the judge had said and smiled. Instead of replying, she simply turned away from Shatilov, sat back down, and rested her cheek on her hand.

Filonenko attempted to discredit Shatilov by asking him questions related to his work in Spain with Franco's forces and his ties to the mysterious Marquis Mendez de Sevilla. (Shatilov had been expelled from France when the French government learned of his military activities in Spain.) In response, Shatilov said that he had met the marquis twice, but that these meetings had no relation to Skoblin. "I am convinced that the events in Spain were directly tied to the Miller case," Filonenko argued.

"How?" Ribet asked.

Filonenko demurred, adding that he would explain it all in his closing argument. Ribet and Strelnikov demanded that Filonenko explain the connection immediately so that they could ask questions and refute the defense's statements.

"You want Spain to distract attention at a time when I would be prevented from rebutting!" Ribet yelled over the din of the courtroom. Judge Delegorgue tried to call the court to order and then suspended the hearing.

When the hearing resumed, Filonenko made a startling announcement: He agreed that Soviet agents had carried out Miller's kidnapping. "However," he added, "the connection with Spain to me is beyond doubt. . . . Mendez was a double agent. The accused had no ties to the Spanish or the Bolsheviks and could not have taken part in Miller's kidnapping!"

At this point, Prosecutor Flach expressed his opposition to the line of questioning, stating that the dossier contained nothing about this Spanish lead.

"The civil attorneys fully agree," Ribet concurred. "The crime we're discussing is Soviet!"

The next witness to testify was General Anton Denikin, who was widely known to have mistrusted Skoblin as far back as the civil war. The former White Army commander pointed out to the court that, on three separate occasions, including the afternoon of September 22, 1937, Skoblin had offered to drive him to Brussels, and Denikin suspected that Skoblin had planned to kill him if presented with the chance.

"You are sure that Nikolai Skoblin is a Soviet agent, yet you have no evidence?" Filonenko inquired.

"Yes."

"Do you know for certain that Nadezhda Plevitskaya was an accomplice in Miller's kidnapping?"

"No."

"Do you think she knew earlier about the crime?"

"I'm convinced she did." A commander of enormous prestige, Denikin came across as a credible witness and considerably aided the prosecution and the Miller family.

The same held for the testimony of the next witness, Colonel Boris Fedoseenko, who discussed why he had served briefly as a Soviet intelligence informant and how he had first alerted General Miller in 1932 to the possibility that Skoblin was a Soviet agent. Fedoseenko told the judge that he was convinced Skoblin had killed Miller with the intention of taking over the ROVS leadership position. However, Fedoseenko had nothing to say about Plevitskaya. His testimony was meant to corroborate earlier testimony about Skoblin's Soviet ties.

Plevitskaya listened to Fedoseenko's testimony and expressed surprise. "This is the first I've seen of this gentleman," she said. "I don't understand how he knows everything so well."

"What do you know about Nadezhda Plevitskaya?" Judge Delegorgue asked Fedoseenko.

"I don't know her, but I always heard how she wore the general's stripes on her trousers." Fedoseenko's reply provoked a wave of laughter in the courtroom.

Plevitskaya smiled and remarked offhandedly to her translator, "It's a pun of some kind."

Colonel Gregory Troshin, once Skoblin's close confidant, was next to testify. Troshin claimed to have heard Skoblin say several times that Miller needed to be removed as ROVS head because he was old and useless. Skoblin's former friend also agreed that Plevitskaya had exerted a large influence over Skoblin, although he noted that she had never been involved in his regimental business. When asked by Strelnikov whether he thought Skoblin was a coward, Troshin answered equivocally, "No, I can't say he was, but it turned out somehow that in difficult moments at the Front, he was absent."

To cap off an already tension-filled day, Ribet sparred with the judge about the French government's alleged involvement in another cover-up linked to the Soviets. This concerned a suspected Chekist named Lydia Grozovskaya, whom French police had arrested in Paris in September 1937 in connection with the Reiss murder. Instead of being kept in prison awaiting trial—as Plevitskaya had been—Grozovskaya had been released on 50,000 francs bail and had then fled the country.[7] Ribet yelled out, "On Marx Dormoy's order!" Judge Delegorgue was furious with Ribet for his outburst and demanded an apology. Ribet demurred, insisting that it was in fact at Dormoy's behest that the police had not monitored Grozovskaya after her release.

Filonenko piped in. "You see, gentlemen of the jury, Grozovskaya was under arrest and still the Soviets agreed to help her. Why? Because she was a Soviet agent. No one helped Plevitskaya escape."

Ignoring Filonenko's comment, Ribet pivoted back to his story about Dormoy, zeroing in not only on the Grozovskaya affair, but also on Dormoy's alleged order that had allowed the *Maria Ulyanova* to leave French waters without being pursued. In the process, Ribet issued a formal demand before Judge Delegorgue that Dormoy be ordered to appear in court the following day.

Judge Delegorgue began the court hearing on day 6 of Plevitskaya's trial—Saturday, December 10—with an announcement: Marx Dormoy had declined to testify. Delegorgue read the text of the ex-minister of the interior's statement, in which he claimed to have known nothing about the Miller case. Even if he did have something to say, Dormoy argued, due to France's separation of powers system, a cabinet minister was answerable only to Parliament and the French electorate, not to judicial bodies. Apparently, nine months before, Dormoy had already set a precedent by refusing to testify in another high-profile criminal case.

Prosecutor Flach, the first court actor to react, disagreed with Dormoy's grounds for refusal, insisting that a French court had the right to summon anyone as a witness, regardless of political status. But Judge Delegorgue had no way to compel Dormoy to appear in his courtroom. The matter was settled. Ribet, who had requested Dormoy's presence, was disappointed but confidently responded, "We'll find the truth without him!"

Schwab, however, tried to prevent Ribet from achieving his goal. Early in the hearing, the defense attorney told the judge he had evidence that the truck at Le Havre was not even Soviet. This revelation caused a sensation in the courtroom. Schwab insisted that the truck in fact belonged to a private company and was usually parked on rue de Paradis, in the tenth arrondissement. Judge Delegorgue immediately ordered a police inquiry into the matter.

The first set of witnesses addressed the topic of the Le Havre trail. Mondanel was called to the stand a second time, and a Sûreté employee named Fournier was summoned as well. In addition, Louis Ducloux, the Sûreté's general controller, was asked to testify because he had questioned Chauvineau at Le Havre on September 23, 1937, about his controversial report. Ducloux stated that Chauvineau had not completed the proper police forms on September 23 and had repeatedly revised the estimate of the time of the truck's arrival at Le Havre. Chauvineau, who was in the courtroom, defended himself, claiming that he had not neglected his duties. Ducloux, he insisted, had scolded him unfairly—not due to any failure on his part, but because of the political inconvenience of the report, which had the potential to harm France's relations with the Soviet Union. For his part, Ducloux maintained that he had only spoken of the Miller case's overall importance. Ribet reminded the court of how Papin's subsequent report had falsely concluded that the Le Havre trail did not present anything of interest to the police. In that way, it constituted a government cover-up.

When Mondanel took the stand, he again stated that he did not remember a meeting with Chauvineau and that no French police officials had been politically pressured. Mondanel also said he did not have jurisdiction over the monitoring of Lydia Grozovskaya. While on the topic of Grozovskaya, Filonenko reminded the jurors that, unlike her, Plevitskaya had not fled from Paris and had voluntarily reported to the police. When Fournier took the stand, he confirmed only that he had seen Chauvineau outside Mondanel's office on September 24, 1937, the day Chauvineau claimed he had met with Mondanel. Fournier could not say for certain whether the two men had actually met.

A witness from later that day, Lieutenant Piatnitsky, loudly testified that he knew how Plevitskaya had communicated with her Soviet handlers. He claimed that she had routinely gone to the cinema and passed her contacts secret information and documents while there. Schwab was unconvinced. "You, I heard, write for the newspapers?" he asked Piatnitsky. The lieutenant indeed worked for *Signal*, a Russian-émigré publication. Schwab told the jurors that Piatnitsky's articles had value only as literary pieces, not as accurate news reports. Piatnitsky pounded his fist against the side of the witness stand in frustration. But Judge Delegorgue also remained unconvinced that Piatnitsky's testimony was credible.

The witness who caused the most sensation that day was Sergei Trotsky, a former White Army officer (no relation to Leon Trotsky). Trotsky spoke emotionally about his alleged knowledge of the Miller kidnapping. He claimed that the plot had been carried out by "an international gang of killers the Soviet government had organized" and that Plevitskaya had been informed about it. He asserted that Pyotr Savin, one of Skoblin's friends, and a Russian émigré named Pavel Koltypin-Liubsky had also been involved. Trotsky claimed further that, in January 1937, Soviet agents had tried to recruit him for the kidnapping operations of two other White generals, who remained unnamed. Judge Delegorgue leaned forward, listening attentively to Trotsky, and then sighed and leaned back in his chair. Trotsky said that a friend of his, a Soviet embassy official whom he refused to name, had told him that Skoblin had taken Miller to the gates of the building at 41–43 Montmorency Boulevard, forced him into the building, and stunned him with a blow to his head. While inside the building, Miller had been forced into a box, but he had defended himself energetically, even injuring a Soviet operative when he pushed open the top of the box with his legs.[8] Once safely locked inside, Miller had been taken by truck to Le Havre.

"Where did you hear this?" the judge asked Trotsky.

Trotsky's face looked puzzled, and he glanced around the courtroom suspiciously. He told the judge that he doubted whether it was possible for him to speak about such sensitive matters before such a large audience.

"You're a former officer," the judge asked him. "Were you injured?"

"Several times. In the legs, chest, and head."

Delegorgue sighed, as if concluding that the witness was deranged. The spectators burst out laughing. "If you want to determine whether I'm incompetent, you can call an expert," Trotsky proposed. But it was too late; he had made a poor impression on the court.

Now it was Schwab's turn to strike the final blow. "Jurors," he cried, "this witness is a symbol of what happens inside the brains of White Russians in Paris! Trotsky appeared before the investigator and gave information to the police. All his information is composed of lies, and to Marchat, he wrote, 'The crime was carried out by the Fourth International in order to compromise the Third International.' Today his imagination ranged even further. Who summoned such a witness?"

Flach and Ribet could only shrug their shoulders. What good was Trotsky's testimony if he refused to name his source? Ironically, given what we now know happened that fateful day in September 1937, Trotsky's account of Miller's abduction seems fairly accurate.

Nocin Epstein, the manager of Caroline's dress shop, also appeared on the stand. Although he did not offer any new information, he behaved as a credible witness and confirmed that Plevitskaya had constantly—and oddly—reminded him that Skoblin was right outside in his car reading the newspaper the whole time. It was the type of evidence, easy for the jurors to digest, that would prove most damaging to Plevitskaya's defense.

For the remainder of day 6, the court heard from two more experts. Their findings further compromised Plevitskaya's defense, and Filonenko and Schwab struggled to mount a viable challenge. The first witness, a financial specialist named Fevrier, testified that the Skoblins' financial records showed that, between 1931 and 1935 in particular, their reported income did not cover their household expenses.

"Skoblin received large sums from General Miller," Filonenko explained.

Fevrier disagreed, noting that "Skoblin received 300 francs per month"—an insignificant sum—"from General Miller." Some spectators snickered.

Filonenko pointed out that Miller was known to have paid additional amounts to Skoblin secretly, as well as to Shatilov. "General Miller's letters attest to this," he observed.

Ribet snidely inquired, "If he received secret sums from General Miller, then was it for his salary or that of his wife?"

Filonenko answered that Shatilov had received payments to cover the costs of ROVS's Spanish operations, and additional compensation for himself. Shatilov, from his seat, yelled, "There was no such thing!" Judge Delegorgue called Shatilov back to the stand. Shatilov said he had received 3,000 francs from Miller to cover the expenses of his three-week trip to Spain and 700 francs upon his return.

Schwab, still trying to cast Shatilov as a kidnapping conspirator, declared that the general had been driving a taxi at the time and had sold Miller on the idea of a Russian battalion in Spain simply to better his financial situation.

Shatilov was livid. "That's false!"

"Be careful," Schwab warned. "I have in my hands letters from General Miller to General Abramov. General Shatilov devised a scheme that required funds of 10,000 to 15,000 francs a month. But General Miller did not make up his mind about it. 'When business revolves around money,' Miller wrote, 'Shatilov is incorrigible.' When he returned from Spain, Shatilov presented Miller with such a bill." Shatilov protested.

Filonenko noted further that, if Shatilov had received funds in such a way from Miller, Skoblin could have as well. Clearly, Filonenko and Schwab were using Shatilov as their analogous example in attempting to persuade the jurors that the funds the Skoblins used to pay for additional household expenses were not from the Soviets, but from ROVS sources.

The next expert, and the day's final witness, was Tastevin (Tsatskin in Russian), who had translated and analyzed documents seized from Skoblin's personal archive and from the Skoblins' hotel room. Tastevin admitted that he had found no documents exposing Skoblin as a Soviet agent. In fact, the documents revealed the opposite, that Skoblin and Plevitskaya were "100 percent anti-Bolshevik." He concluded from reading thick piles of correspondence that Plevitskaya was entrenched in her husband's political activities. However, Tastevin confessed, he could not prove that Skoblin had not simply been using his wife's name in correspondence without her knowledge.

Plevitskaya commented that "General Abramov wrote me, knowing that my husband read my letters. If my husband used my name, it was without first receiving my permission."

Ribet referred to correspondence that Plevitskaya seemed to have been actively involved in. In one letter to Plevitskaya, General Abramov wrote, "Allow me to tell this to Nikolai Vladimirovich [Skoblin], but only to him and no one else."

Tastevin attested that he had found only one letter from Plevitskaya to Miller, in which she wrote about a lecture by recent Soviet defector Ivan Solonevich in Marseille. Tastevin said he was struck by the abundance of documents expressing opposition on the part of ROVS members to Miller's leadership of the organization. Generals Skoblin, Turkul, and Fok were at the center of this opposition, he noted.

Now that Turkul's name had again been mentioned, Schwab tried to divert attention away from Skoblin and Plevitskaya and toward the pro-German Russian émigré. Schwab reprised the many rumors that depicted Turkul as saying or writing that he would remove Miller from office by any means necessary. Ribet counterattacked, exclaiming, "I won't allow such diversions this time! Yesterday, it seemed that we had agreed that the crime was committed by the Soviets. Will you say for the record that you've acknowledged this?"

Schwab and Filonenko declared that they did not reject any hypothesis—that the Soviets, fascists, Spanish, Russian émigrés, or any combination of factions—could have been involved. Plevitskaya's defense attorneys demanded that the court investigate all possible leads with impartiality. Ribet told the jurors that the police had also investigated Turkul as a possible suspect and ruled him out. "The single remaining trail is the Soviet one," Ribet insisted.

Flach agreed. "We don't need a hypothesis, but a certainty. And the only one that interests this court is Plevitskaya. I have no doubt of her guilt."

A bailiff entered the courtroom and handed Judge Delegorgue a document. The judge announced that the police's inquiry of the alleged truck on rue de Paradis had resulted in no new findings. No garages existed on the street, and none of the residents even owned a truck. The spectators laughed. "On the other hand," Delegorgue announced, "there's a report from the Paris police archives confirming that an eight-cylinder, twenty-one-horsepower Ford truck with license plate number 235XSD was registered in Paris on August 13, 1937, in the name of USSR Ambassador Vladimir Potemkin."[9] And with that, the discussion about rue de Paradis ended.

On December 10, the Paris police issued a report about how many Russian observers of Plevitskaya's trial thought that Filonenko had changed his mind about Skoblin. Initially, he had not conceded that Skoblin was a Soviet agent. Now, conceding that Skoblin was working for the Soviets, he was concentrating on proving that Plevitskaya knew little or nothing about her husband's activities and bore no responsibility for them. If the general was indeed a Soviet agent, Filonenko now argued, Plevitskaya most assuredly was not.[10]

Day 7 of Plevitskaya's trial—Monday, December 12—was the last full day of the court examination. The hearing began with Judge Delegorgue reading letters from General Kutepov's widow, Lydia, now residing in Belgrade, and General Nikolai Golovin, who had directed military training courses for ROVS recruits in Paris and Belgrade and could not appear in court. Kutepova wrote that, after her husband's kidnapping, Plevitskaya— as described in chapter 5—had often visited her and received updates about the ongoing police investigation. At the time, Kutepova had not suspected Plevitskaya of spying for the Soviets. But afterward, as she noted in her letter, she had begun to find Skoblin's and Plevitskaya's behavior suspicious. Having seen and spoken with the Skoblins recently in Riga (although she did not offer an exact date), Kutepova had come away with the impression that the couple had acted strangely. Plevitskaya had talked critically about Generals Turkul, Fok, and Miller. She had insisted that Miller was incapable of carrying out his duties and should resign as ROVS head. Kutepova had at that point concluded that the Skoblins must have been in Riga to meet with their Soviet handlers.

Filonenko remarked that Kutepova's letter contained only "impressions and assumptions" about the Skoblins. "How did she come to know about the Skoblins' meeting with Soviet agents in Riga?" he asked.

Golovin's letter addressed a query about why one of Skoblin's notebooks, which the police now possessed, would have contained a drawing of the layout of his Paris apartment. Golovin wrote that he had no idea why Skoblin would have done this. However, he noted that the Skoblins had tried to befriend him and had visited his apartment several times. No one raised the possibility at Plevitskaya's trial, but one explanation for Skoblin's possession of the drawing may have been that the NKVD had planned to bug Golovin's apartment.

When M. Blumenfeld, a court translator and document analyst, testified that day, he informed the court about the most instructive documents he had studied. These included a small notebook owned by Skoblin that had been seized from the couple's hotel room. The notebook contained an apparent key for enciphering correspondence and instructions for doing so.

Among the documents seized from offices of the Society of Gallipolians, which Skoblin had led, there was correspondence addressed both to him and Plevitskaya. This, Blumenfeld claimed, suggested Plevitskaya's considerable involvement in Skoblin's business affairs.

Filonenko still wanted the jurors to view Plevitskaya as a simple peasant, too unlettered to engage in espionage or to comprehend politics. He handed the analyst what he said was a recent letter written by Plevitskaya and asked whether the writing was grammatical. Blumenfeld read the letter and remarked that it contained several grammatical errors. "Could a barely literate woman take part in politics? Could she use a cipher?" Filonenko asked.

Ribet was not impressed. "She wrote the letter in prison, when she began to play the role of an illiterate peasant!" he joked. The spectators laughed.

"Someone who's illiterate probably can't use a cipher," Blumenfeld added. "But Plevitskaya is not a simple peasant woman. She impressed me as a woman with innate intelligence and talent. During the investigation, she understood all the issues perfectly."

"I'm pleased to receive this compliment," Plevitskaya said. "If I am intelligent, then I am not ignoble or mean. I've never been mean in my life, and I have not used my mind for evil. I never lie or play low-down tricks." She then crossed herself and sat down.

Six White Army veterans testified at the hearing on day 7, and none of them provided any specific evidence of Plevitskaya's participating in Miller's kidnapping. The first veteran on the witness stand that day was Lieutenant Alexander Pavlov. For a time, he had been expelled from France, a fact that Plevitskaya's attorneys tried to exploit in discrediting him. Pavlov opined that Miller had been kidnapped by French communists, with the aid of a few Russian émigrés, including Skoblin. "Russian emigration is filled with people who do honorable work, earning their own bread," he declaimed. "But there are scoundrels, like Skoblin, who pretend to be poor. Remember this, Mr. Schwab!"

Judge Delegorgue, who never bothered to hide his accusatory bias against the Skoblins, remarked, "The court and jurors know this well! No one here lumps together Skoblin and Plevitskaya with the Russian émigré community as a whole!"

A second witness, A. Gulevich, was described by the press as a young man who acted as if he was testifying before a political tribunal. "Destroying the Bolsheviks," he exclaimed on the stand, "is the world's most important mission!" But when it came to providing details about Plevitskaya,

Gulevich proved worthless. Plevitskaya merely shrugged her shoulders and said, "I absolutely do not know him!" Gulevich was quickly dismissed from the stand.

Captain A. Baranov, who led a cavalry intelligence unit in the Volunteer Army during the civil war, was the next witness. He recounted a scintillating but vague story about Plevitskaya's close acquaintance in Odessa in 1919 with Chekist officials named Dombrovsky and Shulga. As described in chapter 3, Plevitskaya claimed that she had met Dombrovsky and Shulga only once, when they helped find a new residence for her after Red Army soldiers commandeered her hotel. Juror 2 asked Baranov whether it was typical then for Chekists to find housing for residents expelled from their hotel rooms, and Baranov replied that it certainly was not, implying that Plevitskaya had lied on the stand about the nature of her relations with the Chekists.

Sergei Tverskoi, a tsarist-era prosecutor and White Army veteran who knew General Miller, dredged up an unsubstantiated rumor about Plevitskaya's alleged treachery during World War I. Tverskoi claimed that a fellow officer had evidence that Plevitskaya had conspired with Russian General Vladimir Grigoriev in betraying a Russian-held fortress in Kovno in the summer of 1915. Tverskoi could not provide any further details about this tale. Plevitskaya said that she never knew Grigoriev and had never been at the fortress. Tverskoi also had no way to substantiate the stories he had heard about how, in Berlin in 1927, Max Eitingon had transferred funds to the Skoblins from the Soviets.

Tverskoi, who described Miller as cautious by nature, recalled the general's expressions of regret that Kutepov had not left a note about the secret meeting he was to attend on the day he disappeared. Tverskoi theorized that Miller had left a note on September 22 because he had feared a trap. Filonenko tried to debunk Tverskoi's assessment. "Why didn't Miller inquire before the meeting about whether Strohman and Werner were actual German military agents?" Filonenko asked. "The German embassy would have confirmed that there were no such agents. Could General Miller have left such a note?"

Ribet yelled, "General Miller went to a secret meeting. He couldn't have inquired about such information in advance." Ribet reminded the court that Miller's family and handwriting experts confirmed that he had written the note. Filonenko was persistent, no doubt because he believed that he could still convince the jurors that the note had been forged. "Handwriting experts can make mistakes," he pointed out.

A friend of Skoblin's testified next and testified for the defense. This was Captain Pyotr Savin, who had worked on intelligence missions for

Miller and now managed a restaurant. One reporter described Savin as a "dark-complexioned, sharp-nosed brown-haired man who wore a coat and kept his hat under his arm while on the stand."[11] Overall, it seems that the witness failed to inspire trust in the jurors' minds. During the investigation, Savin had accused Shatilov and Pyotr Koltypin-Liubsky of involvement in Miller's kidnapping. Koltypin-Liubsky had once worked as Vladimir Burtsev's assistant and was expelled from France sometime during the investigation. Now Savin claimed that Marquis Mendez de Sevilla was the main culprit.

Filonenko pointed Savin in the direction he thought was most fruitful and asked him what Koltypin-Liubsky had told him in August 1937. Savin answered that he had learned from Burtsev and Koltypin-Liubsky "about a rumor that, in the second half of September, 'the White Russian emigration would experience a blow to the head.'" He also insisted that both men were double agents, working for the Soviets and the French. He said that at 12:15 p.m. on September 22, Miller had met Mendez, not Skoblin, in a café near ROVS headquarters.

"If the marquis kidnapped Miller, then why did Skoblin flee?" asked Ribet. Savin, who had been in Spain the day Miller was kidnapped, stressed that Skoblin and Miller still cooperated closely up to the day they disappeared. When Filonenko showed Savin Miller's note, Savin predictably argued that it was not in Miller's handwriting and questioned why he would have left behind such a note.

"It was left so that a crime would not go unpunished!" Ribet retorted.

The final defense witness was Madame Leonard, a server at the Serdechny Restaurant. Prompted by Filonenko, Leonard confirmed that the Skoblins often sat at the bar, including on the day of Miller's kidnapping. On a previous evening, when the couple had dined at the bar, Leonard noticed that Skoblin had waited for Plevitskaya to leave the restaurant before handing a package to a man seated behind him. Filonenko's implication here was that Skoblin hid his business affairs from Plevitskaya. But would the jurors find Leonard's testimony compelling?

As the court examination ended, the defense had only two more days to argue its case before the jurors deliberated.

12

THE VERDICT

On December 13, the eighth day of Plevitskaya's trial, dozens lined up early to secure a courtroom seat for the closing arguments. Anticipating this larger crowd, extra guards stood at the entrance, and those who failed to get seats stood outside the door. Plevitskaya entered the defendant's box dressed in the same widow's weeds she had worn every day of her trial, with a fur coat wrapped around her shoulders. She looked pale and avoided glancing at the crowd as she pressed on her temples. She had no formal statements to make today, but her gestures betrayed her nervous state of mind.

The attorneys for the Miller family presented first. After Alexander Strelnikov spoke briefly, his senior colleague, Maurice Ribet, stood and held the floor for approximately half an hour. Ribet spoke clearly and calmly, without raising his voice. As Plevitskaya listened, she often covered her face with her hands. Ribet began by telling jurors why he stood before them. He was representing not only the Miller family's interests, but those of all Russian émigrés in France. The Soviets were continuing to wage war on the Russian emigration, and Ribet had been charged with defending this vulnerable group of immigrants. Ribet pointed out to the jurors that, in contrast to Filonenko, who referred to the case only in theoretical terms, he viewed it as a human drama.

Ribet recounted the chilling events of September 22 and explained how Plevitskaya had supported Skoblin's alibi and betrayed herself. Ribet noted how strange it was that Skoblin had not asked any questions when Matsylev knocked on the Skoblins' hotel room door at 1:30 a.m. on September 23. Although Plevitskaya explained her husband's failure to do so as a matter of having been surprised by Matsylev's appearance, Ribet insisted that it was because the couple had already known about Miller's kidnapping. Skoblin, Ribet asserted, had not worried that his ROVS colleagues would suspect him of betrayal because he had assumed that no one else knew about the secret meeting. Only when he had learned that his colleagues had proof about the meeting and his involvement in it had he run from ROVS headquarters—so admitting that he had "lost the game."

As for Plevitskaya, Ribet went on, she was certain that Skoblin was free from suspicion up to the moment when Matsylev returned to the hotel room asking for him. At this point, she screamed, "Do you suspect him?" and thus revealed unwittingly that she had known beforehand about Skoblin's role in Miller's abduction. "She knew and understood that something catastrophic had happened," Ribet observed. If she had really believed her husband innocent, Ribet continued, she would have waited in her hotel room for him to return, instead of roaming around Paris. During her first police interrogation, Ribet reminded the jury, Plevitskaya had tried to save Skoblin and herself by using a particular timeline. As Ribet explained,

> Skoblin, in his own words, said he had left the Hotel Pax at 11:00 a.m. A lie! At 11:30 a.m., her husband returned and waited outside in his car. A lie! At 12:00 p.m., she left the hotel alone. A lie! They both stayed in the restaurant for forty-five minutes. A lie! At 12:25 p.m., she arrived at Caroline's dress shop. A lie! She met up with her husband on the street at 1:45 p.m. A lie! They arrived together at the train station. Again, a lie, a lie, a lie! Witnesses have destroyed their alibi point by point—the hotelier, the garage attendant, the restaurant workers, the store manager. She refused to call her husband into the store? Hardly. She knew he wasn't on the street. He appeared at the store five minutes after she'd left. She left thinking that Skoblin had driven straight to the train station. This was a huge blunder! Skoblin arrived five minutes after Plevitskaya did. That was the first time they met since he had dropped her off at 11:45 a.m. Skoblin had completed his traitorous business. He was sure of his own impunity. He felt calm.

After enumerating other points made during the trial, including about the repeated warnings that ROVS's Finnish collaborators had given General Miller about a traitor in his midst, Ribet hammered home his strongest point: the consistency with which the prosecution's witnesses had testified to Plevitskaya's awareness of Skoblin's political dealings. "Not one of them doubted that Plevitskaya knew Skoblin was a traitor," Ribet reminded the jurors. He discussed the various pieces of correspondence, such as between General Abramov and Plevitskaya, that showed that the singer had not only been aware of her husband's activities, but took part in them. He referred to the green Bible. As Plevitskaya listened, she lowered her eyes and pursed her lips.

Ribet now turned to the accused. "Nadezhda Vasilievna, it's not too late. Tell us what happened to General Miller. Did you see him alive, as you said you did General Kutepov?" Plevitskaya turned to look at Ribet, tears streaming down her face. Ribet spoke of the many Russians in exile who still cherished their cultural beliefs. "Plevitskaya betrayed those beliefs!" he exclaimed.

Ribet told the court about a seemingly menacing warning that Filonenko had given him "not to get carried away—you don't know what will happen." Posturing before the jury, Ribet asked rhetorically, "Was this a threat? I'm not afraid to speak the truth." He explained once more why he was convinced that the Soviet-made Le Havre trail was the key to solving the Miller kidnapping case. He urged the jurors neither to hate Plevitskaya nor pity her.

In closing, Ribet recounted Plevitskaya's March 1938 meeting with Natalya Miller, when the singer, instead of comforting her friend, selfishly implored her to intervene on her behalf with the examining magistrate and to help free her from jail. Ribet looked at Miller, who was crying. "Revolution destroyed your life," he said sympathetically. "The only thing you had left was your family. And your enemies even took that away from you." Plevitskaya sat motionless in the defendant's box, her hands covering her eyes. Turning from the women to the jurors, Ribet exclaimed, "Yes, French justice will prevail!" When he finished, the courtroom fell silent.

Flach now stood to give his *réquisitoire*, the prosecutor's closing argument. As the chief mouthpiece of the French state, he betrayed a somewhat sharp prejudice about Russian émigrés. "To us middle-class Frenchmen," he told the jurors, "the Russian soul will always remain closed." Flach noted that the French government had allowed thousands of Russian refugees to settle in France. The vast majority of them had toiled honorably, he said. But others had sought the easy life and lost their conscience, the Skoblins among them.

Before narrowing his sights on Plevitskaya, Flach discussed Skoblin's flight from justice. At this point, the prosecutor clarified that, as France's representative, he would not offer an opinion about which foreign entity or political group might have been involved in Miller's abduction. In terms of what or who motivated Skoblin to commit his crime, it did not matter if it was "the Soviets or the Gestapo, a personal goal or not," Flach stressed. The prosecutor reminded the jurors that their most important task was to

determine whether sufficient evidence had been gathered to prove Plevitskaya's involvement.

Plevitskaya's inconsistent alibi was the chief piece of evidence against
her, Flach said, and it proved that she was guilty of complicity. Resort-
ing without hesitation to the most hackneyed of femme fatale stereotypes,
Flach imagined Plevitskaya as having the "voice of a siren," placing unwit-
ting men under her trance. He insisted that Plevitskaya, far from being illiterate, was smart and talented, with feminine wiles that "obviously would
have been difficult to resist, given that she had three husbands." At this moment of levity, the spectators smiled at Plevitskaya's expense. Flach outlined
his interpretation of Plevitskaya's and Skoblin's relations:

> In her marriage to Skoblin, the pair had full agreement and love, and
> they completely trusted each other. The wife wore the general's stripes;
> she was the moving force in the marriage and the evil genius. She knew
> everything and took part in everything. The evidence against her is
> indisputable. She did not take part in Miller's kidnapping, but helped
> her husband design an alibi in advance, in order to impart a sense of
> security. Out of the case materials, Plevitskaya's guilt emerges with
> abundant clarity.

Plevitskaya sighed deeply and lowered her head. Now Flach proceeded
with recommendations to the jurors about how to deliberate. Juries in
the Paris court were known to convict less frequently than judges and to
issue lighter punishments, especially for female defendants. Flach would
have none of this. He stressed that Plevitskaya was guilty as charged and
that there were no extenuating circumstances to justify a lighter sentence.
"Jurors, don't yield to feelings of sympathy," he exclaimed. "I demand life
imprisonment for the accused!"

The spectators were shocked, as they had not expected the prosecutor
to recommend such a harsh sentence. After all, Plevitskaya had apparently
not even laid a hand on Miller and was, even if guilty, only an accomplice.
In addition, the supposed victim's body had not even been found, and
Skoblin, the main perpetrator of the crime, had fled. The entire courtroom
turned to look at Plevitskaya, who angrily shuddered and choked back
tears. Her eyes looked sunken, and her lips shook. She leaned against the
bar and whispered something to Filonenko. Judge Delegorgue called for a
break.

Judge Delegorgue resumed the hearing and called on Jean Schwab
to speak. "Yes, French justice *will* prevail," Schwab proclaimed. But of
course he took an entirely different tack from Ribet's and Flach's, attempt-

ing to plant doubt in the jurors' minds about the strength of the evidence. Curiously, Schwab chose less to defend Plevitskaya as the accused. Instead, he spent more time refuting the validity of the evidence pointing toward the Soviets' participation in Miller's kidnapping and questioning the integrity of those witnesses who had linked the Soviets to the kidnapping and accused Skoblin and Plevitskaya of treachery. "The generals," Schwab argued, "not having an external enemy anymore, focused on the enemy within, themselves!" As Filonenko would do the following day, Schwab argued that the case against Plevitskaya rested solely on innuendo and vague circumstantial evidence, rather than reliable testimony and hard proof. Inside the White Army veterans' community, everyone suspected everyone else of espionage, Schwab contended.

Addressing the jurors, Schwab painted White Army veteran organizations like ROVS as filled with embittered, spy-obsessed men who complained about everything, including General Miller's leadership. He discussed the possibility that Turkul had been involved in Miller's kidnapping, given the former's ties to the Nazi regime. He alluded to Kussonsky's possible involvement as well, a more plausible scenario, considering his suspicious behavior on September 22. Schwab suggested, moreover, that Skoblin might not have fled but might have been abducted and killed.

Further casting doubt on the Le Havre trail, Schwab noted that French investigators had received hundreds of anonymous tips from deranged Russian émigrés who knew nothing about Miller's kidnapping. Such sources claimed to have seen Miller throughout France and Skoblin across Europe. Schwab noted that, in September 1937, other Soviet ships had been docked in French harbors, and he maintained that the truck supposedly carrying Miller could not have reached Le Havre in less than three hours, as Chauvineau and some other witnesses had claimed. "In this case, all hypotheses are possible," Schwab averred.

In his closing remarks, Schwab reminded jurors that, in the dossier, "no document proves that Nikolai Skoblin and Nadezhda Plevitskaya were Soviet agents." He urged jurors to judge "on the basis of their conscience and justice," and said that he did not doubt that, if the jury weighed all the evidence, "they would not convict this forsaken and deceived woman." Plevitskaya, resting her hands on her chest, seemed to be studying the jurors' faces for their reaction to Schwab's arguments. When he returned to his seat, she leaned over and shook his hand.

On the morning of December 14—the last day of Plevitskaya's trial—the nuns at the Petite-Roquette reported that Plevitskaya had sung more wondrously in the choir at the chapel service than ever before.[1] It would seem that the Kursk Nightingale felt reassured she would soon be free to fly away. She might even be able to see her beloved Kolya again!

That afternoon, though, the spectators in the crowded courtroom did not see a woman bursting with confidence. Plevitskaya looked thin and pale, and she had dark circles under her sunken eyes. She entered the courtroom for the last time and avoided looking at the public. As she sat down on the bench, she let out a deep sigh and then covered her face with her hands to avoid the glare of the reporters' flashbulbs.

Before the case was handed to the jurors for their final judgment, Filonenko first needed to present his closing arguments. His speech, which began at 1:20 p.m., lasted nearly three hours—with one five-minute break—and combined sober legal reasoning with impassioned pleas to the jurors for an acquittal. "If you knew the accused as I have these past fifteen months," he began, "you would not even consider the manner of punishment, but would acquit her outright." He emphasized that Plevitskaya was unaware of any kidnapping plot against Miller and that the French investigators had no evidence that she was a spy or had been ordered in any way to take part in Miller's kidnapping.

Filonenko contested the charge of complicity against his client. Under French law, he explained, a person was guilty of complicity only if he had aided the main culprit through a positive, determined act. Furthermore, he had to be aware of what he had done and whether "he and the main culprit had the same idea and intention." Nothing in the dossier proved that Plevitskaya was guilty, Filonenko insisted, and neither did witness testimony. "I asked each witness the question, 'Do you know for certain that Plevitskaya took part in the preparation of Miller's abduction?' And each one answered, 'No, I don't know for certain.' The preliminary investigation did not gather any direct evidence against the accused," Filonenko added. In other words, the prosecution had proved neither Plevitskaya's intention to kidnap Miller nor her participation in the act.

In order to find Plevitskaya guilty as charged, Filonenko continued, French authorities, lacking clear proof, had resorted instead to creating a "climate" or vague impression of Plevitskaya as an evil genius, meddling in her husband's intrigues and fully capable of committing a felony. Filonenko told the jurors that, when the decision had been made in September 1938 to send Plevitskaya's case to trial, "my friends at the Palace of Justice—the advocates, my confreres, and certain magistrates who honor me with their friendship—told me, 'You will have to combat not only the precise charges in the indictment, but, according to a term now in usage, you will have to combat the climate.'" Convicting on the basis of an impression was against French criminal procedure, Filonenko warned the jurors: "It is contrary to your fundamental oath that gives you the formidable powers delegated from the French people to judge without any motives, to judge directly." Prosecutor Flach and Ribet had manufactured a "climate," Filonenko stressed; they had not addressed the law. They were counting on the jurors to succumb to their "psychological infection."

Knowledgeable of France's legal system and political history, Filonenko compared the Plevitskaya trial to the famous Dreyfus Affair (1894–1906), which he viewed as a miscarriage of justice. Filonenko may also have referred to it because Delegorgue had served as the presiding judge in Émile Zola's 1898 trial, which concerned the writer's public defense of Dreyfus. Alfred Dreyfus, a French Jew and an artillery officer, had been accused of giving the German military classified French government documents and had been twice convicted of treason. The case, which exposed widespread anti-Semitism in France, had been highly divisive, but by the 1930s, the vast majority of French argued that Dreyfus had been falsely accused. To support his point about the atmosphere of false claims against Plevitskaya, Filonenko paraphrased an excerpt from *Penguin Island*, a novel by writer Anatole France, who had satirized the behavior of Dreyfus's prosecutors: "The Ministers and the Deputies had suspicions and even certainties, but they had no proofs. The Public Prosecutor said to the Minister of Justice: 'Very little is needed for a political prosecution, but I have nothing at all and that is not enough.'"[2]

Moving from the ideational realm to the factual, Filonenko next detailed how the investigators, with their massive 2,500-page dossier, and then the prosecutor and the Miller family's attorneys created this "climate" against Plevitskaya through a combination of name-calling, specious witness testimony, and misinterpretation of the correspondence between the Skoblins and ROVS officers. Flach had labeled Plevitskaya a "wicked woman" (*méchante*), and *Vozrozhdenie* editor Yuly Semenov had referred to posters proclaiming her a "Red Mother," even though the existence of such posters had never been proven. In fact, Filonenko reminded the jurors, Plevitskaya had defended the tsar in 1917, and her 1926 concert in New York City to raise funds for undernourished Soviet children had helped the same group of people that Herbert Hoover had assisted in 1921 as director of the American Relief Administration. Filonenko criticized White Army veterans such as Generals Erdely and Shatilov for testifying that Plevitskaya controlled Skoblin's actions while offering little to no evidence supporting their accusations. "Skoblin conducted all the business,"

Filonenko asserted. "He maintained the bank accounts, was the leader, drove his wife into the city, gave her money." Similarly, Filonenko criticized Flach for accusing the Skoblins of never working, when Plevitskaya had performed in hundreds of concerts across Europe and in America, and while Skoblin had organized ROVS operations for General Miller, albeit for little pay. And many observers, Filonenko added, had confirmed that the Skoblins had lived within their means.

As for the letters from General Abramov to Plevitskaya, Filonenko explained, these were addressed to her, but likely for Skoblin's eyes only. Sending the letters to Plevitskaya had been a security measure taken by ROVS members to avoid having their secret work exposed, in case the letters fell into the wrong hands. Similarly, Filonenko said, the prosecutor, Ribet, and the investigators had cynically turned the green Bible into a key piece of evidence against Plevitskaya, although they had no proof that it had been used to communicate with the Soviets—as opposed to ROVS members only—or that Plevitskaya had ever encrypted or deciphered communications with it. He admitted that it was possible Skoblin had been a double agent, but investigators had found no documents proving that he or Plevitskaya had spied for the Soviets.

Filonenko informed the jurors that, if the majority of letters he had received from the public earlier in the investigation had assumed Plevitskaya's guilt, more of them now assumed that she was being used as a scapegoat by the French authorities. He reminded jurors of how, during the Russian Civil War, Plevitskaya had saved two of Matsylev's brothers—the same Matsylev who now was one of her accusers. At this point, Plevitskaya glanced hopefully at her defense attorney while swallowing her tears.

For the remainder of his lengthy speech, Filonenko turned to the Miller kidnapping and the accusations about Plevitskaya's alleged role in it. As any defense attorney should, he tried to discredit every major accusation against his client, and he offered his own theories as to who the real culprits might be. Plevitskaya, he maintained, had not lied to investigators about her meeting with the Eitingons on September 20. In the midst of everything else that had happened in her life since September 22, the Eitingon meeting had seemed irrelevant, and she had simply been forgetful. Wouldn't anyone, he asked, after being imprisoned for fifteen months? More than once, Filonenko pointed out that, had Plevitskaya been guilty of complicity, and had she thought Skoblin's notebook, which she was carrying around, contained evidence damning him, she would have thrown it away during her wanderings around Paris on September 23. Nor would she have gone to the police on September 24. She had handed Skoblin's notebook to Liuba

Grigul not to destroy valuable evidence, but simply to empty her purse of nonessentials, as an act of good intent. If Skoblin had been a trained Soviet agent, Filonenko continued, he would not have written a note to himself about a secret meeting with Miller. "You've seen what's in the notebook," he reminded the jurors. "Messages like 'Drop off shirts at the laundry,' 'buy shoes,' . . . 'kidnap General Miller on such-and-such a date.' Don't forget!" he joked. The note referencing General Miller, he insisted, was about a breakfast date that he and Plevitskaya had had with Miller and others on September 20, two days before his kidnapping.

Resuming a more serious tone, Filonenko urged the jurors, "You should acquit Nadezhda Plevitskaya to compensate for the slander and insult she has suffered!"

It could not have been a surprise to those in the courtroom that Filonenko would then revisit his earlier points about why he thought Miller's note had been forged. The defense attorney recapped his litany of arguments. Had he really written the note, Miller, a military man with an exacting mind, would have included more detailed information about the secret meeting and would have told Kussonsky the exact time he wanted him to open it. As the leader of a military organization, Miller would probably not have agreed to attend an intelligence-gathering meeting with foreign agents; he would have been more likely to send a subordinate to such a shady appointment. At the very least, he would have phoned the German embassy for verification. The purpose of the note, Filonenko exclaimed, was not to inform Kussonsky about Miller's secret meeting, but to frame Skoblin, who might have been eliminated. Filonenko then focused on Kussonsky as the person French investigators should have arrested, given his suspicious behavior on September 22 and 23 and his contradictory testimony.

Filonenko admitted that the "Bolsheviks or Red Spanish" could have abducted Miller, but he never acknowledged the Le Havre trail as the route the Soviets had used to transport Miller from Montmorency Boulevard to the *Maria Ulyanova*. He appears to have wanted the jurors to think that, if Skoblin had been working for a left-wing group, it was for Spanish communists not the Soviets.

As for contradictions in Plevitskaya's testimony about the events of September 22, Filonenko noted, they were mainly related to time, and she had not been wearing a watch that day. It had taken her more than an hour to choose a new dress because, as a stage performer, her costumes meant a great deal to her. As for Plevitskaya's changing account of her and Skoblin's route from Caroline's to the train station, Filonenko glossed over its weaknesses and stressed that no evidence supported the prosecution's theory that Plevitskaya had taken a taxi to the station. The driver, after all, had never come forward.

It was now 4:15 p.m., and Filonenko, aware of the passing time, chose to end with an emotional appeal to the jurors. "Last Sunday," he said, "when I was visiting Plevitskaya in jail, the mother superior, who loves this woman with all her heart, said that all the nuns and detainees would be praying today for her acquittal!" Plevitskaya wept quietly while Filonenko spoke these words. The defense attorney finished by reminding the jurors that, if Plevitskaya had really been a Soviet agent, the NKVD would have helped her—as it had Lydia Grozovskaya in the aftermath of the Reiss murder. And after fifteen months in detention, Plevitskaya would have confessed to being a Soviet agent, had she been one and gone unrescued by the NKVD, and it would have been in her interest to denounce her husband as a coward in return for leniency.

Filonenko sat down, looking utterly exhausted. Plevitskaya had turned away from the spectators and continued crying softly, her fur coat falling from her shoulders. Judge Delegorgue asked through her translator whether

Nadezhda Plevitskaya at her trial, Palace of Justice, Paris, December 1938. Courtesy of Roger-Viollet/The Image Works

she desired to give the final word. Plevitskaya stood up, resting both of her hands on the wooden bar. She choked back tears and spoke with difficulty:

> Yes, I . . . want . . . I . . . am an orphan. . . . I have no witnesses. . . .
> One . . . he . . . he [glancing upward] knows . . . knows that I never
> in my life did any harm . . . to anyone. . . . Apart from my love for my
> husband, I have nothing. Let them judge me for this.

The courtroom fell silent. Judge Delegorgue asked the accused to be seated and turned to the jurors. He instructed them to answer seven questions of fact during their deliberation:

1. On September 22, 1937, did an abduction and deprivation of freedom occur on French territory?
2. Did this deprivation of freedom last for more than one month?
3. Was Plevitskaya an accomplice?
4. Was a violent act committed on French soil against General Miller on September 22, 1937?
5. If this was so, then was it committed with malicious intent (premeditated)?
6. If it was, then was it committed in order to lure the victim into a trap?
7. Was Plevitskaya an accomplice in the kidnapping and the violent act?

Delegorgue outlined the jurors' options. If they answered questions three and seven affirmatively, without accounting for extenuating circumstances, then Plevitskaya would be found guilty and sentenced to life imprisonment. If they answered the questions negatively, then Plevitskaya would be acquitted. If they answered question three affirmatively and question seven negatively, or vice versa, and factored in extenuating circumstances, then her punishment could be as severe as twenty years' hard labor or as lenient as six days in prison. He assured the jurors that, if they had any concerns, they could consult with him, the prosecutor, and the defense attorneys.

The jurors retired to their conference room at 4:30 p.m., and Plevitskaya, who had since regained her composure, left the courtroom with her guards. The spectators, the attorneys, and even the remaining guards freely exchanged their opinions about the potential verdict. There seemed to be no consensus about what the jurors would decide, although a majority of the spectators seemed to assume that Plevitskaya would be found guilty. Someone shouted that Plevitskaya would be acquitted. But no one expected a long prison sentence, given the reputation of Paris juries for leniency in cases involving female defendants.

At 5:00 p.m., the jurors asked to see Delegorgue, Flach, and the two defense attorneys, and they all piled into the conference room. Ten minutes later, the defense attorneys reappeared in the courtroom. This time they were quiet and looked worried. A few minutes later, a rumor spread through the courtroom that the jurors had answered the key questions in the affirmative and were now discussing whether to acknowledge the existence of extenuating circumstances, such as the fact that Miller and Skoblin had not been found and that only circumstantial evidence pointed to Plevitskaya as Skoblin's accomplice.

At approximately 5:20 p.m. the jurors returned to the courtroom. The judge warned those present not to make a scene while the verdict was being read. The guards stood in the doorways in case of disorder.

"Bring in the accused!" Judge Delegorgue ordered. Soon Plevitskaya entered the courtroom between two guards. She lingered for a second on the threshold, casting her eyes quickly over the jurors' faces. Then she sat down in the defendant's box.

The foreman stood up and dramatically placed his hand over his heart. He announced that eleven of the twelve jurors had answered yes to all seven questions and that the jury recognized the presence of extenuating circumstances, although he did not detail what they were. Plevitskaya clearly understood what the foreman had said. She had been found guilty. She swayed and then regained her composure. She reached for her throat. Hardening her expression and absently picking at her collar, she sat down on the bench and glanced up.

Next came the sentencing phase. Given the jurors' decision to apply extenuating circumstances, the law afforded them, Judge Delegorgue, and the three assessors a range of choices, from a minimum of five years' hard labor to a maximum of twenty years' hard labor. However, before they left the courtroom to deliberate in the conference room, Flach requested a moment to speak. Granted permission to do so, he reminded the jurors that he had originally requested a guilty verdict with no extenuating circumstances and life imprisonment. Realizing that he would gain the satisfaction of neither, he now urged the jurors to issue Plevitskaya a sentence of twenty years forced labor. "The sentence ought to set an example," he declared, "to let whoever sent this woman to conduct evil activities on our soil know that the hand of French justice can punish without mercy."

Plevitskaya's attorneys defended her. Schwab stood up and pleaded for clemency. Then Filonenko added, "The circumstances of the crime remain unclear. Everything is dark and mysterious. I yield to the verdict. But let Plevitskaya live long enough to see the day when the true culprit will be revealed."

Judge Delegorgue now turned to the accused, who had the right to the last word. It appeared that Plevitskaya had not even prepared a statement about sentencing because she probably had not expected to be in this position. She glanced over at her attorneys, then to the judge, and finally toward the public. In a barely audible voice, she said, "I . . . don't . . . know." Plevitskaya, usually not at a loss for words, had nothing more to say.

It was now 5:30 p.m. The jurors, Judge Delegorgue, and the court assessors retired to the conference room. Plevitskaya remained in the courtroom and conferred quietly with her attorneys. At one point, a flock of photographers swooped down on her. She turned away from the bright flashes and covered her eyes. She and the dozens of others in the courtroom waited twenty minutes for the jury to return.

At 5:50 p.m., the jury filed back in. Judge Delegorgue resumed the hearing and announced the sentence: "Twenty years' hard labor followed by a ten-year exile from France." The hall erupted in cries of disbelief. Plevitskaya covered her forehead with her hand. The interpreter translated for her, but she did not listen. She already knew. She stood erect and glanced up at the ceiling.

Meanwhile, Plevitskaya's defense attorneys did not waste a minute. Schwab immediately informed the court about potential grounds for an appeal. While he, Filonenko, Delegorgue, and Flach had been in the conference room with the jurors, he said, juror 4 had told them of his vote against a conviction and revealed that the other jurors had voted for it. Schwab insisted that juror four's unveiling of this information before the reading of the formal verdict in court was grounds for an appeal. The judge confirmed that this incident had taken place as Schwab claimed and declared that the matter would be reviewed at a later date. Filonenko informed journalists that he would file an appeal on his client's behalf.

Only one more formality remained that day, and it concerned the civil law suit. Having been found guilty in the criminal case, Plevitskaya was automatically found liable for paying compensation to the plaintiffs of the civil law suit. The court presented the Miller family with one franc as a symbol of the damages. At this point, Plevitskaya was in no position to offer a monetary settlement.

The hearing and trial ended shortly after 6:00 p.m. Plevitskaya looked calm. As she walked by Filonenko on her way out, she shook his hand and told him, "It makes no difference to me. I will die soon."

The jurors in Plevitskaya's trial had fulfilled their civic duty, but the process concluded with many questions left unanswered: Miller's and Skoblin's fates, details of the Soviets' kidnapping plot and Plevitskaya's prior knowledge of them, the French government's alleged cover-ups, and Eitingon's political loyalties. Some of these questions would be answered years or decades later, while others would never be. "The trial was strangely inconclusive and muddled," Nabokov incisively wrote in "The Assistant Producer" (1943), his thinly veiled fictionalization of the event. As the great novelist noted, "witnesses did not shine, and the final conviction of the Slavska on a charge of kidnapping was debatable on legal grounds. Irrelevant trifles kept obscuring the main issue."

The Eitingon question, for example, still belongs in the "unanswered" category. In his correspondence to Freud during Plevitskaya's trial and shortly after its conclusion, Eitingon noted that his name had been raised in the trial, but he neglected to write that he and his wife had been with the Skoblins in Paris shortly before Miller's kidnapping. Eitingon claimed in one letter that he did not think the French authorities had collected any evidence supporting Plevitskaya's guilt, although this definitely was not the case. "It somehow felt like a political trial, like the Dreyfus trial," he told Freud. "To be honest I have to say that the grotesque lies in the newspapers didn't annoy me very much. I only felt sorry for the accused Russian singer."[3] As noted in chapter 4, even Eitingon's biographer, a distant relative, has not ruled out the possibility that he and Mirra were Soviet agents.

What is clear is that no one had expected the sentence to be so harsh, despite knowing in advance what the prosecutor's preferences were. The explanation for the sentence was fairly straightforward—even if the jurors questioned whether a preponderance of evidence existed, all but one of them had accepted the prosecutor's reasoning that the court needed to treat this case as a warning to any immigrants who might contemplate committing crimes on French soil.

Unfortunately for Plevitskaya, playing the role of a simple Russian peasant woman proved ineffective. Xenophobia was widespread in France at the time, and so perhaps the jurors would have seen her as less threatening had she spoken in French and acted like a cultured bourgeois woman who had assimilated into Paris life. They might also have given her a more lenient sentence had she confessed, but one can imagine that she still felt loyal to Skoblin and may have been warned through an NKVD intermediary that she needed to remain silent about his Soviet ties in order to protect him. Although Plevitskaya was not convicted of espionage or executed as Mata Hari was in 1917, both cases were used by the French state to set an example. In one, a Dutch exotic dancer was prosecuted during a world war; in the other, a Russian singer was prosecuted on the eve of one. Beware of female foreigners, and female foreigners, beware!

Perhaps there were other reasons as well for Plevitskaya's harsh prison sentence. According to historian Benjamin F. Martin, "La Plevitskaïa had to pay because the prosecution could not place the Soviet Union and the Popular Front in the defendant's dock with her."[4] As mentioned earlier, the French government under Édouard Daladier did not want Plevitskaya's trial to cause any political controversies, either with the Germans or the Soviets. However, French officials who leaned right may have felt that they could have their cake and eat it too by convicting and severely sentencing Plevitskaya—thereby signaling that they knew the Soviets had kidnapped Miller and that they had not been duped on this count. To a lesser extent, Plevitskaya's heavy punishment may also have been meant to give the Miller family and the Russian émigré community some solace by creating the impression that justice had been served.

The news of the verdict made headlines throughout Paris. The socialist daily, *Le Populaire*, portrayed Plevitskaya as the victim of Skoblin's political agenda, as well as that of the French government and right-wing Russian émigrés. The bourgeois jurors had taken out their hatred of the Soviets—and even of the legacy of the French Revolution—on the hapless folk singer, claimed the newspaper.[5] From the right, *Vozrozhdenie* emphasized how Ribet had proven, supposedly beyond a doubt, that the Soviets had kidnapped Miller with Skoblin's help. Plevitskaya, the paper continued, had served as his accomplice, and her attorneys had spent more time defending the interests of the Soviet Union than the accused. In doing so, they had helped condemn her.[6]

Now that Skoblin's and Plevitskaya's ties to Soviet intelligence have been established, we can credit Ribet, Strelnikov, and the French investigators with correctly identifying the Soviets as the organizers and the abductors, Skoblin as the conspirator who lured Miller to his doom, and Plevitskaya as her husband's accomplice, for having defended his alibi. Conversely, whatever their true feelings about Plevitskaya's guilt or lack thereof, Filonenko and Schwab were certainly misguided, or even duplicitous, in their efforts to persuade jurors that the Soviets had not transported Miller to Le Havre.

One aspect of Plevitskaya's talent on stage was her strong sense of timing—knowing just when to apply dynamics in songs, when to use certain facial expressions and body gestures, and how to bow. But in September 1937, her timing was uncharacteristically off. Her alibi failed. She lost her adoring audience and her integrity as a performer. Her last audience, in the Palace of Justice, viewed her as a Red Seductress, not as Mother Russia. She had truly become homeless.

And she was certainly not innocent. Even if we grant that she was unaware of the Miller kidnapping plot before September 22, she at least knew about Skoblin's role by the time Matsylev came knocking on their hotel room door. At no point during the investigation or trial did she confess any knowledge of Skoblin's recruitment by the Soviets or his role in the Miller abduction. These actions alone serve as proof of her complicity and were sufficient grounds for prosecution and punishment. On the other hand, given the fact that investigators found no direct evidence that Plevitskaya was a Soviet agent or that she knew during the afternoon of the 22nd that she was helping Skoblin carry out his part of the kidnapping plot, her punishment still seems—seventy-five years later—to be draconian.

After leaving the Palace of Justice, Plevitskaya returned to the Petite-Roquette. Unless she successfully appealed her case or the French government granted her a pardon, she would serve her sentence in the women's prison in Rennes, the provincial capital of Brittany in northwestern France. A macabre family story is told about a dark premonition Plevitskaya supposedly had before her ordeal. According to her niece, Helene Fournier—the daughter of Skoblin's sister, Tamara Vorobieva—only weeks before Miller's kidnapping, when she was staying with her aunt and uncle in Ozoir-la-Ferrière, Plevitskaya came down to breakfast one morning looking pale. She told her niece, "I had a strange dream. I was in prison, I died, and then my body was buried under its walls."[7]

13

APPEAL

The day her trial ended, Plevitskaya began arranging for her appeal. She insisted that she was innocent and predicted—perhaps based on her fatalistic dream—that she would not survive long in the women's prison in Rennes. Plevitskaya did not lose hope that her conviction would be overturned, but she failed to grasp the immensity of the obstacles in her way. First, the French government supported her conviction from the start and had no reason to overturn it. Secondly, applications for appealing jury judgments in high-profile criminal cases were rarely approved. When they were, the subject of the appeal was more often based on points of law—the grounds for illegality—than on facts.[1] In other words, the party bringing the appeal would need to show that the trial had proceeded irregularly or suffered from flawed reasoning on the part of the court. Would the Court of Cassation agree to review her appeal on this basis?

Lack of money was Plevitskaya's other immediate concern. She owed the French courts 60,000 francs and could afford only bread and water for breakfast at the Petite-Roquette. She could have earned a few francs toiling in a workshop with other inmates, but she chose to remain in her cell.[2] Instead, she tried to sell whatever she could of her and Skoblin's remaining possessions, including her fur coats and sheet music. She even wrote the manager of Caroline's dress shop to arrange for the return of her deposit on the clothes she had bought the day of Miller's kidnapping. It did not seem to matter that Nocin Epstein had testified against her. "I hope, since you're a good Russian man," Plevitskaya reasoned, "you don't wish me evil, after hearing all the lies and slander about me in court." She also hoped to raise funds through friends and acquaintances, some of whom might have been Soviet operatives. For instance, she urged Filonenko to contact her acquaintances in Sofia, Bulgaria, and claimed that they would not hesitate to send her money.

For nearly three months after her trial ended, Plevitskaya's main link with the outside world was Filonenko, who bore the brunt of her frustration. She wrote him letters demanding that he agree to work with advocate Vincent de Moro-Giafferri.[3] She made countless other requests and vented her anger over what White Army veterans, her husband's former brothers-in-arms, had said about her. In an undated letter to Filonenko, Plevitskaya wrote, "You said that you pity me! And now you object to cooperating with a smart Frenchman? Should I just quiet down and die in prison?" She pronounced herself "guilty only of loving":

> I spent seventeen years with my husband, and what he told me was the truth! Who cooperated with the Bolsheviks? Turkul, Abramov, Guchkov. They were all Russian aristocrats! My husband avoided conversations. And only now I understand that he was right—the circle was all made up of untrustworthy people and you didn't know who you were speaking to! You need to exonerate me with Moro-Giafferri's assistance! And let the Bolsheviks—who know that I was not with them, although I will not answer for my husband—feel ashamed! Let them help me, a woman who did no evil to them or anyone else!

Filonenko, Plevitskaya continued, had failed to defend her against these slanderers. "No one says that I harmed General Miller, yet everyone criticized me severely. Why?" Plevitskaya felt compelled to reiterate to Filonenko that she was not a criminal and that Skoblin had never shared his political dealings with her. She was perplexed, she said, by Lydia Kutepova's claims about her and Skoblin's supposedly strange behavior in Riga. Near the end of her letter, Plevitskaya urged Filonenko to "remember Dreyfus!"

Plevitskaya felt that Filonenko was not giving her the attention she deserved. Only five days after her conviction, she scolded him for forgetting "all that I have asked you to do." She begged him to prevent her transfer to Fresnes, a prison in a southern suburb of Paris, where felons appealing their convictions were detained. In one of her rare legal triumphs, Plevitskaya persuaded the director of the Petite-Roquette to keep her there until her appeal was adjudicated. Plevitskaya also pleaded with Filonenko to contact Schwab, who had promised to file a complaint about illegalities at her trial. As always, she lashed out at her detractors and at Judge Delegorgue for believing them. She reasoned that, while she had never harmed anyone and yet had been thrown in prison, White Army veterans, including Miller, had committed evil acts against the Bolsheviks, with the Bolsheviks similarly harming the Whites. "Has Kolya heard about my verdict?" Plevitskaya wondered in her letter to Filonenko. "And if he's really still alive, wouldn't he come running back to me? You know me now! You know that, in the face of death, I told you everything!" In closing, she swore her "eternal fidelity" to her husband and admitted that "all my crimes stem from my love for him."

In her December 19 diary entry, Plevitskaya mentioned receiving a little money from a Russian woman named Marina and wrote about her frustration over her trial's outcome. "I'll never get used to being silent!" she exclaimed. Marina had read in Plevitskaya's memoirs about her first meeting with Tsar Nicholas II and asked the singer about her loyalty to him. Writing in her diary about this conversation, Plevitskaya compared herself to Tsar Nicholas II, who had also been betrayed by his own countrymen. She worried about her impending transfer to the women's prison in Rennes. "How can I work, given my advanced age?" she asked herself. "Prison labor? Such suffering! And for what? Being a smart idiot? In life, I never envied anyone, nor was I ever mean."

On December 21, still awaiting news of her appeal, she composed this poem:

> Slander spread from a dark shadow,
> Truth was covered by a dirty paw,
> A good heart was buried in the ground.
> The heart cried over the grief of a stranger,
> The devil is amusing himself with an unhappy mouse,
> I am in a foreign land—in captivity I languished,
> And forgot my own dear song.

In late December, Plevitskaya's mood darkened even more after Moro-Giafferri wrote that he could not see her unless he first reached an agreement with Filonenko and Schwab.[4] Undeterred, she continued to pressure Filonenko to allow the prestigious attorney to join her defense team. By chance that December, Plevitskaya had met one of Moro-Giafferri's colleagues, the attorney Isidore Franckel, when he came to the Petite-Roquette to see a client.[5] Franckel, an Odessa Jew, fled Russia with his family after the Bolshevik Revolution, eventually settling in Paris. There he became an esteemed defense attorney and the president of the Zionist Federation of France. Like Moro-Giafferri, Franckel defended Herschel Grynszpan, the young murderer of the Nazi diplomat vom Rath.

Franckel's client in the Petite-Roquette was Elena G., Plevitskaya's cell mate and a fellow Russian émigré. Elena, a midwife, was accused of murdering a woman by performing an abortion for her, a crime at the time. Franckel overheard a heated exchange between Plevitskaya and Filonenko. She was berating him for having reassured her during the investigation that the case would not proceed to trial, and then telling her during the trial that she would be exonerated.

"And now you tell me twenty years! That means death!" she exclaimed. "It would be better for me simply to be executed." Filonenko sat there listening to her. "Why are you silent?" Plevitskaya asked. "Say anything! You need to file an appeal. Quickly!"

Filonenko cautioned her that petitioning for a new trial was not a viable option, as juries' decisions were considered final. Plevitskaya then asked him to file a cassation appeal, based on claims that a legal error had been committed, and Filonenko demurred. "So, this means I'll die?" she asked, her voice shaking, like that of an injured animal. "I still want to live! Do you hear me? I want to live, live, live!" The sound of her voice thundered down the hallway. In earshot of Franckel, who had read about her trial in the newspapers, Plevitskaya told Filonenko to mobilize public opinion in France, to appeal to state ministers and even to French president Albert Lebrun. Franckel watched her become hysterical and nearly collapse. Several nuns ran into the room and led her away.

Shortly after witnessing Plevitskaya's outburst that day, Franckel received a letter from the prison. She wished to meet with him to discuss the possibility of his representing her. He hesitated to accept her proposal because the grounds for her appeal were weak. The chances of clemency or even a slight reduction of her long sentence were equally low. Franckel did not know for certain whether Plevitskaya was guilty of serving as an accomplice in Miller's kidnapping, but he felt compelled to accept her anyway as a new client. "I wanted to help her," he recalled. "I knew she was suffering."

Not only was Plevitskaya appealing to the French state and her attorneys for help, but she also turned to her few remaining friends for aid. In a maudlin, self-pitying letter dated December 27, Plevitskaya wrote to Elena G., who had been released by this time.[6] The midwife sent her funds to pay for coffee at the jail's canteen. Plevitskaya stressed that her sorrow knew no bounds. Plevitskaya pictured herself as a martyr, comparing her experience with that of Jesus's suffering on the cross. On the day of her conviction, she had felt "purer and braver" than anyone else in the courtroom. She recounted in her diary how, when she had returned to the Petite-Roquette after the verdict, the nuns and inmates had cried with her. They had prayed for her every day of her trial. "It was where I got my strength, my inner peace," she declared. "Yes, thy will will be done!" She then referred to Jesus's last supper and continued:

> Whose sins do I atone for? I did not commit sins that deserve such great suffering in return! The judges saw me as a strong, evil, smart female criminal. But if only they saw the truth, that I'm a completely helpless, weak, good woman! I'm an uneducated woman who doesn't even know the multiplication table and could never figure out a cipher! My husband was my brain, my motivator, and my divine being! What would Kolya say about what must be done? Kolya would say, "Die, die, one must die!" I didn't need politics. My soul was full of happiness! I wasn't greedy or envious. There was no malice in my heart. Why then was I accused of a crime? Why did the people who had known and loved me do it?

Plevitskaya then told Elena how thin she was getting and how she needed a friend. "I swear to the entire world that I am not guilty!"

On December 29, Plevitskaya frantically wrote Filonenko, first to inform him that prison authorities would be sending her to the Fresnes prison in an uncomfortable prison van. But she had more to say. Plevitskaya criticized Filonenko for rarely visiting her. She asked him to cancel the van and find her sister-in-law Tamara Vorobieva, who could help her. Then she asked him for an even larger favor, and in doing so may have unwittingly betrayed her Soviet ties: "Don't be afraid, dear Maximilian Maximilianovich! I speak the truth! If a courier could be sent to Sofia, then I'll write Abramov's son—I am acquainted with him, but he doesn't know that I know his code name. Kolya somehow told me what it was." (Plevitskaya apparently did not know that, in October 1938, Nikolai Abramov had been accused of espionage and expelled from Bulgaria.[7])

In supporting her appeal, Plevitskaya wanted to include letters written by Captain Foss and General Abramov (Nikolai's father, who was president of ROVS from 1937 to 1938) prior to Miller's kidnapping, and she may have assumed that Nikolai Abramov had copies of them. She planned to show the appeals court that her name had been used in the coded letters only as a decoy, in order to conceal their real purpose, which was to convey information about clandestine ROVS activities in which Skoblin had been involved during 1935 and 1936.[8]

It also seems from Plevitskaya's December 29 letter to Filonenko that she assumed she could get money from her Sofia contact to pay some of her court costs. "We should refute every accusation against me, and this is not hard," she shrilled. "Truth is on our side!" Then she proposed two new appeal strategies. Both, however, involved factual issues and were therefore useless. First, Plevitskaya reckoned, they could use Epstein's testimony about how he had not seen Skoblin in Caroline's dress shop, thereby arguing that Skoblin had been sitting in his car the whole time, where Epstein could not have seen him. Second, Plevitskaya suggested, they could use the testimony of Skoblin's friend Troshin in arguing that she had not been involved in Skoblin's political matters.

In January 1939, Plevitskaya followed up with two letters to Filonenko that further illustrated their strained relations. She chided him for not taking the necessary risks to help her, writing, "You are a noteworthy and experienced professor, a wonderful jurist, but a lazy defense attorney in such complicated cases, despite defending someone who is as pure as a dove." She also lashed out at Ribet and Strelnikov, describing them derisively as "Jew advocates," which is ironic, given that Franckel was Jewish and representing Grynszpan at the time. In the first of these letters, she admitted that, given their recent rift, "I probably won't be seeing you for a long time." Two days later, she wrote Filonenko, asking that he drop her as a client and telling him that she planned to meet with Moro-Giafferri. "You did not defend me from the lies that rained down on me at my trial," she concluded.

Sometime between mid-January and mid-February 1939, Filonenko and Schwab stopped representing Plevitskaya, and Franckel and Moro-Giafferri, together with Louis Sarran and an advocate named Meyer, agreed to serve as her new defense attorneys. Of this group, Franckel apparently had the most contact with her. When he arrived at the entrance to the Petite-Roquette for his first meeting with her, he identified Plevitskaya as his client. The face of the attendant, an old nun, lit up. "So, you're the new advocate!" she cried out. "She told me, the poor thing. How severe they were to her! She's a wonderful woman, and everyone here loves her. She has a heart of gold." The attendant told him that when Plevitskaya first arrived and had some money to spare, she bought coffee, sugar, and bread for several other inmates. "She has a generous nature," she went on. "A Slavic soul."

Plevitskaya and Franckel met in a reception area. He noticed that she had grown thinner and more wrinkled and was looking more exhausted. She appeared in a black dress and worn shoes, with a kerchief on her head and a shawl wrapped around her shoulders. On her once-famous face, he noticed traces of powder and rouge.

"My dear, I didn't think you'd come," she said. "No one wants to know me anymore. How many friends I once had! And suddenly no one's left. I am all alone, as in the grave." Tears formed in her eyes. She asked for cigarettes, but smoking was prohibited, and a nun was watching them through a window. "Don't be afraid," Plevitskaya assured him. "Here all advocates give their clients cigarettes, even those who don't smoke. They serve as money and will buy you anything except your freedom." She continued in a different vein: "Here I pray a great deal, but God doesn't want to listen to me—a sinner. All my life, I entertained people with my songs. But they ruined me, slandered me. The Russians were the worst of all. Everyone turned on me, though I am innocent. But you will save me. I can feel it. God sent you to me, so you could rescue me from this hell."

Franckel told her that he would try to do everything he could to help her. He admitted that finding grounds for an appeal would be very difficult. Barring the appeal, the only other possibility was a pardon. Plevitskaya listened to Franckel, hanging on his every word and breathing hard. "It's true," Franckel said, "that one additional means is left to us." Her eyes widened. "There'd have to be a reexamination of the trial," Franckel continued, "which only the minister of justice can approve. But such an order could happen only with the introduction of new facts that were not available at your trial. In other words, we need a sensational unmasking." Perhaps Plevitskaya had been thinking that the Abramov-Foss correspondence would serve such a purpose. But she and Franckel would first need to follow through with the cassation appeal on a point of law. Franckel recalled that one juror had not indicated his profession in his paperwork. On the other hand, Franckel was apparently not aware of, or did not consider relevant, the procedural error—informing the attorneys of the jury's vote before the formal reading of the verdict in the courtroom—committed by juror 4. Plevitskaya interrupted Franckel and insisted, "Dear, do what you want, but save me. I want to live, live, live!" Before he could retreat, she fell to her knees and kissed his hand.

Whenever Franckel visited her, Plevitskaya referred to Skoblin, whom she believed was still alive and trying to rescue her. On one such visit, she described the last time she had seen him, in the early morning of September 23. There was a knock on the door, she told Franckel. Matsylev had asked Skoblin to accompany him to ROVS. She had wanted to join him, but she thought he would not be gone for long and so decided to stay back in their hotel room waiting for him. She continued her story but confessed nothing to Franckel about her or Skoblin's involvement in Miller's kidnapping. Her tale reached a wistful climax:

> "Where are you taking my husband?" I asked. "I will go with him."
> They said he'd be gone only for an hour or two. Peaceful, but pale, he

followed them out the door, without saying a word, not even glancing
back at me. . . . Oh, if only I'd known! I would've followed him wherever he went, to suffering . . . to death, and done whatever was needed
of me! Why did I leave him alone? This thought torments me. Earlier
I was convinced that he was no longer alive. But now I'm starting to
hope. I'm beginning to think that he's alive and that he'll return to me.

Sometime in the first half of 1939, Franckel recruited Louis Sarran
to serve on Plevitskaya's defense team. Even though he specialized in civil
law and could not speak Russian, Sarran wielded significant influence in
France's legal circles during the 1930s and was therefore potentially valuable to Plevitskaya. At the time, he was a representative of the Union of
French Advocates and the Secretary General of the International Union of
Advocates. His first meeting with Plevitskaya proved awkward, though,
because of the singer's melodramatic behavior, which unnerved the busi-
nesslike Sarran. Noticing the Legion of Honor medal he was wearing, she
addressed him and Franckel as "big Frenchmen" who would save her. She
kneeled to kiss Sarran's hand, and he was taken aback.[9] Nevertheless, he
agreed to serve on her defense team, if only because hers was a high-profile
case and her punishment had been unusually severe.

How did Moro-Giafferri come to join Plevitskaya's defense team?
According to one account, which provides a partial and highly question-
able explanation, Plevitskaya's final break with Filonenko led him to join.[10]
Plevitskaya had asked Filonenko (referred to as "Max") to drop by the Soviet embassy to retrieve some cash and secure an amnesty for her, presumably so she could escape to the USSR. Instead, the risk-averse Filonenko
urged her to confess to the French authorities for the sake of her appeal.
At first she agreed, but then she reconsidered and asked Moro-Giafferri to
serve as her counsel. Moro-Giafferri dissuaded Plevitskaya from pursuing
Filonenko's line of defense, and this is what caused Filonenko to resign. If
this account is true, Filonenko then recorded what Plevitskaya had told him
about her knowledge of the Miller affair, sealed his statement in an envelope, and gave it to a trustworthy acquaintance at the Paris courthouse for
safekeeping—with a Miller-like proviso that it be opened only if something
untoward were to happen to him. (Whether Filonenko actually did do this,
and whether anyone ever found and read his note, remains unknown.) Regardless of this source's accuracy, *Poslednie novosti* was reporting by March
1939 that Moro-Giafferri, Franckel, Meyer, and Sarran were now Plevitskaya's attorneys.[11] However, it appears that Moro-Giafferri played only a
minor role on Plevitskaya's new defense team.

On March 22, a criminal appeals court reviewed Plevitskaya's request, with Meyer representing her. Within weeks, if not days, the court rejected her request, and this legal avenue was now closed. Franckel broke the bad news to Plevitskaya in person. She did not respond emotionally, Franckel recalled, because she had understood that this approach was unlikely to succeed and that it was mainly a tactic to extend her stay in the Petite-Roquette. "She suffered from loneliness," Franckel noted. "She received no letters, no one visited her, and worst of all, not one soul sent her any francs to help support her. She was starving." Plevitskaya accepted as the next strategy a petition requesting a reexamination of her trial.

In the meantime, Franckel visited Plevitskaya often and brought her cigarettes and food. He knew he was breaking the jail's rules, but he could not arrive empty-handed. Once the nuns found cigarettes on Plevitskaya and put her in solitary confinement for a few days. After returning to her cell, she asked Franckel if his wife, Lola, might give her some cosmetics and a scarf that she could wear on Easter. Lola granted her husband's client her wishes, and Plevitskaya wrote her a thank-you letter overflowing with emotion and gratitude.

But despite Franckel's efforts, the Ministry of Justice rejected Plevitskaya's petition for a reexamination of her trial. This loss meant that she could no longer be detained at the Petite-Roquette. On April 4, 1939, she was driven to Fresnes prison and was now only one transfer away from the women's prison in Rennes. During her months in Fresnes, Plevitskaya "turned into an old woman," observed *Poslednie novosti*.[12] She was forced to wear a uniform—a gray striped dress, a coarse cotton shirt, a white cap, thick stockings, and uncomfortable wooden shoes—and was initially prevented from writing her attorneys. She slept in a dormitory room with other inmates. For breakfast, she had bread and coffee without sugar, which she still could not afford; for lunch, she was served vegetable soup. She spent her days making clothes in a workshop, earning only two francs a day, half of which was deducted to pay for her court costs. As a concession, Franckel and Sarran were allowed to visit her twice a month.

On May 10—the day before the Soviets executed General Miller in Moscow—Sarran and Franckel met with Minister of Justice Paul Marchandeau to submit a petition to pardon Plevitskaya, based on her advanced age and frail health.[13] The minister, however, could not make the decision independently. The procedure for reviewing such petitions involved a special commission, which would study the case and make a recommendation; final approval would come from the minister of justice. Franckel recalled that Marchandeau "very attentively listened to us. He promised to support our request, but said that a full pardon was impossible."[14] The advocates had assumed that this would be the case and had petitioned for a partial pardon—commuting her sentence from twenty years' hard labor to solitary confinement. Marchandeau told Franckel and Sarran that he would try his best to reduce Plevitskaya's sentence.

Plevitskaya wrote to Natalya Miller, asking her to honor their long friendship by supporting her application for a pardon. When Franckel and Sarran visited her, Plevitskaya asked them to tell Miller that "I'm suffering for her and thinking of her. She's a wonderful person. She ought to forgive me. She should comfort me in my time of grief and join in my request for a pardon."[15] Not surprisingly, Miller did not reply to Plevitskaya's appeal. When Franckel told Plevitskaya that she should not expect to receive a full pardon, but at best would be granted a lighter sentence, she was disappointed and admitted that she was losing her will to live.

In the end, all of Plevitskaya's appeals were in vain. Two weeks after Franckel and Sarran met with Minister of Justice Marchandeau, the commission unanimously voted against granting Plevitskaya even a partial pardon, and Marchandeau affirmed its decision.[16] Plevitskaya began informing Franckel about her heart problems. But prison officials rejected her request to be hospitalized, and so she was unable to avoid the harsh conditions inside Fresnes.

Soon after learning that she would not be pardoned, Plevitskaya asked Franckel to arrange for a priest to see her. A French priest who had converted to Russian Orthodoxy agreed to come. "That calmed her somewhat," Franckel observed. "But when she was preparing to be transferred to Rennes, she again became aggrieved. She felt she could not remain alone any longer. She was tortured by nightmares. She said she was afraid of rats. She said she couldn't adjust to wearing prison clothes or survive her transfer to Rennes."

"Is this the end, then?" Plevitskaya asked Franckel. "Is it true that nothing will save me now? Oh, I so want to live, so want to still see flowers and the sun!"

14

DEATH OF A NIGHTINGALE

By order of Napoléon III, construction of a women's prison began in Rennes in the early 1860s. *La Maison Centrale de Rennes*, also known as the *Centre Pénetentiaire pour Femmes*, was completed in 1878. Located in the city's center, it is the only prison in France exclusively for women inmates and the largest women's prison in Europe. The architects chose an imposing hexagonal design, conceiving each section as a separate dormitory. A large courtyard stands in the middle of the main structure, with walkways intersecting at its center, where a fountain stands. For over one hundred years, the high stone wall surrounding the nearly two-and-a-half-acre campus has sent a bleak message to prisoners that escape is futile.

Arriving at *La Maison Centrale* on July 3, 1939, Plevitskaya was treated like any other prisoner.[1] In her prison file, wardens noted her release date as September 25, 1957, exactly twenty years from the day of her arrest.[2] Once processed, Plevitskaya changed into her prison uniform, consisting of a long skirt and a blouse, wooden clogs, and a white bonnet. Then she was taken to one of the dormitories. The barred window in her cell was small, making it hard for her to see more than a tiny slice of the sky. During the day, she labored in a prison workshop.

Despite all her earlier protests against being sent there, prisoner 9202 quickly adapted to her new surroundings and was even awarded a special stripe on her sleeve and several perks for her exemplary behavior and industriousness. Plevitskaya sang in the choir and attended services in the chapel. In the interior courtyard, when she was physically able, she walked with other prisoners for her daily exercise. She gained special permission from the Ministry of Justice to write Isidore Franckel.[3] In one letter, she asked Franckel to mail her a copy of her first volume of memoirs, *Dezhkin karagod*, perhaps to remind her of happier times. It seems she had accepted that she would be in prison for the duration of her sentence—or until her death—and, in the meantime, would try to make her stay there tolerable.

However, with each passing month, Plevitskaya's health worsened. She had been in her new residence for barely four weeks when she was admitted to the infirmary on August 10. Doctors diagnosed her with myocarditis, an inflammation of the middle layer of the heart wall. Her eighteen-day stay in the infirmary suggests that her symptoms—such as heart failure, abnormal heart rhythms, and chest pain—were likely severe. Plevitskaya was released and returned to her prison cell on August 28, only six days before France declared war on Germany in response to the Nazi invasion of Poland.

Prison inmates would not have learned much detail about the first months of World War II, as they did not have regular access to newspapers. However, the war soon changed their daily routine, as the government ordered prisons to contribute to the domestic war effort. In the prison workshop, Plevitskaya sewed buttons on soldiers' coats, earning eighteen francs a day.[4] Seven-tenths of her pay was deducted for court costs, and the remaining went toward her personal care.

In December, Plevitskaya contacted Maximilian Filonenko again, probably asking for his renewed financial and legal assistance. Filonenko sent her a brief reply, which appears to have been his last correspondence with her. He had thought over whatever she had communicated to him, he wrote, but felt he could no longer be of any use to her.[5] Around this same time, Plevitskaya learned the outcome of the brief July court hearing in which Skoblin was convicted and sentenced to life in prison in absentia; a fellow inmate had shown her an article about the hearing in a months-old issue of a magazine. Plevitskaya read the piece and wept.[6]

Nineteen forty would prove to be as fateful a year for France and the rest of Europe as it was for Plevitskaya. It began with little happening on the war front, as Hitler had decided to postpone his invasion of France and the Low Countries until the spring.

With the onset of spring, Plevitskaya's health deteriorated further. Franckel's last update about her came around this time from an acquaintance who had recently been released from the Rennes prison. She informed him that Plevitskaya was gravely ill. "The whole day she prays and sings in the church choir," the woman told Franckel. "She told us she was a real singer and even performed for the tsar. But, you know, many inmates boast in prison, and no one believes her stories. But they all love her very much."[7]

Plevitskaya was readmitted to the prison infirmary on April 13 because of an abscess on her left foot and remained there for two months. While undergoing treatment, she accepted that she was dying and felt the need to speak to a priest and to French officials. Her motivation for doing so remains a mystery. Perhaps she was acting on a desire for religious redemption, or making a last-ditch effort to seek clemency from earthly authorities—or a combination of both. By this point, she must have understood that her NKVD contacts would not rescue her and, if they thought of her at all, wanted her to avoid "singing" about them to the French.

The part-Russian Father Gillet was the only Orthodox priest accredited in France to work with prisoners and was likely the same priest who had visited Plevitskaya in the Fresnes prison. Sometime in early May 1940, Gillet called on her and heard what some sources have claimed was her confession, probably the only one a Soviet agent had ever given to a priest.[8] According to an unsubstantiated account, French authorities recorded their conversation; the recording is said to have fallen into the hands of the German occupiers and to have later been used as evidence against NKVD agent Sergei Tretyakov, whom the Gestapo arrested in Paris in 1942.[9]

Whether or not a recording was actually made of Plevitskaya's confession, the story of what happened next is likely true. Plevitskaya asked Father Gillet to contact Sûreté Nationale commissaire Jean Belin, with whom she wanted to speak. On May 9, the priest met with Belin to convey the message that he was the only police officer Plevitskaya trusted and that she needed to speak to him so she could die in peace.[10] The following day, the Germans began their invasion of France, Belgium, the Netherlands, and Luxembourg. But this did not prevent Belin from traveling to Rennes with an interpreter and a police inspector.

Belin had not seen Plevitskaya since her trial and noticed how the once beautiful Slav now looked miserable, thin, wrinkled, and humbled. She was suffering from a serious heart ailment and breathing with difficulty. He asked that they be seated on a divan in the visitor's lounge. A nurse sat beside her with smelling salts in order to revive her in case she passed out. Belin told Plevitskaya that he pitied her, and she told him that she knew she was going to die soon. For several hours, she recounted her life to him. But her focus was on Skoblin:

> I love General Skoblin. He was my great love. I would gladly sacrifice my life for him. I'll die of sadness for never having seen him again, three years after Miller's disappearance. His absence is killing me and it will cause my death. I don't know where he is, as I told the jury at

my trial. Nevertheless, I wish to confess to you alone, so you'll know all that I have hidden from justice until now. My dear husband Skoblin had great ambitions. You know that he was a domineering man. He was also domineering with me. It was impossible for me to question his activities without his objecting. I subordinated myself to him and never contradicted him. I affirm to you that he was a loyal servant to General Kutepov and that for several years he served General Miller no less loyally. His attitude changed in 1933, when Hitler came to power. I heard him turn then and ridicule General Miller, and he wished to take his place as the head of ROVS. He became an avowed enemy of General Miller in 1936, when the majority of the Popular Front favored a rapprochement between France and the USSR. Contrary to General Miller's opinions, Skoblin favored a rapprochement between the White Russians and the Nazis, in the hope that they would intervene in Russia for the reestablishment of the imperial regime. In 1936, Skoblin received a number of envoys among the White Russians in Germany. At the same time, he spoke to me about his conversations with leading Soviets and how he was rallying behind Soviet ideas. I understood at this very moment that Skoblin had betrayed General Miller. He managed my concert tours. I bought him a car and a property in Ozoir-la-Ferriére, near the Armainvilliers Forest.

Given what is now known, that the Soviets had recruited the Skoblins in 1930, it is clear that even in her "confession" to Belin, she had dissembled. She made it seem as if her husband's motivations were purely political, rather than personal—and she failed to tell Belin that she had played a role in persuading Skoblin to work for the Soviets and that she herself was a Soviet agent. Then Plevitskaya began recounting to Belin her narrative about Miller's kidnapping:

Skoblin left me in the morning to attend to his business and met up with me that evening, after dinner. He returned around 10:00 p.m. We went to bed. I noticed that my husband was taciturn. I got the impression that he was running from danger. He did not fall asleep and was not even drowsy around 11:00 p.m. He woke up all in a sweat, like he'd had a nightmare. I embraced him affectionately. He began to cry. "Forgive me, Nadya. I'm miserable. I betrayed the cause," he cried. "I lied to General Miller and told him that I was taking him to a political meeting. I was ordered to take him to a building in St. Cloud, where he'd find himself inside enemy territory. He had accompanied me in all confidence in my car. We arrived in St. Cloud and entered into the designated villa. We were met by three men who spoke Russian and German equally well. General Miller was taken into an adjacent room, while I remained alone in the antechamber. Ten minutes later, I was asked to leave. "Will I be allowed to return to General Miller?" I asked. I entered a small room. General Miller was stretched out on a couch. I did not move. "What are you doing?" I said. "He's sleeping, Your Excellency! We gave him an injection," the man said in fluent French.[11]

Belin noticed that, at this point, Plevitskaya was exhausted. She continued to speak, but she breathed with much more difficulty. "I want to tell you the whole truth," she said, "but I don't have anything more to add. Perhaps I'd have learned more if, at the moment he told me this story, ROVS members hadn't knocked on our door and asked my husband to follow them. It was the last meeting I had with Skoblin. I was arrested and convicted. It's all the same to me. I suffer the most from my separation from Skoblin and won't survive," Plevitskaya concluded.

Belin told her that he would convey her story to his superiors and see if he could help her in some way. He pitied her as a victim because he felt that her only crime was her attachment to Skoblin, who had abandoned her to her tragic fate. Apparently, Belin either did not believe Plevitskaya had ties to the NKVD or he had communist sympathies himself. In his memoirs, he expressed his belief that she had not lied to him. "She had faith in God and sought to earn his pardon," Belin wrote. Reportedly, his superiors viewed Plevitskaya's dramatic story with skepticism because it was full of improbabilities and contradictions.[12] For instance, if Belin correctly related what she told him, she claimed not to have spent the afternoon of September 22, 1937, with Skoblin, and this was patently false.

Readers should therefore not accept at face value Plevitskaya's "confession" to Belin about Skoblin's supposed political transformation and involvement in Miller's kidnapping. It contains half-truths, which are the currency of spies. Even at this late point, in May 1940, Plevitskaya may still have been seeking ways to reduce her prison sentence. Admitting that she had only covered up Skoblin's dirty work rather than confessing to having taken part in the kidnapping plot would make her guilty of an obviously less serious, more pardonable offense. She might have hoped that, if and when the Germans invaded France, Belin might somehow protect her. Moreover, the Germans and Soviets were not enemies yet.

Belin's supervisors in Paris, however, declined to act on the new information, because they had more serious matters to deal with than the rehabilitation of a dying Russian prisoner. The Germans were fast approaching Paris and entered the city on June 14. Within days, they began collecting files and interrogating people of interest to them about the Miller kidnapping case. German military security officials, presumably from the Abwehr, reportedly confiscated the case files from the Paris police as early as June 18.[13]

On June 15, Plevitskaya was discharged from the prison infirmary and returned to her cell. Three days later, the Germans entered Rennes, then located within the German-occupied zone in northern France. They eventually used the prison for detaining female resistance fighters who were not sentenced to death. For now, the French Resistance was in its infancy. One might assume that the Germans, who had only begun setting up shop in Rennes, would have had more important things to do in the provincial capital than investigate Plevitskaya, but they came looking for her in prison before the end of June.

A female guard named Merle recalled this day, when two handsome, French-speaking Germans arrived.[14] They were in charge now, and the French had to follow their orders or face retribution. The Germans told a prison official that they wanted to question the Russian inmate, and Merle was ordered to find Plevitskaya, who was in the courtyard admiring the daisies. Merle led her to the waiting Germans, who interrogated her somewhere in the building. Although there is no record of the meeting, they must have grilled her about her knowledge of Soviet intelligence and NKVD contacts.

For Plevitskaya, already stressed by her health problems, the meeting with the Germans would have been chilling, even if Skoblin, as rumored, had once served as a German agent during the mid-1930s. However, due to her visible illness, she may have persuaded the Germans that she knew nothing valuable about NKVD operations or operatives. Whatever the case, it is not known whether they interrogated her again at the prison, but it seems that she was spared a trip to Abwehr or Gestapo headquarters in Rennes.

A few days later, on July 3, Plevitskaya returned to the infirmary. The abscess on her left foot was now diagnosed as tuberculous osteitis, a cystic growth that had become infected. The doctors feared that the infection would spread. On July 20, she was taken to a hospital on rue Saint-Louis, less than two miles from the prison. Doctors there examined her foot and determined that it was too badly infected to be saved. They were forced to amputate. Plevitskaya remained there for several weeks to give her body time to heal from the surgery.

On September 9, Plevitskaya was discharged from the hospital and returned to the prison infirmary. But her health had not improved at all. Rather the opposite was true. The physician assigned to her in the infirmary, Dr. Porée, certified that she had been readmitted in a state of complete medical deficiency, suffering chiefly from symptoms of heart failure.[15] For nearly a dozen days, Plevitskaya lay bedridden in the infirmary, barely holding on to life. It is not known whether she fell into a coma or expressed any final wishes during her last days. No friends or relatives, not even her two brothers-in-law, Feodosy and Sergei Skoblin, or her sister-in-law, Tamara Vorobieva, rushed to her side to comfort her. They were unaware of her grave condition and might have been restricted from traveling to Rennes even if they had been notified about it.

Dr. Porée and his staff continued to monitor their dying patient, but they did not return her to the hospital. Perhaps they were prevented from doing so or simply assumed that no treatments there could save her. It was wartime, resources were scarce, and Rennes was under enemy occupation. Saving sickly foreign prisoners was not a top priority.

The Kursk Nightingale died at 6:00 p.m. on September 21, 1940, in the prison infirmary. L. Courtel, a female warder, signed the death notice later that day.

On September 24, Plevitskaya's remains were interred with little or no ceremony in a communal plot within the prison grounds. No one was there to eulogize her or to throw a handful of soil onto her coffin, as she herself had done at her mother's funeral in Vinnikovo twenty-five years before. In late November, Feodosy and Sergei wrote the prison director to inquire about the circumstances of her death. They also asked about her belongings and any final wishes she might have expressed before she died, but the director provided no information apart from suggesting that they contact the Ministry of Justice and city hall.[16] Skoblin's brothers said that they had learned of her death only from the newspapers.

The plot where Plevitskaya lay was reportedly located beside the northern wall of the cemetery, between two sections of children's graves marked by small tombstones with etchings of angels. For years, every spring, daisies that she had once admired grew on top of the communal grave. However, Plevitskaya's body may not have rested in peace for long—it may have undergone an autopsy and then been reinterred in the communal grave. It may also have been disposed of elsewhere. On October 12, a representative from the German Military Security office by the last name of Grimm left a handwritten note stating that his office had confiscated the file of "no. 9202, Vinnikova (Skoblin's wife)."[17] Clearly, the Nazis were still curious about her, even after she had shuffled off her mortal coil.

The French rulers of the collaborationist Vichy regime wanted to know more about Plevitskaya as well. On October 26, the procurator's office in Rennes wrote the Rennes prison director to confirm her date of death. In this same letter, the procurator's office informed the prison director about a telegram recently sent by Joseph Chapplain of Vichy's Ministry of Justice to Marshal Pétain, the Vichy head of state, asking, "Could you order an autopsy on the cause of Plevitskaya's death, for she was well known."[18] This letter and telegram prompted Dr. Porée to produce a statement on October 28 confirming the amputation of Plevitskaya's foot, her return to the prison infirmary, and her death on September 21. Notably, he did not mention the cause of death, only that she had returned to the infirmary in a state of complete medical deficiency. But the existence of the telegram does not prove that an autopsy ever occurred, only that it was proposed.

The strongest circumstantial evidence that an autopsy did occur comes from Jean Belin, who later learned that the head of the Gestapo in France, Karl Bömelburg, led a German police inquiry in late 1940 into Plevitskaya's death. Belin claimed that her body was exhumed and autopsied, but he never saw the autopsy report.[19] Decades later, Moscow investigative journalist Arkady Vaksberg agreed. "There is reliable evidence to suggest that the Germans dug up her body two weeks after her death and conducted a postmortem," he concluded. "They did some analyses and then reburied it somewhere else. There is no information as to what the analyses found."[20] The autopsy report, if it ever existed, probably would not have been added to Plevitskaya's prison file anyway, and the French or Germans may have destroyed it for their own political reasons.

Like so many episodes from her life story, Plevitskaya's death is still open to interpretation. Rumors that she had died from unnatural causes began to circulate shortly after her death and persisted for decades. The most sensational one, advanced in the late 1980s by Russian journalist and screenwriter Gely Riabov, was that the Germans had tied her limbs to tanks and dismembered her. Riabov claimed to have had evidence, but his account has never been satisfactorily verified.[21] The Nazis were ruthless and brutal to their enemies, but why would they have bothered to rip Plevitskaya's body apart so gruesomely? In 1940, Germany was not even at war with the USSR yet, so the Nazis had no good reason to send a strong signal to the NKVD by torturing to death one of their former agents, one whom the Soviets had not even deemed worthy of attempting to rescue.

One oft-proposed hypothesis, that the Soviets poisoned Plevitskaya in order to silence her, seems more plausible. She returned from the hospital on rue Saint-Louis in worse condition than she had entered it, so one can imagine her having been poisoned there. However, most of the theories along this line assume that, if she was poisoned by the Soviets, it happened in prison. Whatever the case, according to Vaksberg, Soviet intelligence historians "tend to believe that she was poisoned on orders from Lubyanka because she knew too much about too many people. . . . Exposed and disgraced in émigré circles in Paris, she was of no more use to Moscow, particularly since she had already served her purpose. It was quite easy for them to pay some prison employee to poison her, but not to arrange her escape."[22]

The notion that the NKVD poisoned Plevitskaya—whether in the hospital or in the prison infirmary—is based on solid historical grounds. The Soviet secret police ran a secret toxicology lab nicknamed LAB X, where its technicians formulated deadly poisons that were successfully used for decades to eliminate numerous enemies of the state.[23] Some victims died inside the USSR, while others were killed outside it. General Wrangel may have been poisoned by a Soviet agent, and General Kutepov certainly was. General Miller, as we have seen, was injected with an anesthetic that allowed the Soviets to transport him from Paris to Le Havre. On the other hand, most victims of Soviet poisoning died within hours. Could Plevitskaya have been poisoned gradually—with arsenic, for example—making it seem that she was dying of natural causes? It is possible, but there is no proof.

Although the scenario that Plevitskaya simply died of heart failure and complications resulting from the amputation of her infected foot lacks drama and intrigue, it may have the virtue of being true. Perhaps the staff at the hospital on rue Saint-Louis was merely incompetent or unmotivated to help a gravely ill prisoner at a time when medical resources were scarce. Before arriving at the hospital, Plevitskaya already had a serious heart condition and foot infection. She herself said at least four months before her death that she expected that she would die soon. Losing all hope of seeing her husband again, she wanted to die. It was her final act of free will. The Soviets may very well have considered eliminating her, particularly if they knew that she had confessed to a police officer about the Miller kidnapping. But they may have figured that she was close to dying anyway—and, instead of planning and executing a murder, which could have tipped off the German and the French authorities, they may have let her die of natural causes.

EPILOGUE

In death, Nadezhda Plevitskaya served as the subject of a cautionary tale for Russian émigrés who were desperately homesick: striking a deal with the Soviet secret police did not necessarily lead to your safe return and could even prove fatal. Plevitskaya's and Nikolai Skoblin's Faustian bargain led to their early demise, to General Evgeny Miller's death, and to years of suffering for Miller's family. Burial in an unmarked communal grave on the grounds of a foreign prison was Plevitskaya's final return on her risky investment. Had she managed to repatriate after Miller's kidnapping, her fate would probably have been no better. Under the circumstances, she would likely have been imprisoned in the Soviet Gulag or simply executed.

After Plevitskaya's death, no one in the Russian emigration honored her memory with memorial concerts or a gravestone in a Russian Orthodox cemetery. It did not matter anymore that she had once been a unifying symbol of national pride in Russia and one of Tsar Nicholas II's favorite performers. Nor did it matter that famous singers such as Feodor Chaliapin had mentored her or that renowned musicians such as Sergei Rachmaninoff had performed with her. The Kursk Nightingale would now be remembered as a traitor, no more ethical than an NKVD thug. Vladimir Nabokov's satirical story based on her and Skoblin's life, "The Assistant Producer," serves as a monument to the poor choices the couple made in exile.

Plevitskaya's accusers and all newspapers with the exception of pro-Soviet ones portrayed her at times as a Red Mata Hari and at others as a controlling wife. This sensationalistic description of her persona surely helped to convict her and to sell copy, but it was not wholly accurate. On the one hand, Plevitskaya conformed to this image in superficial ways. She had a strong personality and, in her younger years, men found her highly

287

attractive. Once married to her third husband, Plevitskaya was aware of at least some of Skoblin's activities in ROVS and his work as a Soviet agent provocateur. She herself was an informant for the NKVD, and her foreign concert tours served as a cover for her husband's clandestine work. On the other hand, she did not, as her detractors claimed, direct his spy operations. Skoblin's marching orders came from Moscow. He was the dominant agent, she his helpmate. The use of such stereotypes as "Red seductress" and "shrewish, domineering wife" in describing female Soviet operatives did not cease with Plevitskaya. During the Cold War, they would be applied to others, including Elizabeth Bentley and Ethel Rosenberg.[1]

Plevitskaya, conversely, portrayed herself as a martyr, in league with Alfred Dreyfus, Tsar Nicholas II, and even Jesus. She insisted that she had not known of the Miller kidnapping plot in advance. When she confessed to a French police official shortly before her death, she apparently said that she had first learned about her husband's role in Miller's kidnapping several hours after the fact, when Skoblin told her the night of September 22, 1937, in their hotel room. There is a slight chance that she might have been telling the truth, particularly at a time when she felt that Jean Belin, the official in question, might offer her protection if and when the Germans invaded France. But it is more likely that she knew about the plot in advance. Either way, she had obstructed justice by not cooperating with the investigation and had perjured herself at her trial.

In her prison diaries, her interrogations, and her testimony on the stand, Plevitskaya swore that she had never been interested or involved in politics and had exerted no control over her husband's affairs. In her memoirs, Plevitskaya envisioned herself as a performer, a creator of art and beauty, not a political actor. She wanted readers to see her as a great singer who had sprung from humble beginnings but had not lost her simple, village ways or her strong Russian Orthodox faith. She also stressed how homesick she felt in exile, which no doubt was the case. But at her trial, she failed to persuade her audience that she was still Dezhka. Her widow's costume, her mournful expressions and gestures, and her dramatic narratives all failed to move hearts. Decades before their NKVD files were released, Plevitskaya's fellow Russian émigrés already well understood that she and Skoblin had betrayed them.

Back in the Soviet Union, the NKVD and its successors continued for decades to deny the Soviets' involvement in Miller's kidnapping. For years, Plevitskaya's and Skoblin's lives were not mentioned in the Soviet media. Then, in the 1970s, the regime allowed Plevitskaya's reputation to be at least partly rehabilitated. In 1973, Soviet musicologist I. V. Nestev published a book on the stars of the estrada.[2] In it, he highlighted three female singers who epitomized this genre and, in a sense, had democratized concerts for the masses. One of them was Plevitskaya. Nestev reported that a group of young folklorists in Vinnikovo had created a makeshift museum housing materials about her singing career. Her home had been destroyed by the Germans in 1942, but on its foundation, the village had erected a school, and elderly Vinnikovo residents who knew her or her relatives gathered there to reminisce about her.[3]

Thanks to Mikhail Gorbachev's glasnost reforms during the late 1980s, parts of the secret police archives were briefly declassified. Average citizens came to learn that the Soviets had recruited Skoblin and Plevitskaya in 1930 and that the Skoblins had played roles in Miller's kidnapping. Journalists published books about their intrigues, and television documentaries were produced about them. At this time, Russians were eager to learn about the dark side of the Soviet Union's past, to rehabilitate relatives who had been persecuted in the Great Terror, and to create memorials to Stalin's victims.

However, as the fall of the USSR receded into the past, average Russians grew tired of hearing about old atrocities, including those committed by Stalin and the secret police. At a time when many felt devastated by their country's economic problems and the loss of its superpower status, they sought a new, more positive national identity. Agreeing with this approach, former KGB officer Vladimir Putin, upon becoming president in 2000, revived symbols of Russia's imperial era and even more recent Soviet past and began to censor negative versions of its history.

Perhaps to their credit, instead of eliminating their foreign agents when they are exposed, Putin and the Federal Security Service (FSB), the KGB's successor agency, have been known to welcome them home with open arms. The most famous case on this point is Anna Chapman's. In 2010, the FBI uncovered and deported to Russia the then twenty-eight-year-old businesswoman, along with nine other Russian sleeper agents posted in the New York City area, and Chapman quickly capitalized on the Western media's portrayal of her as a femme fatale. Instead of being shot—the usual treatment for exposed spies during Stalin's Terror—Chapman and the others met privately with Putin shortly after they arrived home. Putin joined them in performing the song "From Where the Motherland Begins," which was featured in *Shield and Sword*, a 1968 film about Soviet intelligence operations during World War II.[4] Chapman later found lucrative work as a fashion model and television talk show host, and was even rumored to have become Putin's mistress.

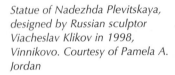

Statue of Nadezhda Plevitskaya, designed by Russian sculptor Viacheslav Klikov in 1998, Vinnikovo. Courtesy of Pamela A. Jordan

As a part of the trend to sanitize Russia's past, Plevitskaya—in the form of a celebrated folk performer, not as Stalin's singing spy or as a criminal—has reappeared as a minor symbol of national identity. Since the early 1990s, at least three biographies about her have been published in Russia, and in 1993 her memoirs were published in Russia for the first time. Several of Plevitskaya's recordings were remastered on compact disc. Her songs are once again being publicly performed, and Kursk hosts a biennial singing competition named in her honor. In 1996, minor planet 4229, discovered by Soviet astrophysicist Lyudmila I. Chernykh in 1971, was given the name "Plevitskaya."

Finally, in the fall of 2009, Plevitskaya's village dedicated a museum to her. Admirably, the museum's exhibits take into account Plevitskaya's entire life, including her criminal trial, and its director is more motivated to provide visitors with accurate information about the singer than to hide her misdeeds. Overall, though, the museum is as much a space for celebrating Russia's folk music traditions as it is for commemorating Plevitskaya's contributions to them. David Remnick, the editor of the *New Yorker* and a noted Russia expert, writes that a common malady in Russian society today is "nostalgia without memory," and so it goes with Plevitskaya.[5]

While Putin remains in power, it is unlikely that his regime will grant researchers renewed access to the intelligence files on Skoblin and Plevitskaya. Vasily Kristoforov, the director of the FSB's archive, stressed that the agency will never declassify documents concerning "ways and means of operational investigative activity," and presumably the Skoblin materials contain such information.[6] Even if they were all opened to public scrutiny, though, they would not necessarily answer every question. Intelligence files are often inaccurate and difficult to decipher. As a result, parts of Plevitskaya's life—particularly from the Civil War to her death in 1940—still remain under wraps, and readers must decide for themselves what actually happened at all too many points along Dezhka's journey.

NOTES

INTRODUCTION

1. Michael Barry Miller, *Shanghai on the Métro: Spies, Intrigue, and the French between the Wars* (Berkeley: University of California Press, 1994), 232.

2. Hubertus F. Jahn, *Patriotic Culture in Russia during World War I* (Ithaca, NY: Cornell University Press, 1995), 100. A novel based on Plevitskaya's life falsely depicts her as a gypsy singer, but its author admits that it is a work of fiction. Ally Hauptmann-Gurski, *La Plevitskaya: A Gypsy Singer's Life in Tsarist Russia and in Exile* (CreateSpace Independent Publishing Platform, 2011).

3. Jahn, *Patriotic Culture*, 100.

4. Nadezhda V. Plevitskaia, *Dezhkin karagod; Moi put' s pesnei: neizvestnye literaturnye proizvedeniia russkoi narodnoi pevitsy*, ed. Irina E. Raksha (Moscow: I. E. Raksha, 1993), 210.

5. Evgenii Primakov et al., eds., *Ocherki istorii rossiiskoi vneshnei razvedki*, vol. 3, *1933–1941* (Moscow: Mezhdunarodnye otnosheniia, 1997), 117.

6. Gary Kern, *A Death in Washington: Walter G. Krivitsky and the Stalin Terror* (New York: Enigma Books, 2003), 272.

7. Christopher Andrew and Vasili Mitrokhin, *The Mitrokhin Archive: The KGB in Europe and the West* (New York: Penguin, 2000).

8. J. Bernard Hutton, *Women in Espionage* (New York: Macmillan, 1971), 15.

9. For example, Geoffrey Bailey, *The Conspirators* (London: Victor Gollancz, 1961); Marina Grey, *Le général meurt à minuit: l'enlèvement des généraux Koutiepov (1930) et Miller (1937)* (Paris: Plon, 1981); Walter Krivitsky, *In Stalin's Secret Service* (New York: Harper & Bros, 1939); and Boris Prianishnikov, *Nezrimaia pautina* (Silver Spring, MD: self-published, 1979).

10. For example, Leonid Mlechin, *Alibi dlia velikoi pevitsy* (Moscow: Geia, 1997); Mlechin, *Set'-Moskva-OGPU-Parizh* (Moscow, 1991); Elena Prokof'eva, *Nadezhda Plevitskaia* (Smolensk: Rusich, 2000); and Varlen L. Strongin, *Nadezhda Plevitskaia: Velikaia pevitsa i agent razvedki* (Moscow: Ast-Press Kniga, 2005).

11. Jeanne Vronskaya with Vladimir Chuguev, *A Biographical Dictionary of the Soviet Union 1917–1988* (Kent, UK: K. G. Saur, 1989), 328–29.

CHAPTER 1

1. Nina Berberova, *The Italics Are Mine* (London: Vintage, 1993), 332–33.

2. *Dezhkin karagod* was first published in Berlin in 1925. Plevitskaya's second and final volume of memoirs, *Moi put' s pesnei* (*My Way with a Song*), was published in 1930 and covered her life from 1909 until 1915. The edition of her two volumes of memoirs that I draw from was published in Moscow in 1993 and edited by Irina E. Raksha. Unless otherwise noted, stories about Plevitskaya's youth, recollections of her youthful emotions, and specific quotations are taken from this edition of her memoirs: Nadezhda V. Plevitskaia, *Dezhkin karagod; Moi put' s pesnei: neizvestnye literaturnye proizvedeniia russkoi narodnoi pevitsy*, ed. Irina E. Raksha (Moscow: I. E. Raksha, 1993).

3. Noted in a brief, unpublished biography of Plevitskaya by I. V. Lotashov, used by guides at the Plevitskaya museum in Vinnikovo (hereafter, Lotashov).

4. An entry in the Trinity Church registry, housed in the State Archive of the Kursk Oblast, notes that, in January 1880, a Nadezhda Vinnikova was three months old. Her exact birth date was not recorded, but she was born on or near September 17 (old Russian calendar), the days when Orthodox believers celebrate the lives of three female saints: Nadezhda, Liubov, and Vera. A Kursk archivist, Yuri Bugrov, who extensively researched Trinity Church's records, confirmed that Plevitskaya was born in 1879. Yuri Bugrov, *Nadezhda Plevitskaia: Udal' i pechal'* (Kursk: Terorgan FSGS, 2006), 17–18. In contrast, the date of birth given in Plevitskaya's prison file from the women's prison in Rennes, France, is September 18, 1886. Archives Departementales d'Ille-et-Vilaine, in Rennes, France, File "Vinikova Nadia (Skobline, dite la Plevitzkaïa), prisoner number: 9202" (*la chemise* no. 8943). I am grateful to Professor Laurence Tauzin of the law faculty of Université de Rennes for securing a photocopy of Plevitskaya's file in 2010.

5. Lotashov, 2.

6. Toby W. Clyman and Judith Vowles, eds., *Russia through Women's Eyes: Autobiographies from Tsarist Russia* (New Haven, CT: Yale University Press, 1996), 15.

7. Ibid., 41.

8. Rose Glickman, "Peasant Women and Their Work," in *The World of the Russian Peasant: Post-Emancipation and Society*, ed. Ben Eklof and Stephen Frank, 45–63 (Boston: Unwin Hyman, 1990), 60.

9. Laura Olson, *Performing Russia: Folk Revival and Russian Identity* (London: RoutledgeCurzon, 2004), 19.

10. Bugrov, *Nadezhda Plevitskaia*, 16.

11. Ibid., 5.

12. Ben Eklof, "Peasants and Schools," in Eklof and Frank, *The World*, 126.

13. Barbara Engel, "The Woman's Side: Male Outmigration and the Family Economy in Kostroma Province," 65–80, in Eklof and Frank, *The World*, 69.

14. Barbara Alpern Engel, *Breaking the Ties That Bind: The Politics of Marital Strife in Late Imperial Russia* (Ithaca, NY: Cornell University Press, 2011), 2.

15. Engel, "The Woman's Side," 69.

16. Bella Merlin, "Tilly Wedekind and Lulu: The Role of Her Life or the Role in Her Life?," in *Auto/biography and Identity: Women, Theatre and Performance*, ed. Maggie B. Gale and Viv Gardner (Manchester and New York: Manchester University Press, 2004), 144.

17. Nadya is a diminutive form of Nadezhda.

18. Mark D. Steinberg, *Petersburg Fin de Siècle* (New Haven, CT: Yale University Press, 2011), 77.

19. G. Breitman, "Iz Kafeshtana k vserossiiskoi izvestnosti," *Novoe russkoe slovo*, September 6, 1974.

20. Louise McReynolds, *Russia at Play: Leisure Activities at the End of the Tsarist Era* (Ithaca, NY, and London: Cornell University Press, 2003), 9.

21. Olson, *Performing Russia*, 19.

22. I. V. Nest'ev, *Zvezdy russkoi estrady: Ocherki o russkikh estradnykh pevitsakh nachala XX veka* (Moscow: Vsesoiuznoe izdatel'stvo "Sovetskii Kompozitor," 1974), 12–13.

23. Ibid.

24. Laura Engelstein, *The Keys to Happiness: Sex and the Search for Modernity in Fin-de-Siècle Russia* (Ithaca, NY: Cornell University Press, 1992), 335.

25. Olson, *Performing Russia*, 16.

26. Background on Yar and Sudakov is drawn from Vladimir Alexandrov, *The Black Russian* (New York: Atlantic Monthly Press, 2013), 71–72.

27. Konstantin Nikolaev, "Populiarnye pesny XX veka v Rossii (1909 god)," accessed June 21, 2015, http://www.stihi.ru/2014/06/09/7081.

28. Vsevolod Meierkhol'd, excerpt from "Veriététes, Cabaret, Übertrett," in appendix of *Dezhkin kararod*, by Nadezhda Plevitskaia (Moscow: Kurskii obastnoi kraevedcheskii muzei, 2011), 194.

29. Leonid Sobinov, "Iz interv'iu," in appendix of *Dezhkin kararod*, by Nadezhda Plevitskaia (Moscow: Kurskii oblastnoi kraevedcheskii muzei, 2011), 194.

CHAPTER 2

1. Plevitskaia, *Dezhkin karagod; Moi put' s pesnei*, 124. Unless otherwise noted, the stories and Plevitskaya's words come from this volume.

2. Ilya Shneider, *Zapiski starogo moskvicha* (Moscow: Sovetskaia Rossiia, 1970), 109.

3. Lotashov, 7.

4. Bugrov, *Nadezhda Plevitskaia*, 17.

5. Ibid., 31.

6. Alexandre Benois, *Reminiscences of the Russian Ballet*, trans. Mary Britnieva (London: Putnam, 1941), 337.

7. Sergei M. Eisenshtein, *Iz avtobiograficheskikh zapisok* (Moscow, 1967), 222.

8. Writer Irina Raksha, whom I interviewed on May 21, 2012, in Moscow, told me that Plevitskaya gave birth to a son in 1915 named Evgeny (nicknamed Zhenya), who was raised by Plevitskaya's sister Maria after the singer left Russia in 1920. Raksha claims to be Plevitskaya's granddaughter through Evgeny. However, the director of the Plevitskaya museum in Vinnikovo, whom I interviewed in May 2012, and an archivist at the state archive in Kursk argue that Raksha is Plevitskaya's grandniece and Maria's granddaughter. Bugrov, *Nadezhda Plevitskaia*, 67. Given the lack of documentation—as well as the singer's health problems, access to reproductive services, and career-mindedness—I assumed that she did not give birth.

9. Engelstein, *The Keys to Happiness*, 342–55.

10. Andrei Sedykh, "Plevitskaia pishet' iz' tiurmy . . . ," *Novoe russkoe slovo*, May 15, 1938. Concerning Plevitskaya's height and build, see Archives de la préfecture de police, Paris (henceforth APP), GA S10 Dossier Skobline, Case No. 59638 ("Audition de Kondratieff èpouse Grigoul," September 24, 1937).

11. Fund 601, File 255, 1910, p. 61, March 28 entry, translated on the website of the Alexander Palace Time Machine, http://www.alexanderpalace.org/palace/ndiaries.html.

12. Nest'ev, *Zvezdy russkoi estrady*, 89.

13. Plevitskaia, *Dezhkin karagod; Moi put' s pesnei*, 142.

14. Lotashov, 7–8.

15. Nest'ev, *Zvezdy russkoi estrady*, 9.

16. Bugrov, *Nadezhda Plevitskaia*, 5.

17. Ibid., 8. For instance, see Yuri Beliaev, "Plevitskaia," *Novoe vremia*, October 29, 1910. Plevitskaya sang gypsy songs occasionally, but they never dominated her repertoire. Nest'ev, *Zvezdy russkoi estrady*, 28–29.

18. Yuri Engel', "Kontsert N. V. Plevitskoi," *Russkie vedomosti*, April 23, 1910, no. 92; quoted in publication by same author: *Glazami sovremennika. Izbrannye stat'i o russkoi muzyke* (Moscow, 1971), 290.

19. Nest'ev, *Zvezdy russkoi estrady*, 18.

20. Lotashov, 6.

21. For background on domestic violence, see Stephen Frank, *Crime, Cultural Conflict, and Justice in Rural Russia, 1856–1914* (Berkeley: University of California Press, 1999), 256–57.

22. Bakhmeteff Archive of Russian & East European Culture, Rare Book & Manuscript Library, Columbia University (henceforth BA), Maximilian M. Filonenko Papers, Box 12, Folder 1, "Clippings US Tour" (*Ten Russian Folksongs from the Repertoire of Nadiejda Plevitzkaia*, trans. Kurt Schindler, 1926).

23. Nest'ev, *Zvezdy russkoi estrady*, 72.

24. Bugrov, *Nadezhda Plevitskaia*, 8.

25. Alexander Kuprin, "Sluchainaia zametka pisatelia. Plevitskaia" (1913). In appendix of *Dezhkin karagod* by Nadezhda Plevitskaia, 196–97.

26. Nest'ev, *Zvezdy russkoi estrady*, 104. Examples of village songs that Plevits-kaya sang more often beginning in 1914 included "Luchinushka," "Vo piru byla," "Ty vzoidi, solntse krasnoe," and also a number of wedding and singing circle songs from the Kursk region.

27. Nest'ev, *Zvezdy russkoi estrady*, 85; and N. V. Velidor, "Plevitskaia o svoikh pesniakh," *Utro Rossii*, October 21, 1910.

28. Nest'ev found Piatnitskii's letter in the Russian State Archive of Literature and Art (TsGali), fond Piatnitskii, no. 2001, op. 1, ed. khr. 28.

29. Bugrov, *Nadezhda Plevitskaia*, 31.

30. Nest'ev, *Zvezdy russkoi estrady*, 87.

31. Ibid., 89.

32. Lotashov, 5. Some sources spell the accompanist's name "Zaremba" instead of "Zarema," and he sometimes used the name Rozenvasser.

33. McReynolds, *Russia at Play*, 240.

34. Ibid.

35. Nest'ev, *Zvezdy russkoi estrady*, 82, 105. In 1914, newspapers reported that Plevitskaya began to perform in costumes modeled on clothing of Kursk women peasants and to perform mainly peasant songs. See, for example, "Khronika teatra i muzyki," *Gazeta Den'*, April 13, 1914. Note, however, according to another source, she began doing this in 1913. See Elizaveta Uvarova et al., *Estrada v Rossii. XX Vek: entsiklopediia* (Moscow: OLMA-Press, 2004), 507.

36. Nest'ev, *Zvezdy russkoi estrady*, 73.

37. BA, Filonenko Papers, Box 12, Folder "NV Plevitskaia Skoblin (clippings: Eastern European Tour)" (no title or author, *Za svobodu*, December 22, 1924).

38. Nest'ev, *Zvezdy russkoi estrady*, 35.

39. Ibid., 109.

40. Ibid., 90.

41. Sergei Mamontov, excerpt from *Kaplia zhivoi vody* (1910). In appendix of *Dezhkin kararod* by Nadezhda Plevitskaia, 195–56.

42. Shneider, *Zapiski*, 110.

43. Bugrov, *Nadezhda Plevitskaia*, 5.

44. Ibid., 74.

45. Shneider, *Zapiski*, 112.

46. Lotashov, 8.

47. Interview with Irina Raksha in her Moscow apartment, May 21, 2012.

48. Engelstein, *The Keys to Happiness*, 32, 41; Engel, *Breaking the Ties*, 4.

49. Bugrov, *Nadezhda Plevitskaia*, 17.

50. V. L. Strongin, *Nadezhda Plevitskaia: Velikaia pevitsa i agent razvedki* (Moscow: AST-Press Kniga, 2005), 110–12.

51. David R. Stone, *A Military History of Russia: From Ivan the Terrible to the War in Chechnya* (Westport, CT: Praeger Security International, 2006), 162–68, 175.

52. N. P. V., "Protsesse N. V. Plevitskoi," *Poslednie novosti*, December 13, 1938, 2.

53. Nest'ev, *Zvezdy russkoi estrady*, 90.

54. Jahn, *Patriotic Culture*, 100.

55. Shneider, *Zapiski*, 112–15. In his memoirs, Shneider wrongly identified Shangin as Plevitskaya's husband. His story about the circumstances surrounding how she learned of Shangin's death differs somewhat from Plevitskaya's account. Shneider claimed that he helped her arrange a concert in Dvinsk, close to where Shangin was posted, but it was canceled due to renewed fighting. Plevitskaya learned of Shangin's death at the staff headquarters, Shneider recalled. Shangin reportedly was wounded in his abdomen and was briefly treated in a military hospital. Plevitskaya arrived that night, a few hours after he had died in the morning.

56. Jahn, *Patriotic Culture*, 101.

57. Ibid., 206.

58. Ibid., 212.

59. Vladimir Gardin, excerpt from *Vospominaniia*, in appendix of *Dezhkin kararod* by Nadezhda Plevitskaia, 198–202. In 1918, the two films were combined into one and renamed *Agaf'ia*. Plevitskaya appeared in at least two other films, although these were produced elsewhere and she played minor roles in them. Bugrov, *Nadezhda Plevitskaia*, 5.

60. Excerpt from article by Plevitskaya in the journal *Kulisy*, no. 5, 1917; Bugrov, *Nadezhda Plevitskaia*, 23.

CHAPTER 3

1. Strongin, *Nadezhda Plevitskaia*, 144.

2. "Protsess N. V. Plevitskoi," *Poslednie novosti*, December 8, 1938, 2.

3. "Segodnia Kontsert Nadezhdy Vasil'evny Plevitskoi," *Svobodnaia rech'*, no. 30, August 11, 1917; Shneider, *Zapiski*, 118.

4. Irina Solodova, the director of the Plevitskaya Museum in Vinnikovo, gave me a photocopy of the marriage registry in which Plevitskaya and Levitsky's marriage record appears.

5. Shneider, *Zapiski*, 114.

6. Bugrov, *Nadezhda Plevitskaia*, 18.

7. Shneider, *Zapiski*, 115–16. Another document, a transcript of a conversation between a Russian émigré woman and Grand Duchess Olga Alexandrovna in 1937 or 1938, contains a statement by the grand duchess about this meeting: Archive, Holy Trinity Orthodox Seminary, Jordanville, New York (henceforth HTOS), ROVS, Box 18, Folder 4.

8. Paul Robinson, *The White Russian Army in Exile 1921–1941* (Oxford: Clarendon Press, 2002), 8.

9. Harold Shurkman, ed., *The Blackwell Encyclopedia of the Russian Revolution* (Oxford: Basil Blackwell, 1988), 145.

10. Robinson, *The White Russian Army in Exile*, 5–6.

11. Peter Kenez, *Civil War in Southern Russia, 1919–1920: The Defeat of the Whites* (Berkeley: University of California Press, 1977), 24.

12. Denikin's quotation appears in W. Bruce Lincoln, *Red Victory: A History of the Russian Civil War* (New York: Touchstone Books, 1989), 86.

13. "Protsess N. V. Plevitskoi," *Poslednie novosti*, December 6, 1938, 2.

14. Nest'ev, *Zvezdy russkoi estrady*, 91–92; *Izvestiia Kurskogo Soveta*, no. 28 (April 16, 1918).

15. Bugrov, *Nadezhda Plevitskaia*, 10.

16. "Pokhishchenie gen. E. K. Millera," *Vozrozhdenie*, November 26, 1937.

17. Igor V. Nezhnyi, *Byloe pered glazami: teatral'nye vospominaniia* (Moscow: Vserossiiskoe teatral'noe obshchestvo, 1963), 72.

18. Hoover Institution Archives, Stanford University, Stanford, CA (henceforth HIA), Boris I. Nicolaevsky Collection, Box 299, Folder 4 (P. Trubnikov, "Plevitskaia—'Khitrushchaia Dezhka,'" unknown publication, September 27, 1937).

19. George Leggett, *The Cheka: Lenin's Political Police* (Oxford: Clarendon Press, 1981), 198–200.

20. "Ischeznovenie E. K. Millera," *Poslednie novosti*, December 3, 1937, 1.

21. "Protsess N. V. Plevitskoi," *Poslednie novosti*, December 13, 1938, 2. Baranov also testified about the rumor that posters advertising Plevitskaya's Kursk concerts called her "Our Red Mother." Two other sources claim that Plevitskaya had a sexual relationship with Shulga: Grey, *Le général meurt à minuit*, 140; and Strongin, *Nadezhda Plevitskaia*, 151–55.

22. BA, Aleksandr Vasil'evich Miakin Memoirs. Miakin incorrectly writes that Plevitskaya met Levitsky during the civil war, which began in 1918.

23. HIA, Boris Prianishnikov Papers, Box 3, Folder "Skoblin and Plevitskaia 2," (excerpts from *Iz sviatoi obiteli v Arfianki*, by Lev Kamyshnikov).

24. "Protsess N. V. Plevitskoi," *Poslednie novosti*, December 13, 1938, 2.

25. HTOS, ROVS, Box 12, Folder 4 (typed document written in French by a Madame Kharitonoff, undated).

26. HTOS, ROVS, Box 18, Folder 4. The same ROVS file contains an anonymous, undated note that is handwritten in French. It appears to be written by the sister of a ROVS official, who reported that, while Kharitonova said she saw Plevitskaya at a Cheka prison in Kursk, Soren swore she saw her in an Odessa prison.

27. Leggett, *The Cheka*, 348.

28. Ibid., 198; Orlando Figes, *A People's Tragedy: A History of the Russian Revolution* (New York: Viking, 1997), 647.

29. Tammy M. Proctor, *Female Intelligence: Women and Espionage in the First World War* (New York: New York University Press, 2003), 123–44.

30. HIA, Volkov Papers, Box 18, Folder 1 ("Gen. Miller Zhiv i nakhoditsia," *Novia zaria*, late January or early February 1938, 2); BA, Filonenko Papers, Box 11,

Folder "Case Files—Plevitskaia Skoblin, N. V. 2" (copy of letter from Plevitskaya
to the editor of *Poslednie novosti*, February 1, 1938).

31. Bugrov, *Nadezhda Plevitskaia*, 18; Prince Alexander Ratiev, *To, chto sokhra-nila mne pamiat'* (Sofia, 1999).

32. The first account is that of a Captain M. of the Markov Artillery Division of
the Volunteer Army. Sometime between July and September 1919, near the town
of Fatezh, Plevitskaya was following Levitsky and his Red Army platoon. Levitsky's
platoon came under White attack, and a division of mounted White intelligence
officers burst into the village. The division commander, Captain Kaliansky, seized
Levitsky and his wife, who was dressed as a nurse, and rudely cursed her. She
proudly threw back her head and exclaimed: "Do you know whom you're speak-ing to? I am Nadezhda Vasilievna Plevitskaya!" Kaliansky then led her to the bat-talion's staff quarters. "Zagadochnoe ischeznovenie gen. E. K. Millera," *Poslednie
novosti*, September 29, 1937, 2.

A second account confirms that Plevitskaya and Levitsky joined up with the
Whites in the late summer of 1919. At Plevitskaya's trial, Staff Captain Pyotr Lit-vinenko, who in 1919 headed a detachment of mounted intelligence officers in
the Second Kornilov Shock Regiment, said that his unit had detained Plevitskaya
and Levitsky. Plevitskaya agreed that she had seen Litvinenko from a distance, but
instead of admitting that she had been captured by the Whites, she euphemistically
said she had "transferred to the front" where the Second Kornilov Shock Regiment
was based. She also tried to convince the court that Litvinenko was an officer in the
First Regiment, questioning whether he could have witnessed her and Levitsky's
"transfer." Defending his remarks, Litvinenko reaffirmed that he was attached to
the Second Regiment at the time. "Protsess N. V. Plevitskoi," *Poslednie novosti*,
December 11, 1938, 2.

In a 1936 book on the Kornilov Shock Regiment, Mikhail N. Levitov, a former
battalion commander of the Second Kornilov Shock Regiment, outlined two other
versions of the story of how Levitsky, along with Plevitskaya, came to be with the
Volunteer Army again. One version resembles Litvinenko's account, although it
identifies Colonel Peschanik-Klenovoi, not Captain Kaliansky, as the commanding
officer who found Plevitskaya and Levitsky. In the second, Plevitskaya and Levitsky
were encountered on September 4, 1919, en route to a town in the Kursk region
called Safronovka. A unit of intelligence officers seized some Red Army ordnance
and detained several people who had been with the Reds, including Plevitskaya.
Mikhail N. Levitov, "Kornilovtsy v bioakh letom-osen'iu 1919 goda," in *Ko-rnilovskii udarnyi polk* (Paris, 1936).

33. "Zagadochnoe ischeznovenie gen. E. K. Millera," *Poslednie novosti*, Septem-ber 29, 1937, 2.

34. Bugrov, *Nadezhda Plevitskaia*, 18; Ratiev, *To, chto sokhranila mne pamiat'*.

35. Kenez, *Civil War in Southern Russia*, 218.

36. BA, Filonenko Papers, Box 12, Folder 1 (Nadezhda Plevitskaia, "Na Per-ekope," unknown newspaper, undated).

37. M. A. Kritskii, Nikolai V. Skoblin, and N. N. Golovin, *Kornilovskii udarnyi polk* (Paris: Impr. "Val," 1936), chap. 25, 167–68.

38. Nadezhda Plevitskaia, "Na Perekope."

39. Ibid.

40. Prianishnikov, *Nezrimaia pautina*, 16.

41. For more on the hospital narrative, see Grey, *Le général meurt à minuit*, 142. Information on height is found in Alexander M. Orlov, *The March of Time: Reminiscences*, ed. Phillip Knightley (London: St. Ermin's Press, 2004), 193.

42. HIA, Prianishnikov Papers, Box 3, Folder "Skoblin and Plevitskaia (biographical information)" (article by E. Messner in *Novoe russkoe slovo*, October 17, 1937). Plevitskaya and Skoblin may have first met earlier than the fall of 1920, during one of her Perekop concerts. HIA, Nicolaevsky Collection, Box 299, Folder 4 ("Brillianty Nadezhdy Plevitskoi," undated newspaper article). In a fanciful narrative, Skoblin was said to have rescued her from the Reds, who were preparing to execute her, in the summer or early fall of 1919 near Fatezh, in the Kursk region. Strongin, *Nadezhda Plevitskaia*, 157.

43. HIA, Nicolaevsky Collection, Box 299, Folder 7 (P. Tastevin, secretary, "Rapport: Affaire de Miller," December 14, 1937; henceforth Tastevin Report, December 14, 1937).

44. Biographical information about Skoblin: "Iz proshlogo Skoblina," *Novoe russkoe slovo*, December 1, 1937; HIA, Maria Vrangel' Collection, Box 8, Folder 9 ("Kratkiiabiografiia: Komandira Kornilovskogo Udarnogo polka Generala-Maiora Skoblina, na osnovanii ego podlinnogo posluzhnogo opioka," November 23, 1932, Paris); HTOS, V. K. Abdank-Kossovskii Papers, Box 16 ("Kniga gen. Skoblina," undated newspaper article); Armen Gasparian, *General Skoblin: Legenda razvedki* (Moscow: Veche, 2012); Dmitry Lekhovich, *Belye protiv krasnykh: Sud'ba generala Antona Denikina* (Moscow: Voskresen'e, 1992), 308.

45. Grey, *Le général meurt à minuit*, 205.

46. Messner cited in Prianishnikov Papers; and "Po delu ob ischeznovenii gen. Miller oprosheno 150 lits," *Novaia zaria*, October 20, 1937, 3.

47. Lekhovich, *Belye protiv krasnykh*, 308.

48. Bailey, *The Conspirators*, 121; see also Gasparian, *General Skoblin*, 11.

49. Lincoln, *Red Victory*, 86, 446; V. A. Zolotarev, ed., *Russkaia voennaia emigratsiia 20-x-40-x godov: dokumenty i materialy Tom 1: Tak nachinalos' izgnan'e 1920–1922 gg. Kniga vtoraia Na chuzhbine* (Moscow: Izdatel'stvo "Geia," 1998), 682.

50. HIA, Nicolaevsky Collection, Box 299, Folder 5 ("Deiatel'nost', sviazi i sluzhba Skoblina v ROVSe i v Chatiakh I-go Aermeiskago Kurpusa," Erdely Commission Report, February 4, 1938).

51. Vladimir L. Burtsev, *Bol'shevitskie gangstery v Parizhe* (Paris: self-published, 1939), 64.

52. HIA, Prianishnikov Papers, Box 3, Folder "Skoblin and Plevitskaia (biographical information)" (I. F. Patronov, "Skoblin za 20 let," *Illiustratsionnaia Rossiia*, December 21, 1937, excerpted in *Novoe russkoe slovo*, December 10, 1937).

53. General A. I. Denikin, with an introduction by Alan Wood, *The White Army* (Cambridge, UK: Ian Faulkner Publishing, 1992), 315.

54. Lincoln, *Red Victory*, 446–48.

55. Marc Raeff, *Russia Abroad: A Cultural History of the Russian Emigration 1919–1939* (New York: Oxford University Press, 1990), 24.

56. Miakin memoirs.

57. Georgii Grebenshchikov, "Nadezhda Plevitskaia (iz dnevnika)," *Novoe russkoe slovo*, March 30, 1926. I would like to thank Professor Robert Shenk for supplying me with information about U.S. vessels and Admiral McCully; e-mail message from Professor Shenk, January 8, 2013. See also Robert Shenk, *America's Black Sea Fleet: The U.S. Navy amidst War and Revolution, 1919–1923* (Annapolis, MD: U.S. Naval Institute, 2012), 69–87.

CHAPTER 4

1. Feodor Chaliapin, *Man and Mask: Forty Years in the Life of a Singer*, trans. Phyllis Megroz (London: Victor Gollancz, 1932), 304.

2. Robinson, *The White Russian Army in Exile*, 32.

3. Dmitrii Meisner, *Mirazhi i deistvitel'nost': Zapiski emigranta* (Moscow: Izdatel'stvo Agenstva Novosti, 1966), 107.

4. Bugrov, *Nadezhda Plevitskaia*, 33.

5. Grey, *Le général meurt à minuit*, 142.

6. Tatiana Varsher, "Moi vstrechi s Plevitskoi i Skoblinym," *Novoe russkoe slovo*, May 19, 1939.

7. Bugrov, *Nadezhda Plevitskaia*, 33.

8. Ibid., 34.

9. BA, Filonenko Papers, Box 11 (first notebook of Plevitskaya prison diaries, approximately p. 30, fall 1937).

10. Ibid.

11. Vladimir Alexandrov, *The Black Russian*, 191–92.

12. BA, Aleksandr Vasil'evich Miakin Memoirs (essay on Nadezhda V. Plevitskaia).

13. HIA, Nicolaevsky Collection, Box 299, Folder 4 (undated, no author, "Brillianty Nadezhdy Plevitskoi.").

14. BA, Filonenko Papers, Box 12, Folder "NV Plevitskaia Skoblin (clippings: Eastern European Tour)" (*Russkoe delo*, Sofia, March 12, 1921).

15. Robinson, *The White Russian Army in Exile*, 40.

16. Ibid., 45.

17. Paul Robinson, *Grand Duke Nikolai Nikolaevich, Supreme Commander of the Russian Army* (DeKalb: Northern Illinois University Press, 2014), 326.

18. Robinson, *The White Russian Army in Exile*, 46.

19. Bugrov, *Nadezhda Plevitskaia*, 34.

20. V. A. Zolotarev, ed., *Russkaia voennaia emigratsiia 20-x-40x-godov: dokumenty i materialy Tom 4: Raskol 1924-1925* (Moscow: Izdatel'stvo "Geia," 2010), 257–66.

21. Robinson, *The White Russian Army in Exile*, 66.

22. Ibid., 70.

23. "Iz proshlogo Skoblina," *Novoe russkoe slovo*, December 1, 1937.

24. Bugrov, *Nadezhda Plevitskaia*, 34.

25. BA, Filonenko Papers, Box 12, Folder "NV Plevitskaia Skoblin (clippings: Eastern European Tour)" (Nadezhda Plevitskaia, "Elka na Pernik," *Rus'*, January 24, 1924).

26. Excerpt from Strok's memoirs quoted in Bugrov, *Nadezhda Plevitskaia*, 73.

27. BA, Filonenko Papers, Box 12, Folder "NV Plevitskaia Skoblin (clippings: Eastern European Tour)."

28. BA, Filonenko Papers, Box 12, Folder "NV Plevitskaia Skoblin (clippings: Eastern European Tour)" (Baian, "Chudesnaia kurianka," *Vremya*, February 12, 1923).

29. HIA, Prianishnikov Papers, Box 3, Folder "Skoblin and Plevitskaia (biographical information)" ("Zarubezhnaia kar'era N. V. Plevitskoi").

30. BA, Filonenko Papers, Box 12, Folder "NV Plevitskaia Skoblin (clippings: Eastern European Tour)" (Sviatoslav Kamburov, "N. V. Plevitskaia," *Rus'*, August 19, 1923).

31. "Po delu ob ischeznovenii gen. Miller oprosheno 150 lits," *Novaia zaria*, October 20, 1937, 3.

32. Bugrov, *Nadezhda Plevitskaia*, 34; Leonard Mikhailov, "ROVS terpit porazhenie," *Nedelia*, no. 50 (December 11–17, 1989): 11; Vladimir Antonov, "Nadezhda Plevitskaia—'kurskii solovei' sovetskoi razvedki," *Nezavisimoe voennoe obozrenie*, February 19, 2010.

33. Lesley Milne, *Mikhail Bulgakov: In Dialogue with Time; A Critical Biography* (Cambridge: Cambridge University Press, 1990), 144.

34. Bugrov, *Nadezhda Plevitskaia*, 34.

35. Ibid., 37.

36. HIA, Prianishnikov Papers, Box 3, Folder "Skoblin and Plevitskaia (biographical information)" ("Zarubezhnaia kar'era N. V. Plevitskoi").

37. HIA, Prianishnikov Papers, Box 3, Folder "Skoblin and Plevitskaia (biographical information)" (excerpt from article by N. Piatnitskii in *Signal*, November 1, 1937).

38. APP, GA S10 Dossier Skobline, Case No. 59638 (letter from the director of general intelligence to the Paris prefect of police, April 3, 1931, "Nicolas Skobline et sa femme à la demande de la Sûreté Générale"); henceforth APP, letter of April 3, 1931.

39. Ibid.

40. Boris Raymond and David R. Jones, *The Russian Diaspora, 1917–1941* (Lanham, MD, and London: Scarecrow Press, 2000), 24.

41. Robinson, *The White Russian Army in Exile*, 94–95.

42. Clifford Rosenberg, *Policing Paris: The Origins of Modern Immigration Control between the Wars* (Ithaca, NY: Cornell University Press, 2006), 65.

43. Robert Harold Johnston, *New Mecca, New Babylon: Paris and the Russian Exiles, 1920–1945* (Montreal and Kingston: McGill-Queen's Press, 1988), 26.

44. Ibid., 77–78.

45. APP, letter of April 3, 1931.

46. Raeff, *Russia Abroad*, 4.

47. Johnston, *New Mecca*, 6.

48. Ibid., 72.

49. Sally Cline, *Zelda Fitzgerald: Her Voice in Paradise* (New York: Arcade Publishing, 2004), 178–79.

50. Ulla E. Dydo and William Rice, *Gertrude Stein: The Language That Rises* (Evanston, IL: Northwestern University Press, 2008), 99–100, 186.

51. Ernest Hemingway, "Paris Is Full of Russians," *Toronto Star*, February 22, 1922.

52. Robinson, *The White Russian Army in Exile*, 29.

53. Ibid., 30.

54. Johnston, *New Mecca*, 36.

55. Robinson, *The White Russian Army in Exile*, 17.

56. Johnston, *New Mecca*, 22.

57. Ibid., 91–92.

58. "Pokhishchenie gen. Millera," *Vozrozhdenie*, October 29, 1937, 5.

59. Jean Belin, *Trente ans de Sûreté Nationale* (Paris: Bibliotèque France Soir, 1950), 241.

60. Robinson, *The White Russian Army in Exile*, 101.

61. Norman Polmar and Thomas B. Allen, *Spy Book: The Encyclopedia of Espionage* (New York: Random House, 1998), 479.

62. Phillip Knightley, "Introduction," in Orlov, *March of Time*, 13.

63. Christopher Andrew and Oleg Gordievsky, *KGB: The Inside Story of Its Foreign Operations from Lenin to Gorbachev* (New York: HarperCollins, 1990), 150.

64. Andrew and Mitrokhin, *The Mitrokhin Archive*, 54.

65. Klim Degtiarev and Aleksandr Kolpakidi, eds., *Vneshniaia razvedka SSSR: INO, SVR, PGU* (Moscow: EKSMO, 2009), 11.

66. Zolotarev, *Russkaia voennaia emigratsiia Tom 1*, 113–31: No. 143 "Sovmestnyi doklad general-leitentanta Ia. A. Slashchova i kapitana B. N. Voinakhovskogo na zadannye im v VChK voprosy," Moscow, November 13, 1921.

67. Ibid., No. 140: "Otvety generala A. S. Mil'kovskogo na zadannye emu v VChK voprosy," Moscow, November 10, 1921; ibid., 681–84: No. 305 "Svodka Inostrannogo otdela GPU o deiatel'nosti russkoi voennoi emigratsii v Bolgarii," November 10, 1922.

68. Andrew and Mitrokhin, *The Mitrokhin Archive*, 45–46.

69. Robinson, *The White Russian Army in Exile*, 140–41.

70. Evgenii M. Primakov et al., eds., *Ocherki istorii rossiiskoi vneshnei razvedki*, vol. 2, *1917–1933* (Moscow: Mezhdunarodnye otnosheniia, 1997), 84. See also Viacheslav V. Kostikov, *Ne budem proklinat' izgnan'e . . . Puti i sud'by russkoi emigratsii* (Moscow: Mezhdunarodnye Otnosheniia, 1990), 367; Robinson, *The White Russian Army in Exile*, 142; and Paul W. Blackstock, *The Secret Road to World War Two: Soviet versus Western Intelligence, 1921–1939* (Chicago: Quadrangle Books, 1969), 159–69.

71. Robinson, *The White Russian Army in Exile*, 163.

72. Andrew and Gordievsky, *KGB*, 150.

73. Emil Draitser, *Stalin's Romeo Spy: The Remarkable Rise and Fall of the KGB's Most Daring Operative* (Evanston, IL: Northwestern University Press, 2010), 5.

74. Peter Gay, *Freud: A Life for Our Time* (New York: Norton, 2006), 383.

75. Bugrov, *Nadezhda Plevitskaia*, 37.

76. Mary-Kay Wilmers, *The Eitingons: A Twentieth Century Story* (London: Faber & Faber, 2009), 186.

77. Ibid., 241.

78. See Stephen Schwartz, "Intellectuals and Assassins: Annals of Stalin's Killerati," *New York Times Book Review*, January 24, 1988, 3, 30–31; Theodore H. Draper, "The Mystery of Max Eitingon," *New York Review of Books*, April 14, 1988, 32–43; Walter Laqueur, Vitaly Rapoport, Stephen Schwartz, and reply by Theodore H. Draper, "'The Mystery of Max Eitingon': An Exchange," *New York Review of Books*, June 16, 1988, 50–55; Robert Conquest, "Max Eitingon: Another View," *New York Times Book Review*, July 3, 1988, 22–23; and Pierre Broue and reply by Theodore H. Draper, "More Eitingon Mystery," *New York Review of Books*, August 8, 1988. More recently, Stephen Schwartz renewed the debate in a review of Wilmers's book: Stephen Schwartz, "Commie Dearest: The Tangled Web of the KGB and the Eitingon Clan," *Weekly Standard*, September 13, 2010.

79. Wilmers, *The Eitingons*, 194, 200–201.

80. See Wilmers for accurate information on Leonid Eitingon. Two Russian researchers, Vitaly Rapoport (who immigrated to the United States in 1980) and Yuri Alexeev (who was still in the USSR when their report was published), published a report about the Red Army in which they falsely claimed that Naum and Max were brothers; they also assumed that Max was an NKVD operative. See Vitaly Rapoport and Yuri Alexeev, *High Treason: Essays on the History of the Red Army, 1918–1938*, ed. Vladimir G. Treml, ed. and trans. Bruce Adams (Durham, NC: Duke University Press, 1985), 391–92. John J. Dziak also assumed that Max (wrongly called "Mark") was Naum's brother: *Chekisty: A History of the KGB* (Lexington, MA: Lexington Books, 1988), 100–102.

81. Before marrying Max, Mirra Eitingon had twice been married; her second husband was Boris Khariton, with whom she had a son, the future Soviet atomic weapons scientist, Yuli Khariton. She may have been connected to Soviet intelligence through Yuli. See Isabella Ginor and Gideon Remez, "Her Son, the Atomic

Scientist: Mirra Birens, Yuli Khariton, and Max Eitingon's Services for the Soviets," *Journal of Modern Jewish Studies* 11, no. 1 (March 2012): 39–59.

82. Orlov, *March of Time*, 193–94.

83. Rene Sais, "Malen'kiu fel'eton," *Novoe vremia*, September 3, 1925. For biographical information on Polevitskaya, see http://www.kino-teatr.ru/kino/acter/w/sov/36911/bio (accessed May 26, 2015).

84. The story is outlined in Shneider, *Zapiski starogo moskvicha*, 118–19.

85. Simon Morrison, *Lina & Serge: The Love & Wars of Lina Prokofiev* (New York: Houghton Mifflin Harcourt, 2013), 119.

86. Alexander Tumanov, *The Life and Artistry of Maria Olenina-d'Alheim*, trans. Christopher Barnes (Calgary: University of Alberta Press, 2000), 221.

87. Gasparian, *General Skoblin*, 33. The story about Afanasiev's meeting with Dzerzhinsky could bolster an alternative interpretation, that Dzerzhinsky rejected Plevitskaya's request to return to Russia because the Soviet secret services had plans to recruit her and Skoblin as agents in Europe at some later date. Andrew and Gordievsky, *KGB*, 152.

88. In his memoirs, Besedovsky identified a "Vladimir Ianovitch" as the OGPU director (*rezident*) in the Soviet embassy in Paris, so this is likely the same person whom Besedovsky named in his testimony at Plevitskaya's trial. See Grigory Bessedovsky, *Revelations of a Soviet Diplomat*, trans. Matthew Norgate (London: Williams & Norgate, 1931), 243; and N. P. V., "Protsess N. V. Plevitskoi," *Poslednie novosti*, December 10, 1938.

89. Varsher, "Moi vstrechi s Plevitskoi i Skoblinym."

90. Bugrov, *Nadezhda Plevitskaia*, 36.

91. "Po delu ob ischeznovenii gen. Miller oprosheno 150 lits," *Novaia zaria*, October 20, 1937, 3.

92. A handwritten draft of *Moi put' s pesnei* is preserved in the M. M. Filonenko Papers, BA. The handwriting in the manuscript appears to be Skoblin's and resembles the handwriting in the declarations the Skoblins made to the Soviets in Berlin in January 1931 (see chapter 6).

93. Barrie Martyn, *Rachmaninoff: Composer, Pianist, Conductor* (Aldershot, England: Scholar Press, 1990), 355n32; Bugrov, *Nadezhda Plevitskaia*, 36.

94. BA, Filonenko Papers, Box 11, Plevitskaya diary, 27; Bugrov, *Nadezhda Plevitskaia*, 36.

95. A. Pogodin, "Sviataia Rus'," *Novoe vremia* (Bulgaria), December 25, 1924.

96. Al. Petrunkevich, "Russkaia dusha," *Vozrozhdenie*, June 29, 1925.

97. Nikolai Ber, "Bibliografia," *Vremya*, January 9, 1925.

98. BA, Filonenko Papers, Box 12, Folder "NV Plevitskaia Skoblin (clippings: Eastern European Tour)."

99. L. Aleksandrov, "N. V. Plevitskaia," *Poslednaia izvestiia* (Riga), October 22, 1924.

100. P. Khrushchev, "N. V. Plevitskaia," *Poslednaia izvestiia*, November 7, 1924.

101. HIA, Prianishnikov Papers, Box 3, Folder "Skoblin and Plevitskaia (bio info)" (excerpt from 1924 article in *Le Petit Parisien*).

102. BA, Filonenko Papers, Box 12, Folder "NV Plevitskaia Skoblin (clippings: Eastern European Tour)" (Ali Khan, "N. V. Plevitskaia," unknown newspaper and date).

103. Lollii Lev'ov, "Nashe russkoe," *Vozrozhdenie*, December 2, 1925.

104. "U steny," *Russkoe vremya* (Paris), October 21, 1925.

105. Max Harrison, *Rachmaninoff: Life, Works, Recordings* (London, New York: Continuum, 2005), 248.

106. Ibid., 262.

107. Marie Turbow Lampard, "Sergei Konenkov: An Introduction," in *The Uncommon Vision of Sergei Konenkov 1874–1971: A Russian Sculptor and His Times*, ed. Marie Turbow Lampard, John E. Bowlt, and Wendy R. Salmond, 3–54 (New Brunswick, NJ: Rutgers University Press, 2001), 32.

108. Sergei T. Konenkov, *Moi vek: Vospominaniia* (Moscow: Izdatel'stvo politicheskoi literatury, 1988), 261.

109. Ibid.

110. V. L. Il'in, "B gostiakh u 'Dezhki,'" *Novoe russkoe slovo*, January 1, 1926.

111. "Music," column by Samuel Chotzinoff, *World* (newspaper), March 13, 1926.

112. "Blestiashchii uspekh Nadezhdy Plevitskoi," *Novoe russkoe slovo*, March 14, 1926.

113. BA, Filonenko Papers, Box 12, Folder 2 (Herman George Scheffauer, "Plevitzka's Voice").

114. BA, Filonenko Papers, Box 12, Folder 1 (booklet of songs from Plevitskaya's repertoire, trans. Kurt Schindler).

115. Georgii Grebenshchikov, "Nadezhda Plevitskaia (iz dnevnika)," *Novoe russkoe slovo*, March 30, 1926.

116. "Teatr i muzyka: Edinyi front," *Novoe russkoe slovo*, April 16, 1927.

117. "Her Farewell Concert," *New York Times*, April 13, 1927.

118. Lydia Nadezhina, "Proshchalnyi kontsert Plevitskoi," *Russkii golos*, April 21, 1927.

119. HTOS, ROVS, Box 18, Folder 4 (note in French about the deposition of Staff Captain P. D. Litvinenko, October 12, 1937).

120. Bugrov, *Nadezhda Plevitskaia*, 37; Strongin, *Nadezhda Plevitskaia*, 201. Another source claims that the Skoblins used a Soviet front organization called the Union for the Return to the USSR to benefit Soviet children. See HIA, Nicolaevsky Papers, Box 299, Folder 7 (P. Tastevin, secretaire, "Rapport Affaire de Miller," December 14, 1937; henceforth Tastevin Report, December 14, 1937).

121. HTOS, ROVS, Box 18, Folder 4 (letter from S. Ughet in New York to Karl Karlovich Miller, November 3, 1937). Thank you to Lazar Fleishman for his insights about the "Bolshevik" nature of the Amtorg; e-mail message from Lazar Fleishman to author, January 13, 2013.

122. HIA, Prianishnikov Papers, Box 3, Folder "Skoblin and Plevitskaya (biographical information)" (article in *Vozrozhdenie*, November 19, 1937, excerpted in "Dopolnitel'nye svedeniia o Skoblinykh").

123. Strongin, *Nadezhda Plevitskaia*, 202.

124. HTOS, ROVS, Box 18, Folder 4 (A. Stoupenkoff, "La Plevitskaya a un concert bolchévique," French translation of an article in *Novoe russkoe slovo*, October 23, 1937).

125. HIA, Petr Berngardovich Struve Papers, Box 31, Folder 65.

126. "Pokhishchenie gen. E. K. Millera," *Vozrozhdenie*, October 15, 1937, 8.

127. Several of Plevitskaya's 1927 concerts are listed in the following reference book: L. A. Mnukhin and T. L. Gladkova, eds., *Russkoe zarubezh'e: khronika nauchoi, kul'urnoi i obshchestvennoi zhizni, 1920–1940, Fransiia*, vol. 1 (Paris: YMCA-Press; Moscow: Eksmo, 1995).

128. Bugrov, *Nadezhda Plevitskaia*, 42.

129. P. V., "V gostiakh u N. V. Plevitskoi," *Ekho* (Kovno, Lithuania), July 7, 1927.

130. "N. V. Plevitskaia," *Segodnya vecherom*, July 23, 1927.

131. Prianishnikov, *Nezrimaia pautina*, 22.

132. Bugrov, *Nadezhda Plevitskaia*, 42; Lekhovich, *Belye protiv krasnykh*, 309.

133. Brian Boyd, *Vladimir Nabokov: The American Years* (Princeton: Princeton University Press, 1993), 59.

134. Excerpt from Vladimir Nabokov, "The Assistant Producer," in *The Stories of Vladimir Nabokov* (New York: Random House, 1995).

135. Nest'ev, *Zvezdy russkoi estrady*, 96.

136. HIA, Prianishnikov Papers, Box 3, Folder "Skoblin and Plevitskaia (biographical information)." Gasparian claims that the farm was not a vineyard and was located in the Var department in southeastern France. Gasparian, *General Skoblin*, 38–39.

137. N. P. V., "Zagadochnoe ischeznovenie gen. E. K. Millera," *Poslednie novosti*, October 6, 1937, 1; "Po delu ob ischeznovenii gen. Miller oprosheno 150 lits," *Novaia zaria*, October 20, 1937, 3.

CHAPTER 5

1. Andrew and Gordievsky, *KGB*, 151.

2. Bessedovsky, *Revelations of a Soviet Diplomat*, 244.

3. Orlov, *March of Time*, 163.

4. Ibid., 165.

5. Primakov et al., *Ocherki istorii rossiiskoi vneshnei razvedki*, vol. 3, 112.

6. Oleg Kapchinskii, "Pokhishchenie generala Kutepova. Ego podgotovil i osushchestvil razvedchik-nelegal Iakov Serebrianskii," *Nezavisimaia gazeta*, January 2, 2002, 16.

7. Andrew and Mitrokhin, *The Mitrokhin Archive*, 54.

8. One source claims that Major General Boris Steifon, Kutepov's former chief of staff, betrayed Kutepov to the Soviets. Reportedly, Steifon told Kutepov shortly before January 26 that two representatives from an underground anti-Soviet cell in the USSR—who were actually two OGPU operatives—needed to see him and would pick him up in a taxi at a designated time. Andrew and Gordievsky, *KGB*, 151–52. However, there is no strong proof that Steifon was a Soviet agent. Robinson, *The White Russian Army in Exile*, 145.

9. Pascal Krop, *Les secrets de l'espionnage français de 1870 à nos jours* (Paris: Grande Bibliotèque Payot, 1995), 346; Aleksandr Ivanovich Kolpakidi and Dmitrii Prokhorov, *KGB: spetsoperatsii sovetskoĭ razvedki* (Moscow: Olimp Ástrel' Izdatel'stvo AST, 2000), 59.

10. Kolpakidi and Prokhorov, *KGB*, 60. The Paris police dossier on the Kutepov case contains a newspaper article about a Soviet embassy officer in Berlin named Andre Fikner, who had confessed to participating in Kutepov's abduction and to knowing that he had been chloroformed. APP, Dossier Affaire Koutiepoff, Case No. 238142 (no author, "Un diplomate soviétique confesse avoir machine l'enlèvement de Koutiepoff en janvier dernier à Paris," unidentified newspaper, 1938).

11. On how Kutepov might have died, see Andrew and Gordievsky, *KGB*, 151; Johnston, *New Mecca*, 101–4; Kapchinskii, "Pokhishchenie generala Kutepova," 16; Kolpakidi and Prokhorov, *KGB*, 59–61; Krop, *Les secrets de l'espionnage français*, 346–47; Mlechin, *Set'-Moskva-OGU-Parizh*, 21; and Orlov, *March of Time*, 166, 171.

12. Kolpakidi and Prokhorov, *KGB*, 59.

13. Krop, *Les secrets de l'espionnage français*, 346.

14. Orlov, *March of Time*, 166.

15. On February 3, 1930, the Soviet government newspaper *Izvestiya* falsely reported that Kutepov had stolen ROVS money and escaped to South America.

16. Orlov, *March of Time*, 167.

17. In the September 22, 1965, issue of *Krasnaia zvezda*, the flagship newspaper of the Soviet Red Army, an obituary of Sergei V. Puzitsky, an operative in OGPU's counterintelligence branch, noted that he "had brilliantly carried out an operation involving the arrest of Kutepov and a number of other White Guardist organizers and initiators of foreign military intervention and the civil war." K. Shimenov, "Moi dopolneniia k romanu," *Krasnaia zvezda*, September 22, 1965.

18. Primakov et al., *Ocherki istorii rossiiskoi vneshnei razvedki*, vol. 3, 113.

19. Andrew and Mitrokhin, *The Mitrokhin Archive*, 54.

20. Pavel Sudoplatov and Anatoli Sudoplatov, with Jerrold L. Schecter and Leona P. Schecter, *Special Tasks: The Memoirs of an Unwanted Witness—A Soviet Spymaster* (New York: Little, Brown, 1994), 91.

21. See, for example, Andrew and Gordievsky, *KGB*, 152–53, 163–64; Dziak, *Chekisty*, 111–13; and Krivitsky, *In Stalin's Secret Service*, 237–40. One Russian

intelligence researcher argues that Skoblin and Plevitskaya were recruited by the Soviet secret police at the end of the 1920s and participated in Kutepov's kidnapping. Igor Simbirtsev, *Spetssluzhby pervykh let SSSR 1923–1939 na puti k bol'shomu terroru* (Moscow: Tsentr poligraf, 2008), 182.

22. HIA, Volkov Papers, Box 18, Folder 1 (article in *Novaia zaria*, undated).

23. Tastevin Report, December 14, 1937.

24. "Zagadochnoe ischeznovenie gen. E. K. Millera," *Poslednie novosti*, September 29, 1937, 1.

25. Robinson, *The White Russian Army in Exile*, 185.

26. Andrew and Gordievsky, *KGB*, 152.

27. A. M. Boreiko, "General Skoblin: Iz Kornilovskogo polka v Sovetskuiu razvedku," in *Istoricheskie chteniia na Lubianke 2004 g: Rukovoditeli i sotrudniki spetsslubzhb Rossii*, ed. I. Iu. Bazhenov, 100–107 (Moscow: Obshestvo Izuchenia Istorii Otechestvennika Spetsluzhb, 2004), 102.

28. Miller, *Shanghai on the Métro*, 137.

29. Archives nationales, Paris, France, F/7/15976/1 "Communication des documents par extrait Section du XXeme Siècle," Archives du fichier central de la direction générale de la police, dit fonds "Panthéon" (1880–1945) (henceforth AN, Panthéon, F/7/15976/1), Folder "Miller procès de la Plevitskaia enlèvement du général Miller" (intelligence report no. 4145, Préfecture de Police, August 4, 1930, re: Russian General Dragomiroff).

30. AN, Panthéon, F/7/15976/1, Folder "Miller procès de la Plevitskaia enlèvement du général Miller" (Paris police report, March 26, 1930).

31. AN, Panthéon, F/7/15976/1, Folder "Miller procès de la Plevitskaia enlèvement du général Miller" (intelligence report, Préfecture de Police, September 1930, dossier 8.079).

32. "Zagadochnoe ischeznovenie gen. E. K. Millera," *Poslednie novosti*, September 30, 1937, 2.

33. Janet Flanner, *Paris Was Yesterday*, ed. Irving Drutman (New York: Harcourt Brace Jovanovich, 1972), 207.

34. Eugen Weber, *The Hollow Years: France in the 1930s* (New York: Norton, 1994), 65.

35. N. P. V., "Zagadochnoe ischeznovenie gen. E. K. Millera," *Poslednie novosti*, October 6, 1937, 1; "Po delu ob ischeznovenii gen. Miller oprosheno 150 lits," *Novaia zaria*, October 20, 1937, 3.

36. "Zagadochnoe ischeznovenie gen. E. K. Millera," *Poslednie novosti*, September 29, 1937, 2.

37. "Zagadochnoe ischeznovenie gen. E. K. Millera," *Poslednie novosti*, September 30, 1937, 1.

38. Igor Damaskin with Geoffrey Elliot, *Kitty Harris: The Spy with Seventeen Names* (London: St. Ermin's Press, 2001), 80–82.

39. Primakov et al., *Ocherki istorii rossiiskoi vneshnei razvedki*, vol. 3, 115–16.

40. Ibid., vol. 2, 85.

41. B. G. Strukov, "Bor'ba OGPU protiv Rossiiskoi politicheschoi emigratsii," in *Istoricheskie chteniia na lubianke 1999 god: Otechestvennye spetsluzhby v 1920-1930-x godakh*, ed. A. Zdanovich et al., 94–100 (Moscow: FSBRF and Novgorod State University, 2000).

42. Unless otherwise noted, the narrative about Kovalsky's recruitment of the Skoblins relies on the following sources, containing excerpts from OGPU/NKVD files related to Skoblin's recruitment and Miller's kidnapping: V. Syrokomskii, "Neizvestnye stranitsy istorii sovetskoi razvedki," *Nedelia*, no. 48 (November 27–December 3, 1989): 1; Leonid Mikhailov, "General daet soglasie," *Nedelia*, no. 48 (November 27–December 3, 1989): 10–11; Mikhailov, "Fermer soobshchaet iz Parizha," *Nedelia*, no. 49 (1989): 14–16; Mlechin, *Alibi dlia velikoi pevitsy*, 34–67; and Mlechin, *Set'-Moskva-OGPU-Parizh*, 29–37.

43. Plevitskaia, *Dezhkin karagod; Moi put' s pesnei*, 81.

44. Morrison, *Lina & Serge*, 121.

45. Bugrov, *Nadezhda Plevitskaia*, 50.

46. Mikhailov, "General daet soglasie," 11.

47. Ibid.

48. Ibid., 10.

49. Mlechin, *Alibi dlia velikoi pevitsy*, 66.

50. Mikhailov, "General daet soglasie," 11.

51. Miller, *Shanghai on the Métro*, 137.

52. Mlechin, *Set'-Moskva-OGPU-Parizh*, 51–52.

53. Mikhailov, "Fermer soobshchaet iz Parizha," 14. According to Boreiko, on November 24, Skoblin attended a meeting where Miller announced a secret mobilization of White Army veterans. Skoblin was asked to be involved in the organization. Boreiko, "General Skoblin," 102.

54. Vladimir Antonov, "Nadezhda Plevitskaia—'kurskii solovei' sovetskoi razvedki," *Nezavisimoe voennoe obozrenie*, February 19, 2010.

55. Mikhailov, "Fermer soobshchaet iz Parizha," 14.

56. Mlechin, *Set'-Moskva-OGPU-Parizh*, 52–54.

57. Ibid., 53–54.

58. Ibid., 54.

59. Ibid., 54–56.

60. Ibid., 57.

61. According to one story, in 1931, Plevitskaya asked former impresario Mekler to arrange a concert tour of the USSR. N. P. V., "Delo Plevitskoi," *Poslednie novosti*, October 15, 1938. A second account, by Saikis A. Oskanian, claimed that Russian émigrés in Berlin offered to arrange a Soviet concert tour, but that Plevitskaya told them that this would be impossible: HTOS, Ob"edinenie Chinov Kornilovskogo Udarnogo Polka Records, Box 18, Folder 4. Oskanian served under Skoblin during the civil war. In Berlin, Oskanian helped arrange some of Plevitskaya's concerts and often saw the Eitingons.

62. Mlechin, *Alibi dlia velikoi pevitsy*, 71.

63. Mikhailov, "Fermer soobshchaet iz Parizha," 15.

CHAPTER 6

1. Andrew Hussey, *Paris: The Secret History* (New York: Viking, 2006), 338.

2. Johnston, *New Mecca*, 25.

3. AN, Panthéon, F/7/15976/1, Folder "Miller procès de la Plevitskaia enlèvement du général Miller" (Paris police report of January 13, 1931, on Miller's interview in the *Sunday Times*; and Paris police report of January 19, 1931).

4. APP, GA S10 Dossier Skobline, Case No. 59638 (letter dated March 10, 1931, from the president of the Council/Ministry of the Interior to the prefect of police, Paris; and letter dated March 20, 1931, from the president of Council/Ministry of the Interior to the prefect of police).

5. APP, GA S10 Dossier Skobline, Case No. 59638 (letter from the director of general intelligence to the prefect of police, April 3, 1931, file no. 293.481).

6. Mlechin, *Alibi dlia velikoi pevitsy*, 100–101.

7. Boreiko, "General Skoblin," 101.

8. Mlechin, *Alibi dlia velikoi pevitsy*, 101.

9. Mikhailov, "Fermer soobshchaet iz Parizha," 15; Mlechin, *Set'-Moskva-OGPU-Parizh*, 67–78, 94–97; Mlechin, *Alibi dlia velikoi pevitsy*, 86–98, 109–11.

10. Mikhailov, "Fermer soobshchaet iz Parizha," 15.

11. "Zagadochnoe ischeznovenie gen. E. K. Millera," *Poslednie novosti*, September 29, 1937, 2.

12. Plevitskaya's 1930s concerts are listed in Mnukhin and Gladkova, *Russkoe zarubezh'e.*

13. Robinson, *The White Russian Army in Exile*, 184.

14. Ibid., 198.

15. After World War II, U.S. and British intelligence agencies suspected that Turkul was a Soviet agent while he was working for a German military intelligence (Abwehr) network under the leadership of Richard Kauder (alias Klatt). The Soviets had infiltrated this network. Authors Mark Aarons and John Loftus claim that Turkul was a Soviet agent in *Unholy Trinity: The Vatican, the Nazis, and the Swiss Banks*, rev. ed. (New York: St. Martin's, 1998). However, based on my own research and correspondence with historian Paul Robinson (e-mail message on May 21, 2013), I determined that there is still insufficient evidence on which to form a judgment. See also Arnold M. Silver, "Questions, Questions, Questions: Memories of Oberusel," *Intelligence and National Security* 8, no. 2 (April 1993); and the National Archives, Kew, KV 2/1591, "Anton TURKUL: Russian" (the Secret Intelligence Service/MI6 concluded that Turkul's involvement with Soviet intelligence "was never established"), at http://discovery.nationalarchives.gov.uk/details/r/C11190776 (accessed June 6, 2015).

16. Robinson, *The White Russian Army in Exile*, 196–97.

17. HTOS, Ob"edinenie Chinov Kornilovskogo Udarnogo Polka Records, Box 1, Folder 17 (text of Miller's speech on July 12, 1931, in honor of the Kornilov Shock Regiment).

18. Mlechin, *Set'-Moskva-OGPU-Parizh*, 111.

19. Ibid., 112.

20. Primakov et al., *Ocherki istorii rossiiskoi vneshnei razvedki*, vol. 3, 117–18; Mikhailov, "Fermer soobshchaet iz Parizha," 16; Mlechin, *Set'-Moskva-OGPU-Parizh*, 155–56; Degtiarev and Kolpakidi, eds., *Vneshniaia razvedka SSSR*, 48. According to Pavel Sudoplatov, Skoblin's principal controller was Sergei Shpigelglas of OGPU's Foreign Department. Sudoplatov et al., *Special Tasks*, 36.

21. Igor Zavadsky-Krasnopolsky created an independent intelligence-gathering network called RIS, and he and his associates reportedly provided services for the Paris police, ROVS, the Bolsheviks, and anyone else who was willing to pay. Skoblin often met with Zavadsky-Krasnopolsky in Paris cafés, but it appears that the former was more interested in keeping tabs on the latter for the Soviets than in carrying out planned actions. Grey, *Le général meurt à minuit*, 62; and Miller, *Shanghai on the Métro*, 132–33, 136–38.

22. Mikhailov, "Fermer soobshchaet iz Parizha," 16.

23. Interview with M. A. Stolypine, "Unir Tous Les Émigrés pour le livrer aux Soviets," *Le Jour*, October 5, 1937, 5.

24. Belin, *Trente ans de Sûreté Nationale*, 242.

25. HIA, Nicolaevsky Collection, Box 299, Folder 6 (Erdely Commission Report, February 4, 1938).

26. HIA, Nicolaevsky Collection, Box 299, Folder 7 (COTE IV, "Scellé no. 3-Miller").

27. HIA, Nicolaevsky Collection, Box 299, Folder 7 ("Scellé no. 94: Lettre de December 15, 1933, de Miller à Colonel Matsyleff," Perquisitions rue de la Faisanderie).

28. HIA, Nicolaevsky Collection, Box 299, Folder 7 (COTE III, "Projet d'un soulément en U.R.S.S.").

29. Robinson, *The White Russian Army in Exile*, 176; and A. V. Okorokov, *Fashizm i russkaia emigratsiia 1920–1945 gg.* (Moscow: Rusaki, 2002), 21.

30. Robinson, *The White Russian Army in Exile*, 221–23.

31. Strongin, *Nadezhda Plevitskaia*, 249–52; A. F. Kiselev, ed., *Politicheskaia istoriia russkoe emigratsii: 1920–1940 gg.: dokumenty i materialy* (Moscow: Gumanitarnoe izdatel'stvo Tsentr VLADOS, 1999), 39.

32. Robinson, *The White Russian Army in Exile*, 221.

33. Bailey, *The Conspirators*, 131.

34. Belin, *Trente ans de Sûreté Nationale*, 247.

35. Krivitsky, *In Stalin's Secret Service*, 236–37; and Robert Conquest, *The Great Terror: A Reassessment* (New York: Oxford University Press, 2008), 198.

36. Mikhailov, "ROVS terpit porazhenie," 10.

37. Prianishnikov, *Nezrimaia pautina*, 228–30.

38. HIA, Nicolaevsky Collection, Box 299, Folder 7 (COTE VI, Scellé 5-Miller-Domicile, "Extrait d'une letter, en date du 14 Septembre 1933, addressee par Severoff à Ivan Ivanovitch").

39. Andrew and Gordievsky, *KGB*, 153; Vladislav I. Goldin and John W. Long, "Resistance and Retribution: The Life and Fate of General E. K. Miller," *Revolutionary Russia* 12, no. 2 (1999): 27.

40. Prianishnikov, *Nezrimaia pautina*, 227.

41. Prianishnikov, "Gibel' generala E. K. Millera, 4. 'Vnutrenniaia liniia'opekaet emigratsiiu," *Novoe russkoe slovo*, September 13, 1962. Shatilov was also accused of being a Bolshevik traitor, but no convincing evidence was ever found to support this allegation. HIA, Prianishnikov Papers, Box 2, Folder "Gen. P. N. Shatilov" (excerpt of article by R. Kh. in *Novoe russkoe slovo*, October 24, 1937).

42. HIA, Prianishnikov Papers, Box 3, Folder "Skoblin and Plevitskaya 1 (biographical information)" (text of article in *Chasovoi*, May 1933, in "Prazdniki Kornilovskogo Polka").

43. Viktor A. Larionov's memoirs (excerpt), "Plevitskaia i Skoblin," *Novaia zaria*, December 17, 1938.

44. Grey, *Le général meurt à minuit*, 148.

45. Ibid., 147–49.

46. Leonid Livak, *Russian Émigrés in the Intellectual and Literary Life of Interwar France* (Montreal and Kingston: McGill-Queen's University Press, 2010), 29–30.

47. Rosenberg, *Policing Paris*, 87.

48. Primakov et al., *Ocherki istorii rossiiskoi vneshnei razvedki*, vol. 3, 115–16.

49. On Mireille Abbiate, see Andrew and Mitrokhin, *The Mitrokhin Archive*, 98, 103.

50. Primakov et al., *Ocherki istorii rossiiskoi vneshnei razvedki*, vol. 3, 115.

51. Andrew Meier, *The Lost Spy: An American in Stalin's Secret Service* (New York: Norton, 2008), 162–66.

52. "Switzes Set Free by French Court," *New York Times*, April 18, 1935; "Paris Spy Verdict Upheld," *New York Times*, July 27, 1935.

53. Douglas Porch, *The French Secret Services: A History of French Intelligence from the Dreyfus Affair to the Gulf War* (New York: Macmillan, 1995), 124.

54. HTOS, Ob"edinenie Chinov Kornilovskogo Udarnogo Polka Records, Box 12, Folder 11 (text of 1934 speech by General Miller).

55. HIA, Nicolaevsky Collection, Box 299, Folder 7, "Scellé 5-Miller-Domicile-Cote X."

56. Prianishnikov, "Gibel' generala E. K. Millera, 7. Boevaia rabota ROVS-a pri gen. E. K. Millera," *Novoe russkoe slovo*, September 19, 1962.

57. Viktor A. Larionov's memoirs (excerpt), "Plevitskaia i Skoblin," *Novaia zaria*, December 17, 1938.

58. Mikhailov, "ROVS terpit porazhenie," 11.

59. Ibid.; Robinson, *The White Russian Army in Exile*, 190 (writes that the operation occurred in June, not July), and Andrew and Gordievsky, *KGB*, 153.

60. AN, Panthéon, F/7/15976/1, Folder "Miller procès de la Plevitskaia enlèvement du général Miller" (Paris police report, July 2, 1934, on the break-in at Miller's apartment).

61. "Zagadochnoe ischeznovenie gen. E. K. Millera," *Poslednie novosti*, September 29, 1937, 1.

62. Andrew and Mitrokhin, *The Mitrokhin Archive*, 98.

63. BA, Filonenko Papers, Box 12, Folder "Mr. and Mrs. Skoblin auto accident" (draft of letter dated March 14, 1935, from Filonenko to unnamed prosecutor).

64. BA, Filonenko Papers, Box 12, Folder "Plevitskaia Skoblin, N. V. (clippings: Eastern European Tour)" (article in Kishenev newspaper, January 6, 1935).

65. V. A. Larionov's memoirs (excerpt), "Plevitskaia i Skoblin," *Novaia zaria*, December 17, 1938.

66. "Zagadochnoe ischeznovenie gen. E. K. Millera," *Poslednie novosti*, September 29, 1937, 1.

67. HIA, Nicolaevsky Collection, Box 299, Folder 5 ("Deiatel'nost', sviazi i sluzhba Skoblina v ROVSe i v Chatiakh I-go Aermeiskago Kurpusa," in the Erdely Commission Report, February 4, 1938).

68. K. P., "X—XX i gen. Miller," *Edinyi front*, February 10–23, 1935.

69. Mikhailov, "ROVS terpit porazhenie," 10.

70. Ibid., 10–11.

71. Meier, *The Lost Spy*, 165.

72. Mikhailov, "ROVS terpit porazhenie," 10–11.

73. Ibid.

74. Robinson, *The White Russian Army in Exile*, 198–99.

75. Ibid.

76. BA, Filonenko Papers, Box 12, Folder "Mr. and Mrs. Skoblin (auto accident)."

77. Mikhailov, "ROVS terpit porazhenie," 11.

78. HIA, Nicolaevsky Collection, Box 299, Folder 4 ("Kuda privel 'Put' s pesnei' Nadezhdu Plevitskaiu," *Segodnya vecherom*, no. 221 undated).

79. Andrei Sedykh, "Plevitskaya pishet' iz' tiurmy . . . ," *Novoe russkoe slovo*, May 15, 1938.

80. "Zagadochnoe ischeznovenie gen. E. K. Millera," *Poslednie novosti*, September 29, 1937, 2.

81. HIA, Prianishnikov Papers, Box 3, Folder 1 "Skoblin and Plevitskaia (biographical information)" (excerpt of March 1935 *Chasovoi* article, issue no. 145).

82. Boreiko, "General Skoblin," 104.

83. Larionov's memoirs (excerpt), "Plevitskaia i Skoblin," *Novaia zaria*, December 17, 1938.

84. Grey, *Le général meurt à minuit*, 186.

85. Prianishnikov, "Gibel' generala E. K. Millera, 9. General E. K. Miller i 'vnutrenniaia liniia,'" *Novoe russkoe slovo*, September 19, 1962; Maurice Ribet, *L'enlèvement du Général de Miller par le Général Skobline; le procès de la Plevitzkaïa. Plaidoirie de Me. Maurice Ribet* (Paris: Imprimerie du Palais, 1939).

86. Bailey, *The Conspirators*, 131.

87. Prianishnikov, "Gibel' generala E. K. Millera, 8. General E. K. Miller i Skoblin," *Novoe russkoe slovo*, September 20, 1962.

88. Robinson, *The White Russian Army in Exile*, 190.

89. For the NTSNP's warning of Miller about Skoblin's provocateur activities within the Inner Line, see "Gen. Skoblin i 'Vnutrenniaia liniia,'" *Poslednie novosti*, October 6, 1937, 1.

90. APP, GA S10 Dossier Skobline, Case No. 59638, Folder "Mme. Skobline Rapports Divers" (Paris police report, September 26, 1937). This report mentions a police report of August 31, 1935, in which Theodosienko (possibly a misspelling of Fedoseenko), described as a Russian chauffeur and police informant, identified Skoblin as a Soviet agent.

91. HIA, Nicolaevsky Collection, Box 299, Folder 7 (COTE XX, Scellé 5-Miller-Domicile, "Extrait d'une letter de DOBROVOLSKY à Miller en date du 26 août 1935").

92. Ribet, *Plaidoirie*, 22.

93. HIA, Nicolaevsky Collection, Box 299, Folder 7 (COTE XXXV, Scellé Miller-Domicile, "Extrait d'une lettre de Miller à Dobrovolsky en date du Ier Novembre 1935").

94. HIA, Prianishnikov Papers, Box 3, Folder "Skoblin and Plevitskaia 1 (biographical information)" (article in *Chasovoi*, September 1935, excerpted in "Prazdniki Kornilovskogo Polka").

95. Nicolas Ross, *Saint-Alexandre-Nevski: Centre spirituel de l'émigration russe 1918–1939* (Paris: Éditions des Syrtes, 2011), 484–86.

96. HIA, Prianishnikov Papers, Box 3, Folder "Skoblin and Plevitskaia (biographical information)" (article in *Chasovoi*, October–November 1935, excerpted in "Prazdniki Kornilovskogo Polka").

97. Robinson, *The White Russian Army in Exile*, 202–5.

98. Ibid., 203, 204n5; Mlechin, *Set'-Moskva-OGPU-Parizh*, 120, 165.

99. Prianishnikov, *Nezrimaia pautina*, 246–47.

100. Paul Paillole, *Services spécialaux, 1935–1945* (Paris: Editions Robert Laffont, 1975), 48.

101. Ibid., 49.

102. Ibid.

103. Grey, *Le général meurt à minuit*, 187.

104. Fonds du Moscou, National Archives of France, Fontainebleau: Box 0019940502 Code n1: 9722 Localisation: 237083 (report information number C.2718 of March 17, 1936, by the French Ministry of the Interior to the French Minister of War).

105. Robinson, *The White Russian Army in Exile*, 190. Correspondence continued between Miller and Dobrovolsky, and between Dobrovolsky and Skoblin, up through August 1937, suggesting that Miller and Skoblin—for their separate purposes—wanted to maintain contact with Dobrovolsky. HIA, Nicolaevsky Collection, Box 299, Folder 7 (Cote XXXXV, Scellé Pax, "Extrait d'une letter de Dobrovolsky à Skobline en date du 14 Août 1937").

106. Prianishnikov, *Nezrimaia pautina*, 267.

107. HIA, Prianishnikov Papers, Box 3, Folder "Skoblin and Plevitskaia 1 (biographical information)" (article in *Chasovoi*, October 1, 1936, excerpted in "Prazdniki Korniloskogo Polka").

108. HIA, Prianishnikov Papers, Box 3, Folder "Skoblin and Plevitskaia 1 (biographical information)" (article in *Chasovoi*, December 20, 1936, excerpted in "Prazdnizi Kornilovskogo Polka").

109. Prianishnikov, *Nezrimaia pautina*, 267.

110. Robinson, *The White Russian Army in Exile*, 225.

111. Viacheslav V. Kostikov, *Ne budem proklinat' izgnan'e . . . Puti i sud'by russkoi emigratsii* (Moscow: Mezhdunarodnye Otnosheniia, 1990), 375–77.

112. Mikhail Kol'tsov, "Tri pezety—chisten'kimi," *Pravda*, September 10, 1937, 5.

113. N. P. V., "Zagadochnoe ischeznovenie E. K. Millera," *Poslednie novosti*, October 6, 1937, 1.

114. HIA, Nicolaevsky Collection, Box 299, Folder 5 ("Deiatel'nost', sviazi i sluzhba Skoblina v ROVSe i v Chatiakh I-go Aermeiskago Kurpusa," Erdely Commission Report, February 4, 1938).

115. Ibid.

116. Robinson, *The White Russian Army in Exile*, 208.

117. Bailey, *The Conspirators*, 132.

118. Ribet, *Plaidoirie*, 22.

119. HIA, Nicolaevsky Collection, Box 299, Folder 7 (letter of January 25, 1937, to Severin Cesarovich from Skoblin).

120. Robert Tucker, *Stalin in Power: The Revolution from Above, 1928–1941* (New York: Norton, 1992), 379.

121. Walter Schellenberg, *The Labyrinth*, trans. Louis Hagen (Boston: Da Capo, 2000), 25–28; Wilhelm Höttl, *Secret Front: Nazi Political Espionage 1938–45* (New York: Enigma Books, 2003), 66–71; Krivitsky, *In Stalin's Secret Service*, 237. Pavel Sudoplatov writes that Skoblin's NKVD file does not contain any reference to German intelligence apart from how Skoblin had lured Miller to a secret meeting in September 1937 with NKVD operatives posing as Germans. Sudoplatov, *Special Tasks*, 90–91. For more on Skoblin's alleged involvement in the Tukhachevsky affair, see Paillole, *Services spécialaux*, 46–52; John Erickson, *The Soviet High Command: A Military-Political History, 1918–1941*, 3rd ed. (London: Frank Cass, 2001), 434–35, 471–72; F. Sergeev, "Delo Tukhachevskogo," *Nedelia*, no. 7 (1989), 10–11; and Rapoport and Alexeev, *High Treason*, 258–62.

122. In addition, fictionalized accounts, such as the one appearing in Victor Alexandrov's 1964 *The Tukhachevsky Affair*—which portrays Skoblin as a quadruple agent on the payroll of ROVS, the Nazis, the Soviets, and the Belgians—misinform more than enlighten readers. Victor Alexandrov, *The Tukhachevsky Affair*, trans. John Hewish (Englewood Cliffs, NJ: Prentice Hall, 1964).

123. Schellenberg, *The Labyrinth*, 25. There is also testimonial evidence from the Miller kidnapping investigation that in the summer of 1936, when accompanying

Plevitskaya to her July 12 concert in London, Skoblin secretly met with Vitovt Putna, a Soviet military attaché at the London embassy. Stalin later implicated Putna in the Tukhachevsky conspiracy, and Putna was executed in 1937. For sources referring to Skoblin's alleged meeting with Putna, see HIA, Nicolaevsky Papers, Box 299, Folder 7 (P. Tastevin, secretary, "Rapport: Affaire de Miller," December 14, 1937; henceforth "Tastevin Report," December 14, 1937); and "Pokhishchenie gen. E. K. Millera," *Vozrozhdenie*, October 29, 1937, 2. *Vozrozhdenie* argued that the actual reason Skoblin met with Putna was to gauge for the NKVD Putna's loyalty to Stalin, that Skoblin found Putna disloyal, and, as a result, that the Stalin regime soon after recalled Putna to Moscow. However, based on his sources, former head of the Provisional Government, Alexander Kerensky, insisted that Skoblin had not met with Putna. "Ischeznovenie gen. E. K. Millera," *Poslednie novosti*, November 23, 1937, 2. There is also unsubstantiated evidence that Skoblin may have met Tukhachevsky. In *Services spécialaux 1935–1945*, Paillole notes (pp. 47–48) that, during his brief visit to Paris in early February 1936, Tukhachevsky queried French officials about their knowledge of Miller and Skoblin and, on the principle of maintaining contact with one's adversaries, said that he had met in London with one of Miller's envoys, possibly Skoblin.

124. Conquest, *The Great Terror*, 198.

125. At a 1989 roundtable discussion in Moscow, the head of the International Department of the Soviet Communist Party's Central Committee claimed to have seen some materials he said were compiled by Schellenberg on Tukhachevsky and others. V. Falin, "Dva raznykh dogovora," *Argumenty i fakty*, no. 33 (August 19, 1989): 5; Tucker, *Stalin in Power*, 383.

126. Krivitsky, *In Stalin's Secret Service*, 237.

127. Nikolai Abramov, "The New Version of the 'Tukhachevsky Affair,'" *New Times*, no. 13 (March 23–April 3, 1989): 37.

128. Grey, *Le général meurt à minuit*, 243.

129. Letter from Nadezhda Plevitskaya to Ivan Bunin, February 19, 1937. The letter is in the Bunin collection at the Leeds Russian archive, housed at the Leeds University Library, UK. Many thanks to Edythe Haber and Leeds archivist Richard Davies for their help.

130. HIA, Nicolaevsky Collection, Box 299, Folder 7 (COTE XLI, Scellé 19-Ozoir, "Lettre date de Berlin, 14 Février 1937, addressee à Paul Alexeevitch par A. de Lampe").

131. Ribet, *Plaidoirie*, 22.

132. Robinson, *The White Russian Army in Exile*, 200, 208.

133. HIA, Nicolaevsky Collection, Box 299, Folder 7 ("Affaire Skobline," letter from Troshin to Skoblin, c. 1937).

134. HIA, Nicolaevsky Collection, Box 299, Folder 7 (report, "Le Commissaire de Police André Roches attaché à la Direction de la Police Judiciaire," February 8, 1938; henceforth Roches Report, February 8, 1938).

135. HIA, Nicolaevsky Collection, Box 299, Folder 7 (excerpt of letter, April 16, 1937, from Miller to Abramov, Scellé 5—Miller-Domicile-Cote XXXV).

136. HIA, Nicolaevsky Collection, Box 299, Folder 7 (COTE XXIII, Scellé 25-Faisanderie-Ière Perquisition, "Extrait d'une letter de Matzeleff au general Zinkevitch en date du 4 Juin 1937").

137. Prianishnikov, *Nezrimaia pautina*, 308.

138. AN, Panthéon, F/7/15976/1, Folder "Miller procès de la Plevitskaia enlevement du général Miller" (police report, October 2, 1937).

139. Tastevin Report, December 14, 1937.

140. "Pokhishchenie gen. E. K. Millera," *Vozrozhdenie*, October 27, 1937, 2.

141. "Zagadochnoe ischeznovenie gen. E. K. Millera," *Poslednie novosti*, September 30, 1937, 1.

142. Gasparian, *General Skoblin*, 219.

143. Prianishnikov, *Nezrimaia pautina*, 271.

144. Gasparian, *General Skoblin*, 219.

145. Tastevin Report, December 14, 1937.

146. Ribet, *Plaidoirie*, 24.

147. Ibid., 25.

148. Robinson, *The White Russian Army in Exile*, 206–8; and Gasparian, *General Skoblin*, 178–85.

149. HIA, Prianishnikov Papers, Box 5, Folder "Affaire Miller (II)" ("Au Sujet du Role Joue par Mme. Skobline dite 'Plevitskzkaia'").

CHAPTER 7

1. Orlov, *March of Time*, 191. Miller had already survived several threats to his life, including a bombing of ROVS headquarters and a 1933 assassination attempt. In August 1933, the Sûreté Générale received an anonymous tip claiming that Miller and Shatilov were being targeted by a group named Front Unique, which consisted of Russian anarchists and communists and was likely a Chekist front organization. AN, Panthéon, F/7/15976/1, Folder "Miller procès de la Plevitskaia enlèvement du général Miller" (letter of August 21, 1933, from the Ministry of the Interior/Director of the Sûreté Générale to the prefect of police).

2. Primakov et al., *Ocherki istorii rossiiskoi vneshnei razvedki*, vol. 3, 115.

3. David R. Shearer and Vladimir Khaustov, eds., *Stalin and the Lubianka: A Documentary History of the Political Police and Security Organs in the Soviet Union, 1922–1953* (New Haven, CT: Yale University Press, 2015), 197–98 (document 107). Despite the arguments of NKVD defector Walter Krivitsky and others, the Soviets probably did not base their decision to kidnap Miller on what he may have known about Skoblin's alleged role in the Tukhachevsky affair. Krivitsky, *In Stalin's Secret Service*, 213; Bailey, *The Conspirators*, 260–61; Grey, *Le général meurt à minuit*, 210; Erickson, *The Soviet High Command*, 471–72.

4. Kolpakidi and Prokhorov, *KGB*, 67; John Costello and Oleg Tsarev, *Deadly Illusions: The KGB Orlov Dossier Reveals Stalin's Master Spy* (New York: Crown,

1993), 471n14. *Ded* reference mentioned in Nikolai Petrov, "Konets agenta '13,'" *Moskovskie novosti*, no. 86 (December 17–24, 1995): 9.

5. Sudoplatov, *Special Tasks*, 37.
6. Orlov, *March of Time*, 193.
7. Krivitsky, *In Stalin's Secret Service*, 213.
8. Kern, *A Death in Washington*, 87.
9. Krivitsky, *In Stalin's Secret Service*, 213.
10. In an official Russian government account of the Miller kidnapping, Evgeny M. Primakov identified Shpigelglas, Georgii Kosenko (Kislov), Veniamin Grazhul', and Mikhail Grigor'ev as participants in the Miller kidnapping in addition to Skoblin. Primakov et al., *Ocherki istorii rossiiskoi vneshnei razvedki*, vol. 3, 118. Sudoplatov and Orlov both said that Kosenko and Shpigelglas played the roles of the Germans in the Miller operation: Sudoplatov, *Special Tasks*, 91; Orlov, *March of Time*, 196. For more on participants in the Miller operation, see Kolpakidi and Prokhorov, *KGB*, 68; Boris Volodarsky, *Stalin's Agent: The Life & Death of Alexander Orlov* (Oxford: Oxford University Press, 2015), 267–68; and Petrov, "Konets agenta '13,'" 9. Orlov reportedly confided to former Soviet intelligence officer Mikhail Feoktistov that he had taken part in Miller's kidnapping, "although he had fallen out with Yezhov because he said he had disapproved of the whole operation." Costello and Tsarev, *Deadly Illusions*, 297.

11. Kolpakidi and Prokhorov, *KGB*, 68; Vladimir Antonov, "Tragediia razvedchika Glinskogo," *Nezavisimoe voennoe obozrenie*, December 21, 2012.
12. Costello and Tsarev, *Deadly Illusions*, 471n14; and Orlov, *March of Time*, 195.
13. Andrew and Mitrokhin, *The Mitrokhin Archive*, 99.
14. Ibid., 98.
15. Orlov, *March of Time*, 194.
16. Bailey, *The Conspirators*, 262. In 1935, Miller had stopped employing a security guard, mainly as a cost-saving measure.
17. Orlov assumed that Plevitskaya "was privy to the whole operation" in advance, but Sudoplatov maintained that she believed Shpigelglas to be just one of Skoblin's friends and remained oblivious to what lay ahead. Orlov, *March of Time*, 195; Sudoplatov, *Special Tasks*, 37. Plevitskaya never publicly admitted her role in the plot. However, in a 1939 letter written by White Army colonel Georgy Poliansky that recounts Plevitskaya's alleged confession in February 1939 to an unidentified woman named Valya, Skoblin told Plevitskaya only that he and Miller had a top-secret meeting to attend and warned her of the need to construct an alibi. BA, Filonenko Papers, Box 11, Folder "Plevitskaia Skoblin, N. V. 1." (Poliansky letter dated February 12, 1939). I cannot confirm whether this letter accurately reflects Plevitskaya's thoughts, words, or deeds. However, it is intriguing that Filonenko, Plevitskaya's attorney, placed it in his archive. On the back of the envelope in which the Poliansky letter came, another researcher earlier identified Valya as Princess Shakhovskaya, who was Filonenko's wife in 1939 and the former wife of

Poliansky; however, Tanya Chebotarev, archivist at the Bakhmeteff Archive, noted that Shakhovskaya's first name was Varvara, while "Valya" usually is a nickname for Valentina. E-mail message from Chebotarev to author, September 4, 2013.

18. Costello and Tsarev, *Deadly Illusions*, 297–98.

19. Karl Schlögel, *Moscow, 1937*, trans. Rodney Livingstone (Cambridge, UK, and Malden, MA: Polity Press, 2012), 198–208.

20. Orlov, *March of Time*, 195.

21. Ibid.

22. HIA, Prianishnikov Papers, Box 5, Folder Affaire Miller (II), "Au Sujet du Role Joue par Mme. Skobline dite 'Plevitskzkaia.'"

23. BA, Aleksandr Vasil'evich Miakin Memoirs.

24. "Zagadochnoe ischeznovenie gen. E. K. Millera," *Poslednie novosti*, September 29, 1937, 2.

25. "Le Général Miller A Disparu Depuis Mercredi," *Le Journal*, September 24, 1937, 1.

26. "Zagadochnoe ischeznovenie gen. E. K. Millera," *Poslednie novosti*, September 25, 1937, 1.

27. Evgeny Novitsky, "Pis'ma v redaktsiiu," *Novoe russkoe slovo*, November 17, 1967, 4.

28. S. Rozhdestvensky, "Tridtsatiletie pokhishcheniia Generala E. K. Millera," *Novoe russkoe slovo*, October 17, 1967, 2, 6; Lekhovich, *Belye protiv krasnykh*, 317.

29. "V sem'e general Millera," *Vozrozhdenie*, October 8, 1937, 5.

30. Ibid.

31. Wilmers, *The Eitingons*, 242; Bugrov, *Nadezhda Plevitskaia*, 61.

32. "V sem'e general Millera," *Vozrozhdenie*, October 8, 1937, 5.

33. Grey, *Le général meurt à minuit*, 213.

34. Roches Report, February 8, 1938.

35. AN, Panthéon, F/7/15976/1, Folder "Miller procès de la Plevitskaia enlèvement du général Miller" (Paris police report, September 24, 1937, on Miller's disappearance); Roches Report, February 8, 1938. Miller arrived at ROVS headquarters at 10:30 a.m. according to a statement by Vasily Asmolov: APP, GA S10 Dossier Skobline, Case No. 59638 ("Declaration de M. Asmoloff," September 23, 1937; henceforth "Declaration de M. Asmoloff," September 23, 1937).

36. Roches Report, February 8, 1938.

37. Ibid.

38. Boreiko, "General Skoblin," 107n20.

39. Rozhdestvensky, "Tridtsatiletie pokhishcheniia Generala E. K. Millera," 2, 6.

40. A. P., "Pamiati general E. K. Millera," *Russkaia mysl'*, October 9, 1962.

41. "Erdely Commission Report," February 4, 1938.

42. Plevitskaya told the police that she and Skoblin had left the hotel later than they did, because she wanted to convince investigators that they had arrived at the Serdechny restaurant closer to noon. The first time she was questioned by police,

she said that Skoblin returned from the garage at 11:30 a.m. and waited for her to emerge from the hotel at around 12:10 p.m., and that they arrived at the restaurant at 12:15 p.m. APP, CBFB GA S10 Dossier Skobline ("Audition de la Dame SKO-BLINE, September 24, 1937"; henceforth "Audition de la Dame SKOBLINE," September 24, 1937).

43. "Zagadochnoe ischeznovenie gen. E. K. Millera," *Poslednie novosti*, September 26, 1937, 1.

44. APP, GA S10 Dossier Skobline, Case No. 59638 ("Audition de EPSTEIN," September 24, 1937; henceforth "Audition de EPSTEIN," September 24, 1937).

45. "Audition de EPSTEIN," September 24, 1937.

46. Ibid.

47. Burtsev, *Bol'shevitskie gangstery v Parizhe*, 19.

48. N. P. V., "Delo Plevitskoi," *Poslednie novosti*, October 15, 1938.

49. Roches Report, February 8, 1938. A French businessman told the police that he had seen a man who looked like Miller in a car of a foreign make, with two others, one of whom he identified as Skoblin. "Zagadochnoe ischeznovenie gen. E. K. Millera," *Poslednie novosti*, September 28, 1937, 1.

50. Burtsev, *Bol'shevitskie gangstery v Parizhe*, 78; Lekhovich, *Belye protiv krasnykh*, 312.

51. "Skoblin i razstrel' Tukhachevskogo i Putny," *Vozrozhdenie*, October 22, 1937, 13.

52. Primakov et al., *Ocherki istorii rossiiskoi vneshnei razvedki*, vol. 3, 118.

53. Orlov, *March of Time*, 196. The Poliansky letter contains a similar description but assumes that Skoblin was oblivious to the plot before entering the building. A number of other sources—varying in reliability—offer similar narratives about Miller's abduction but include other details. See, for example, Burtsev, *Bol'shevitskie gangstery v Parizhe*, 22; Kolpakidi and Prokhorov, *KGB*, 68, 118; Costello and Tsarev, *Deadly Illusions*, 471n14; Mlechin, *Alibi dlia velikoi pevitsy*, 142–43; and Sudoplatov, *Special Tasks*, 36–37, 91. A witness (reportedly a member of the Society of Gallipolians) who was standing on a balcony overlooking 41 Montmorency at the time of Miller's abduction claimed that he saw Skoblin and Miller outside the building with a large, tall man. Skoblin motioned Miller to enter the building, the three men entered, and that was the last this witness saw of them. Lekhovich, *Belye protiv krasnykh*, 312; Rozhdestvensky, "Tridtsatiletie pokhishcheniia Generala E. K. Millera," 2, 6.

54. "Delo Plevitskaia," *Novaia zaria*, November 3, 1938, 2.

55. Ribet, *Plaidoirie*, 29; Orlov, *March of Time*, 195.

56. For accounts of Miller's imprisonment and execution based on documents preserved in NKVD files, see Mikhailov, "ROVS terpit porazhenie," 12; B. Kraevskii, "Pokhishchenie Generala E. K. Millera," *Vestnik Russkogo Khristianskogo Dvizheniia* 178 (1998): 159–82; Goldin and Long, "Resistance and Retribution," 19–40; and Gennady Barabtarlo, "Life's Sequel," *Nabokov Studies* 8 (2004): 1–21. Text of several of Miller's letters written in the NKVD prison and of the decrees

ordering Miller's conviction and execution are published in A. F. Kiselev, ed., *Politicheskaia istoriia russkoi emigratsii, 1920–1940 gg. dokumenty i materialy* (Moscow: Vlados, 1999), 50–60; Kraevskii, 162–80; Barabtarlo, 5–18; and Kolpakidi and Prokhorov, *KGB*, 65–85. Barabtarlo writes (p. 18) that the three documents pertaining to Miller's trial and execution

> are paper-clipped together with both Miller's and Skoblin's letters and put in a blue file within the general folder, which is inscribed, "This material was shown to comrade Abakumov [Soviet Minister of State Security] on March 5, 1949," signed illegibly. All documents pertaining to the case, including the interrogation records, etc., were destroyed after Miller's murder, and the surviving ones translated here were attached to an entirely different case.

One of the more fantastical narratives of the Miller abduction is outlined in *Sinfonia en Rojo Mayor* by Dr. Iosif M. Landovskii (or Landowsky). The book's contents and Landovskii himself are almost certainly fabrications. The book manuscript reportedly was found on Landovskii's body shortly after he died on a Soviet battlefield during World War II and was published in Spain in 1953: Iosif M. Landovskii, *Sinfonia en Rojo Mayor* (Madrid: Editorial NOS, 1953). According to this source, Landovskii was the NKVD doctor who injected Miller. However, in this version of the abduction story, instead of being shipped to Leningrad on the *Maria Ulyanova*, Miller was first flown to Spain and then placed on board another Soviet ship for Leningrad. The book features the text of alleged conversations between Landovskii and Miller. Finally, Miller was to have died when Landovskii gave him a lethal injection on board the ship, apparently to spare him a painful death.

57. "Gen. Miller zhiv i nakhoditsia v SSSR," *Novaia zaria*, October 1937, 2.

58. Translation by Barabtarlo, "Life's Sequel," 6.

59. The Soviet secret police had used this strategy before. For instance, in 1923, the OGPU captured former Ukrainian nationalist general Yurko Tutyunnik in a TREST-style operation and forced him to write letters to Ukrainian nationalists exiled abroad "saying that their struggle was hopeless and that he had aligned himself irrevocably with the Soviet cause." Tutyunnik was eventually executed. Andrew and Mitrokhin, *The Mitrokhin Archive*, 42–43.

60. Mikhailov, "ROVS terpit porazhenie," 12.

61. David Satter, *It Was a Long Time Ago, and It Never Happened Anyway: Russia and the Communist Past* (New Haven, CT: Yale University Press, 2012), 56.

62. Roches Report, February 8, 1938. The Poliansky letter contains a very different and implausible explanation of what happened at this point, which is not surprising, given that it was reportedly based on Plevitskaya's perspective: "Skoblin went to Caroline's, picked up his wife, and they drove to North Station. Along the way he told her, 'I think Miller was kidnapped.' His lips were trembling, and he had lost his composure. He asked Plevitskaya to go to the train platform alone, while he collected himself."

63. "Zagadochnoe ischeznovenie gen. E. K. Millera," *Poslednie novosti*, September 26, 1937, 1.

64. Grey, *Le général meurt à minuit*, 218; "Zagadochnoe ischeznovenie gen. E. K. Millera," *Poslednie novosti*, September 26, 1937, 1.

65. "Sobytiia 22-go sentiabria 1937 goda," Erdely Commission Report, February 4, 1938.

66. Grey, *Le général meurt à minuit*, 18. The author of the Poliansky letter claims that Plevitskaya suffered an attack of colitis.

67. Roches Report, February 8, 1938.

68. Ibid., 4; Bugrov, *Nadezhda Plevitskaia*, 67; APP, GA S10 Dossier Skobline, Case No. 59638 (police report, October 1, 1937). After Plevitskaya's trial, Kussonsky moved to Brussels; when the Germans occupied the city, they arrested and imprisoned him, and he died in prison in August 1941. One Russian researcher alleged that, under duress, Kussonsky had confessed his ties to Soviet intelligence, which led to his death. Simbirtsev, *Spetssluzhby pervykh let SSSR*, 182–83, 190.

69. APP, GA S10 Dossier Skobline, Case No. 59638 ("Audition de sieur GRIGOUL Pierre," September 23, 1937; henceforth "Audition de sieur GRIGOUL Pierre," September 23, 1937).

70. "Sobytiia 22-go sentiabria 1937 goda," Erdely Commission Report, February 4, 1938.

71. Ibid.

72. Ibid.

73. AN, Panthéon, F/7/15976/1, Folder "Miller procès de la Plevitskaia enlèvement du général Miller" (Gregory Troshin's statement to André Roches, September 23, 1937; hereafter, "TROCHINE Grégoire Statement," September 23, 1937).

74. "Sobytiia 22-go sentiabria 1937 goda," Erdely Commission Report, February 4, 1938.

75. "V sem'e generala Millera," *Vozrozhdenie*, October 8, 1937, 5.

76. "TROCHINE Grégoire Statement," September 23, 1937.

77. APP, GA S10 Dossier Skobline, Case No. 59638 ("Nouvelle audition de Mme. Skobline," September 24, 1937; henceforth "Nouvelle audition de Mme. Skobline," September 24, 1937).

78. Grey, *Le général meurt à minuit*, 221.

79. "Nouvelle audition de Mme. Skobline," September 24, 1937.

80. "TROCHINE Grégoire Statement," September 23, 1937.

81. Grey, *Le général meurt à minuit*, 221.

82. "Declaration de M. Asmoloff," September 23, 1937.

83. Ibid.; Roches Report, February 8, 1938.

84. Roches Report, February 8, 1938.

85. Ibid.

86. Ibid; N. P. V., "Ischeznovenie gen. E. K. Millera," *Poslednie novosti*, November 26, 1937.

87. Miller, *Shanghai on the Métro*, 136.

88. Bugrov, *Nadezhda Plevitskaia*, 67.

89. "Sobytiia 22-go sentiabria 1937 goda," Erdely Commission Report, February 4, 1938.

90. Roches Report, February 8, 1938.

91. "Declaration de M. Asmoloff," September 23, 1937.

92. Matsylev's testimony about what he had told Skoblin changed somewhat. Initially, he said he had told Skoblin that Miller had vanished, but at Plevitskaia's trial, he said only that they were worried about him. "Sobytiia 22-go sentiabria 1937 goda," Erdely Commission Report, February 4, 1938; N. P. V., "Protsess N. V. Plevitskoi," *Poslednie novosti*, December 8, 1938, 2.

93. "Sobytiia 22-go sentiabria 1937 goda," Erdely Commission Report, February 4, 1938.

94. "Nouvelle audition de Mme. Skobline," September 24, 1937.

95. N. P. V., "Zagadochnoe ischeznovenie gen. E. K. Millera," *Poslednie novosti*, October 2, 1937, 4.

96. "Sobytiia 22-go sentiabria 1937 goda," Erdely Commission Report, February 4, 1938.

97. N. P. V., "Protsess N. V. Plevitskoi," *Poslednie novosti*, December 8, 1938, 2.

98. "Sobytiia 22-go sentiabria 1937 goda," Erdely Commission Report, February 4, 1938.

99. This section is based on testimony by Kussonsky and Kedrov about their confrontation with Skoblin as outlined in "Sobytiia 22-go sentiabria 1937 goda," Erdely Commission Report, February 4, 1938. See also a transcript of the conversation in Ig. Opishnia, "Chto izvestno o pokhishchenii generala Millera," *Russkoe voskresenie*, July 14, 1955.

100. Polkovnik S. Matsylev, "Raz'iasnenie," *Chasovoi*, no. 198 (October 20, 1937): 20.

CHAPTER 8

1. N. P. V., "Protsess N. V. Plevitskoi," *Poslednie novosti*, December 8, 1938, 2.

2. "Sobytiia 22-go sentiabria 1937 goda," Erdely Commission Report, February 4, 1938.

3. Ibid.

4. Ibid.

5. "Nouvelle audition de Mme. Skobline," September 24, 1937.

6. "Sobytiia 22-go sentiabria 1937 goda," Erdely Commission Report, February 4, 1938.

7. Ibid.

8. Roches Report, February 8, 1938.

9. "Sobytiia 22-go sentiabria 1937 goda," Erdely Commission Report, February 4, 1938.

10. One witness, Boris Lentz, swore that on rue du Colisée at around 2:30 a.m., he saw a man, possibly Skoblin, try opening car doors until he found an unlocked car, hopped into it, started it up, and drove in the direction of avenue des Champs-Élysées. This would have taken him in the wrong direction down a one-way street. When Lentz read in the papers about Miller, he contacted the police, although his testimony was not used at trial, because investigators ultimately concluded that his report was inaccurate. "Zagadochnoe ischeznovenie gen. E. K. Millera," *Poslednie novosti*, September 25, 1937, 4.

11. Ibid.

12. Roches Report, February 8, 1938.

13. Grey, *Le général meurt à minuit*, 245–46.

14. "Csarist Is Arrested as Soviet Spy; He Confessed, Say Paris Gestapo," *New York Times*, August 5, 1942, 2.

15. Orlov, *March of Time*, 201–2; Costello and Tsarev, *Deadly Illusions*, 297, 314, 471n14, and 472n15.

16. Orlov, *March of Time*, 207–8.

17. N. P. V., "Ischeznovenie gen. E. K. Millera," *Poslednie novosti*, October 28, 1937, 1.

18. Grey, *Le général meurt à minuit*, 239; the article appeared in the October 15, 1937, issue of *Gringoire*, in the section titled "Repetez-le."

19. "Gen. Miller zhiv i nakhoditsia v SSSR," *Novaia zaria*, October 1937, 2. Another unsubstantiated story about Skoblin's life in the USSR was outlined in Grey, *Le général meurt à minuit*, 240: In 1946, Polish communist agents who were arrested in Belgium reportedly confirmed that Skoblin passed through Spain and then onto the USSR, and that he had once served as a liaison agent between the Pasionaria, Isidora Dolores Ibárruri Gómez, a communist politician and Republican leader during the Spanish Civil War, and Red general El Campesino.

20. Elisabeth K. Poretsky, *Our Own People: A Memoir of "Ignace Reiss" and His Friends* (Ann Arbor: University of Michigan Press, 1970), 193.

21. Alexandrov, *The Tukhachevsky Affair*, 179–80.

22. Victor Serge, *The Case of Comrade Tulayev*, translated from the French by Roger Trase (London: Journeyman, 1993).

23. Mikhail Kol'tsov, "Bumagi Generala Foka," *Pravda*, September 29, 1937, 5; "Otkliki na ischeznovenie belogvardeiskikh generalov Millera i Skoblina," *Pravda*, September 30, 1937. In *Pravda*'s first article about the Miller kidnapping, "Ischeznovenie Belogvardeiskogo Generala Millera," published on p. 5 of the September 24, 1937, issue (no author), the Soviet press agency TASS did not include any disinformation; the article seems to be straight-up reportage.

24. Hiroaki Kuromiya and Andrzej Pepłoński, "Stalin, Espionage, and Counter-espionage," in *Stalin and Europe: Imitation and Domination, 1928–1953*, ed. Timothy Snyder and Ray Brandon (New York: Oxford University Press, 2014), 85.

25. Damaskin, *Kitty Harris*, 153.

26. Degtiarev and Kolpakidi, *Vneshniaia razvedka SSSR*, 90.

27. Primakov et al., *Ocherki istorii rossiiskoi vneshnei razvedki*, vol. 3, 119. Stanislav Glinsky, who may have been involved in the early planning of the operation, was arrested and executed in the fall of 1937, and G. Z. Besedovsky testified at Plevitskaya's trial that Grazhul, alias Beletsky, had also been killed. Antonov, "Tragediia razvedchika Glinskogo"; N. P. V., "Protsess N. V. Plevitskoi," *Poslednie novosti*, December 10, 1938. According to Volodarsky, Grazhul (Beletsky) was not executed shortly after the Miller kidnapping but was instead dismissed from the NKVD in 1946. Volodarsky, *Stalin's Agent*, 268.

28. Kern, *A Death in Washington*, 52.

29. Primakov et al., *Ocherki istorii rossiiskoi vneshnei razvedki*, vol. 3, 118.

30. Ibid.; Costello and Tsarev, *Deadly Illusions*, 297, 299, 314, 471n14, and 472n15; Sudoplatov, *Special Tasks*, 37; Mlechin, *Set'-Moskva-OGPU-Parizh*, 193; Kolpakidi and Prokhorov, *KGB*, 69; Andrew and Gordievsky, *KGB*, 163–64. In May 1938 correspondence to Shpigelglas, Orlov referred to a plane he had chartered for whisking away FARMER (Skoblin's code name). Costello and Tsarev, *Deadly Illusions*, 472n15. However, after he defected, Orlov never admitted his role in the operation in his interview with U.S. officials or in his memoirs. (In his memoirs, Orlov wrote that, instead of being flown to Spain, Skoblin, in November 1937, "was smuggled aboard a Soviet cargo ship bound for Leningrad." Orlov did not reveal Skoblin's fate after that. Orlov, *March of Time*, 207.)

31. Nikolai Petrov, "Konets agenta '13,'" *Moskovskie novosti*, no. 86 (December 17–24, 1995): 9; Nikolai Petrov, "Master individual'nogo terrora: Portret Eitingona, kollegi Sudoplatova," *Novaia gazeta*, February 26, 2014; Bugrov, *Nadezhda Plevitskaia*, 60; Gasparian, *General Skoblin*, 358.

32. Petrov, "Konets agenta '13'"; Volodarsky, *Stalin's Agent*, 270.

33. Volodarsky, *Stalin's Agent*, 270–72.

34. Ibid., 271; Costello and Tsarev, *Deadly Illusions*, 430, 472n15.

35. Volodarsky, *Stalin's Agent*, 271.

36. The text of the letter is published in at least four publications: Kiselev, ed., *Politicheskaia istoriia russkoi emigratsii, 1920–1940 gg.*, 60–61; Arkady Vaksberg, *Toxic Politics: The Secret History of the Kremlin's Poison Laboratory* (Santa Barbara, CA: ABC-CLIO, 2011), 53–54; Kraevskii, "Pokhishchenie generala E. K. Millera," 167–68; and Barabtarlo, "Life's Sequel," 8–9. The English translation of Skoblin's letter is Barabtarlo's. Comrade Stakh's identity has not been revealed. Volodarsky (p. 628 n. 136) and Vaksberg (p. 53) think that it could have been Stanislav Glinsky, who might have once been Skoblin's case officer.

37. The USSR was technically created in 1922, not 1917, the year of the Bolshevik Revolution. However, for many Soviet citizens, this distinction was immaterial. Apparently Skoblin felt the same.

38. Kraevskii, "Pokhishchenie generala E. K. Millera," 167; Barabtarlo, "Life's Sequel," 7–8; Vaksberg, *Toxic Politics*, 53; V. Naumov and A. Kraiushkin, "Zakliuchennyi pod nomerom 110," *Moskovskie novosti*, no. 63 (760) (December 1994): 20.

39. Petrov, "Konets agenta '13,'" 9; Petrov, "Ubiistvo Ignatiia Reisa," *Moskovskie novosti*, no. 63, September 17–24, 1995, 21.

40. Irma Kudrova, *The Death of a Poet: The Last Days of Marina Tsvetaeva* (New York: Overlook Duckworth, 2004), 20.

41. Ibid., 220.

42. Ibid., 72–92; Schlögel, *Moscow 1937*, 476–77.

43. Schlögel, *Moscow 1937*, 515.

44. Ibid., 513.

CHAPTER 9

1. Roches Report, February 8, 1938.

2. Malcolm Anderson, *In Thrall to Political Change: Police and Gendarmerie in France* (Oxford: Oxford University Press, 2011), 174. The type of investigation that was used in the Miller/Plevitskaya case was formally called a "Commission Rogatoire," which was led by an examining magistrate (*juge d'instruction*), who was based in the prosecutor's office. The examining magistrate ensures that the evidence collected by investigators is accurate and thus makes it more likely to be upheld by a trial judge.

3. Grey, *Le général meurt à minuit*, 151.

4. "Sobytiia 22-go sentiabria 1937 goda," Erdely Commission Report, February 4, 1938.

5. Grey, *Le général meurt à minuit*, 151.

6. APP, GA S10 Dossier Skobline, Case No. 59638 ("Audition de Mme. KOUDRATIEFF épouse Grigoul," September 24, 1937).

7. APP, GA S10 Dossier Skobline, Case No. 59638 ("Audition de sieur GRIGOUL Pierre," September 23, 1937; henceforth "Audition de sieur GRIGOUL Pierre," September 23, 1937).

8. "Zagadochnoe ischeznovenie gen. E. K. Millera," *Poslednie novosti*, September 24, 1937, 1.

9. Whether Chekunov, who was born in Russia in 1875 and settled in France in 1926, ever had formal medical training is unclear. According to Paris police files, he obtained drugs illegally and was practicing illegally. APP, GA S10 Dossier Skobline, Case No. 59638 (Paris Police biography of "TSCHEKOUNOFF Iwan").

10. "Zagadochnoe ischeznovenie gen. E. K. Millera," *Poslednie novosti*, September 27, 1937, 1.

11. The Poliansky letter, February 12, 1939 (see note 17 in chapter 7).

12. Mlechin, *Set'-Moskva-OGPU-Parizh*, 191.

13. "Nouvelle audition de Mme. Skobline," September 24, 1937.

14. Grey, *Le général meurt à minuit*, 152; Ginor and Remez, "Her Son, the Atomic Scientist," 40.

15. Grey, *Le général meurt à minuit*, 152.

16. According to one account, before dropping her off at the Society of Gallipolians, Raigorodsky drove Plevitskaya to Église d'Auteuil, a church located at 4 rue Corot—near Montmorency Boulevard. She left the car and was approached by two men who were unknown to Raigorodsky. He overheard one of them say in Russian, "Don't worry, Nadezhda Vasilievna, everything will be fine. And Russia won't forget you." Prianishnikov, *Nezrimaia pautina*, 285–86; HIA, Prianishnikov Papers, Box 3, Folder "Skoblin and Plevitskaia 1 (biographical information)" (report about Prianishnikov's meeting with journalist Andrei Sedykh on October 6, 1976). In 1937, Raigorodsky apparently confided what he had overheard only to Sedykh. Raigorodsky made Sedykh promise not to reveal his secret. At their 1976 meeting, sometime after Raigorodsky's death, Sedykh told Raigorodsky's secret to Prianishnikov, who published it in his book.

The second account is outlined in the February 1939 Poliansky letter (see earlier citation). According to this account, once they were alone again in their hotel room on the night of September 22, Skoblin told Plevitskaya everything that had happened that day. They agreed that, if something unexpected occurred, an NKVD operative, Petya Khramov, would serve as their go-between and would meet Plevitskaya opposite Caroline's in two days around 10:00 a.m. This meeting happened when "R." (presumably Raigorodsky) was driving Plevitskaya to the Society of Gallipolians and Plevitskaya spotted NKVD operative Petya Khramov at his post, near Caroline's dress shop. R. drove them around, and at this point, Khramov told her that Skoblin had gone up to Tretyakov's apartment after fleeing ROVS's headquarters. Tretyakov then drove Skoblin to the Soviet embassy. Plevitskaya asked Khramov to take her to the embassy, but he refused because it was under tight surveillance. The Poliansky letter is the earliest piece of evidence supporting the theory that Tretyakov had hidden Skoblin in his apartment. It also corroborates Alexander Orlov's narrative in *March of Time* about how Skoblin hid in the Soviet embassy for a time after Miller's kidnapping.

17. The narrative about Plevitskaya's visit on September 24 to the Society of Gallipolians and subsequent police interrogation and arrest is based on "Zagadochnoe ischeznovenie gen. E. K. Millera," *Poslednie novosti*, September 25, 1937, 1; and "Pokhishchenie gen. E. K. Millera," *Vozrozhdenie*, October 8, 1937, 7.

18. AN, Panthéon, F/7/15976/1, Folder "Miller procès de la Plevitskaia enlèvement du général Miller" (police report, September 24, 1937).

19. "V sem'e generala Millera," *Vozrozhdenie*, October 8, 1937, 5.

20. Wilmers, *The Eitingons*, 250.

21. "Zagadochnoe ischeznovenie gen. E. K. Millera," *Poslednie novosti*, September 26, 1937, 1.

22. Ibid.

23. Roches Report, February 8, 1938.

24. The materials used for this section include copies of two statements made by Plevitskaya at her interrogation on September 24, 1937; a statement made by Epstein on September 24; and a summary of the confrontation between the two

of them on September 24. "Audition de la Dame SKOBLINE," September 24, 1937; "Nouvelle audition de Mme. Skobline," September 24, 1937; "Audition de Epstein," September 24, 1937; and "Confrontation between M. Epstein and Mme. Plevitskaya," September 24, 1937. All four reports are in APP, GA S10 Dossier Skobline, Case No. 59638, Folder "enlèvement général Miller sans derogation."

25. "Zagadochnoe ischeznovenie gen. E. K. Millera," *Poslednie novosti*, September 26, 1937, 1.

26. "Nouvelle Audition de Mme. Skobline," September 24, 1937. Depending on the source, Zarubin's name is spelled differently, including "Tserulian."

27. Ibid.

28. Ribet, *Plaidoirie*, 12.

29. "Zagadochnoe ischeznovenie gen. E. K. Millera," *Poslednie novosti*, September 26, 1937, 1.

30. "Zagadochnoe ischeznovenie gen. E. K. Millera," *Poslednie novosti*, September 25, 1937, 1; "Zagadochnoe ischeznovenie gen. E. K. Millera," *Poslednie novosti*, September 26, 1937, 1.

31. The role of accomplices in the committing of crimes is defined in Article 121-7 of the current French Criminal Code and is nearly identical to that found in Article 60 of the existing code in 1937: "The accomplice to a felony or a misdemeanor is the person who knowingly, by aiding and abetting, facilitates its preparation or commission" (official French government translation of the French Criminal Code: www.legifrance.gouv.fr/content/download/1957/13715/.../Code_33 .pdf). In Article 121-6 of the French Criminal Code, an accomplice "is punishable as a perpetrator." French prosecutors and judges were in a bind when it came to prosecuting Plevitskaya because Miller and Skoblin were never found. They partly circumvented the problem by indicting (and later convicting) Skoblin in absentia as the principal perpetrator of the crime. However, they were also challenged by the fact that investigators lacked information about the planning of Miller's kidnapping. "*The act of complicity* must be positive and intentional, and occur at the time of the offence. This poses particular problems in the area of aiding and abetting. The requirement of a positive act means that the accomplice is actively engaged in facilitating the offence. Where there is only passive acquiescence, then there is no liability." John Bell, Sophie Boyron, and Simon Whittaker, *Principles of French Law* (Oxford: Oxford University Press, 2008), 231.

Another obstacle for the prosecution was proving intent. Bell, Boyron, and Whittaker (p. 222) state, "The deliberate intention to commit a wrong is labeled *dol* in French and involves both knowledge that something is prohibited and yet the deliberate willingness to bring about the prohibited actions. . . . An imprecise intention exists where the offender wishes to commit the actions in question but either is uncertain of the result which will be achieved by them or finds that it is more serious than anticipated. In both cases, French law treats the results as intended because the acts which led to them were intended." In the Plevitskaya case, French investigators and prosecutors tried to overcome these obstacles by arguing that Plevitskaya had deliberately lied in her statements to police about her actions on September 22, 1937, and that her awareness of and involvement in Skoblin's political activities over the years set the pattern for her involvement in the Miller kidnapping.

32. "Po delu ob ischeznovenii gen. Millera oprosheno 150 lits," *Novaia zaria*, October 20, 1937, 3.

33. "Zagadochnoe ischeznovenie gen. E. K. Millera," *Poslednie novosti*, September 26, 1937, 1.

34. BA, Filonenko Papers, Box 11, Folder "Case Files—Plevitskaia Skoblin, N. V. 1." (copy of a typed brief by Maurice Ribet to Judge Pierre Marchat, undated).

35. Information about the Petite-Roquette comes from the website "La Roquette," https://sites.google.com/site/laroquette/la-petite-roquette (accessed August 10, 2013); and from I. L. Frenkel', "Poslednye dni Plevitskoi," *Novoe russkoe slovo*, August 23, 1942. When Paris came under Nazi occupation, female resistance fighters were imprisoned in the Petite-Roquette. Finally, in 1974, the facility was demolished.

36. BA, Filonenko Papers, Box 11, Folder "Case files—Plevitskaia Skoblin, N. V. 2" (copy of letter from Maximilian Filonenko to Pierre Marchat, February 24, 1938).

37. APP, General Skoblin Dossier Progisoire 59638 (Note no. C/11, police intelligence report on ties between Plevitskaya, Basile Bezzoubikoff, and Mme. Timofeef-Peters, January 4, 1938).

38. HIA, Volkov Papers, Box 18, Folder 1 ("'Maria Ul'ianova' vernulas' v Gavr," *Novaia zaria*, no date [ca. July 1938], 2).

39. Jean Dax, "Skobline avait inscrit dans la bible verte les preuves de sa culpabilité," *Le Petit Journal*, November 8, 1937, 1.

40. Vaksberg, *Toxic Politics*, 54–55.

CHAPTER 10

1. In 1937, foreigners, who made up nearly 8 percent of France's total population, committed 21 percent of murders. Johnston, *New Mecca*, 144. Also that year, more than fifteen politically motivated violent attacks occurred, several of which were perpetrated by foreigners. Rosenberg, *Policing Paris*, 100.

2. "Zagadochnoe ischeznovenie gen. E. K. Millera," *Poslednie novosti*, September 26, 1937, 5.

3. Johnston, *New Mecca*, 142. Chautemp's premiership lasted to March 1938. He was replaced by Socialist politician Léon Blum. Blum served until April 1938 and was succeeded by Radical Party politician Édouard Daladier, who left office in March 1940.

4. Ibid., 145.

5. "Zagadochnoe ischeznovenie gen. E. K. Millera," *Poslednie novosti*, September 30, 1937, 1.

6. "Obrashchenie N. N. Millera k prezidentu respubliki," *Poslednie novosti*, October 16, 1937, 1.

7. "N. V. Plevitskaia podderzhivaet obrashchenie N. N. Millera k prezidentu Lebrenu," *Poslednie novosti*, October 17, 1937, 1.

8. Sudoplatov, *Special Tasks*, 36–37.

9. "Le Général Miller A Disparu Depuis Mercredi," *Le Journal*, September 24, 1937, 1.

10. Roches Report, February 8, 1938.

11. According to one source, Daladier tried in vain to convince Léon Blum—the former Socialist prime minister who was now vice premier—to intervene and prevent the *Maria Ulyanova* from leaving French waters. Paillole, *Services spécialaux, 1935–1945*, 50.

12. In 1937, there were two Soviet ambassadors to France, which created some confusion. Vladimir Potemkin had been the ambassador from November 1934 to April 1937, when he was recalled to Moscow, five months before Miller was kidnapped, to fill the position of assistant commissar for foreign affairs. The Soviet ambassador at the time of Miller's kidnapping was Yakov Surits. "Potemkin Withdrawn," *Montreal Gazette*, April 5, 1937.

13. Lekhovich, *Belye protiv krasnykh*, 313.

14. BA, Filonenko Papers, Box 11, Folder "Plevitskaia-Skoblin, N. V. (clippings: trial)" ("L'Enquête Piétine . . . ," unnamed French newspaper, ca. September 30, 1937).

15. "Delo Plevitskoi," *Novaia zaria*, November 3, 1938, 2.

16. Alfred Morain, *The Underworld of Paris: Secrets of the Sûreté* (New York: E. P. Dutton, 1931), 165.

17. Ibid.

18. Flanner, *Paris Was Yesterday*, 164.

19. Tastevin Report, December 14, 1937.

20. Comments by Levitov, Vozovik, Turkul, and Erdely are outlined in Ribet, *Plaidoirie*.

21. "Zagadochnoe ischeznovenie gen. E. K. Millera," *Poslednie novosti*, September 30, 1937, 1.

22. AN, Panthéon, F/7/15976/1, Folder "Miller procès de la Plevitskaia enlèvement du général Miller" (Paris police report, October 4, 1937, about Boris Solonevich).

23. Tastevin Report, December 14, 1937.

24. Jacqueline Hodgson, *French Criminal Justice: A Comparative Account of the Investigation and Prosecution of Crime in France* (Oxford and Portland, OR: Hart Publishing, 2006), 21.

25. Ibid., 221.

26. Andrew West et al., *The French Legal System: An Introduction* (London: Foumat Publishing, 1992), 259.

27. Hodgson, *French Criminal Justice*, 24.

28. "Pokhishchenie gen. E. K. Millera," *Vozrozhdenie*, November 12, 1937.

29. Russian émigré Count de Witte claimed that he overheard Sergei Tretyakov say that Filonenko had agreed to represent Plevitskaya after he came into contact with a Soviet agent, who presumably promised him a salary for his defense work. Grey, *Le général meurt à minuit*, 227. But why would Tretyakov, who was an NKVD agent, make such a careless remark?

A second account that seems to support the theory that Filonenko was on the Soviets' payroll is in the Poliansky letter. According to its author, Valya, Plevitskaya had received a letter when she was in jail from an author identified only as "POSL" (short for "embassy" in Russian), advising her to invite "Max" (Filonenko) as her defense attorney.

On November 11, 1937, Filonenko reported to the police and newspapers that his apartment had been robbed early that morning, although the thief failed to steal anything valuable. Paul Rachard, "Et voici un telephone qui cess de fonctionner," *Le Petit Journal*, November 12, 1937, A. It is plausible that a Soviet operative had broken into his apartment to install listening devices, as Mireille Abbiate had done in Miller's apartment in 1934. If this was the case, then it suggests that Filonenko was not a Soviet operative.

30. Andrei Sedykh, "Plevitskaia bol'she ne verit Skoblinu," *Novoe russkoe slovo*, October 10, 1937.

31. Belin, *Trente ans de Sûreté Nationale*, 248.

32. BA, Filonenko Papers, Box 11, Folder "Case Files—Plevitskaia Skoblin, N. V. 1" ("La Lettre de Miller").

33. "Ischeznovenie gen. E. K. Millera," *Poslednie novosti*, December 7, 1937.

34. BA, Filonenko Papers, Box 11, Folder "Case Files—Plevitskaia Skoblin, N. V. 2" (copy of letter from Filonenko to Marchat, January 26, 1938).

35. "Une demonstration 'academique' et une confrontation pour rien," *L'Oeuvre*, March 2, 1938.

36. See, for example, BA, Filonenko Papers, Box 11, Folder "Case Files—Plevitskaia Skoblin, N. V. 3" (copy of defense memorandum by Filonenko, December 7, 1937).

37. Unless otherwise noted, the information on Plevitskaya's interrogations on October 1 and 2 comes from Ribet, *Plaiadoire*, 31; "Zagadochnoe ischeznovenie gen. E. K. Millera," *Poslednie novosti*, October 2, 1937, 1; "Zagadochnoe ischeznovenie gen. E. K. Millera," *Poslednie novosti*, October 3, 1937, 1; and "Po delu ob ischeznovenii gen. Millera oprosheno 150 lits," *Novaia zaria*, October 20, 1937, 3.

38. "Metr Ribet o vinovnosti Plevitskoi," *Vozrozhdenie*, November 5, 1937, 5.

39. "Zagadochnoe ischeznovenie gen. E. K. Millera," *Poslednie novosti*, October 2, 1937, 1.

40. AN, Panthéon, F/7/15976/1, Folder "Miller procès de la Plevitskaia enlèvement du général Miller" (police report, October 14, 1937).

41. "Zagadochnoe ischeznovenie gen. E. K. Millera," *Poslednie novosti*, October 2, 1937, 1.

42. Ribet, *Plaiadoire*, 31.

43. "Zagadochnoe ischeznovenie gen. E. K. Millera," *Poslednie novosti*, October 3, 1937, 1; "Zagadochnoe ischeznovenie gen. E. K. Millera," *Poslednie novosti*, October 7, 1937, 1.

44. "Pokhishchenie gen. E. K. Miller," *Vozrozhdenie*, October 8, 1937, 1.

45. BA, Filonenko Papers, Box 11, Folder "Case Files—Plevitskaia Skoblin, N. V. 2" (copy of letter from Filonenko to Marchat, October 2, 1937).

46. The photo was featured in the Russian television documentary, "Nadezhda Plevitskaia—Krasnaia-Belaia istoria," produced by RusNasledie documentary film company, 2009, http://www.youtube.com (accessed February 10, 2012).

47. N. P. V., "Ischeznovenie gen. E. K. Millera," *Poslednie novosti*, November 6, 1937, 1.

48. APP, GA S10 Dossier Skobline, Case No. 59638 (police report, October 28, 1937).

49. N. P. V., "Ischeznovenie gen. E. K. Millera," *Poslednie novosti*, October 28, 1937, 1; Albert Ch.-Morice, "La Disparition du Général Miller: Où est question d'une bible verte . . . ," *Le Journal*, October 28, 1937.

50. K. L., "Ischeznovenie gen. E. K. Millera," *Poslednie novosti*, November 10, 1937, 2; N. P. V., "Ischeznovenie gen. E. K. Millera," *Poslednie novosti*, January 5, 1938, 1.

51. N. P. V., "Ischeznovenie gen. E. K. Millera," *Poslednie novosti*, November 6, 1937, 1; Jean Dax, "Skobline avait inscrit dans la bible verte les preuves de sa culpabilité," *Le Petit Journal*, November 8, 1937, 1.

52. BA, Filonenko Papers, Box 11, Folder "Case Files—Plevitskaia Skoblin, N. V. 2" (copy of letter from Filonenko to Marchat, December 2, 1937.

53. BA, Filonenko Papers, Box 11, Folder "Case Files—Plevitskaia Skoblin, N. V. 2" (copy of undated letter from Filonenko to Marchat re: the green Bible).

54. "Zagadochnoe ischeznovenie gen. E. K. Millera," *Poslednie novosti*, September 30, 1937, 2.

55. BA, Filonenko Papers, Box 11, Folder "Case Files—Plevitskaia Skoblin, N. V. 2" (Filonenko's memorandum about court hearing, addressed to Marchat, December 14, 1937).

56. Tastevin Report, December 14, 1937.

57. K. L., "Ischeznovenie gen. E. K. Millera," *Poslednie novosti*, January 5, 1938, 1.

58. AN, Panthéon, F/7/15976/1, Folder "Enlèvement de Miller successeur du général Koutiepoff No. 5" (Paris police report, January 13, 1938); N. P. V., "Ischeznovenie gen. E. K. Millera," *Poslednie novosti*, January 29, 1938.

59. N. P. V.," Ischeznovenie gen. E. K. Millera," *Poslednie novosti*, January 29, 1938, 2.

60. Ibid.

61. Ibid.

62. BA, Filonenko Papers, Box 11, Folder "Case Files—Plevitskaia Skoblin, N. V. 2" (copy of letter from Plevitskaya to the editor of *Poslednie novosti*, February 1, 1938).

63. HIA, Volkov Papers, Box 18, Folder 1 ("Gen. Miller Zhiv i nakhoditsia," *Novia zaria*, late January or early February, 1938, 2).

64. Roches Report, February 8, 1938.

65. Burtsev, *Bol'shevitskie gangstery v Parizhe*, 81.

66. Petr Savin, *Gibel' Generala Millera: Rabota GPU, "Vozhdei" i "Druzhei" po ravalu ROVS* (Paris: Imprimerie Moderne, 1939); Prianishnikov, *Nezrimaia pautina*, 313–14, 365. According to Prianishnikov, Savin and other members of ROVS's Inner Line hid documents from investigators.

67. AN, Panthéon, F/7/15976/1, Folder "Gen. Miller procès de la Plevitskaia Rapports divers et coupures de presse" (Paris police report on Captain Savine, February 25, 1938).

68. Robinson, *The White Russian Army in Exile*, 210–11.

69. Erdely Commission Report, February 4, 1938.

70. Reportage, including partial transcripts of this two-day session, appears in N. P. V., "Ischeznovenie gen. E. K. Millera," *Poslednie novosti*, March 1, 1938, 2; N. P. V., "Ischeznovenie gen. E. K. Millera," *Poslednie novosti*, March 2, 1938, 1, 2.

71. BA, Filonenko Papers, Box 11, Folder "Case Files—Plevitskaia Skoblin, N. V. 2" (copy of memorandum from Filonenko to Marchat, March 3, 1938.

72. Sedykh, "Plevitskaya pishet' iz' tiurmy . . ."

73. Ibid.

74. "Delo N. V. Plevitskoi," *Poslednie novosti*, May 13, 1938, 2.

75. Ibid.

76. AN, Panthéon, F/7/15976/1, Folder "Gen. Miller procès de la Plevitskaia Rapports divers et coupures de presse" (Paris police report on rumors about the Miller kidnapping, June 2, 1938).

77. APP, GA S10 Dossier Skobline, Case No. 59638 (Paris police memorandum on the Miller case, June 21, 1938).

78. HIA, Volkov Papers, Box 18, Folder 1 (A. S., "'Maria Ul'ianova' vernulas' v Gavr," *Novaia zaria*, ca. July 1938, 2). Apparently, parts of Plevitskaya's diary were never sold; the original diary is preserved in BA, Filonenko Papers, Box 11.

79. BA, Filonenko Papers, Box 11, Folder 'Case Files—Plevitskaia Skoblin, N. V. 1' (copy of a memorandum by Filonenko to the Prosecutor's Office, August 4, 1938).

80. "Delo Plevitskoi," *Poslednie novosti*, August 29, 1938, 2.

81. BA, Filonenko Papers, Box 11, Folder "Case Files—Plevitskaia Skoblin, N. V. 2" (copy of a memorandum from Plevitskaya's defense team to the Paris Court, August 26, 1938).

82. AN, Panthéon, F/7/15976/1, Folder "Gen. Miller procès de la Plevitskaia Rapports divers et coupures de presse" (Paris police report on the Miller case, September 6, 1938). See also N. P. V., "Delo Plevitskoi," *Poslednie novosti*, September 7, 1938, 2.

83. John Glad, *Russia Abroad: Writers, History, Politics* (Tenafly, NJ, and Washington, DC: Hermitage & Birchbark Press, 1999), 308.

84. See Julie Fette, *Exclusions: Practicing Prejudice in French Law and Medicine, 1920–1945* (Ithaca, NY: Cornell University Press, 2012), 118.

85. "Vincent de Moro-Giafferi, Lawyer, Dies; Defended 'Bluebeard' and vom Rath Killer," *New York Times*, November 23, 1956. Note that, on his stationery, the attorney spelled his last name "de Moro-Giafferri," but the *New York Times* spelled it using only one *r*.

86. Richard Davies and G. S. Smith, "D. S. Mirsky: Twenty-Two Letters (1926–34) to Salomeya Halpern; Seven Letters (1930) to Vera Suvchinskaya (Traill)," *Oxford Slavonic Papers* 30 (1997): 97.

87. N. P. V., "Delo Plevitskoi," *Poslednie novosti*, November 11, 1938, 2. Other sources reported Plevitskaya as saying that she had last seen Max Eitingon in July 1937, instead of July 1936.

88. BA, Filonenko Papers, Box 11, Folder "Case Files—Plevitskaia Skoblin, N. V. 1" (letter from Filonenko to Princess Marie of Greece, December 9, 1938; response from Princess Marie to Filonenko, December 10, 1938).

CHAPTER 11

1. Four sources were used in reconstructing Plevitskaya's trial: (1) the transcript and reportage of the trial in *Poslednie novosti*, from December 6 to 16, 1938; (2) trial reportage in *Vozrozhdenie* on December 2, 9, and 16, 1938; (3) AN, 334 AP 72 Fond Bluet (1918–1966) "Cour d'assises de la Seine . . . Mme Skobine (1938)" (the transcript of parts of Plevitskaya's trial that was produced by the Paris stenography firm, Bluet Brothers, preserved on microfilm); and (4) the minutes of Plevitskaya's trial taken by the Paris police, copies of which are filed in two places in Paris: APP, GA S10 Dossier Skobline, Case No. 59638; and AN, Panthéon, F/7/15976/1 (Enlèvement de Miller successeur du général Koutiepoff. No. 5).

2. Sarah Maza, *Violette Nozière: A Story of Murder in 1930s Paris* (Berkeley and Los Angeles: University of California Press, 2011), 232–33. Since the 1940s, French jury trials have consisted of nine jurors, but during the 1930s, twelve jurors were impaneled. At Plevitskaya's trial, jurors decided both the guilt and punishment of the accused.

3. Grey, *Le général meurt à minuit*, 125; Johnston, *New Mecca*, 145.

4. "L'Enlèvement du Général de Miller Aux Assises de la Seine," *L'Action Française*, December 6, 1938.

5. Wilmers, *The Eitingons*, 258.

6. Maurice-Ivan Sicard, *Les Crimes du Guépéou en France* (Paris: Le Bureau de Presse de l'Exposition Internationale "Le bolchévisme contre l'Europe," 1942), 17.

7. In his memoirs, former Soviet diplomat and defector Alexander Barmine wrote that Grozovskaya worked as his stenographer for a few months in 1933, and he had suspected that she was an OGPU operative. In 1937, Barmine read in the Paris newspapers about Grozovskaya's arrest, release from custody, and escape from

the authorities. See Alexander Barmine, *One Who Survived: The Life Story of a Russian under the Soviets* (New York: Putnam, 1945), 232–33.

8. Robert Danger, "Au Procès de la Plevitzkaia: Les confrontations policières continuent sans resultant," *L'Oeuvre*, December 11, 1938.

9. As noted in chapter 10, Potemkin resigned as Soviet ambassador in April 1937 and was replaced by Yakov Surits. The Soviets may have intentionally included Potemkin's name on the registration for the truck chosen specifically for Miller's abduction.

10. APP, GA S10 Dossier Skobline, Case No. 59638 (police report on Mme. Skobline's trial, December 10, 1938).

11. N. P. V., "Protsess N. V. Plevitskoi," *Poslednie novosti*, December 13, 1938, 5.

CHAPTER 12

1. I. L. Frenkel', "Poslednye dni Plevitskoi," *Novoe russkoe slovo*, August 23 and 24, 1942.

2. Anatole France, *L'Île des Pingouins* (Paris: Modern Library, 1908). The English translation used is posted on Project Gutenberg, http://www.gutenberg.org/files/1930/1930-h/1930-h.htm (accessed August 18, 2013).

3. Wilmers, *The Eitingons*, 263.

4. Benjamin F. Martin, *France in 1938* (Baton Rouge: Louisiana State University Press, 2005), 181.

5. Johnston, *New Mecca*, 146.

6. Lev Liubimov, "Plevitskaya prigovorina k 20-ti godam kotorzhnykh rabot," *Vozrozhdenie*, December 16, 1938.

7. Grey, *La général mort à minuit*, 149.

CHAPTER 13

1. Catherine Elliott, Eric Jeanpierre, and Catherine Vernon, *French Legal System*, 2nd ed. (Essex, England: Pearson Education, 2006), 111.

2. Ibid.

3. Several of Plevitskaya's letters to Filonenko are stored with her prison diary in BA, Filonenko Papers, Box 11.

4. BA, Filonenko Papers, Box 11, Folder "Prison Diaries 1937–39" (letter from V. de Moro-Giafferri to Plevitskaya, December 26, 1938).

5. The information about Franckel's interactions with Plevitskaya comes from an article he wrote in a Russian-language newspaper published in New York City; he was living in the United States during most of World War II. I. L. Frenkel',

"Poslednye dni Plevitskoi," *Novoe russkoe slovo*, August 23, 1942. I received additional biographical information about Isidore Franckel from Franckel's grandson, Philip L. Franckel, a New York attorney, and the latter's website, http://www.franckel.com. Many thanks to Philip Franckel and his father, Alexander S. Franckel (Isidore's son), for answering my queries.

6. "Delo Plevitskoi," *Poslednie novosti*, March 10, 1939, 3.

7. Robinson, *The White Russian Army in Exile*, 211.

8. For more information on these controversial letters, including reports written by General Abramov and Captain Foss in March 1939, see BA, Aleksei Petrovich Arkhangel'skii Papers, Box 3, Folder "Delo Skoblina & Plevetskoi" [*sic*].

9. Frenkel', "Poslednye dni Plevitskoi."

10. The Poliansky letter, February 12, 1939.

11. "Delo Plevitskoi," *Poslednie novosti*, March 10, 1939, 3; "Delo Plevitskoi," *Poslednie novosti*, March 22, 1939, 2.

12. Andrei Sedykh, "Plevitskaia na tiurme," *Poslednie novosti*, June 2, 1939, 3.

13. "Delo Plevitskoi," *Poslednie novosti*, May 11, 1939, 4.

14. Frenkel', "Poslednye dni Plevitskoi."

15. Sedykh, "Plevitskaia na tiurme."

16. "Delo Plevitskoi," *Poslednie novosti*, July 17, 1939, 3.

CHAPTER 14

1. In addition to Plevitskaya's prison file, the most complete account of Plevitskaya's fourteen months in the Central Prison in Rennes is found in Grey, *Le général meurt à minuit*, 157–66.

2. Archives Departementales d'Ille-et-Vilaine, Rennes, File "Vinikova Nadia (Skobline, dite la Plevitzkaïa), prisoner number: 9202" (la chemise no. 8943).

3. "Plevitskaia na katorge," *Poslednie novosti*, December 28, 1939, 3.

4. Ibid.

5. BA, Filonenko Papers, Box 11 (letter from Filonenko to Plevitskaya, December 19, 1939).

6. "Plevitskaia na katorge," 3.

7. Frenkel', "Poslednye dni Plevitskoi." Russian émigré writer Nina Berberova wrote in her memoirs that, around ten years after the singer's death, one of Plevitskaya's attorneys told her that, from her prison cell shortly before her death, Plevitskaya had "confessed everything to him—that is, that she was her husband's accomplice in the kidnapping of Miller." Berberova, *The Italics Are Mine*, 333. If Berberova has correctly recalled this conversation, then the attorney she spoke with could have been Filonenko or Franckel, with whom Plevitskaya had the strongest rapport. Unfortunately, Berberova's account cannot be corroborated. Nothing in Filonenko's papers suggests that he and Plevitskaya met after early 1939. As for Franckel, he and his family fled from Paris for the south of France in the summer

of 1940 to escape the Nazis. They lived in the United States from 1942 to 1945, returning to Paris after the city was liberated. Plevitskaya might have confessed to Franckel in 1939 or the first half of 1940, and then he might have spoken with Berberova around 1950. However, in his 1942 *Novoe russkoe slovo* article, he wrote that he was still restricted by attorney-client confidentiality, as stipulated by French law, and so was limited in what he could divulge about his clients. It is possible, though, that he no longer felt restricted by attorney-client confidentiality around eight years later and was willing to tell Berberova about Plevitskaya's confession.

8. Grey, *Le général meurt à minuit*, 159; Mikhailov, "ROVS terpit porazhenie," 12.

9. Mikhailov, "ROVS terpit porazhenie," 12.

10. Belin's narrative about his meeting with Plevitskaya appears in the French version of his memoirs, not in the English-language version. Belin, *Trente ans de Sûreté Nationale*, 248–49. Belin investigated some of France's most notorious murder cases as an officer for the Prefecture of Police and the Sûreté Générale. He was not a Nazi collaborator during the Occupation. Michel Aubouin, Arnaud Teyssier, and Jean Tulard, eds., *Histoire et Dictionnaire de la Police du Moyen Âge à Nos Jours* (Paris: Robert Laffont, 2005), 568–69. Two other sources refer to Belin's account of his 1940 meeting with Plevitskaya: Grey, *Le général meurt à minuit*, 159–61; and Prianishnikov, *Nezrimaia pautina*, 375.

11. The account that Plevitskaya gave to Belin in 1940 resembles the one outlined in the Poliansky letter of February 1939 in which Poliansky relays information that a woman named Valya said she had heard directly from Plevitskaya that same month.

12. Grey, *Le général meurt à minuit*, 162.

13. Ibid., 10.

14. Ibid., 162–63.

15. Statement signed by Dr. Porée and dated October 28, 1940; original is in Plevitskaya's prison file.

16. Letter from Feodosy and Sergei Skoblin to the director of la Prison Centrale de Rennes, dated November 25, 1940; and presumably a handwritten draft from the director dated November 26, 1940. Letters are found in Plevitskaya's prison file.

17. The note is now stored in Plevitskaya's prison file. Its author signed it simply "Grimm," with no first name. It could possibly have been the signature of Friedrich Grimm, an attorney in the German Foreign Ministry who had served as Germany's legal representative in Grynszpan's case before the boy was extradited to Germany in July 1940. It is not clear how much of Plevitskaya's prison file the Germans had confiscated. French intelligence officer Paul Paillole argues that the Germans had shown interest in Plevitskaya's death because of Skoblin's involvement in the Tukhachevsky affair. Paillole, *Services spécialaux*, 51.

18. The letter dated October 26, 1940, is located in Plevitskaya's prison file.

19. Belin, *Trente ans de Sûreté Nationale*, 251–52.

20. Vaksberg, *Toxic Politics*, 54–55.

21. Armen S. Gasparian, *OGPU protiv ROVS: Tainaia voina v Parizhe, 1924–1939 gg.* (Moscow: Veche, 2008), 185; and Gasparian, *General Skoblin*, 296.

22. Vaksberg, *Toxic Politics*, 54–55.

23. Vadim J. Birstein, *The Perversion of Knowledge: The True Story of Soviet Science* (Boulder, CO: Westview Press, 2004); Sudoplatov, *Special Tasks*, 269–70, 278–84; Vaksberg, *Toxic Politics*; and Boris Volodarsky, *The KGB's Poison Factory: From Lenin to Litvinenko* (London: Frontline Books, 2009), 32–38.

EPILOGUE

1. Kathryn S. Olmsted, "Blond Queens, Red Spiders and Neurotic Old Maids: Gender and Espionage in the Early Cold War," *Intelligence and National Security* 19, no. 1 (Spring 2004): 87.

2. I. V. Nest'ev, *Zvezdy russkoi estrady: Ocherki o russkikh estradnykh pevitsakh nachala XX veka* (Moscow: Sovetskii Kompozitor, 1974).

3. Ibid., 116.

4. "Anna Chapman Joins Putin for Spy Singalong," *The Week* (UK), July 26, 2010.

5. David Remnick, "Danse Macabre: Scandal at the Bolshoi Ballet," *New Yorker*, March 18, 2013.

6. Clifford J. Levy, "Nationalism of Putin's Era Veils Sins of Stalin's," *New York Times*, November 27, 2008.

BIBLIOGRAPHY

ARCHIVES

1. Archives nationales, Paris, France (AN).
   Archives du fichier central de la direction générale de la police, dit Fonds "Panthéon" (1880–1945): F/7/15976/1 enlèvement du général Miller
   334 AP Fonds Bluet (1918–1966)
2. Centre des archives contemporaines de Moscou (CAC) de Fontainebleau ("fonds de Moscou"), France.
3. Archives de la préfecture de police, Paris (APP).
   Dossier Affaire Koutiepoff
   GA S10 Dossier Affaire Skobline
4. Archives Departementales d'Ille-et-Vilaine, Rennes, France.
5. Bakhmeteff Archive, Rare Book and Manuscript Library, Butler Library, Columbia University, New York, New York (BA).
   Aleksei Petrovich Arkhangel'skii Papers
   Maximilian M. Filonenko Papers
   Aleksandr Vasil'evich Miakin Memoirs
6. Holy Trinity Orthodox Seminary, Jordanville, New York (HTOS).
   V. K. Abdank-Kossovskii Papers
   Ob"edinenie Chinov Kornilovskogo Udarnogo Polka Records
   Russkii Obshe-voinskii soiuz Records 1919–1986
7. Hoover Institution Archives, Stanford University, Stanford, California (HIA).
   Boris I. Nicolaevsky Collection
   Boris Prianishnikov Papers
   Boris N. Volkov Papers
   Maria Vrangel' Collection
8. State Archives of the Kursk Region (Oblast), Russia.

NEWSPAPERS OFTEN CITED

L'Action Française
L'Humanité
Le Journal
Le Matin
New York Times
Novaia zaria
Novoe russkoe slovo (New York Russian-language émigré newspaper)
L'Oeuvre
Le Petit Journal
Le Populaire
Poslednie novosti (Russian-language émigré newspaper in Paris)
Vozrozhdenie (Russian-language émigré newspaper in Paris)

BOOKS AND PERIODICALS

Aarons, Mark, and John Loftus. *Unholy Trinity: The Vatican, the Nazis, and the Swiss Banks*. Rev. ed. New York: St. Martin's, 1998.

Abramov, Nikolai. "The New Version of the 'Tukhachevsky Affair.'" *New Times*, no. 13 (March 23–April 3, 1989): 37.

Alexandrov, Victor. *The Tukhachevsky Affair*. Translated from the French by John Hewish. Englewood Cliffs, NJ: Prentice Hall, 1964.

Alexandrov, Vladimir. *The Black Russian*. New York: Atlantic Monthly Press, 2013.

Anderson, Malcolm. *In Thrall to Political Change: Police and Gendarmerie in France*. Oxford: Oxford University Press, 2011.

Andrew, Christopher, and Oleg Gordievsky. *KGB: The Inside Story of Its Foreign Operations from Lenin to Gorbachev*. New York: HarperCollins, 1990.

Andrew, Christopher, and Vasili Mitrokhin. *The Mitrokhin Archive: The KGB in Europe and the West*. New York: Penguin, 2000.

Antonov, Vladimir. "Nadezhda Plevitskaia—'kurskii solovei' sovetskoi razvedki." *Nezavisimoe voennoe obozrenie*, February 19, 2010.

———. "Tragediia razvedchika Glinskogo." *Nezavisimoe voennoe obozrenie*, December 21, 2012.

Aubouin, Michel, Arnaud Teyssier, and Jean Tulard, eds. *Histoire et Dictionnaire de la Police du Moyen Âge à Nos Jours*. Paris: Robert Laffont, 2005.

Bailey, Geoffrey. *The Conspirators*. London: Victor Gollancz, 1961.

Barabtarlo, Gennady. "Life's Sequel." *Nabokov Studies* 8 (2004): 1–21.

Barmine, Alexander. *One Who Survived: The Life Story of a Russian under the Soviets*. New York: Putnam, 1945.

Belin, Jean. *Trente ans de Sûreté Nationale*. Paris: Bibliotèque France Soir, 1950.

Bell, John, Sophie Boyron, and Simon Whittaker. *Principles of French Law*. Oxford: Oxford University Press, 2008.

Benois, Alexandre. *Reminiscences of the Russian Ballet.* Trans. Mary Britnieva. London: Putnam, 1941.

Berberova, Nina. *The Italics Are Mine*. London: Vintage, 1993.

Berlière, Jean-Marc. *Le Monde des polices en France*. Paris: Editions Complexe, 1996.

Bessedovsky, Grigory. *Revelations of a Soviet Diplomat*. Trans. Matthew Norgate. London: Williams & Norgate, 1931.

Birstein, Vadim J. *The Perversion of Knowledge: The True Story of Soviet Science*. Boulder, CO: Westview Press, 2004.

Blackstock, Paul W. *The Secret Road to World War Two: Soviet versus Western Intelligence, 1921–1939*. Chicago: Quadrangle Books, 1969.

Boreiko, A. M. "General Skoblin: Iz Kornilovskogo polka v Sovetskuiu razvedku." In *Istoricheskie chteniia na Lubianke 2004 g.: Rukovoditeli i sotrudniki spetssluzhb Rossii*, ed. I. Iu. Bazhenov, 100–107. Moscow: Obshestvo Izuchenia Istorii Otechestvennika Spetsluzhb, 2004.

Boyd, Brian. *Vladimir Nabokov: The American Years*. Princeton, NJ: Princeton University Press, 1993.

Bugrov, Yuri. *Nadezhda Plevitskaia: Udal' I pechal'*. Kursk: Territorial'nyi organ Federal'noi sluzhby rosudarstvennoi statistiki po Kurskoi oblasti, 2006.

Burgess, Greg. *Refuge in the Land of Liberty: France and Its Refugees from the Revolution to the End of Asylum, 1787–1939*. Basingstoke, UK, and New York: Palgrave Macmillan, 2008.

Burtsev, Vladimir L. *Bol'shevitskie gangstery v Parizhe*. Paris: Izdanie avtora [self-published book], 1939.

Carley, Michael Jabara. *Silent Conflict: A Hidden History of Early Soviet-Western Relations*. Lanham, MD: Rowman & Littlefield, 2014.

Chaliapin, Feodor. *Man and Mask: Forty Years in the Life of a Singer*. Trans. Phyllis Megroz. London: Victor Gollancz, 1932.

Chubakov, V. N., ed. *Nezabytye moguli: Rossiiskoe zarubezh'e: nekrologi 1917–1997*. Moscow: Pashkov Dom, 1999.

Cline, Sally. *Zelda Fitzgerald: Her Voice in Paradise* New York: Arcade Publishing, 2004.

Clyman, Toby W., and Judith Vowles, eds. *Russia through Women's Eyes: Autobiographies from Tsarist Russia*. New Haven, CT: Yale University Press, 1996.

Conquest, Robert. *The Great Terror: A Reassessment*. New York: Oxford University Press, 2008.

Costello, John, and Oleg Tsarev. *Deadly Illusions: The KGB Orlov Dossier Reveals Stalin's Master Spy*. New York: Crown Publishers, 1993.

Damaskin, Igor, with Geoffrey Elliot. *Kitty Harris: The Spy with Seventeen Names*. London: St. Ermin's Press, 2001.

Davies, Richard, and G. S. Smith. "D. S. Mirsky: Twenty-Two Letters (1926–34) to Salomeya Halpern; Seven Letters (1930) to Vera Suvchinskaya (Traill)." *Oxford Slavonic Papers* 30 (1997): 97.

Degtiarev, Klim, and Aleksandr Kolpakidi, eds. *Vneshniaia razvedka SSSR: INO, SVR, PGU.* Moscow: EKSMO, 2009.

Denikin, General A. I., with an introduction by Alan Wood. *The White Army.* Cambridge, UK: Ian Faulkner Publishing, 1992.

Draitser, Emil. *Stalin's Romeo Spy: The Remarkable Rise and Fall of the KGB's Most Daring Operative.* Evanston, IL: Northwestern University Press, 2010.

Draper, Theodore. "The Mystery of Max Eitingon," *New York Review of Books*, April 14, 1988, 32–43.

Dydo, Ulla E., and William Rice. *Gertrude Stein: The Language That Rises.* Evanston, IL: Northwestern University Press, 2008.

Dziak, John J. *Chekisty: A History of the KGB.* New York: Ivy Books, 1988.

Efron, Ariadna. *No Love without Poetry: The Memoirs of Marina Tsvetaeva's Daughter.* Trans. Diane Nemec Ignashev. Evanston, IL: Northwestern University Press, 2009.

Eisenshtein, Sergei M. *Iz avtobiograficheskikh zapisok.* Moscow, 1967.

Eklof, Ben. "Peasants and Schools." In *The World of the Russian Peasant: Post Emancipation Culture and Society*, ed. Ben Eklof and Stephen Frank, 115–32. Boston: Unwin Hyman, 1990.

Elliott, Catherine, Eric Jeanpierre, and Catherine Vernon. *French Legal System.* 2nd ed. Essex, England: Pearson Education, 2006.

Engel, Barbara Alpern. *Breaking the Ties That Bind: The Politics of Marital Strife in Late Imperial Russia.* Ithaca, NY: Cornell University Press, 2012.

———. "The Woman's Side: Male Outmigration and the Family Economy in Kostroma Province." In *The World of the Russian Peasant: Post-Emancipation Culture and Society*, ed. Ben Eklof and Stephen Frank, 65–80. Boston: Unwin Hyman, 1990.

Engelstein, Laura. *The Keys to Happiness: Sex and the Search for Modernity in Fin-de-Siècle Russia.* Ithaca, NY: Cornell University Press, 1992.

Erickson, John. *The Soviet High Command: A Military-Political History, 1918–1941.* 3rd ed. London: Frank Cass, 2001.

Falin, V. "Dva raznykh dogovora." *Argumenty i fakty*, no. 33 (August 19, 1989): 5.

Fedor, Julie. *Russia and the Cult of State Security: The Chekist Tradition, from Lenin to Putin.* London and New York: Routledge, 2011.

Fedorenko, A. A. *Russkaia emigratsiia pervoi volny (desiat' portretov).* Balashikha: Voenno-technicheskii universitet pre spetsstroe Rossii, 2008.

Fette, Julie. *Exclusions: Practicing Prejudice in French Law and Medicine, 1920–1945.* Ithaca, NY: Cornell University Press, 2012.

Figes, Orlando. *A People's Tragedy: A History of the Russian Revolution.* New York: Viking, 1996.

Flanner, Janet. *Paris Was Yesterday.* Ed. Irving Drutman. New York: Harcourt Brace Jovanovich, 1972.

France, Anatole. *L'Île des Pingouins.* Paris: Modern Library, 1908.

Frank, Stephen. *Crime, Cultural Conflict, and Justice in Rural Russia, 1856–1914.* Berkeley: University of California Press, 1999.

Frenkel', I. L. "Poslednye dni Plevitskoi." *Novoe russkoe slovo*, August 23 and 24, 1942.

Gasparian, Armen S. *General Skoblin: Legenda razvedki*. Moscow: Veche, 2012.

———. *OGPU protiv ROVS: Tainaia voina v Parizhe, 1924–1939 gg*. Moscow: Veche, 2008.

Gay, Peter. *Freud: A Life for Our Time*. New York: Norton, 2006.

Gerhart, Genevra. *The Russian's World: Life and Language*. 2nd ed. Orlando: Harcourt, Rinehart & Winston, 1994.

Ginor, Isabella, and Gideon Remez. "Her Son, the Atomic Scientist: Mirra Birens, Yuli Khariton, and Max Eitingon's Services for the Soviets." *Journal of Modern Jewish Studies* 11, no. 1 (March 2012): 39–59.

Glad, John. *Russia Abroad: Writers, History, Politics*. Tenafly, NJ, and Washington, DC: Hermitage & Birchbark Press, 1999.

Glickman, Rose. "Peasant Women and Their Work." In *The World of the Russian Peasant: Post-Emancipation Culture and Society*, ed. Ben Eklof and Stephen Frank, 45–63. Boston: Unwin Hyman, 1990.

Goldin, Vladislav I., and John W. Long. "Resistance and Retribution: The Life and Fate of General E. K. Miller." *Revolutionary Russia* 12, no. 2 (1999): 19–40.

Grey, Marina. *Le général meurt à minuit: l'enlèvement des généraux Koutiepov (1930) et Miller (1937)*. Paris: Plon, 1981.

Harrison, Max. *Rachmaninoff: Life, Works, Recordings*. London, New York: Continuum, 2005.

Hauptmann-Gurski, Ally. *La Plevitskaya: A Gypsy Singer's Life in Tsarist Russia and in Exile*. Rev. ed. CreateSpace Independent Publishing Platform, 2011.

Haynes, John Earl, Harvey Klehr, and Alexander Vassiliev. *Spies: The Rise and Fall of the KGB in America*. New Haven, CT: Yale University Press, 2009.

Hemingway, Ernest. "Paris Is Full of Russians." *Toronto Star*, February 22, 1922.

Hodgson Jacqueline. *French Criminal Justice: A Comparative Account of the Investigation and Prosecution of Crime in France*. Oxford and Portland, OR: Hart Publishing, 2006.

Höttl, Wilhelm. *Secret Front: Nazi Political Espionage 1938–45*. New York: Enigma Books, 2003.

Hussey, Andrew. *Paris: The Secret History*. New York: Viking, 2006.

Hutton, J. Bernard. *Women in Espionage*. New York: Macmillan, 1971.

Jahn, Hubertus F. *Patriotic Culture in Russia during World War I*. Ithaca, NY: Cornell University Press, 1995.

Jensen, Marc, and Nikita Petrov. "Mass Terror at the Court: The Military Collegium of the USSR." *Europe-Asia Studies* 58, no. 4 (June 2006): 589–602.

Johnston, Robert Harold. *New Mecca, New Babylon: Paris and the Russian Exiles, 1920–1945*. Montreal and Kingston: McGill-Queen's Press, 1988.

Kenez, Peter. *Civil War in Southern Russia, 1919–1920: The Defeat of the Whites*. Berkeley: University of California Press, 1977.

Kern, Gary. *A Death in Washington: Walter G. Krivitsky and the Stalin Terror*. New York: Enigma Books, 2003.

Kirsch, Jonathan. *The Short, Strange Life of Herschel Grynszpan: A Boy Avenger, a Nazi Diplomat, and a Murder in Paris*. New York: Liveright, 2013.

Kiselev, A. F., ed. *Politicheskaia istoriia russkoi emigratsii 1920–1940 gg. dokumenty i materialy*. Moscow: Gumanitarnoe izd. Tsentr VLADOS, 1999.

Kolpakidi, Aleksandr Ivanovich, and Dmitrii Prokhorov. *KGB: spetsoperatsii sovetskoĭ razvedki*. Moscow: Olimp Ástrel' Izdatel'stvo AST, 2000.

Konenkov, Sergei T. *Moi vek: Vospominaniia*. Moscow: Izdatel'stvo politicheskoi literatury, 1988.

Kostikov, Viacheslav V. *Ne budem proklinat' izgnan'e . . . Puti i sud'by russkoi emigratsii*. Moscow: Mezhdunarodnye Otnosheniia, 1990.

Kraevskii, B. "Pokhishchenie Generala E. K. Millera." *Vestnik Russkogo Khristianskogo Dvizheniia* 178 (1998): 159–82.

Kritskii, M. A., Nikolai V. Skoblin, and N. N. Golovin. *Kornilovskii udarnyi polk*. Paris: Impr. "Val," 1936.

Krivitsky, Walter. *In Stalin's Secret Service*. New York: Harper & Bros, 1939.

Krop, Pascal. *Les secrets de l'espionnage français de 1870 à nos jours*. Paris: Grande Bibliotèque Payot, 1995.

Kudrova, Irma. *The Death of a Poet: The Last Days of Marina Tsvetaeva*. New York: Overlook Duckworth, 2004.

Kuromiya, Hiroaki, and Andrzej Pepłoński. "Stalin, Espionage, and Counterespionage." In *Stalin and Europe: Imitation and Domination, 1928–1953*, ed. Timothy Snyder and Ray Brandon, 73–91. New York: Oxford University Press, 2014.

Lampard, Marie Turbow, John E. Bowlt, and Wendy R. Salmond, eds. *The Uncommon Vision of Sergei Konenkov 1874–1971: A Russian Sculptor and His Times*. New Brunswick, NJ: Rutgers University Press, 2001.

Landovskii, Iosif M. *Sinfonia en Rojo Mayor*. Madrid: Editorial NOS, 1953.

Laqueur, Walter. "The Strange Lives of Nicholas Skoblin." *Encounter* 72 (March 1989): 11–20.

Leggett, George. *The Cheka: Lenin's Political Police*. Oxford: Clarendon Press, 1981.

Lekhovich, Dmitry V. *Belye protiv krasnykh: Sud'ba generala Antona Denikina*. Moscow: Voskresen'e, 1992.

Leonov, S. V. "Istoriia sovetskikh spetssluzhb 1917–1938 gg. v noveishei istoriografii (1991–2006)." In *Trudy obshchestva izucheniia istorii otechestvennykh spetssluzhb, t. 3*. Moscow: Kuchkove pole, 2007.

Levitov, Mikhail N. *Kornilovskii udarnyi polk*. Paris, 1936.

———. *Materialy dlia istorii Kornilovskogo udarnogo polka*. Paris, 1974.

Levy, Clifford J. "Nationalism of Putin's Era Veils Sins of Stalin's." *New York Times*, November 27, 2008.

Lewis, Mary Dewhurst. *The Boundaries of the Republic: Migrant Rights and the Limits of Universalism in France, 1918–1940*. Stanford, CA: Stanford University Press, 2007.

Lincoln, W. Bruce. *Red Victory: A History of the Russian Civil War*. New York: Touchstone Books, 1989.

Livak, Leonid. *Russian Émigrés in the Intellectual and Literary Life of Interwar France*. Montreal and Kingston: McGill-Queen's University Press, 2010.

Lukes, Igor. *Czechoslovakia between Stalin and Hitler: The Diplomacy of Edvard Benes in the 1930s*. New York and Oxford: Oxford University Press, 1996.

Martin, Benjamin F. *France in 1938*. Baton Rouge: Louisiana State University Press, 2005.

Martyn, Barrie. *Rachmaninoff: Composer, Pianist, Conductor*. Aldershot, England: Scholar Press, 1990.

Massie, Suzanne. *Land of the Firebird: The Beauty of Old Russia*. First Touchstone edition. New York: Simon & Schuster, 1982.

Maza, Sarah. *Violette Nozière: A Story of Murder in 1930s Paris*. Berkeley and Los Angeles: University of California Press, 2011.

McIntosh, Elizabeth P. *Sisterhood of Spies: Women of the OSS*. Annapolis, MD: Naval Institute Press, 1998.

McReynolds, Louise. *Russia at Play: Leisure Activities at the End of the Tsarist Era*. Ithaca, NY, and London: Cornell University Press, 2003.

Meier, Andrew. *The Lost Spy: An American in Stalin's Secret Service*. New York: Norton, 2008.

Meisner, Dmitrii. *Mirazhi i deistvitel'nost'. Zapiski emigranta*. Moscow: Izdatel'stvo Agenstva Pechati Novosti, 1966.

Merlin, Bella. "Tilly Wedekind and Lulu: The Role of Her Life or the Role in Her Life?" In *Auto/biography and Identity: Women, Theatre and Performance*, ed. Maggie B. Gale and Viv Gardner, 126–52. Manchester, UK, and New York: Manchester University Press, 2004.

Mikhailov, Leonid. "Fermer soobshchaet iz Parizha." *Nedelia* (supplement of *Izvestiya*), no. 49 (December 4–10, 1989): 14–16.

———. "ROVS terpit porazhenie." *Nedelia*, no. 50 (December 11–17, 1989): 10–12.

Miller, Michael Barry. *Shanghai on the Métro: Spies, Intrigue, and the French between the Wars*. Berkeley: University of California Press, 1994.

Milne, Lesley. *Mikhail Bulgakov: In Dialogue with Time: A Critical Biography*. Cambridge: Cambridge University Press, 1990.

Mironov, Boris. "The Russian Peasant Commune after the Reforms of the 1860s." In *The World of the Russian Peasant: Post-Emancipation Culture and Society*, ed. Ben Eklof and Stephen Frank, 7–44. Boston: Unwin Hyman, 1990.

Mlechin, Leonid. *Alibi dlia velikoi pevitsy*. Moscow: Geia, 1997.

———. *Set'-Moskva-OGPU-Parizh*. Moscow, 1991.

Mnukhin, L. A., and T. L. Gladkova, eds. *Russkoe zarubezh'e: khronika nauchoi, kul'urnoi i obshchestvennoi zhizni, 1920–1940, Fransiia*, vols. 1–3. Paris: YMCA-Press; Moscow: Eksmo, 1995–1997.

Morain, Alfred. *The Underworld of Paris: Secrets of the Sûreté*. New York: E. P. Dutton, 1931.

Morrison, Simon. *Lina & Serge: The Love & Wars of Lina Prokofiev*. New York: Houghton Mifflin Harcourt, 2013.

Mulley, Clare. *The Spy Who Loved: The Secrets and Lives of Christine Granville.* New York: St. Martin's, 2012.

Nabokov, Vladimir. "The Assistant Producer." In *The Stories of Vladimir Nabokov.* New York: Random House, 1995.

Naumov, V., and A. Kraiushkin. "Zakliuchennyi pod nomerom 110." *Moskovskie novosti,* no. 63 (760) (December 1994): 20.

Nest'ev, I. V. *Zvezdy russkoi estrady: Ocherki o russkikh estradnykh pevitsakh nachala XX veka.* Moscow: Vsesoiuznoe izdatel'stvo "Sovetskii Kompozitor," 1974.

Nezhnyi, Igor V. *Byloe pered glazami: teatral'nye vospominaniia.* Moscow: Vserossiiskoe teatral'noe obshchestvo, 1963.

Okorokov, A. V. *Fashizm i russkaia emigratsiia 1920–1945 gg.* Moscow: Rusaki, 2002.

Olmsted, Kathryn S. "Blond Queens, Red Spiders and Neurotic Old Maids: Gender and Espionage in the Early Cold War." *Intelligence and National Security* 19, no. 1 (Spring 2004): 78–94.

———. *Red Spy Queen: A Biography of Elizabeth Bentley.* Chapel Hill: University of North Carolina Press, 2002.

Olson, Laura. *Performing Russia: Folk Revival and Russian Identity.* London: RoutledgeCurzon, 2004.

Orlov, Alexander. *The March of Time: Reminiscences.* Ed. Phillip Knightley. London: St. Ermin's Press, 2004.

Paillole, Paul. *Services spécialaux, 1935–1945.* Paris: Editions Robert Laffont, 1975.

Petrov, Nikolai. "Konets agenta '13.'" *Moskovskie novosti,* December 17–24, 1995, 9.

———. "Master individual'nogo terrora: Portret Eitingona, kollegi Sudoplatova." *Novaia gazeta,* February 26, 2014.

———. "Ubiistvo Ignatiia Reisa." *Moskovskie novosti,* September 17–24, 1995, 21.

Plevitskaia, Nadezhda V. *Dezhkin kararod.* Moscow: Kurskii oblastnoi kraevedcheskii muzei, 2011.

———. *Dezhkin karagod; Moi put' s pesnei: neizvestnye literaturnye proizvedeniia russkoi narodnoi pevitsy.* Ed. Irina E. Raksha. Moscow: I. E. Raksha, 1993.

Polmar, Norman, and Thomas B. Allen. *Spy Book: The Encyclopedia of Espionage.* New York: Random House, 1998.

Porch, Douglas. *The French Secret Services: A History of French Intelligence from the Dreyfus Affair to the Gulf War.* New York: Macmillan Press, 1995.

Poretsky, Elisabeth K. *Our Own People: A Memoir of "Ignace Reiss" and His Friends.* Ann Arbor: University of Michigan Press, 1970.

Prianishnikov, Boris. *Nezrimaia pautina.* Silver Spring, MD: self-published, 1979.

Primakov, Evgenii M., et al., eds. *Ocherki istorii rossiiskoi vneshnei razvedki,* vol. 2, *1917–1933,* and vol. 3, *1933–1941.* Moscow: Mezhdunarodnye otnosheniia, 1997.

Pringle, Robert W. *Dictionary of Russian and Soviet Intelligence.* Lanham, MD: Scarecrow Press, 2006.

Proctor, Tammy. *Female Intelligence: Women and Espionage in the First World War.* New York: New York University Press, 2003.

Prokof'eva, Elena. *Nadezhda Plevitskaia.* Smolensk: Rusich, 2000.

Raeff, Marc. *Russia Abroad: A Cultural History of the Russian Emigration 1919–1939.* New York: Oxford University Press, 1990.

Rapoport, Vitaly, and Yuri Alexeev. *High Treason: Essays on the History of the Red Army, 1918–1938.* Ed. Vladimir G. Treml, ed. and trans. Bruce Adams. Durham, NC: Duke University Press, 1985.

Ratiev, Prince Alexander. *To, chto sokhranila mne pamiat'.* Sofia, 1999.

Raymond, Boris, and David R. Jones. *The Russian Diaspora, 1917–1941.* Lanham, MD, and London: Scarecrow Press, 2000.

Remnick, David. "Danse Macabre: Scandal at the Bolshoi Ballet." *New Yorker,* March 18, 2013.

Ribet, Maurice. *L'enlèvement du Général de Miller par le Général Skolbine; le procès de la Plevitzkaïa. Plaidoirie de Me. Maurice Ribet.* Paris: Imprimerie du Palais, 1939.

Rice, James L. *Freud's Russia: National Identity in the Evolution of Psychoanalysis.* New York: Transaction Books, 1993.

Richelson, Jeffrey T. *A Century of Spies: Intelligence in the Twentieth Century.* New York: Oxford University Press, 1995.

Robinson, Paul. *Grand Duke Nikolai Nikolaevich, Supreme Commander of the Russian Army.* DeKalb: Northern Illinois University Press, 2014.

———. *The White Russian Army in Exile 1920–1941.* Oxford: Clarendon Press, 2002.

Rosenberg, Clifford. *Policing Paris: The Origins of Modern Immigration Control between the Wars.* Ithaca, NY: Cornell University Press, 2006.

Ross, Nicolas. *Saint-Alexandre-Nevski: Centre spirituel de l'émigration russe 1918–1939.* Paris: Éditions des Syrtes, 2011.

Satter, David. *It Was a Long Time Ago, and It Never Happened Anyway: Russia and the Communist Past.* New Haven, CT: Yale University Press, 2012.

Savin, Petr. *Gibel' Generala Millera: Rabota GPU, "Vozhdei" i "Druzhei" po ravalu ROVS.* Paris: Imprimerie Moderne, 1939.

Schellenberg, Walter. *The Labyrinth.* Trans. Louis Hagen. Boston: Da Capo, 2000.

Schlögel, Karl. *Moscow, 1937.* Trans. Rodney Livingstone. Cambridge, UK, and Malden, MA: Polity Press, 2012.

Schwartz, Stephen. "Commie Dearest: The Tangled Web of the KGB and the Eitingon Clan." *Weekly Standard,* September 13, 2010.

———. "Intellectuals and Assassins: Annals of Stalin's Killerati." *New York Times Book Review,* January 24, 1988, 3, 30–31.

Scott, Eric. "The Nineteenth Century Russian Gypsy Choir and the Performance of Otherness." BPS Working Papers Series, Summer 2008.

Serge, Victor. *The Case of Comrade Tulayev.* Translated from the French by Roger Trase. London: Journeyman, 1993.

Sergeev, F. "Delo Tukhachevskogo." *Nedelia,* no. 7 (1989): 10–11.

Shearer, David R., and Vladimir Khaustov, eds. *Stalin and the Lubianka: A Documentary History of the Political Police and Security Organs in the Soviet Union, 1922–1953.* New Haven, CT: Yale University Press, 2015.

Shenk, Robert. *America's Black Sea Fleet: The U.S. Navy amidst War and Revolution, 1919–1923.* Annapolis, MD: U.S. Naval Institute, 2012.

Shmelev, Anatol. *Tracking a Diaspora: Émigrés from Russia and Eastern Europe in the Repositories.* West Hazleton, PA: Haworth Information Press, 2006.

Shneider, Ilya. *Zapiski starogo moskvicha.* Moscow: Sovetskaia Rossiia, 1970.

Shurkman, Harold, ed. *The Blackwell Encyclopedia of the Russian Revolution.* Oxford: Basil Blackwell, 1988.

Sicard, Maurice-Ivan. *Les Crimes du Guépéou en France.* Paris: Le Bureau de Presse de l'Exposition Internationale "Le bolchévisme contre l'Europe," 1942.

Silver, Arnold M. "Questions, Questions, Questions: Memories of Oberusel." *Intelligence and National Security* 8, no. 2 (April 1993), https://www.cia.gov/library/center-for-the-study-of-intelligence/kent-csi/vol37no4/html/v37i4a07p_0001.htm.

Simbirtsev, Igor. *Spetssluzhby pervykh let SSSR 1923–1939 na puti k bol'shomu terroru.* Moscow: Tsentr poligraf, 2008.

Smith, Gerald Stanton. *D. S. Mirsky: A Russian-English Life, 1890–1939.* New York: Oxford University Press, 2000.

Sobinov, Leonid V. *Tom vtoroi.Stat'i, rechi, vyskazyvaniia.* Moscow: Izdatel'stvo Iskusstvo, 1970.

Stead, Philip John. *The Police of France.* New York: Macmillan, 1983.

Steinberg, Mark D. *Petersburg Fin de Siècle.* New Haven, CT: Yale University Press, 2011.

Stone, David R. *A Military History of Russia: From Ivan the Terrible to the War in Chechnya.* Westport, CT: Praeger Security International, 2006.

Strongin, Varlen L. *Nadezhda Plevitskaia: Velikaia pevitsa i agent razvedki.* Moscow: Ast-Press Kniga, 2005.

Strukov, B. G. "Bor'ba OGPU protiv Rossiiskoi politicheschoi emigratsii." In *Istoricheskie chteniia na lubianke 1999 god: Otechestvennye spetsluzhby v 1920–1930-x godakh,* ed. A. Zdanovich et al., 94–100. Moscow: FSBRF and Novgorod State University, 2000.

Sudoplatov, Pavel, and Anatoli Sudoplatov, with Jerrold L. and Leona P. Schecter. *Special Tasks: The Memoirs of an Unwanted Witness—A Soviet Spymaster.* New York: Little, Brown, 1994.

Syrokomskii, V. "Neizvestnye stranitsy istorii sovetskoi razvedki." *Nedelia* (supplement of *Izvestiya*), November 27–December 3, 1989 (no. 48), 1, pp. 10–11.

Tucker, Robert. *Stalin in Power: The Revolution from Above, 1928–1941.* New York: Norton, 1992.

Tumanov, Alexander. *The Life and Artistry of Maria Olenina-d'Alheim.* Trans. Christopher Barnes. Calgary: University of Alberta Press, 2000.

Uvarova, Elizaveta Dmitrievna, et al., eds. *Estrada v Rossii. XX Vek: entsiklopediia.* Moscow: OLMA-Press, 2004.

Vaksberg, Arkady. *Toxic Politics: The Secret History of the Kremlin's Poison Laboratory.* Santa Barbara, CA: ABC-CLIO, 2011.

Varganova, Vera, ed. *Russkie narodnye pesni.* Moscow: Pravda, 1988.

Veglia, Patrick, and Delphine Folliet, eds. *Les étrangers en France. Guide des sources d'archives publiques et privées XIXe–XXe siècles, tome IV.* Paris: Génériques, direction des Archives de France, 2005.

Volodarsky, Boris. *The KGB's Poison Factory: From Lenin to Litvinenko.* London: Frontline Books, 2009.

———. *Stalin's Agent: The Life and Death of Alexander Orlov.* Oxford: Oxford University Press, 2015.

Vronskaya, Jeanne, with Vladimir Chuguev. *A Biographical Dictionary of the Soviet Union 1917–1988.* Kent, UK: K. G. Saur, 1989.

Weber, Eugen. *The Hollow Years: France in the 1930s.* New York: Norton, 1994.

Werner, Ruth. *Sonya's Report: The Fascinating Autobiography of One of Russia's Most Remarkable Secret Agents.* London: Chatto & Windus, 1991.

West, Andrew, et al. *The French Legal System: An Introduction.* London: Foumat Publishing, 1992.

Wheelwright, Julie. "Poisoned Honey: The Myth of Women in Espionage." *Queen's Quarterly* 100, no. 2 (Summer 1993): 291–309.

White, Rosie. *Violent Femmes: Women as Spies in Popular Culture.* London and New York: Routledge, 2007.

Wilmers, Mary-Kay. *The Eitingons: A Twentieth Century Story.* London: Faber & Faber, 2009.

Zolotarev, V. A., ed. *Russkaia voennaia emigratsiia 20-x-40-x godov: dokumenty i materialy.* 4 vols. Moscow: Izdatel'stvo "Geia," 1998–2010.

WEBSITES AND RESOURCES

Olga Matich et al., "House of Anastasia Vialtseva, 22 Karpovka Embankment. Karpovka: The Unique Little River of St. Petersburg Modernism." Mapping St. Petersburg Project, Department of Slavic Languages and Literatures, University of California, Berkeley, http://stpetersburg.berkeley.edu/polina/polina_sing1 .html.

Fund 601, File 255. 1910, p. 61, March 28 entry, translated on the website of the Alexander Palace Time Machine, http://www.alexanderpalace.org/palace/ ndiaries.html.

Web site with biographical information for Elena Polevitskaya, http://www.kino -teatr.ru/kino/acter/w/sov/36911/bio.

National Archives, Kew, KV 2/1591, "Anton TURKUL: Russian," http://discov ery.nationalarchives.gov.uk/details/r/C11190776.

"Nadezhda Plevitskaia—Krasnaia-Belaia istoria." Russian television documentary produced by RusNasledie in 2009; accessed on www.youtube.com, February 10, 2012.

Information about the Petite-Roquette comes from the website La Roquette, https://sites.google.com/site/laroquette/la-petite-roquette.

Web pages maintained by DePaul University about Saint-Lazare Prison: https://vincentiancollections.depaul.edu/saintlazare/footnotes/Pages/steinheil.aspx and https://vincentiancollections.depaul.edu/saintlazare/footnotes/Pages/Caillaux .aspx.

Website with biographical information about Isidore Franckel, maintained by his grandson, Philip L. Franckel: http://www.franckel.com.

INDEX

353

ABOUT THE AUTHOR

Pamela A. Jordan is an assistant professor of politics and global affairs at Southern New Hampshire University and a center associate at the Davis Center for Russian and Eurasian Studies, Harvard University. Before repatriating to the United States in 2011, she was a tenured associate professor of history at the University of Saskatchewan. Her previous publications include *Defending Rights in Russia: Lawyers, the State, and Legal Reform in the Post-Soviet Era* (2005) and articles in such scholarly journals as *African Studies Quarterly*, the *American Journal of Comparative Law*, *Canadian Slavonic Papers*, *Demokratizatsiya: The Journal of Post-Soviet Democratization*, *Europe-Asia Studies*, and the *Journal of Communist Studies and Transition Politics*. In addition to working in academe, Jordan served as the executive director of the NGO Committee on Disarmament in New York City and as a program assistant at the Kennan Institute for Advanced Russian Studies, the Wilson Center (Smithsonian Institution), in Washington, DC. She lives with her husband and daughter in Nashua, New Hampshire.